Writing for Immortality

Writing for Immortality

Women and the Emergence of High Literary
Culture in America

Anne E. Boyd

The Johns Hopkins University Press
Baltimore and London

© 2004 The Johns Hopkins University Press
All rights reserved. Published 2004
Printed in the United States of America on acid-free paper
9 8 7 6 5 4 3 2 1

The Johns Hopkins University Press
2715 North Charles Street
Baltimore, Maryland 21218-4363
www.press.jhu.edu

Library of Congress Cataloging-in-Publication Data
Boyd, Anne E., 1969–
    Writing for immortality: women and the emergence of high literary
culture in America / Anne E. Boyd.
       p.   cm.
Includes bibliographical references (p.) and index.
    ISBN 0-8018-7875-6 (hardcover : alk. paper)
    1. American literature — Women authors — History and criticism.
2. Women and literature — United States — History — 19th century.
3. Alcott, Louisa May, 1832–1888 — Criticism and interpretation.
4. Phelps, Elizabeth Stuart, 1844–1911 — Criticism and interpretation.
5. Stoddard, Elizabeth, 1823–1902 — Criticism and interpretation.
6. Woolson, Constance Fenimore, 1840–1894 — Criticism and
interpretation. 7. American literature — 19th century — History and
criticism. 8. United States — Intellectual life — 1865–1918. 9. Canon
(Literature) I. Title.
PS217.W64B69 2004
810.9′9287′09034 — dc22   2003019050

A catalog record for this book is available from the British Library.

For Emma

Contents

Acknowledgments

My special thanks go first and foremost to the many individuals who supported me through my graduate studies and early career as an assistant professor. My parents, Roger Boyd, Beverly Rude, and Bert Rude, have always buoyed me up during times of doubt. Their encouragement over the years made my goals in an uncertain academic climate seem reachable. At Purdue University, my dissertation advisers, Leonard Neufeldt, Susan Curtis, Cheryl Oreovicz, and Robert Lamb, deserve my deep appreciation for their careful reading and their invaluable feedback. Their advice and encouragement made an incalculable difference. I also wish to thank my fellow graduate students, especially Rebecca Saulsbury, Gwen Tarbox, Tom Pendergast, and Jacob Jones, who were supportive comrades in arms. At the University of New Orleans, my current home, I wish to thank all of my colleagues, who have offered support and encouragement in many thoughtful ways. I am grateful to count among my friends the extraordinary Rachel Kaul, Michelle Byrne, Stephanie Stanley, and Lauren Fox, all of whom have spurred me on over the years and provided encouragement for my work. Paul Rioux's companionship and affection have centered me and given me the joy of my life. This book is very much about women's struggles to preserve their ambitions and individuality without sacrificing love and companionship. I feel fortunate to have found such a relationship with Paul.

Many friends and colleagues devoted their time, energy, and expertise to reading drafts of chapters or even the entire manuscript. I am grateful for their willingness to take time out of their very busy lives to give me much-needed feedback; their comments were always useful and encouraging. My special thanks to Susan Curtis, Catherine Loomis, Gary Richards, Nancy Easterlin, John Hazlett, Rebecca Saulsbury, and Lisa Radinovsky. To Sharon Dean, who generously read a large portion of the manuscript and offered encouragement and advice, I am particularly grateful. Other members of the Constance Fenimore Woolson Society, especially Kathleen Diffley, Cheryl Torsney, Caroline Gebhard, and Kris Comment, provided valuable support and guidance over the years. At an early stage in the process of finding a publisher, Nina Baym, Leonard Neufeldt, and Susan

Curtis were very kind to read drafts of my book proposal and to offer suggestions. Attendees at the New Frontiers in Early American Literature conference at the University of Virginia in 2002 enthusiastically responded to my ideas, asked valuable questions, and gave me the motivation I needed at a crucial stage.

I cannot fully express the extent of my gratitude to Robert J. Brugger, Melody Herr, the anonymous reader, the editorial board, and the faculty board at the Johns Hopkins University Press for finding value in my work and recommending its publication. I also appreciate the efforts of Carol Ehrlich, my manuscript editor, whose thoroughness and expertise made this a more polished book. For financial assistance, I am grateful to the Purdue Research Foundation and to the College of Liberal Arts and the English Department at the University of New Orleans.

For permission to reprint images or quote from materials in their collections, I am grateful to the following archives and libraries: Department of Manuscripts, Huntington Library, San Marino, CA; Beinecke Rare Book and Manuscript Library, Yale University, New Haven, CT; Beverly Historical Society, Beverly, MA; Boston Public Library, Department of Rare Books and Manuscripts, Boston, MA; Houghton Library, Harvard University, Cambridge, MA; Concord Free Public Library, Concord, MA; American Antiquarian Society, Worcester, MA; Western Reserve Historical Society, Cleveland, OH; Manuscripts Division, Department of Rare Books and Special Collections, Princeton University Library, Princeton, NJ; Rare and Manuscript Collections, Carl A. Kroch Library, Cornell University, Ithaca, NY; Rare Book and Manuscript Library, Butler Library, Columbia University, New York, NY; New York Public Library, New York, NY; Shelley Collection, Rare Books, University Libraries, Pennsylvania State University, University Park, PA; Clifton Waller Barrett Library, University of Virginia, Charlottesville, VA; and Abernethy Library, Special Collections, Middlebury College, Middlebury, VT. For help in acquiring the materials I needed for illustrations, I wish to thank Elizabeth Lewis. And photographer Harriet Bloom was a godsend; for her generous flexibility I am thankful.

Portions of chapters 1 and 4 first appeared in an earlier form in the journal *American Studies* as " 'What! Has she got into the *"Atlantic"*?': Women Writers, the *Atlantic Monthly*, and the Formation of the American Canon" (39, no. 3 [1998]: 5–36); © 1998 Mid-American Studies Association. A portion of chapter 4 appeared in *Constance Fenimore Woolson's Nineteenth Century: Essays*, ed. Victoria Brehm (Detroit: Wayne State University Press, 2001), as "Anticipating James, Anticipating Grief: Constance Fenimore Woolson's ' "Miss Grief." ' " I am grateful for permission to republish these passages.

Writing for Immortality

New Ambitions

In her article "The Transitional American Woman," published in the *Atlantic Monthly* in 1880, Kate Wells paints a critical portrait of the new generation of women who were leaving their homes in great numbers to engage in self-directed pursuits. In their decision to emphasize their own development rather than live only for others, these postbellum American women were making a major break with the past. "Formerly, to be a good housekeeper, an anxious mother, an obedient wife, was the *ne plus ultra* of female endeavor, — to be all this for others' sakes. Now it is to be more than one is, for one's own sake," she complains. Wells portrays a radical transformation in the way women viewed their lives as they became doctors, women's rights activists, or simply unmarried women. What united them, Wells observes, was their "ambition": "Women do not care for their home as they did; it is no longer the focus of all their endeavors. . . . Daughters must have art studios outside of their home; [and] authoresses must have a study near by."[1] As she suggests, women's new ambitions were prominently visible in the areas of art and literature, and many other commentators of the era also focused on women's participation in the literary world as marking a radical departure from previous gender norms. Wells's article was part of the forefront of what would become a common cultural lament about the advent of the "New Woman." But the seeds of this shift had already been planted in the 1860s and 1870s. In fact, during and after the Civil War, a convergence of cultural factors led some women — primarily white, middle class, and from the Northeast — to envision a place for themselves in the high literary culture that began to emerge in the pages of the *Atlantic Monthly* and elsewhere.

What did it mean for postbellum women to look to the field of literature to realize their ambitions? Certainly many women had already become famous as authors. In fact, the realm of literature was deemed by many male critics and writers to be dominated by women, who had extended their powerful roles as wives and mothers into the public sphere. The prominent female authors of the antebellum era generally had subscribed to the idea that being a good wife and mother was, as Wells indicated, "the *ne plus ultra*" of their existence. And even those women writers who weren't married viewed their authorial identities as secondary to their roles as women. As Catharine Maria Sedgwick insisted, "My *author* existence has always seemed something accidental, extraneous, and independent of my inner self." She claimed that her life was "so woven into the fabric of others that I seem to have had no separate, individual existence."[2]

During and after the Civil War, however, some women writers began to view authorship much differently, namely as a central part of their identities, leading to the development of new ambitions as they sought to fulfill their potential as artists. They lived and wrote not only for others but "for one's own sake," in Wells's words. For example, Constance Fenimore Woolson (1840–94) claimed, "The best of me goes into my writing," conveying comfort with her devotion to her work. Elizabeth Stuart Phelps (1844–1911) similarly declared her commitment to literary pursuits: "my time and vitality have always been distinctly the property of my ideals of literary art." Another marker of this generation's dedication to art was their high ambitions. While revising her novel *Moods*, Louisa May Alcott (1832–88) wrote in her journal that she was " 'living for immortality.' " And Elizabeth Stoddard (1823–1902) confessed that she desired to be "compare[d] . . . with Shakespeare, Milton[,] Dante & Co."[3] As each of these brief quotes suggests, alternative conceptions of authorship were becoming available to women. These four authors, who form the focus of this study, were part of a new generation of women writers who committed themselves to lives as artists and exhibited the highest aims available to them, dreaming of immortality as members of America's emerging high literary culture.

Antebellum women writers such as Sedgwick, Fanny Fern, Harriet Beecher

Stowe, and Lydia Sigourney had established authorship as a respectable profession for women. They had claimed the authority to contribute to discussions of national importance and had written some of the most popular works of the century, participating in the formation of a national conscience and identity and thereby expanding the range of acceptable roles for women. Some of their writings also challenged or revised traditional concepts of womanhood. But such authors, who broadened the scope of what was thought to be appropriate subject matter for women writers, were also essentially united in their acceptance of the taboo against women openly expressing or even harboring ambitions as artists. They wrote for God, family, or society and often thought of themselves — and were thought of by their culture — as "scribblers" (a term that signifies modest literary aims and implies that writing is a pastime rather than an artistic endeavor). They generally adhered to a republican model of authorship and viewed their roles as those of educators and moral inculcators, adopting authorial stances that some male authors — such as Washington Irving, William Cullen Bryant, and James Fenimore Cooper — had begun to abandon as early as the 1810s and 1820s in favor of a democratic ideal of the individualistic author. This democratic model, influenced by European romanticism, remained culturally unavailable to women, who continued to be viewed and to view themselves as representatives of their sex rather than as unique individuals. Creative women writers of the antebellum era were united in their adherence to an ideal of duty to others, which was culturally sanctioned for them as women and also meshed with the republican model of authorship. This cultural mantra of self-sacrifice for women, which most women deeply internalized, prevented them from adopting the democratic model of individualistic authorship and from seeing themselves as potential "artists." Of course, the altruistic ideals of republican or domestic authorship remained potent for many women writers throughout the nineteenth century, but during the antebellum years these were the primary models available to women as public authors. It wasn't until the 1860s and 1870s that the competing model of the woman artist, which had been born in France and England, became accessible to American women writers.

The fact that antebellum women writers did not conceive of themselves as artists has been recognized by many scholars, such as Nina Baym, who writes in *Woman's Fiction* that they "conceptualized authorship as a profession rather than a calling, as work and not art." Even Judith Fetterley, who asserts that midcentury women's writing often displays "self-consciousness and self-confidence," argues that the "comfort these women felt in the act of writing derives from the fact that they did not . . . think of themselves primarily as artists."[4] A few scholars have also alluded in passing to the radical change in women writers' perceptions of themselves that would occur after the Civil War. Baym observes that "[w]omen authors tended not to think of themselves as artists or justify themselves in the language of art until the 1870s and after." Elaine Showalter refers to postbellum women writers beginning to feel "free to present themselves as artists." And Joanne Dobson notes, "The 1870s saw the beginnings of a new and often quite divergent ethos in women's writing," as writers such as Phelps and Woolson were "more self-consciously artistic in their literary endeavors."[5] But no one has yet examined how and why this alternative model of authorship became available to women. This, therefore, is my primary objective in this book.

In order to sketch the main outlines of this cultural and literary development, I examine the lives and works of four representatives of this generation: Alcott, Phelps, Stoddard, and Woolson. Only by considering them as a group can we fully comprehend the ways in which women seized upon this era's opportunities to contribute to America's burgeoning high culture. For example, studies of these authors individually have noted Charlotte Brontë's influence on both Alcott and Stoddard, as well as George Eliot's impact on both Phelps and Woolson. By recognizing the connections between the ambitions and models adopted by these contemporaries, we can see such phenomena not as discrete and isolated happenings but as symptomatic of broader changes in the perspectives of American women writers.

Examining these authors together brings some striking crosscurrents into focus, such as feelings of difference from other women, the intertextuality of their works with those of European women writers, high artistic ambitions, fears of being rejected because of those ambitions, belief in the sufferings of genius, and conflicted relationships with their male peers and mentors. However, these four authors did not form a tight-knit network of writers. Although they shared some mutual friends and knew about each other, they did not regularly read and comment on each other's works; neither did they correspond nor directly support each other. But they were products of their age, deriving inspiration from similar sources. Most importantly, they all felt that there would be room for women writers to participate in the realm of high literature beginning to form in America. They believed that they were part of an unprecedented historical moment on the cusp of women's realization of their full potential, and they recognized their difficulties in realizing their ambitions as ones that they shared with each other and other women of their generation. For example, after a visit with Stoddard,

Woolson wrote to their mutual friend, Edmund Clarence Stedman, "Why do literary women break down so?" And when Alcott's sister (a visual artist) embarked on a new "adventure" as a wife, Alcott wrote to a friend that she hoped May would "prove 'Avis' in the wrong," referring to Phelps's novel *The Story of Avis*, which depicts an artist heroine whose career is nullified by her duties as a wife and mother.[6] Both Woolson and Alcott understood that they shared with their sister writers and artists many experiences, such as physical and mental hardships and the choice between matrimony and art, prominent themes in their works. These perceived similarities make it obvious that Woolson and Alcott knew their experiences and ambitions were not isolated phenomena. Their stories counter Elizabeth Ammons's assertion that there were only "scattered individuals" who "struggled with . . . issues of gender and art" before the 1890s.[7] Alcott, Phelps, Stoddard, and Woolson struggled with those issues beginning in the 1860s and extending through the 1880s and 1890s, and they were aware of themselves as belonging to a generation of women attempting to enter the field of high literature at a specific historical moment and suffering the same dilemmas and difficulties as a result.

Other women writers who began to write and/or publish in the 1860s and 1870s also wrestled with the taboo against women developing ambitions as artists. Although not all proclaimed the same high ambitions as Alcott, Phelps, Stoddard, and Woolson, their careers exhibit many similarities with the group under examination here. Rebecca Harding Davis (1831–1910) is a good example. Her stories about women artists tend to reflect the belief that women who pursue genius for its own sake are selfish and foolish. However, many aspects of her life and her works further amplify women's changing authorial identities. She had one of the highest literary reputations of any American woman writer of her day and examined the difficulties of women's pursuit of artistry in her works. Other contemporary figures who were inspired by the emerging model of the woman artist and/or participated in America's high literary culture include Helen Hunt Jackson (1830–85), Emily Dickinson (1830–86), Harriet Prescott Spofford (1835–1921), Charlotte Forten Grimké (1837–1914), Sarah Piatt (1836–1919), Sarah Orne Jewett (1849–1909), Emma Lazarus (1849–87), and Sherwood Bonner (1849–83). In short, Alcott, Phelps, Stoddard, and Woolson do not form an exclusive group; rather their lives and works are indicative of broader phenomena.

However, this longer list of writers is, in some respects, exclusive. For example, it suggests that the emerging model of female artistry was available almost exclusively to white women. Grimké is the only person of color among them, and her access to high literary culture, while facilitated by some powerful white men, was quite limited. In terms of ethnicity, these writers are also quite uniform, with the additional exception of Lazarus, who was Jewish. However, the fact that these two women harbored high ambitions for literary fame suggests the reach of this new idea of the woman writer across social barriers. Indeed, many of these women were well outside the circles of cultural privilege that established America's early high literary culture, namely the elite literati in Boston and New York. Regionally they are a fairly diverse group: Piatt and Bonner were from the deep South; Davis grew up in what is now West Virginia; Woolson grew up in Ohio; while Alcott, Phelps, Stoddard, Spofford, Dickinson, Grimké, and Jewett all were raised in the Northeast. One thing that clearly unites all of these women, however, is middle-class or genteel cultural status. Although some came from very wealthy backgrounds — as did Lazarus, Dickinson, and Jewett — and some struggled for at least part of their lives to obtain financial security — as did Alcott, Grimké, Jackson, Phelps, Bonner, and Woolson — they all would be considered privileged in terms of class. None of them struggled up from the kind of impoverished background that, say, Frederick Douglass or Walt Whitman did. Not to diminish these men's achievements, but the kind of self-education and self-support that they practiced was even more difficult for women to obtain. A certain degree of privilege in terms of education and exposure to literature and the arts was necessary in order for women to formulate serious ambitions. They had to be aware of the successes of George Sand and Charlotte Brontë, or be exposed to the ideas of Ralph Waldo Emerson and the European romantics, or read high cultural periodicals like *Harper's* and the *Atlantic Monthly*. And they had to be free from hard labor, inside or outside the home, in order to find time to write. Such things, of course, were granted primarily to women of the white middle class in New England, although it is important to recognize the deviations from this rule that would become even more pronounced in succeeding generations.[8]

My decision to concentrate on four authors was driven first and foremost by my desire to combine an analysis of the crosscurrents among women writers of this generation with in-depth analyses of their careers and works. I chose to focus primarily on Alcott, Phelps, Stoddard, and Woolson because significant groundwork had been laid by previous scholars, helping me to recognize some of the interconnections between them;[9] republication of their texts was under way, particularly their works about women and artistry;[10] they offered striking similarities *and* differences, allowing for a complex composite portrait; and these four seemed particularly deserving of (re)examination. When I began this project, Alcott was viewed primarily as a children's author or a writer of protofeminist sensation stories. It is still the case that little attention has been paid to her artistic ambitions. The same is true of Phelps. And although Stoddard and Woolson are undergoing a modest renaissance, their extraordinarily accomplished works remain on the margins of American literary scholarship. Most importantly, none of these four writers has been significantly examined in the context of their contemporaries and the cultural debates about women and genius of the last half of the nineteenth century.

There are surely other women writers of this generation who possessed high ambitions but who remain unknown because they were not successful at gaining the attention of editors, publishers, critics, or the reading public. And given the taboos against women's ambitions, others may remain unknown simply because they did not publish or did not act on their desires for literary recognition or achievement. Two women who certainly belong to the category of apprehensive yet clearly very accomplished women of genius are Dickinson and Alice James, sister of Henry and William James. Both women cultivated very remarkable literary lives, which they kept secret owing to their reluctance to be known publicly (or even to their families) as authors. Their discomfort with combining the identities of woman and artist suggest how many women continued to internalize cultural strictures against literary ambitions at the same time that some women were finding ways to overcome or circumvent such taboos.

My decision not to focus on Dickinson or Jewett but to limit my discussion of them to occasional points of comparison or contrast warrants further explanation. No doubt, some readers will feel that one or both of these writers deserves a prominent place in a study of nineteenth-century women's literary ambitions. The most significant factor that sets Dickinson apart is, of course, her decision not to publish and participate fully in the literary world of her day. As a result, she avoided many of the obstacles that other female authors encountered as they attempted to establish themselves as highly regarded literary artists. So although Dickinson's view of herself as a poet certainly reflects the reformulation of women writers' identities, for the most part she does not fit the picture I am drawing. Jewett, however, participated in many of the conversations discussed in this book, but I want to emphasize that a whole generation of women writers was redefining the possibilities for women authors and, in some cases, articulating much higher ambitions than she did. She was not the "single historical exhibit" Richard Brodhead claims her to be, nor did she alone "establish . . . the normative model for women's high-artistic literary identity in America."[11] Therefore, my choice not to place Dickinson or Jewett in the foreground rests primarily on the fact that they have been more widely accepted and recognized as "artists" than have any other nineteenth-century American women writers, overshadowing the contributions of others. In fact, one or the other has often been held up as the sole example of the serious woman writer in America. Such myopia has certainly fueled the perception that American women writers did not adopt serious artistic aims on the same scale that their European sisters did or that only a few, exceptional female authors deserve serious scrutiny.

The critical emphasis on Dickinson and Jewett has also left the impression that American high literary culture had no place for women and that women believed it was off-limits to them. The examples of Alcott, Phelps, Stoddard, and Woolson offer much evidence to the contrary. In fact, recognizing the efforts of this era of women writers to make room for themselves in the emerging high literary culture can help us to reenvision women's participation in American literature beyond the separate spheres model, which assumes differentiated realms of male and female authors. More recently, challengers have begun to break down the private/public dichotomy in nineteenth-century American literary culture. One strategy has been to show the social and intellectual engagement of antebellum women's writings. Beginning with Jane Tompkins's idea of "cultural work," scholars have developed the argument that women writers, in Baym's words, "were demolishing whatever imaginative and intellectual boundaries their culture may have been trying to maintain between domestic and public worlds." The writers Baym surveys in *American Women Writers and the Work of History, 1790–1860* "were claiming on behalf of all women the rights to know and opine on the world outside the home, as well as to circulate their knowledge and opinions among the public." Scholars have therefore reclaimed many nineteenth-century women writers working outside the realm of domestic fiction and advice literature and contributing more overtly to a national literary culture. Thus scholars are more and more attempting to "understand how men and women lived in the same historical moment," in the words of Monika M. Elbert, making it "more productive to see where and how their roles converged and how their interactions created a national culture in flux rather than . . . dwell[ing] on a separatist notion of the genders living apart or without interaction."[12]

However, despite these productive developments in critical thinking about American literary culture, one important aspect of the separate spheres model has not been adequately overturned, namely the assumption that the realm of high literature was always an exclusively male preserve defined in opposition to Nathaniel Hawthorne's "damned mob of scribbling women." Even some of the most discerning studies destabilizing the boundaries between private and public, domestic and canonical, tend to presuppose the existence of a "homosocial high culture," as Lora Romero does in *Home Fronts*. Michael Newbury, in *Figuring Authorship in Antebellum America*, makes a powerful argument for the injection of class and race concerns into the separate spheres debate but does not challenge the association of women's literature with mass production, which Hawthorne and other male writers used to "damn it to a kind of subliterary or even antiliterary status."[13] In such studies, female writers continue to represent middlebrow domestic literature while male writers represent high literature, however much cross-influence between the two groups may be exhibited. In most studies, women writers before the 1890s continue to be figured as domestic or professional and as indubitably cut off from the realm of "high" literature. However, a reconstruction of the cultural matrix out of which nineteenth-century high culture grew reveals that competing visions of American authorship and genius were diverse enough to allow some women to develop the ambition to be included in this more elite sphere of literature. Essentially, a two-tiered high literary culture was conceived, with the top rank reserved for the most accomplished male writers, such as Hawthorne and Emerson, who could claim the distinction of an "American Shakespeare," and just below them a broader stratum of authors clustered around the high literary magazines emerging in the 1860s–1880s. It was to this latter group that women writers were provisionally admitted before the backlash against women writers at the turn of the century.

In short, Alcott, Phelps, Stoddard, and Woolson did not confine themselves as writers to a so-called woman's sphere. They were clearly adopting models of authorship that previously had been considered available only to men, at least in the United States. While they did not attempt to transcend gender completely, and they always perceived of themselves as *women* artists, they did dare to tread on what historically has been perceived as a male preserve of high literature. In fact, as the realm of high literature began to take shape in America in the 1860s and 1870s, it was not at all clear that women would be excluded from its construction. Alcott, Phelps, Stoddard, and Woolson came of age as authors during a particular moment of opportunity for female authors, when the idealistic impulses of the post-Jacksonian era and of romantic thought made it possible for them to feel that achieving the status of artist was within their province as American women. Ultimately, though, the dynamics of cultural exclusion that solidified the gendered split in the literary world, particularly by the 1890s, eclipsed the ambitions and achievements of postbellum women writers. I therefore agree with Elbert, in her introduction to *Separate Spheres No More*, where she allows that, even though her aim is to show the intersections between men's and women's spheres, "the concept of separate spheres still applies to nineteenth-century literature to some degree." It is important that we recognize both the power of separate spheres ideology *and* its inadequacy to explain the whole of women's and men's lives in the nineteenth century.[14]

As I claim that women desired entrance into America's high literature, the question that has troubled scholars resurrecting women's neglected literary traditions inevitably arises — "is it any good?"[15] Discussing my project with various colleagues over the years, one of the most frequent questions I received was, now that you have established these women's ambitions to be recognized on a par with the Brontës or Hawthorne, will you also argue that their works deserve to be valued as highly as those of such widely regarded authors? Lawrence Buell and Sandra Zagarell did so for Elizabeth Stoddard, writing that "next to Melville and Hawthorne, [hers] was the most strikingly original voice in the mid-nineteenth-century American novel."[16] But few other scholars have been so bold in declaring the artistic achievements of these four authors. While I agree with Buell and Zagarell's assessment and would like to extend it to other women writers' works, that is not one of my main goals. In fact, I consciously have avoided overtly making any such claims because they rest on the assumption that such worth is deducible by comparison to previously and presumably universally acknowledged "masters." Therefore, if I shy away from declaring that I have "unearthed a forgotten Jane Austen or George Eliot, or hit upon [works] . . . I would propose to set alongside *The Scarlet Letter*," as Baym definitively avowed she had not when she first wrote *Woman's Fiction*,[17] it is not because I believe these women's works to be of less literary value than those of "major" authors. Rather, it is because I question the basis on which such judgments are often made. My goal first and foremost is to understand these women's lives, careers, and writings about gender and genius in their historical context, which does not exclude aesthetic considerations. I have tried my best to historicize such issues rather than approach them from a contemporary perspective.

One of my aims, therefore, is to reconstruct the context of literary value and vocation that allowed postbellum women writers to glimpse the possibility of contributing to America's emerging high literature. Of course, my hope is that by acknowledging and appreciating their efforts to make such a contribution and by examining their rich texts, which exhibit such ambitions, we can learn to value their works anew for their boldness, their individuality, their participation in the tradition of women's artist narratives (which has been largely perceived as a product of French and English writers), and their participation in the cult of "great" works (which has been deemed the province of male writers). Alcott, Phelps, Stoddard, and Woolson each displayed their own serious intent as artists by taking as the subject of their writings the production of high art, exploring the ways women artists develop and pursue their ambitions, and creating artist heroines who exhibit and gain recognition for their genius. They also trespassed on the masculine realm of high art by writing within and against the romantic tradition and participating in the emergence of realism, two subjects that I have been unable to fully explore here. As I explain in the Conclusion, this important subject must wait for my next study.

In Chapter 1 I lay the groundwork for the book by exploring the particular cultural moment in which Alcott, Phelps, Stoddard, and Woolson developed their ambitions, focusing on the cultural/literary factors and the influences in their personal lives that combined to provide an opportunity for these women to view themselves as potential participants in the emerging high literary culture. Chapter 2 examines the difficulties ambitious women writers encountered in combining the identities of woman and artist, which became a rich theme for their writings, paying special attention to their narratives of women's artistry and the ways in which these works contribute to the European women's *Künstlerroman* tradition. In Chapter 3 I examine how Alcott, Phelps, Stoddard, and Woolson constructed their identities as artists, confronting their culture's taboos against women's ambitions and beliefs about female genius; and in Chapter 4, I investigate their desires for serious recognition from the literary elite and their relationships with the men who controlled the high literary world. In the Conclusion, I turn to the question of their lasting reputations and the issue of how we can reconfigure the literary canon to recognize this long-submerged generation of pioneering female literary artists.

CHAPTER ONE

Solving the "old riddle of the Sphinx"

Discovering the Self as Artist

Near the beginning of her first novel, *Anne* (1880), Constance Fenimore Wool-son describes the central problem for her young heroine: "Anne never analyzed herself at all. She had never lived for herself or in herself." Anne is unconscious, unaware of who she is or what she wants from life. Later, at a pivotal point in the novel when Anne is grown and trying to accept that the man she loves is married to another, she passes a mirror and stops to contemplate her reflection. In this moment, "The world, with all its associations . . . drops . . . like a garment, and [she] is left alone facing the problem of [her] own existence. It is the old riddle of the Sphinx."[1] The same riddle also confronts many of Louisa May Alcott's, Elizabeth Stuart Phelps's, and Elizabeth Stoddard's heroines. In Alcott's first novel, *Moods* (1864), the heroine is "an enigma to herself," and to everyone else. In Stoddard's story "The Prescription," a doctor advises a young wife suffering from a mysterious illness: "Comprehend yourself, . . . to do this is necessary in your case."[2] For these authors, the greatest difficulty confronting women in the nineteenth century was self-discovery.

For Alcott, Phelps, Stoddard, and Woolson, the "old riddle of the Sphinx" was solved as they discovered their ambitions to be artists. They spent much of their lives trying to find ways to cultivate an identity that young women were not generally encouraged by nineteenth-century American culture to adopt. The central drama of their lives was this struggle to overcome the obstacles of their society's prejudices against women becoming serious artists. This book, therefore, is motivated by an effort to understand how the world in which they lived made it possible for them to develop serious ambitions as artists (in spite of the barriers it put in their way), how they found a way to circumvent their culture's taboos against women's artistry, and how their struggles, experiences, and art initiated a tradition of American women's literary artistry.

In their attempts to fashion identities as serious artists, Alcott, Phelps, Stoddard, and Woolson were embarking on a lifelong journey more suited to the kinds of lives privileged men had led. In his *Atlantic* essay "Literature as an Art" (1867), Thomas Wentworth Higginson described what he believed it took to create the kind of serious literature of which he had elsewhere deemed women incapable. The requirements he listed for producing such art were far beyond the reach of those who were not wealthy, educated, and male. "To pursue literature as an art," he wrote, is "to devote one's life to perfecting the manner, as well as the matter, of one's work; to expatriate one's self long years for it, like Motley; . . . to live and die only to transfuse external nature into human words, like Thoreau; to chase dreams for a lifetime, like Hawthorne; to labor tranquilly and see a nation imbued with one's thoughts, like Emerson."[3] To become a creator of literary art meant dedicating one's life to such a pursuit. Women in nineteenth-century America were not supposed to dedicate their lives to anything but their homes and families. For a woman to adopt the aim of creating high literature would require a radical transformation in cultural expectations for female behavior and in her self-perception. In Higginson's eyes, and those of most of his contemporaries, the serious pursuit of art required seclusion, commitment, studiousness, inspiration, and even expatriation.

None of the four women writers who are the subject of this study built a cabin in the woods like Thoreau and lived in self-sufficient seclusion to discover her true relation to nature. They typically did not have the luxury of a study like Emerson's, in which he could shut himself up in seclusion from his family members. And unlike Hawthorne, none of them had a wife on whom they could rely to cook their meals and mend their clothes, allowing them the time to chase their dreams. While their husbands and fathers possessed studies and had wives and daughters to care for them, these women had to find their own spaces and time in which to "labor tranquilly." Their lives were not wholly their own. Alcott was devoted to her younger sister and to her parents in their old age; Phelps had family responsibilities to her father and younger siblings; Stoddard was married and had two sons; and Woolson was her invalid mother's companion for the first decade of her career. So they all had to eke out a writer's existence in moments snatched from their other responsibilities. But none of these women felt compelled to always place family and duty before their writing, as Catharine Sedgwick, Harriet Beecher Stowe, Fanny Fern, and other antebellum women writers did. By cultivating lives as artists, which their culture had previously deemed a male privilege, they tried to overcome the association of women's writings with the popular and dared to imagine a place for themselves in the pantheon of American literature, which would become, but was not yet designated, all-male. The gendered split of high and low literary spheres, as potent as it became by the end of the nineteenth century, was only vaguely defined at midcentury and therefore allowed some women to imagine lives as "artists." While "the American genius" envisioned by critics unquestionably would be male, and many believed that he had already been found in Hawthorne, it seemed entirely possible that one or more female writers would rise to a position not exactly parallel with his but analogous to that attained by some exemplary women abroad. "We have no Elizabeth Browning, Bronte, George Sand or Miss Bremer," Stoddard wrote in 1854, but she and other women of her generation during and after the Civil War hoped that America soon would.[4]

What was the cultural climate, and what were the personal backgrounds that allowed these writers to develop the ambition to approximate the achievement of a female Hawthorne or an American Brontë? As yet the intellectual climate was sufficiently fluid that these women were able to feel optimistic about their prospects, even though the dominant strain of nineteenth-century literary nationalism presupposed a purely "manly" literature. Although the barriers were real enough, it was possible for some women to develop dreams of literary greatness. While some voices decried "the entrance of the Amazonian mania into literature," as one writer for the *North American Review* did, fearing "to be overtaken, and branded, and cruelly mauled . . . [by] this clapper-clawing from fair, but not gentle hands," other voices signaled the potential of women's inclusion. One was Margaret Fuller's in *Woman in the Nineteenth Century* (1845), where she writes, "The world, at large, is readier to let woman learn and manifest the capacities of her nature than it ever was before, and here [in America] is a less encumbered field and freer air than any where else."[5] In this declaration, Fuller combines the optimism of exceptionalist American democracy with the promise provided by the achievements of extraordinary European and British women who had eroded prejudices against women's abilities. This is the kind of ferment out of which the ambitions of Alcott, Phelps, Stoddard, and Woolson grew. The democratic discourses of American genius and individualism, Transcendentalism, and European romanticism, combined with the examples of female geniuses in Europe and opportunities for literary professionalization in America, helped to create an atmosphere of potential and possibility for women writers. Out of this fertile cultural ground and supportive families grew the first generation of American women to develop ambitions to pursue careers as serious artists.

Discourses of American Genius and Individualism

As Alcott, Phelps, Stoddard, and Woolson began to envision lives as artists, they were inspired to do so by the varied discussions that proliferated in nineteenth-century periodicals and books about the advent of an American genius who would rival those of Europe yet realize the promise of American democracy. Emerson's ideas, as the culmination of these discussions, particularly influenced this generation of women writers. His inspirational exhortations to Americans to trust their own thoughts and resist cultural pressures to conform took on a significance for these young women that he probably did not intend. His theories grew out of a ferment of ideas about a native literature, democracy, and liberal individualism, which together allowed women to imagine themselves as entities separate from their relationships to others and to begin to conceive of genius — at once otherworldly *and* near at hand — as something within their reach.

In the eighteenth century, public discourse about a national literature centered on a republican model of literature in which works written by ordinary (male) citizens would contribute to the social good. Writing was conceived as part of the mission to promote an enlightened citizenry. In this volatile period, though, many feared that this ideal would be short-lived and predicted grave consequences if the European model of *belles lettres* prevailed at the expense of an educated populace. Despite such concerns, however, as the Republic shifted to a democracy in the early nineteenth century, a "liberal" model of literature composed of masterpieces produced by "men of genius" gained currency. Central to this liberal model is the modern concept of the author that developed in eighteenth-century Europe, when "the inspiration for a work came to be regarded as emanating not from outside or above, but from within the writer himself. 'Inspiration' came to be explicated in terms of *original genius.*"[6] In the context of the literary marketplace, which both validated the author's originality in the form of copyright laws and provided an ethos of commodification against which the inspired author defined himself, German and British romantics initiated a new development in the ideal of the "artist" by claiming that he was not merely a copier of nature; rather, his creativity mirrored the power of the Creator. In the words of Thomas Carlyle, he was "a prophet, or . . . a Priest, continually unfolding the Godlike to men."[7] The proponents of this romantic cult of genius believed that a few chosen men could act as "prophets" to the rest of humanity.

This romantic ideal found a significant following in America at the same time that the ethos of Jacksonian individualism exerted its influence on American ideology, creating tensions between democratic and elitist tendencies in popular conceptions of a national literature. On the one hand, the writer as artist began to represent another, higher realm than that inhabited by ordinary men. The rhetoric that proliferated in the journals and magazines that sprang up in Boston and New York "to foster American genius" exhibited the elusive and divine qualities of art elevated above the masses.[8] The artist had the capacity "not merely to narrate or describe, . . . but to create out of nothing," the *North American Review* declared in its description of Hawthorne's "genius." According to James Russell Lowell, "genius in Art is that supreme organizing and idealizing faculty which . . . apes creation." Hawthorne, in his story "A Select Party" (1844), summed up, perhaps ironically, Americans' hopes for "the Master Genius, for whom our country is looking anxiously into the mist of time, as destined to fulfill the great mission of creating an American literature." From such a genius, he wrote, "we are to receive our first great original work, which shall do all that remains to be achieved for our glory among the nations."[9]

As Hawthorne's story indicates, the greatest concern of most authors and critics was that while America showed great promise it had not yet produced a genius to rival those of Europe. According to a review in *Harper's* in 1857, "Surrounding influences [in American life] were hostile rather than sustaining to [writers'] genius."[10] The prevailing perception was that the industrialization of American society, the increasing emphasis on business, and the accumulation of wealth were creating a hospitable environment for the development of genius in some fields, but not in art or literature. In addition, some felt that the public had embraced works of a decidedly inferior nature, making aspirants to literary genius despair of finding a large enough audience to sustain them. Because, many critics believed, the masses had proven their indifference toward great literature, the American genius, when he did appear, would fail to gain the public's support. Such was Melville's argument in "Hawthorne and His Mosses" (1850), where he depicts Hawthorne as an "American Shiloh," a messiah figure who goes unrecognized by the people, who are looking in all the wrong places for "genius." It was precisely this line of thinking that led Hawthorne to decry the "damned mob of scribbling women" who were robbing him of an audience. In other words, the public was comprised largely of female readers who prized "trash," as Hawthorne called it, rather than the art produced by men of genius.[11] The increasing emphasis on the arts and culture as constituting a realm separate from the hustle and bustle of society led to an elitist notion of the genius embraced particularly by those male writers, such as Poe, Melville, and Hawthorne, who felt themselves to be languishing owing to the public's neglect.

This view, overemphasized as it has been, does help to explain significant developments in antebellum literary culture. But, as scholars have shown, it is not entirely accurate. Even Hawthorne's "pose" in "The Custom House" as "[t]he respectable man of letters [who] supposedly never wrote for money . . . and addressed his work to a select group of peers" was a fiction calculated to win him a wider audience.[12] The publication of *The Scarlet Letter* solidified this fiction and his (limited) success. His newfound status was based on the mystique of his earlier neglect; it was as an underappreciated genius, not as a writer who appealed to the public, that he came to represent the zenith of American literary achievement.

But this association of the aloof male artist-author with the emergence of a national literature has obscured the many attacks against literary elitism, some of them from the very authors associated with ideals of high literature. For while many American authors complained about the reception of the "genius," suggesting an antipopulist exclusivity, they nonetheless ardently stressed the representativeness and individualism of the American author-genius in a way that allowed for the possibility that he could rise up anywhere. Emerson declared in "The American Scholar" (1837) that "genius" was "not the privilege of here and there a favorite, but the sound estate of every man." Even Melville, the American Ishmael himself, rejected the idea of the elitist genius who was removed from the masses of ordinary men. He called specifically for a halt to the near worship of Shakespeare as "unapproachable." "[W]hat sort of a belief is this for an American, a man who is bound to carry republican progressiveness into Literature, as well as into Life?" Indeed, "Shakespeares are this day being born on the banks of the Ohio."[13]

This strain of thought about the author-artist is closely allied with Jacksonian individualism, a development that had a tremendous impact on American women. By and large, this new worship of the individual was reserved for white males while others were still yoked by external constraints (from social customs to actual chains) that were guaranteed by law. But at the same time, the boundaries between conventionally masculine and feminine traits began to blur, mixing autonomy or separation from society and a deep sense of responsibility to others. With the waning of external authority initiated by the revolutionary generation, Americans feared that the pendulum was swinging too far in the direction of democratic equality and individualism. Male and female children alike were instilled with a sense of "self-control" and a "capacity for self-government" that linked autonomy and dependence.[14] At the same time, evangelical Protestants forever changed American Christianity by successfully linking the two views of the self as autonomous (free from ministerial authority to form a personal relationship with God) and the self as submissive to the ultimate authority of the Creator.

This dialogic view of the individual, which grew with the rise of democracy and evangelicalism in the early nineteenth century, is paralleled by the tensions that existed in the discourse on the American genius. Take, for instance, the European romantic emphasis on the artist as a divinely inspired creator, which seems to lead to an exclusive notion of the artist as male, since women were not granted access to the divine.[15] When read in an American context, this concept of the artist as divinely inspired took on a democratic emphasis. Because of the Protestant evangelical movement in America, with its romanticized vision of the priesthood of the individual believer, the idea of the artist as "prophet" or "priest" did not necessarily carry the same elitist coloring that it did in Europe. In the democratic grain, the common man or woman was perceived as possessing the ability to understand or at least catch glimpses of God's design, indicating the capacity for genius. Therefore, although European romanticism on its own had a much more limited ability to inspire women writers, the mixture of romanticism, democracy, and Protestantism, which resulted in American Transcendentalism, proved to be more liberating, as Fuller proved with *Woman in the Nineteenth Century*.

While Hawthorne's elitist disdain for the public and the women writers it lionized remained hidden in his private correspondence, Emerson's views of the artist and his role in society were widely disseminated and had more impact on nineteenth-century discourses of American genius than any other thinker's.

Fuller called his influence "deep-rooted, increasing, and, over the younger portion of the community, far greater than that of any other person." According to Rebecca Harding Davis, he received widespread "worship" in the North and South as an "American prophet." Even to the fiercely southern Sherwood Bonner, his "genius" was "strongly national in its most distinguishing characteristics," suggesting that his influence crossed sectional as well as gender divides.[16] His understanding of the self-reliant artist-author, which was heavily influenced by the cult of democratic individualism and the liberalization of Christianity, linked self-abnegation and self-assertion, communal responsibility and solitude. According to Emerson, the individual must shut out the rest of humanity to receive the divine inspiration of genius. But the ultimate goal and responsibility of the artist is to communicate that inspiration to the world. In his lecture "Genius," Emerson explains that "genius is always representative. The men of genius are watchers set on the towers to report of their outlook to you and me. Do not describe him as detached and aloof; if he is, he is no genius. Genius is the most communicative of all things." Far from being an outsider, the artist is a leader of the (ideally receptive) masses. He is also, Emerson implies, an integral member of the community, an embodiment of the whole.[17] Therefore, Emerson's ideas about the genius combined elitist and democratic tendencies in an idealistic view of the artist who doesn't pursue art for art's sake but art for humanity's and truth's sake. This blurring of the distinction between high artistic ideals and social responsibility is what made Emerson's idea of the artist accessible to some women who responded to his combination of individualism and altruism.

There has been much disagreement, however, about how receptive Emerson was to the idea that women needed liberation from tradition and social conformity as much as men did. In particular, many scholars have noted the masculine rhetoric of Transcendentalism, especially in "Self-Reliance," where Emerson sums up his admonition to American society by declaring that it "is in conspiracy against the manhood of every one of its members," and in *Walden,* where Thoreau seems to reserve his message for the "[t]he mass of men [who] lead lives of quiet desperation." Transcendentalism, the argument goes, excluded women as a class by emphasizing the maleness of the individual who desired seclusion even from family members and pursued self-reliance as both intellectual and economic enterprise. Emerson and Thoreau both sought, personally and culturally, to create a new man, what they called a "true" man, to replace the wasted shell of a man preoccupied with business and materialistic ambition. As an 1839 entry in Emerson's journal makes clear, his early project of creating a true individual could not include women: "I wish to be a true & free man, & therefore would not be a woman, or a king, or a clergyman, each of which classes in the present order of things is a slave." Autonomy, he was aware, was available only to white males; women were still "slaves" in a paternalistic order. For the most part, however, such explicitly exclusionary language did not enter into Emerson's public lectures and printed essays. And in later years, his admiration for and support of women poets like Helen Hunt Jackson and Emma Lazarus suggests that he may have recognized the potential for women to become his ideal "poet." In his many letters to Lazarus, beginning in 1868, Emerson gave her the same advice that resounds in "The Poet" and "The American Scholar," showing his recognition of women's striving for genius.[18]

Recent debate has also centered on the question of Emerson's relationship to Fuller and to the women's rights movement after her death. While some have argued forcefully for Fuller's feminist influence on Emerson and his support of women's liberation, others have made strong arguments concerning the limitations of his professed support. Jeffrey Steele, for one, claims that Emerson "embrace[ed] parts of Fuller's feminist program" but was ultimately unable to grant Fuller and women generally the capacity for prophetic insight, which he equated with masculinity. Certainly, Emerson's thinking about women's rights is important to any discussion of his influence on women writers, but if we take our cues from the writers themselves, we see little concern with Emerson's position on the issue. Instead, it appears that women writers coming of age in the 1850s and 1860s were more attuned to his Transcendentalist essays, such as "Self-Reliance," than to his lecture to the Women's Rights Convention in 1855, which was not published until after his death. Although there was disagreement among those in attendance about how supportive Emerson was of their cause, the effect of many of his other lectures, which did not specifically mention women, was strikingly inspirational to women. One woman told him after his lecture on "Power," "In listening to you, Mr. Emerson, no achievement seemed impossible; it was as though I might remove mountains." In these lectures and his published essays, he spoke to a general public well beyond the ivy-covered walls of elite male privilege. As Steele writes, in spite of Emerson's limitations, he deserves credit "for developing a model of personal transformation that opened the door toward female liberation." This was certainly the case for Fuller, as it was for the next generation of women. Ultimately, women writers who read and attended Emerson's lectures felt licensed by his iconoclastic message to imagine themselves as artists.[19]

The Transcendentalist ideal of self-reliance and concept of the artist were imbued with the same tension between duty and self that American women felt. At its core, Transcendentalism favored intellectual nonconformity and resistance to social dictates concerning styles of worship and living. Marginalized by society yet expected to conform to society's definitions of womanhood, women confronted many of the same issues that Emerson and Thoreau identified. Were not women also living lives of "quiet desperation"? Did they not also need to free themselves from the opinions of others to discover their true relations as individuals to nature? In fact, if Transcendentalism is largely about the crisis of male identity in an age of burgeoning capitalism, women were just as stifled, if not more so, by society's expectations for them and, therefore, more in need of a transforming ideology. If self-reliance proposed a new "true" man, it also seemed, to some women, to call forth a new "true" woman.

As social relations between men and women gradually changed and women's educational opportunities and involvement in the public sphere increased, Transcendental self-reliance spoke to more and more women, first to Fuller's generation and increasingly to the Civil War and postbellum generation of Alcott, Phelps, Stoddard, and Woolson. Fuller's *Woman in the Nineteenth Century* provides the prime example of how Transcendentalist ideology could be used to help women shun society's definitions of who they should be and look inward to discover their "true" natures. Fuller's call for a "greater range of occupation" for women "to rouse their latent powers" echoed the beliefs of Emerson and Thoreau that identity and vocation were linked. But most importantly, she adapted the idea of Emersonian self-reliance, which entailed both autonomy and submission to a higher authority (God or nature), by arguing that women needed to stop seeing men as having authority over them and instead to locate it solely with God. She wanted women "to live, *first* for God's sake" and to have an unmediated relationship with God.[20] By doing so, women would join the ranks of individuals, each answering his or her own higher calling. While self-reliance was a radical proposal for women, it was one that women could justify as not mere willful independence or simple self-assertion; by seeing herself as beholden only to God, a woman could find new powers within herself. Just as well as any man, she could claim to be worthy of the title "prophet," "artist," or "genius." Fuller argued that the best male poets and artists incorporated the "feminine principle." Therefore, it was a small leap for her to claim that women were "especially capable" of the "sight" that is equated with the poet's creative inspiration.[21]

Phelps, especially, reveals her indebtedness to Fuller's ideas in her essay "The

True Woman" (1871), where she described the "scarecrow" of the "true woman," which told women they must live through others, precluding them from discovering their own individuality. She wrote, "We manufacturerd a model of womanly excellence — and that means the model most to man's convenience — and dragged the sex to it with a persistent, complacent, stupid, and stupefying good faith, which is to-day the greatest obstacle in the way of our perception of the important circumstance that we really know next to nothing of what we are about." Echoing Fuller's *Woman*, Phelps argued that society itself had to change for women to unlock the mystery of who they really were and of what they were really capable. Society must open the fields of "politics, art, literature, [and] trade" to women; it must judge them by the same standards as it does men; it must not see them solely as mothers; and it must allow them to become less self-sacrificing and more "self-reliant." Phelps believed, as did Fuller, that a redefinition of womanhood would not ignore gender differences but would nonetheless expand the possibilities for women.[22]

Like Fuller, this later generation of women writers also revered Emerson and counted him foremost among their cultural "gods." Alcott claimed that she had had "Mr. Emerson for an intellectual god all [of her] life," and Woolson declared him "one of my gods." Charlotte Forten Grimké's reverence for him began when she heard him lecture and she eagerly absorbed "the golden words which fell from the poet-philosopher's lips." Many women writers made pilgrimages to meet the Sage of Concord, including Phelps, Bonner, Lazarus, and Sarah Orne Jewett. The reclusive Emily Dickinson may have met him in Amherst, where he delivered a lecture and was a guest in her brother's home. In honor of this occasion she declared, "It must have been as if he had come from where dreams are born!"[23] Having received a copy of his *Poems* when she was eighteen, Dickinson was certainly greatly influenced by his ideas of the poet and self-reliance, which permeate much of her poetry, as they do much of Jewett's work. Jewett delighted in one day meeting on a busy street the "great Emerson, serene, remote / Like one adventuring on a sea of thought." Later she would become an intimate friend of his family's, as would Lazarus. As a young woman, Lazarus had been bold enough to send him her first book of poems and ask, as Bonner did, "You, sir, have helped so many struggling souls — will you help me?" While Bonner received only an invitation to visit, Lazarus become his protégé, and he became to her a "wise" father figure. Upon his death, she memorialized their relationship in her poem "To R.W.E.," calling him "Master and father!"[24]

Alcott's idolization of Emerson was even more intense than Lazarus's. Alcott grew up under his influence, her father being one of his best friends. As she later wrote to her father, "though I am no M. Fuller I have loved my Master all my life, & know that he did more for me than any man except my old papa." After his death, Alcott declared that in his books "I have found the truest delight, the best inspiration of my life." She was one of the "Many a thoughtful young man and woman [who] owe to Emerson the spark that kindled their highest aspirations." Most tellingly, Alcott sent a copy of Emerson's *Essays* to a young woman who was looking for advice on how to live. Alcott marked her favorite essays, including "Self-Reliance," saying, "they did much for me." Indeed, as she was developing her ambitions as an author, she copied Emerson's ideas on genius and self-reliance into her scrapbook: "To believe your own thought, to believe that what is true for you in your private heart, is true for all men, — that is genius."[25] In other words, the confidence and courage that Emerson preached reached across the divide of gender for Alcott, making her feel that genius was not reserved only for men and that she could seek to cultivate it as well.

Most importantly, Emerson's ideas provided the intellectual support that women writers needed to accept their differences from other women and to transform their unique identities into art. Alcott's first and most ambitious novel, *Moods*, begins with his words, "Life is a train of moods," which provide the central theme for this novel about a young woman's painful process of self-discovery. Stoddard also began one of her novels, *Two Men* (1865), with an epigraph from Emerson: "Nature, as we know her, is no saint. The light of the Church, the Ascetics, Gentoos, and corn-eaters, she does not distinguish by any favor. She comes eating and drinking and sinning. Her darlings — the great, the strong, the beautiful — are not children of our law; do not come out of the Sunday-School, nor weigh their food, nor punctually keep the Commandments." This quote from Emerson's essay "Experience" legitimates the idiosyncrasy of her characters and probably gave Stoddard a way to understand her own difference and individuality. Writing to her friend Margaret Sweat, she indicated she "lately [had] been sitting at the feet of Emerson." Although she objected to the fact that his philosophy "beg[an] and end[ed] in self," she insisted, "I like him, he is a wonderful spurer [*sic*] on to self-culture." Clearly, Stoddard did not feel, as a woman, excluded from his message. One entry in her writer's journal reads simply, "Emerson is not original, but makes the originality of others appear in his pages." Although she does not name the work she is reading, her assessment of his influence is noteworthy. Recognizing that he himself was not particularly an original artist, she located the power of his influence to inspire originality in

American authors. For example, in "Self-Reliance," Emerson exhorts, "Insist on yourself; never imitate," and he asks, "Where is the master who could have taught Shakespeare? . . . Every great man is a unique. . . . Shakespeare will never be made by the study of Shakespeare." Such passages point the way toward originality for the inspired reader.[26]

For Woolson, Emerson's writings grew in importance as she developed as a writer. She wrote that although Emerson had "been thrown at me all [my] life; . . . only within the last few years has he dawned upon *me*, and words can hardly express my ~~admiration for~~ no; belief in *some* of his Essays. The sum of all earthly wisdom seems to me embodied in his 'Nature'; 'Essays[']; '*Second Series.*' . . . I have two sentences of his copied and hung up on my wall at this moment. They help me when I feel disheartened, as nothing else does." Unfortunately, she does not quote the lines. Several years later she wrote that although she did not have those words pinned to her wall anymore, Emerson's works had always been her "Bible." She was writing to Edmund Clarence Stedman about his essay on Emerson, in which he wrote, "Every American has something of Emerson in him." She felt that, despite her residence in Europe, she was an "American" writer too.[27] For male and female writers of her generation, Emerson represented the quintessential American author because he was the primary articulator of the duty of individuals to value their unique perspectives. By justifying their desires to devote themselves to a literature that was a natural extension of their original selves, Emerson's concept of the American author helped father the succeeding generation of women writers.

"The triumphs of female authorship"

Of course, Woolson and her contemporaries would not have been able to develop their high ambitions without important literary mothers as well. In addition to Transcendentalism, the many financial and literary successes of women writers in America and abroad inspired a new generation of American women writers to strive for artistry. Fuller hailed "the triumphs of female authorship" and "the shining names of famous women [that] have cast light upon the path of the sex," giving younger women the courage to follow in their footsteps. She recognized that before women writers as a class could gain equal respect, some exemplary women would have to pave the way and prove that women were capable of genius. The fact that some had done so should now open the way for others, particularly in America, she felt. "Even without equal freedom with the other sex, they have already shown themselves [capable of great insight], and should these faculties have free play, I believe they will open new, deeper and purer sources of joyous inspiration than have as yet refreshed the earth."[28]

In America in the 1850s, public authorship was increasingly perceived as a feminine realm, corresponding to the rise in female readership, although, as Lawrence Buell records in *New England Literary Culture*, only 26.6 percent of New England writers during the antebellum and Civil War years were women. But Americans generally felt that women were invading the realm of literature en masse, as the quotation about "the entrance of the Amazonian mania into literature" from the *North American Review* suggests. Another such suggestion comes from Richard Henry Stoddard. When his wife, Elizabeth Stoddard, was finishing up a new work in the 1860s, he wrote to a fellow literary man, "It is a novel, of course, for all the women the world over are writing novels now a day[s]."[29] Perhaps referring to her husband's feelings, Elizabeth Stoddard wrote as early as 1855, "The Literary Female is abroad, and the souls of the literary men are tried." Recognizing the threat that women writers posed to men, Stoddard understood that the examples of those who went before her were both inspirational and empowering: "I like to chronicle the success of a woman. If there be any so valiant as to trench on the domain appropriated by men to themselves, I hasten to do them honor. And I say — O courageous woman!" Woolson echoed these sentiments in her poem "To George Eliot" (1876), in which she wrote, "A myriad women light have seen, / And courage taken because *thou* hast been!"[30] It was important for women who were developing identities as artists to have models like Eliot to give them the faith that what they dared was indeed possible for women.

In *Woman*, Fuller had mentioned, in particular, Madame de Staël, and in 1845, she was the world's foremost "triumph of female authorship," apart from Fuller herself. But a host of other women writers would soon distinguish themselves in France and Britain, and for Civil War–era and postbellum women writers, these women of genius were particularly influential. Although Alcott, Phelps, Stoddard, and Woolson each had their own unique literary tastes, three women writers, in particular, appear most often on their short lists of favorite authors: George Sand, Charlotte Brontë, and George Eliot. Dickinson, who considered Barrett Browning and Sand "queens" and hung portraits of these two and Eliot on the walls of her room, was representative rather than unusual in her choice of role models.[31] The successes of these five women writers from England and France forced the critics to contemplate and, in many cases, reevaluate their biases about women's genius and gave aspiring women writers in America new goals to shoot for. And the heroines of these writers, especially Jane Eyre and Aurora Leigh, were young women with whom Alcott, Phelps, Stoddard, and Woolson could identify, sharing their sense of individuality, self-doubt, strong-mindedness, and high aspirations.

While the works of these European women writers were certainly influential, it was perhaps their biographies that most inspired their American successors. Numerous articles appeared in America chronicling their lives as well as their literary feats. The publicizing of their private lives may have been a burden to them, but it also made them well known to aspiring American women writers. European women writers who had gained the critics' and public's admiration were magical, larger-than-life, glorious exceptions to the perceived rule of woman's inferiority to man. But to hear about their personal lives and read passages of their writings alongside autobiographical details made them human and made the heights they had reached appear more accessible.

The first European woman writer to become widely known for her intellectual prowess, Madame de Staël (1776–1817), was believed to be the best educated and the most articulate and philosophical woman of her age. Her novel *Corinne, or Italy* (1807) made her the most famous woman writer of her age. As Theophilus Parsons wrote in the *North American Review* in 1820, no woman "has displayed a mind of such power and extent, so well cultivated and filled; no one has done so much to vindicate the intellectual equality of woman with man." Although her reputation waned over the century, a reviewer for *Appletons'* declared in 1881 that "for upward of three quarters of a century she has been accepted as the greatest of literary women."[32] She was particularly inspirational to Barrett Browning, Sand, and Eliot, as well as to American antebellum intellectual women like Lydia Maria Child, who wrote a biography of her, and to Fuller, who was known as the "Yankee Corinne." But postbellum women writers felt de Staël's influence as well. Alcott listed her as one of her favorite authors; Stoddard's heroine of *The Morgesons* (1862) translates *Corinne;* and Woolson wrote her story "At the Château of Corinne" (1886) about de Staël's failed legacy to late-nineteenth-century women writers, who suffered from even greater prejudice than de Staël had. In her biography of de Staël, Child depicted hers as a painful life because she was too much of an anomaly to find happiness in her society. As Ellen Moers writes, "the myth of Corinne persisted as both inspiration and warning" to later women writers.[33] With her extraordinary abilities and audacity in daring to invade the male sphere of genius, de Staël opened the door through which other women would pass. But because her ostracism was so severe, she did not provide a model that American women felt comfortable following.

Neither did de Staël's fellow Frenchwoman, George Sand (1804–76), who was considered even more brilliant and daring than her predecessor. She left her husband, donned men's clothes, and enjoyed her newfound freedom by smoking and having affairs. In order to have full access to the literary world, she also adopted a male pseudonym. Her early novels protested the restraints that marriage placed on women and shocked the public because of their frank subject matter, but these works also astonished reviewers with their genius. Critics often accorded her the highest praise of any woman author of her age, but they rarely overlooked what was widely viewed as the immorality of her personal life. The censure she received for taking such a bold path was severe and longstanding.[34] As a result of the public outcry over Sand, young women were forbidden to read her novels. To admire her was scandalous. As the respectable Julia Ward Howe wrote in the *Atlantic* in 1861, "Was she not to all of us, in our early years, a name of doubt, dread, and enchantment?" By daring the seemingly impossible, she inspired girls with dreams of fame, passion, and power. But, as Howe insisted, she was always to be the exception: "The world knows that [her] life . . . is no example for women to follow." Howe admitted that "the popular mind" had distorted her image, making her "a monster." But critics softened their views of her somewhat in the wake of her publication of *Histoire de ma vie* (1854–55), in which she presented herself as sincere, humble, and the victim of circumstance. In her later life, she retired to her family and became more respectable, leaving the critics little to condemn. In the *Galaxy* in 1870, Justin McCarthy claimed that although she had been deemed "a sort of feminine fiend," her literary triumphs had made her "the most influential writer of our day," male or female. "There is hardly a woman's heart anywhere in the civilized world which has not felt the vibration of George Sand's thrilling voice" and "been stirred by emotions of doubt or fear or repining or ambition," he asserted.[35] Sand's illustrious career had a profound effect on Stoddard, who considered her "a true prophet of what a woman can be." Alcott included Sand among her favorite authors, and Woolson counted her as one of her chief literary influences. Lazarus's opinion of Sand was a common one: she possessed "the most curious combination of genius, force, cleverness, generosity, . . . vanity, vulgarity & immorality ever seen." Nonetheless, Lazarus considered her "a truly great & noble woman, whom with all her faults one must love &

admire."[36] Like de Staël's, Sand's audacity was thrilling, and her power as a writer was unparalleled. But she was so exceptional in her eschewal of femininity that most American women found her example forbidding.

Unlike de Staël and Sand, the British women writers of the Victorian era who commanded almost universal admiration — Brontë, Barrett Browning, and Eliot — provided what were considered by many to be more appropriate models of the woman of genius. Charlotte Brontë (1816–55), who had caused a sensation with *Jane Eyre* in 1847, was widely admired and respected. The novel, published under the name Currer Bell, was voraciously read and discussed by the American public, creating a "Jane Eyre fever," as the *North American Review* put it.[37] Reviewers focused on a main conundrum posed by Brontë's work: was a woman capable of producing the "masculine" effects that distinguished a work of art? While *Jane Eyre* had a tremendous impact on Civil War and postbellum women writers, Charlotte Brontë's biography was just as, if not more, influential. After her death in 1855, Elizabeth Gaskell took up the task of defending Brontë against her critics, who continued to challenge her claim to womanliness. Gaskell's *Life of Charlotte Brontë* (1857) told the story of an isolated, tragic genius who embodied self-sacrifice and filial duty. As Margaret Sweat, a friend of Elizabeth Stoddard's, wrote in the *North American Review*, Charlotte's inner life was one of "steady self-denial and struggle" at war with intense desires for "action" and "change." The sisters' desolate lives on the moors devoted to their demanding father and unstable brother gave birth to novels that were, Sweat felt, "the very outpouring of pent-up passion, the cry of fettered hearts, the panting of hungry intellects, restrained by the iron despotism of adverse and unconquerable circumstance."[38] Their lives, therefore, became the ideal of woman's tragic genius, mythic in its suffering and isolation.

Gaskell's biography had an enormous impact on the women who read it and who sympathized with Charlotte Brontë's struggles. Stoddard told her readers in her *Daily Alta California* column that she had always had "a Jane Eyre mania," but that her "interest [in Charlotte Brontë] culminated while I read her biography by Mrs. Gaskell. Patience and pain ruled her [Brontë's] life, and brought to perfection her wonderful genius." Stoddard's only depiction of a woman writer, in her story "Collected by a Valetudinarian," is a composite of Brontë and herself, suggesting how much she thought of herself as a successor to Brontë. And her novel *The Morgesons* was clearly inspired, in part, by *Jane Eyre*. When Alcott, at age twenty-five, finished reading Gaskell's biography, she also recorded her reaction to the "sad" story: "So full of talent; and after working long, just as success, love, and happiness come, she dies." Alcott could not help comparing herself to Brontë. "Wonder if I shall ever be famous enough for people to care to read my story and struggles," she wrote. "I can't be a C.B., but I may do a little something yet."[39] Although it was yet difficult to imagine achieving Brontë's stature, reading about her hardships and success gave Stoddard and Alcott a model for perseverance through their own difficulties on the road to renown as authors. *Jane Eyre* was also a favorite of Dickinson's, as it was of Harriet Prescott Spofford's, who wrote an introduction to an 1898 edition of the novel. And Jewett made a pilgrimage with Annie Fields to the Brontës' homestead in 1892.

The Brontë sisters' successors Elizabeth Barrett Browning (1806–61) and George Eliot (1819–80) had careers that, while not fraught with the public condemnation the Brontë sisters endured, were nonetheless marked by similar difficulties. Barrett Browning and Eliot were widely recognized as the most accomplished woman poet and novelist, respectively, of their day. Reviews of their works invariably addressed the question of whether a woman could achieve mastery in poetry or serious fiction, and their works were taken as the most shining examples of female capabilities. Some critics insisted on placing them not only above all others of their sex but among the best writers in general. "Mrs. Browning is sometimes spoken of as ranking among the first female poets," C. C. Everett wrote in the *North American Review*. "To many this would not seem great commendation." But he declared that Barrett Browning's "place is not merely in the front rank of our female poets, but of our poets." Edward Eggleston, in the *Critic*, argued that Eliot had forever changed the genre of the novel, as Shakespeare did drama and Molière did comedy. He paid her the utmost compliment by discussing her not as a woman novelist but as one of the foremost practitioners of her art, if not the foremost.[40]

Elizabeth Barrett Browning was in many ways the most unproblematic model for the nineteenth-century woman artist. Although she faced the severe attacks of critics who ridiculed her for trespassing on the male realm of poetry, her contemporaries mythologized her into a saintly, pure woman and poet. She was probably better educated than any previous woman writer, and her early literary efforts were criticized for their erudition. But when, in 1846, she married Robert Browning, she became in the public's eyes less of an ambitious female poet trying to rival Milton and more of a "woman." Many perceived her marriage as having a positive effect on her poetry, making it more appropriately devoted to women's themes. While she had attempted to achieve the immortal stature of male poets, for many she remained firmly within the "earthly" bounds of a woman's existence by becoming a wife and mother and writing about those experiences. An accomplished poet who also epitomized womanhood, Barrett Browning thus embodied the cultural ideal of female authorship. She did not neglect her duty to her husband and child in her search for greatness, and she ultimately did not force society to question its most deeply held beliefs about womanhood. "What author of our times has held more loyally to the great aims of authorship than Elizabeth Browning," a reviewer for *Putnam's* asked; "and yet where shall we look for a more womanly woman than she?" In the *Atlantic*, Kate Field portrayed Barrett Browning as the invalid genius, "[i]mprisoned" at home, unable and not wanting to venture beyond her sphere as Sand had done. A kind of Virgin Mother, she was the antithesis of Sand's Magdalen. "Sinless in life, *her* death, then, was without sting," Field concluded.[41]

Barrett Browning's *Aurora Leigh* (1857), a novelistic prose poem about a young woman's quest for poetic genius, spoke to many young women writers who were struggling through the same dilemma, including Dickinson, who often quoted the work in her letters and possessed two marked copies of the book. Stoddard, who reviewed *Aurora Leigh* in her *Daily Alta California* column, criticized Barrett Browning's execution but thought her "a great and glorious woman," as did Phelps, on whom the book made a dramatic impression. Reading *Aurora Leigh* at the age of sixteen, Phelps claimed, "opened for me . . . the world of letters as a Paradise from which no flaming sword could ever exile me." "I owe to her, distinctly," she wrote, "the first visible aspiration (ambition is too low a word) to do some honest, hard work of my own in the World Beautiful, and for it." Charlotte Forten Grimké was equally "bewitched" by *Aurora Leigh*. She sums up the power that this book and those of other European women of genius had to speak to her and other aspiring young women: "May thy sublime and noble nature strengthen me for life's labor! I cannot but believe it will." Barrett Browning's work, in which was embodied her "noble nature," could inspire a young woman like Grimké to desire to discover her own power and to achieve similar feats.[42]

But it was George Eliot, more universally praised than any previous woman writer, who set the highest standard for women who desired to follow in her footsteps. In America, she was held up by nearly all critics not only as the greatest woman novelist but also as one of the finest novelists to have written in the English language. According to a eulogy in *The Spectator*, which was reprinted in America in *Appletons'*, she ranked second only to Scott in the art of the novel, although she was still compared to other female authors. Her books "will long continue to be counted the greatest achievements of any Englishwoman's, and, perhaps, even of any woman's brain," the eulogist asserted.[43] Despite the intense interest in her private life (her cohabitation with the married critic George Lewes caused much furor), she nonetheless transcended her identity as a woman and would always be known by her pseudonym. She stood for all that was serious and respectable in literature.

Many women writers felt, like Dickinson, who claimed Eliot as "*my* George Eliot," that woman's fullest potential was reached in her works. Woolson counted Eliot among her chief literary models, and she declared *The Mill on the Floss* "the favorite novel of my mature years." Woolson's admiration of Eliot is conveyed in her poem "To George Eliot" (1876), which was published in the *New Century for Woman*. This short-lived periodical commemorated women's highest achievements and aimed to inspire American women, who were celebrating their nation's centennial, to partake in the new century of opportunity that was dawning. The poem reads, in part:

> We dwell upon thy pages, not alone
> The beauty of thy rose, we see, as finely traced
> As roses drawn by other woman-hands
> Who spend their lives in shaping them, but faced
> We find ourselves with giant's work, that stands
> Above us as a mountain lifts its brow,
> Grand, unapproachable, yet clear in view
> To lowliest eyes that upward look.

Eliot could create womanly beauty, yet she was also a "giant" who surpassed all other women. She combined the delicate, feminine "rose," a common metaphor for women's writing that conveys its delicate and perishable nature, with the masculine solidity of the mountain. Eliot therefore proved herself capable of both creating feminine beauty in the small details and constructing grand masterworks that would endure as long as mountains. Lazarus used similar imagery to describe the experience of reading a biography of Eliot: "it is like being on top of a mountain—such intellectual & moral greatness combined, I have never felt equaled."[44] This idea that her genius was the result of a perfect confluence of mind and heart was echoed by Phelps, for whom Eliot was the consummate artist. Phelps became an ardent student of her work, giving lectures on her novels, corresponding with her, and publishing many articles on her. Eliot was "the greatest woman of literary history," Phelps wrote, "if not the greatest woman of the world." What made her so was her "massive power of personal tenderness," which combined with "the instinct of an artist." She gave "to the world of men and women . . . the interpretation of a great mind through a great heart."[45] For Phelps and many others, she was the complete woman artist, not simply because, like Barrett Browning, she experienced the love of a wife and mother, but because she embodied woman's most basic instincts as an artist. Her personal life, therefore, was secondary in the public's eye to her great achievements as a novelist. She was simultaneously woman and artist, proving that the two identities could be complementary rather than contradictory.

With these examples before them, Alcott, Phelps, Stoddard, and Woolson hoped they would earn a seat next to these artists in the gallery of immortal literary women. Nineteenth-century Americans and Europeans envisioned two separate literary firmaments: one for men and one for women, each possessing its own qualifications for entry. While male writers hoped to be ranked by their fellows as American geniuses representative of the best this country had produced, the most an American female writer could hope for was to be recognized as a woman of genius representative of the best her countrywomen or perhaps her sex were capable of. As Julia Ward Howe advised George Sand, "[t]he shades of the Poets will greet thee as they greeted Dante and Virgil," but "there is a gallery of great women . . . where thou must sit."[46] Nineteenth-century Americans' and Europeans' understanding of women geniuses suggests the widespread cultural influence of Greek and Roman mythology. In ancient schemata of the otherworld, female entities could be all-powerful, but male deities reigned supreme. The woman of genius, therefore, could be a latter-day reflection of Hera, but she could not directly compete with Zeus. It was this model of the literary firmament, therefore, that attracted this generation of women writers, and it was next to these European women of genius who had achieved the status of cultural goddesses that Alcott, Phelps, Stoddard, and Woolson hoped to be recognized. When Stoddard claimed, "We have no Elizabeth Browning, Bronte, George Sand," she also sensed the possibility that America soon could. It was, therefore, in large part because of these precursors' achievements (and their triumph over tremendous personal difficulties) that Civil War– and postbellum-era women writers could begin to imagine ascending to such heights themselves.

The field of American women writers, however, was not quite as barren as Stoddard believed. Fuller, Child, Lydia Sigourney, Catharine Sedgwick, Fanny Fern, Harriet Beecher Stowe, and many others had helped to open the field for women writing in America. The question was what kind of writers American women could be. While women writers generally held on to republican ideals of authorship, writing for the public good rather than for selfish motives or high ideals of art, it is also apparent that some women adopted this altruistic stance to legitimate their entrance into the public sphere, in much the same way that Hawthorne adopted his of the alienated artist. Just as Hawthorne abandoned his wooing of the market when it proved unsuccessful, some women writers abandoned or never fully developed high ambitions as they discovered that the American literary marketplace would not reward them.

Two good examples of such women writers are Fuller and Child. Both excelled as intellectuals and writers. However, Fuller never fully developed the ambition to make her mark as a creative writer, and Child abandoned her dreams of romantic genius early on. Despite her claims in *Woman in the Nineteenth Century* that women should and could excel as creators, Fuller was unable to find a form that gave her free expression. A revealing passage from Fuller's memoirs suggests the extent to which she felt stifled as a woman writer:

> For all the tides of life that flow within me, I am dumb and ineffectual when it comes to casting my thought into a form. No old one suits me. If I could invent one, it seems the pleasure of creation would make it possible for me to write. . . . One should be either private or public. I love best to be a woman; but womanhood is at present too straitly-bounded to give me scope. At hours, I live truly as a woman; at others, I should stifle; as, on the other hand, I should palsy when I would play the artist.

Fuller felt that no genre would allow her to fully express herself. Fiction, a genre associated with women's private lives, did not appeal to the intellectual Fuller, and poetry was too much linked with a masculine ideal of romantic genius for her. Therefore, although her treatise *Woman* was an intellectual influence on later women writers, Fuller did not provide a model of the creative artist for them. Helen Gray Cone's essay "Woman in American Literature" (1890) summed up her reputation in the nineteenth century: "hers was a powerful genius, but, by the irony of fate, a genius not prompt to clothe itself in the written word." The legacy she left behind, Cone wrote, was one of "hampered power, of force that has never found its proper outlet."[47]

In comparison to Fuller, Child more easily adopted the romantic model of authorship as she wrote her first novel, *Hobomok* (1824). Child wrote at a time when "American literature" was still an open field; only Washington Irving was an established author, and James Fenimore Cooper had just begun his career. As a witness to the dawning of a national literature in the liberal tradition, made up of great works of romantic genius, she believed she could participate in it, but not as a woman writer. Hence she used a "male persona" in her preface and as the narrator of her novel. "Child apparently felt free enough to think of herself as a man," Molly Vaux writes, "but not free enough to write openly, that is, ambitiously, as a woman." Having gained fame for her novel, however, the previously unknown Child could no longer write as a man. Her response was to revert to a position, as Carolyn Karcher argues, as "a woman writer, seeking moral influence and economic independence rather than intellectual greatness." Although she started her career much like Sand, whom she thought of as her "twin sister," her marriage and increasing commitment to social causes caused her to drop her masquerade as the male author and hence her pose as the romantic creator.[48]

Even Child and Fuller, the antebellum women writers who seem to have been most inspired by romantic notions of discovering the artist within, could not escape the overpowering image of the artist/creator as male. Child and Fuller felt strongly that the exclusion of women from the production of art was not natural, and they hoped that in time women would overcome their reluctance to act as creators. But, as Susan Phinney Conrad argues, "the function of literary 'women of letters' was to analyze, not create romantic art. . . . Their social and intellectual orientations, in combination, had created an apparently unbridgeable gap between 'woman's sphere' and the far-ranging, even unlimited, terrain of the artist-hero."[49] In addition, the cultural matrix in which Child and Fuller wrote had not yet sufficiently imagined the possibility of a woman of genius who could realize her potential and gain the public's respect. With only de Staël and Sand as their models, it is no wonder that Fuller and Child did not conceive of their potential as women writers in the same way as did later women writers, who had Brontë, Barrett Browning, and Eliot as models. As a result, Fuller and Child were unable to effect a marriage of woman and artist that could become a legacy for later women writers because they felt that to be a creator was the most aggressive assertion of individuality. To become such a creator was sure to spark intense resistance from a culture that believed society was held together at its very core by the self-sacrifices of its daughters, wives, and mothers.

Nevertheless, their successors in the 1850s, writers like Fern, Stowe, and many others, made authorship a respectable and in some cases even a lucrative profession for women. In "Woman in American Literature," Cone also wrote about the influence that Stowe's success had on women writers: "In the face of the fact that the one American book which had stormed Europe was the work of a woman, the old tone of patronage became ridiculous, the old sense of ordained and inevitable weakness on the part of the 'female writer' became obsolete. Women henceforth . . . were enabled, consciously or unconsciously, to hold the pen more firmly, to move it more freely."[50] Antebellum women writers blurred the boundaries between the domestic sphere and the outside world, legitimating women's involvement in the public realm and thereby decreasing the anxiety many women felt about being published authors. These women drew on two kinds of arguments to legitimate a more active role in society. The first argument, based on natural rights theory from the Enlightenment and a cornerstone of republican and democratic ideology, was that all human beings, including women, possessed individual rights as citizens. Proponents of this view believed that each woman possessed her own individual personality, needs, desires, beliefs, and opinions, just like a man, and therefore she deserved the same rights and opportunities that men received. The other argument, which gained currency in the 1820s and 1850s, claimed that traits more commonly possessed by women than men, such as benevolence and a strong moral compass, made their involvement in the corrupt public sphere essential.

It was during the 1820s and 1830s, while the Enlightenment's ideal of gender equality still held considerable sway in America, that Child had developed her early ambitions, believing that her gender did not automatically exclude her from pursuing genius. In 1828, Sarah Josepha Hale, the foremost female editor in America, promoted the idea in her *Ladies' Magazine* that "There is no sex in talents, in genius." The notion of gender equality that grew out of the Enlightenment, therefore, enabled some women to envision themselves as creators and intellectuals. As Nina Baym writes, female authors born before 1790 "were activated or enabled by an Enlightenment republicanism whose tenets guaranteed women intellectual parity with men and offered them the chance to serve their nation if they developed their minds." Women were viewed as similar to men, especially mentally, and therefore in need of a formal education, especially as they were increasingly allotted the responsibility of raising children to become good citizens. But women's special mission still confined them to the domestic sphere.[51] Therefore, it was difficult for women to participate in the public debates about American literature and genius while they subscribed to this ideal, hence Child's masquerade as a man when she wrote *Hobomok*.

In the 1840s and 1850s, however, American women both built upon and transformed the Enlightenment understanding of gender to formulate a new, Victorian ideal of womanhood that many women felt granted them greater power in shaping cultural discourse. Hale was again a key proponent of the new ideal, which emphasized sexual difference and extolled women's special abilities and virtues as the inculcators of a moral citizenry. This separatist rhetoric helped pave the way for women's entrance into the public sphere as editors and authors. However, the Victorian ideal legitimized a public role for women based on the premise that their minds were fundamentally different from (and ultimately better than) men's, leading to a notion of a separate literary market for women.

It was important that women first saw themselves as having a public role to play and a right to contribute to the construction of the nation's cultural identity. Once they had become not simply marginal participants but, as Stowe had with *Uncle Tom's Cabin,* central contributors to the public sphere and literary marketplace, many more could begin to think seriously about becoming "creators of culture."[52] Women had to see themselves as formulators of public opinion before they could begin to think about being formulators of art. And once women writers had become key players in the literary marketplace, they might be allowed, some believed, to participate in the establishment of a national high literature. But as long as women legitimated their participation in the public role of authorship by claiming it as an extension of their maternal and domestic duties, they would not see themselves as contributors to the national high literature.

With the establishment of the *Atlantic Monthly* in 1857, however, a new opportunity for participation in the formation of the nation's high culture presented itself to women. The magazine created a stable market for artistic literature and was seemingly hospitable to women writers. Despite the fact that those who were received warmly by the magazine in its early years had all but disappeared by the end of the century when its foremost male contributors were canonized, from 1857 to the 1870s, when Alcott, Phelps, Stoddard, and Woolson began their careers, there seemed to be a place for women not only in the pages of the magazine but in the ranks of the prestigious authors associated with it. Ellen Olney Kirk, writing in *The National Exposition Souvenir: What America Owes to Women* (1893), claimed, "In the same way that Putnam's Magazine had brought into notice men destined to make a permanent name in letters, the Atlantic Monthly was now [in the late 1850s] to give a strong impulse to American literature in general and to open a field where women in particular were to take high honors." Although the purpose of Kirk's book was to recognize women's achievements in various fields and therefore it tended to downplay the barriers to women's success, the sense that the *Atlantic* and the high realm of American literature that it was enshrining were an "open field" in which women could win "high honors" was a potent one. Cone echoed Kirk's sentiments in her essay "Woman in American Literature," when she wrote, "The encouragement of the great magazines, from the first friendly to women writers, is an important factor in their development," mentioning specifically *Harper's* and the *Atlantic*, the latter which "opened a new outlet for literary work of a high grade."[53] In addition to Stowe, many women writers, including Child and Rose Terry Cooke, published in the *Atlantic* during its first few years. Although all pieces were published anonymously, it was clear that the fiction department, in particular, was hospitable to women writers, as the magazine courted female readers to help establish financial viability.

In addition to the significant number of women publishing fiction in the *Atlantic*, the successes of two widely celebrated female contributors were particularly influential for aspiring women writers. Both Harriet Prescott Spofford and Rebecca Harding Davis, previously unknown authors, became famous with their first stories published in the *Atlantic*. Spofford made her spectacular debut in the magazine in 1859. The editors were so astonished by her story "In a Cellar" when they first received it, according to Thomas Wentworth Higginson, that he "had to be called in to satisfy them that a demure little Yankee girl could have written it." When it was published, it was quickly declared "the most popular which had appeared in the magazine." It was for this reason that Spofford was accorded the tremendous privilege of an invitation to a special dinner hosted by the Saturday Club (the all-male club that established the *Atlantic*) for Harriet Beecher Stowe in 1859, prior to Stowe's departure for Europe. (Only two other women were invited — Cooke and Julia Ward Howe — but they declined.)[54] Other stories by Spofford appeared in the magazine, and she published many books, the earliest of which the *Atlantic* reviewers accorded very high praise. The success of Spofford was a sign that the *Atlantic* had the power to confer serious recognition on its contributors, even young women who otherwise had little access to privilege or power in the literary world. And lest her case be deemed an exception, that of Davis proved the point. Her success is even more extraordinary because she lacked any connection to the literary world, whereas Spofford had been a student of Higginson's. As another previously unpublished and even more powerless woman, this time from the South, Davis experienced her meteoric rise to fame with the publication of "Life in the Iron Mills" in the *Atlantic* in 1862. The story of her instant fame was widely spread and is still well known today. Both Phelps and Alcott were aware of the successes of Spofford and Davis and read their early stories in the *Atlantic*. Alcott made a special effort to meet Davis during her 1862 visit to Boston to meet the *Atlantic* luminaries and recorded in her journal that Davis's new novel "has made a stir, and is very good." Late in her life, Phelps acknowledged both Spofford's "Amber Gods" and Davis's "Life in the Iron Mills" as having had a formative influence on her when she first read them in the *Atlantic*.[55] Spofford's and Davis's stories made a strong impression because readers could not believe they were written by women (owing to Spofford's worldliness and Davis's stark realism). In addition, the successes of these two obscure women writers suggested that others could follow in their footsteps into the new tier of high literary culture that was opening up just below the great Hawthorne, Emerson, John Greenleaf Whittier, Henry Wadsworth Longfellow, Oliver Wendell Holmes, and James Russell Lowell, who formed the core of the *Atlantic*'s canon.

Discovering the Self as Artist

While American individualism, Transcendentalism, the examples of earlier women writers, and the inclusion of women in the pages of the *Atlantic Monthly* created the cultural climate that enabled women of the Civil War and postbellum years to envision contributing to America's emerging high literature, young women also needed encouragement closer to home in order to begin to imagine themselves as artists. Most families raised their girls to live for others rather than for themselves, creating the greatest obstacle to self-discovery. Phelps, like others before her, including Fuller and John Stuart Mill, identified the essential dilemma for women as the tension between self-sacrifice and self-reliance. In her essay "Unhappy Girls," she wrote that although "[i]ndividuality is the birthright of each human soul, . . . society crushes [it] out of women," as did the family, she argued, by expecting that only sons had the duty to develop their talents and share them with the world.

> It is a selfish affection, a sickly sentimentality, and a terrible error of parental judgment which says to the young man: "Go, life is before you; cut your way; leave your mark; make for yourself an honest independence and an honored name. . . ." And to the young woman: "My dear, we cannot spare you now; wait a while . . . wait a lifetime perhaps. Give us yourself—your young energies, and ingenuities . . . your gifts and graces . . . your opportunities of growth and gain; your chance of usefulness or fame. . . ."

It was exactly this restraining of young women, Phelps believed, that prevented them from attempting great things in life and art. "Suppose that Raphael had refused to gaze into the divine eyes of the Sistine Mary because his mother advised him not to. Or that Milton had not entered Paradise because his father thought he'd better not," she reasoned. This was precisely what happened to women. Raised to think only of others, they were discouraged from seeing themselves as individuals capable of great feats and sublime insights, thereby depriving the world of future Raphaels or Miltons.[56] Although Phelps was still railing against these social and familial pressures in 1871, we can see in her early life, as well as those of Alcott, Stoddard, and Woolson, examples to the contrary. Each of them found in their families enough encouragement to break away from the expectation that women were supposed to devote themselves to the service of others. Instead, they were supported to varying degrees in their development of independence, individuality, and ambition to be artists.

A certain amount of rejection of society's gender codes was necessary for women to understand themselves as artists. In fact, it appears that a strong bond with a mother who, to some extent, had set aside society's definition of women's abilities was an important source of strength for this generation of women writers. While later New Women asserted their individuality by separating from their mothers,[57] Alcott, Phelps, and Woolson (Stoddard is an exception) found in their mothers a role model for autonomy and authorship. These four women also shared many other similarities in their personalities and upbringing that helped them form identities as artists, such as opportunities for self-development and work outside the home during the Civil War, exposure to the outside world through travel, feelings of uniqueness and difference from other women, desires for independence, and a restlessness or ambition to live self-directed and intellectually fulfilling lives.[58] In addition, there were external forces, what R. Ochse, in *Before the Gates of Excellence*, calls "stress" or conditions that leave one feeling powerless, that led these women to pursue lives as artists. Artists manage stress, Ochse argues, by mastering their special talents, thereby regaining control over their lives. Examples of such stress include financial need or the death of one or both parents, factors that played a role in the lives of all four of the writers examined here.[59] To these I would add society's prejudices about women's abilities. While such prejudices certainly acted as barriers to developing literary ambitions for many women writers, for Alcott, Phelps, Stoddard, and Woolson, combating society's ideas about womanhood was a basic motivator; it helped define them as artists.

All four came to understand themselves very early on as different from other girls. As young women they developed a craving to participate in a revolutionary moment of women's expanding opportunities and abilities. They went through intense periods of self-discovery as adolescents and young women, wrestling with their unconventionality and the feeling that they did not fit in with other women or their communities. All four could be described as "tomboys," who often preferred running "wild" and rejected traditional female activities, much like Jewett, who described herself as a "wild and shy" child. "I always thought I must have been a deer or a horse in some former state," Alcott recollected about her childhood. She continued, "No boy could be my friend till I had beaten him in a race, and no girl if she refused to climb trees, leap fences, and be a tomboy." Likewise, Phelps called herself a "tomboy" in her autobiography and described an incident in which a man stopped her one day and told her that "little girls should not walk fences." She only looked at him "with contempt."[60]

Stoddard and Alcott, especially, felt "moody" and ill-tempered, not sweet and cheerful, as girls were supposed to be. They noticed that their sisters possessed sunny dispositions in contrast to their own. Stoddard thought her sister, Anne, was "not one bit like me — there's no devil in her. [N]o ginger hot in the mouth." By contrasting herself with her mild-mannered sister, Stoddard discovered her own "devil," which she would come to see as necessary for the woman artist. Like Hawthorne, who appreciated Fanny Fern's *Ruth Hall* because she wrote "as if the devil was in her," Stoddard believed that women had to set themselves apart from ordinary women in order to be good writers. The young Alcott found it more difficult to embrace the "devil" in her. Her diary exhibits her painful struggles to curb her temper and moods. At the age of twelve she recorded *"A Sample of Our Lessons,"* in which a teacher's interview of her reveals her feelings of difference: "What is gentleness? Kindness, patience, and care for other people's feelings. / Who has it? Father and Anna [her sister]. / Who means to have it? Louisa, if she can." At the age of fifty, Alcott inserted a note at this point in the diary indicating that she had tried all her life "without any great success" to learn these lessons about "self-denial." While her sisters Anna and Lizzy embodied the selflessness and sweetness that her father prized, she had to learn to accept her lack of feminine deference to authority. Although "some people complain[ed]" that Louisa and her youngest sister, May, an artist, were "brusque," Child, a friend of their mother's, considered them simply "straightforward and sincere," two qualities that served them well as artists.[61]

Alcott's, Phelps's, Stoddard's, and Woolson's essential feelings of difference from other girls also centered on their disdain for women's domestic tasks. For example, Phelps described in her autobiography how she protested against domestic duties and how, as a "girl who is never 'domestic,' " she was a "trial" to her family. She recalled the desperation she felt as a young woman who would rather be reading or writing than helping with the spring sewing: "To this day I cannot hear the thick chu-chunk! of heavy wheels on March mud without a sudden mechanical echo of that wild, young outcry: 'Must I cut out underclothes for-ever? . . . Is *this* LIFE?'" Wanting to be an artist required a rejection of the domestic tasks linked with womanhood. Accordingly, Phelps reportedly held up a painter's brush and a thimble to a friend and told her, "It is a choice between the two." In her autobiography, she also described her first literary effort at the age of thirteen as a manifestation of her "determin[ation] to become an individual." Even Dickinson, who managed to keep up her extensive household duties while nurturing a largely secret life as a poet, resented the time such duties took away from her writing. She once complained, "my hands but *two* — not four, or five as they ought to be — and so *many* wants — and me so *very* handy — and my time of so *little* account — and my writing so *very* needless — and really I came to the conclusion that I should be a villain unparalleled if I took but an inch of time for so unholy a purpose as writing a friendly letter." Although letter writing was a thoroughly sanctioned activity for women, Dickinson summed up the tension she felt in her daily life between her desire to write, a solitary activity, and her family's expectations of her. For a young woman to decline to perform even the smallest tasks for her family made her a "villain," or, as Phelps felt for preferring to write over doing household chores, a "burglar."[62]

Alcott, Phelps, and Woolson also decided early in life against marriage and in favor of financial self-sufficiency. In 1860, Alcott wrote in her journal, after a visit to her newly married sister, "Very sweet and pretty, but I'd rather be a free spinster and paddle my own canoe." Being self-reliant meant first of all making one's own money. Stoddard remembered, when she was contracted as a colum-nist early in her career, "I was the first female wage-earner that I had known, and it gave me a curious sense of independence" (despite her married status). When Phelps received her first payment for a published piece, she recalled, she felt a "sense of dignity" at becoming a "wage-earner," which for her was closely tied to feelings of self-worth. "I felt that I had suddenly acquired value — to myself, to my family, and to the world." This sense of value could not be achieved at home. It required recognition from the outside world, and financial compensation for her work was part of that recognition. Elsewhere in her autobiography Phelps claimed that she was "proud to say that I have always been a working woman" and "could take care of myself." Alcott similarly described her desire for financial independence in a letter to her father in 1856: "I am very well and very happy.

Things go smoothly, and I think I shall come out right, and prove that though an *Alcott* I *can* support myself. I like the independent feeling; and though not an easy life, it is a free one, and I enjoy it. . . . I will make a battering-ram of my head and make a way through this rough-and-tumble world." These women saw that in order to be self-reliant, they had to earn money in addition to committing themselves to the pursuit of excellence in their writing, hence their twin goals of achieving serious recognition as artists and financial security.[63] As this generation began their careers, the motivation to support themselves (and/or their families) was part of the artist identities they were developing.

Although most women of the Civil War and postbellum years remained tied to their families of origin, increasing numbers of them did not start families of their own. Although there were twenty thousand more women than men in the United States in 1850, that number rose to fifty thousand by 1870 and continued to rise in the next decade. In New England, the disparity was especially pronounced. Stoddard married before the Civil War, but the war probably influenced Alcott, Phelps, and Woolson not to marry or at least reinforced their decisions not to. Phelps lost her beau, Lieutenant Samuel Hopkins Thompson, at Antietam, a factor that contributed to her decision to launch a literary career. Indeed, as Susan Coultrap-McQuin writes, "His death would echo through her fiction for many years." Her first published story for adults, "A Sacrifice Consumed" (1864), was about this loss. Phelps claimed in her autobiography that when she wrote this story she had no distinct plan to start a career as an author, and "had my first story been refused, or even the second or the third, I should have written no more." But the success of this story, born out of her loss of a potential husband, opened up a new path for her. Woolson may also have lost a beau, Colonel Zeph Spaulding, to the war. Cheryl Torsney writes that Woolson had "a soldier boyfriend, . . . who returned from action a changed man." Later, Woolson wrote that her feelings for Spaulding were due to the "glamor [*sic*] that the war threw over the young officers who left their homes to fight," and, as Sharon Dean writes, "She never expressed regret over her broken relationship with [him]." The war, however, probably interrupted an affair that may otherwise have led to marriage and certainly changed the direction of her life.[64]

While many women felt forced into independence by the war's casualties, others saw spinsterhood as a tremendous opportunity, as Alcott, Phelps, and Woolson did. In her essay "Happy Women" (1868), Alcott celebrated the "superior women who, from various causes, remain single, and devote themselves to some earnest work; espousing philanthropy, art, literature, music, medicine, . . . remaining as faithful to and as happy in their choice as married women with husbands and homes." By calling these women "superior," Alcott plays upon the common reference to "superfluous women," to which she strongly objected. "Never was there so splendid an opportunity for women to enjoy their liberty and prove that they deserve it b[y] using it wisely," she declared.[65] Although the four writers of this study tried out different occupations and looked for the path in which their true talents lay, ultimately they turned to writing, an accessible medium that required little formal training and could be practiced at home. What was needed, though, were special circumstances and encouragement to pursue the lofty goals of excellence and literary laurels.

The first and foremost influence on the development of the self as artist is a family that prizes literature, perhaps even a family that can provide a sense of literary heritage for its daughters. For Alcott, Phelps, and Woolson, this was most certainly true. Scholars have noted the (conflicted) role models that literary and intellectual fathers provided their talented daughters in the cases of Fuller, Stowe, Dickinson, and Jewett. But the role of literary mothers has not been adequately explored as crucial to the development of women authors. It is abundantly clear that Alcott, Phelps, and Woolson all benefited immensely from their mothers' support and example. Mary Kelley has documented the lack of positive female models for antebellum women writers, arguing that "the absence of 'distinguished' women, in fact the invisibility of females in their ancestry, contributed to and heightened their insecurity and sense of illegitimacy as public writers."[66] In order to gain a sense of legitimacy not only as writers but as potential artists, the next generation of women writers learned from the examples of their talented, thwarted mothers, who hoped their daughters would achieve what had not been possible for them.

Woolson's mother, Hannah Cooper Pomeroy, bequeathed her daughter an illustrious literary heritage. She was a niece of James Fenimore Cooper, from whom Woolson received her middle name and her early pen name "Fenimore." When Woolson began her literary career, she allied herself with this legacy, and throughout her life she prized her relations with her aunts, Cooper's daughters, one of whom, Susan Fenimore Cooper, was also a published author. Some of Woolson's early publications were essays about Cooperstown, her uncle, and the Cooper family. Identifying herself with this family lineage, which included women, gave her confidence and immediate clout. She inherited her pride in her

Cooper ancestry from her mother, who had been a writer herself. Although Hannah never published any of her writings, she nonetheless provided an important model and source of support for her daughter.[67]

Woolson early on developed an interest in literature and the habit of writing. She later claimed that in her youth when she received her copies of the *Atlantic*, she first turned to the book reviews, indicating her desire to follow developments in the literary world and study the literary craft. But she did not begin her career until after her father's death in August 1869. Her first publication appeared almost a year later, and it was at that point that she began to write in earnest, publishing essays and stories in *Harper's* and other reputable journals, as well as a column on New York for the *Daily Cleveland Herald*. Why she did not publish earlier is not clear. Perhaps after her father's death she needed to support herself and her mother. But her desire for an independent life, which was always strong, was instilled in her quite early and nurtured by her family, who considered her both very talented and unconventional. According to her sister, Clara, Woolson's "literary talent . . . led her to do things that those *not* thus gifted, did not do." Her mother often warned her, Clara wrote, not to carry her uncorked inkstand up and down the stairs for fear she would "spoil one of [her] pretty new dresses." One day, she did exactly that, tripping down the stairs and spilling ink all over "a lovely grey costume." As this letter conveys, while her family made sport of her preference for literature over personal appearance, they valued her individuality and took pride in their "gifted" family member. Woolson's mother was an especially important source of support for the ten years the two lived together after her father's death. Three years after her mother died, Woolson wrote, "I look back and see how wonderfully good to me Mother was when I was finishing 'Anne' [her first novel]. She was always pleasant and kind, never put me on the defensive, as one may say; never said 'don't!' or tried to make me do anything I didn't want to!" By never saying "don't!" her mother revealed her difference from the more typical parents admonished by Phelps in "Unhappy Girls." Hannah Woolson likely understood her daughter's talent and ambition from personal experience, and she did not stand in her way.[68]

Woolson also probably developed a stronger sense of her individuality through her experiences during the Civil War. She participated in the war effort from the home front, working for the United States Sanitary Commission. She wrote to Stedman years later that she had received a letter from Hawthorne in response to hers asking for an autograph when she was "postmistress at a Sanitary Fair." These fairs were conducted by the commission to raise money for the war hospitals and relief efforts, and Hawthorne's autograph presumably would have been sold for that purpose. (Alcott was also active with the commission, contributing "poems, stories, hand-sewn flags, and clothing for the Boston fair.") Woolson was deeply affected by the excitement and horror of the time. She later recalled, in another letter to Stedman, that "the war was the heart and spirit of my life, and everything has seemed tame to me since." And although she did not begin her writing career until the 1870s, her travels through the South during that decade made the effects of the war a prominent theme in her early stories.[69]

Throughout the 1870s, Woolson steadily developed her literary reputation, hoping to become known all over the country, as she revealed in 1875 to the southern poet Paul Hamilton Hayne: "I thank you sincerely for any notices you may write of my little volume [her first collection of stories, *Castle Nowhere*], and feel especially pleased that your words may be read in the south and southwest, where I am entirely unknown." Although she earlier had difficulty coming before the public (as she confided to her childhood friend — "I have had to get used to my pen, and to 'speaking in public' as it were"), she was now feeling confidence in her abilities. When her mother died in 1879, Woolson was devastated by her loss. "She had been my all for many years. I did not know how to live without her," she wrote to Hayne. Yet the void left by her mother opened up new opportunities, and Woolson entered a new phase in her life and career. She traveled to Europe, a dream of hers since childhood. For the rest of her life, she lived there, traveling extensively and pursuing the vocation of an artist in the company of Henry James and others. Although her mother was once her "all," Woolson conveyed to her nephew that now literature was everything to her: "It is dangerous to ask a writer of novels about novels! He may swamp you with the ocean of his words. The truth is, that, to a writer, the subject is so vast, — really his whole life's interest." Clearly, she was referring to herself, although she used the masculine pronoun, which was common in many women writers' references to the "writer" or "artist." Now, without parents, husband, or children, she was free to identify herself solely as an author.[70]

Elizabeth Stuart Phelps, born in 1844, also inherited her desire to pursue the arts from her mother, who died when Elizabeth was only eight years old. In tribute to her mother, Phelps discarded her given name, Mary Gray Phelps, and took her mother's. The first Elizabeth Stuart Phelps had become a popular author of Sunday school tales and novels, so by taking her mother's name, she essentially took up her career as well. This strong link with her mother gave Phelps a model to follow throughout her life and influenced her decisions as a woman and a writer. Her mother first published short stories and articles at age sixteen or seventeen under the pseudonym H. Trusta. But it was after her marriage in 1842 to Austin Phelps that she published her most popular works, all of which continued to appear under her pseudonym. During the first year of its publication, *The Sunny Side; or, A Country Minister's Wife* (1851) sold one hundred thousand copies. Her next two works, *A Peep at "Number Five"; or, A Chapter in the Life of a City Pastor* and *The Angel Over the Right Shoulder*, were published in the following year and also sold well. She was very proud of her achievement as an author, but, according to her daughter, it came at a steep price. The latter wrote in her autobiography, "Her 'Sunnyside' had already reached a circulation of one hundred thousand copies, and she was following it fast—too fast—by other books for which the critics and the publishers clamored. Her last book and her last baby came together, and killed her." Forever after Phelps would attribute her mother's death to the demands of maintaining both a family and a literary career, a mistake she did not want to repeat.[71]

As a prelude to her mother's posthumously published book, *The Last Leaf from Sunny Side*, Austin Phelps, her father, published a "memorial" to his wife that portrays her as at once a sympathetic figure struggling to find her true mission in life and a larger-than-life ideal mother. The impact of this portrait on the daughter must have been immense. Austin Phelps argues that all of her life his wife wrestled with her love of the arts, fearing that her "indulgence of those refined tastes" conflicted with her life as a Christian. But she eventually came to understand that suppressing her true talents made her depressed and unfit to contribute to the happiness of others. She once wrote to a friend, "I learned at last to be happy as God would have me be. I found out, that He who made me knew better than I, what He made me for; and that He had not given me tastes, and inclinations, and talents, all in themselves innocent, to be suppressed." By reconciling her Christian beliefs with her creative desires, she paved the way for her daughter to accept her own similar inclinations. In fact, one of her mother's deathbed requests was that "her daughter might be carefully instructed in the fine arts."[72]

Phelps's recorded memories of her mother, which convey awe for an almost saintlike creature, echo her father's tribute. Whatever her talents, Austin Phelps wrote, she was above all a "true wife and mother," whose "literary pursuits . . . were religiously subordinated to her duties 'at home.'" In her autobiography, Phelps similarly depicted her mother as committed to her family first and her own career second and as unusually accomplished in both respects. Phelps wrote of how her mother "achieved the difficult reconciliation between genius and domestic life," insisting, "I cannot remember one hour in which her children needed her and did not find her."[73] The first Elizabeth Stuart Phelps, therefore, was representative of the antebellum woman writer who understood her talents as secondary to her familial duties and as only to be used in the service of God's design. Although her daughter's generation would also call upon the sense of a divine calling to become writers, the difference was that the mother understood her God as a paternal, authoritative figure whom she served, while her daughter, more in keeping with Emerson and Fuller, would feel sanctioned to unfold the divine within herself. In the end, however, Phelps's mother looms over her autobiography like the shadow of an unfulfilled promise, a Christ figure who gave up her life so that the daughter could fulfill hers. The daughter felt that she had to live out the promise that had been extinguished with her mother's premature death, which she understood as a direct result of the unresolved conflict between genius and domesticity.

Ultimately, Phelps's mother provided both a guide and a warning to her. Phelps explained that she learned a valuable lesson from her mother: "I have sometimes been glad, as my time came to face the long question which life puts to-day to all women who think and feel . . . that I had those early visions of my own to look upon."[74] The question was whether to try to combine a literary career (or any other single-minded pursuit) with marriage. Phelps held her mother's tragic fate always before her as a guide. It is very telling that while her mother had been too modest or fearful to put her real name before the public's eye, Phelps took her mother's name for both personal and public use. In a sense, she took up the identity of the woman behind the domestic writer H. Trusta, who moralized about women's conventional role. Phelps became a different type of woman, one that her mother could not envision. The daughter was first and foremost an author and an artist. While her first literary efforts (Sunday school books for children) mirrored her mother's, her more mature writing branched out in new directions. And she devoted her life to perfecting her art, a mission she also saw as commensurate with her life as a Christian.

Unfortunately, in her mother's absence there was no one left to support Phelps's developing ambition. In fact, her family (father, stepmother, and younger brothers) appear to have provided only obstacles to the young writer. They expected her to fulfill her household duties and watch over her brothers. Phelps remembered that she shared her writing with no one, undoubtedly because of their disapproval. For many years she was given no place of her own in which to write, and she described in her autobiography the great lengths to which she had to go to secure enough peace and quiet to bring pen to paper. Whereas her father secluded himself in his study, she was not accorded the same privilege but was instead expected to assist *his* endeavors by keeping her brothers occupied and quiet. Her role in the household was to be a supportive caretaker, much like the "unhappy girls" she later wrote about. When she did find time to write, the only place she was afforded any peace was in an abandoned, unheated room; significantly, she took refuge there under the warmth of her mother's old fur cape. Only after *The Gates Ajar* (1868) made her famous was she granted her own space in the household in which to write.[75]

Like Phelps, Alcott (who was born in 1832) was provided with the example of a brilliant mother whose talents were sacrificed to her husband and children. But Alcott's family was more supportive of her early development as an author. Indeed, her family was considered extraordinary by those who knew the Alcotts when Louisa was growing up, and her early life provides a fascinating study of how a young woman could come to understand herself as an artist in nineteenth-century America. The Alcotts can be credited with instilling in their daughters a sense of freedom and purpose in life that inspired two out of the four daughters to pursue lives as artists (Louisa as an author and May as a visual artist). Although the Alcotts had no sons to send forth into the world, and Louisa felt herself to be the "son of the house going to war" as she went off to nurse soldiers in the Civil War, it would be inaccurate to suppose that the Alcotts simply projected ambitions onto Louisa that they would have harbored for a son. Bronson Alcott's ideas about childhood, which were well received by his friend Emerson, reveal a striking gender neutrality that would belie any such notions. Most Alcott scholars have condemned Bronson for placing heavy burdens on Louisa, citing his neglect of financial matters, which made it necessary for her to churn out less serious writings to support her family and prevented her from reaching her full potential as an author. While there is some truth to this view, Bronson's ideas on the inherent genius of every child, male or female, also suggest that he instilled in his daughter a liberating philosophy that gave her faith to pursue life as an artist. To him, genius was a "flaming Herald" sent from God to "revive in Humanity the lost idea of its destiny." Each human being was born with this divine spark, but, unfortunately, fear and intolerance stifled children's potential. It was the job of the teacher — the role Bronson adopted — to awaken the genius of children and to nurture it into fruition. In this role, he made no distinction between the genius granted to boys and to girls; he looked to both sexes for messages from above.[76]

Bronson also conveyed to Louisa the pride he felt in her abilities and accomplishments. On her fourteenth birthday, she received from her father a book into which he had copied her original poetry, a clear sanction and appreciation of her imaginative writing. When she was only twelve years old, he wrote that she "will make a way, perhaps fame in the world" with her "ready genius." When she went to Europe in 1865, Bronson praised "the Genius that draws so skillfully" descriptions of places she visited, descriptions that he proudly read to Emerson and encouraged her to publish. "Dont [*sic*] name your writing 'poor scribble,' " he told her; "write away about whatever interests you: all is delightful to me, and will be so suggestive to you on your return. May you have the health, leisure, comforts, as you have the Genius to shape them into fair volumes, for the wider circle of readers."[77] There is no question that Bronson, throughout his life, explicitly urged Louisa to have faith in her abilities and take pride in her writing, which he consistently deemed worthy of publication. In stark contrast to the parents in Phelps's "Unhappy Girls," Bronson Alcott encouraged his daughters to gaze straight into the divine and make "honored name[s]" for themselves.

As the Alcott children grew up, Bronson practiced his theories and methods of instruction on them, making the home a schoolroom or, as Cynthia Barton puts it, a "laboratory." Conversations, reading and discussing the classics, telling stories, acting out scenes from their favorite Dickens novels, and putting on plays Louisa had written were some of the activities the Alcotts fostered in this household imbued with a republican emphasis on education and a romantic belief in imagination. Unlike Phelps's father, Bronson welcomed his children into his study, encouraging them to play there and to read his books, in which Alcott even remembered scribbling. The study, filled with busts of the great thinkers, was not an exclusive sphere of patriarchal privilege and seclusion but a place where daughters were welcome and books were accessible.[78]

While her father's idealism seemed to provide an opportunity for Alcott to explore her own peculiar genius, his beliefs were nonetheless so all-consuming that they also had a pernicious effect on her family. In his relentless search for the divine within himself, he shut out his family and the material world to the point that he neglected his responsibilities, forcing others to carry more than their share of the burden of earthly existence. He was well known for his refusal to engage in any work that he felt compromised his beliefs, which was just about everything other than teaching and chopping wood. When his teaching methods came under attack, the family subsisted on the charity of friends and relatives until the girls were old enough to contribute to the family's income by sewing, teaching, and, in Louisa's case, writing. But in his family's eyes, he posed an even greater threat to their survival by desiring separation. Throughout Louisa's childhood, her family appears to have been a very unstable one. In her satirical account of the utopian experiment Fruitlands, which nearly destroyed her family, she poked fun at how "some call of the Oversoul wafted all the men away" when it came time to bring in the grain. But the threat of desertion was potentially more than temporary. When Bronson was casting about for the new project that would eventually become Fruitlands, Emerson noted, "He is quite ready at any moment to abandon his present residence & employment, his country, nay, his wife & children, on very short notice, to put any dream into practice."[79]

The Alcott family exemplifies the hidden matrix of support that is required when one individual in the family is as devoted to the pursuit of genius as Bronson Alcott was. When asked once to define "philosopher," Louisa responded, "A man up in a balloon with his family at the strings tugging to pull him down." Her metaphor conveys the mutual effort that was required of family members to keep Bronson earthbound and the family intact. While some would prefer to call him simply selfish, Bronson was trying to fulfill the Transcendentalist ideal of self-reliance. As Louisa was painfully aware, when taken to its logical extreme, self-reliance really meant reliance on others and required the self-sacrifice of family members. She watched her mother give up everything — a comfortable life, her independence, control over her life, and her own separate identity — to Bronson's idealism. She watched as her mother was allotted the care of worldly matters, despite her own spiritual and philosophical nature, while her husband and his friends lived in the metaphysical realm. Abigail was left at home while he attended the meetings of the Transcendental Club, and she was excluded from the intellectual discussions at Fruitlands. As she wrote to a friend, "higher intelligences . . . admit me sometimes to their debates when the carnal things are to be discussed." The women Louisa saw participating in the world of ideas were usually single women, like Fuller and Elizabeth Peabody, both of whom were friends of her family and teaching assistants to her father. The message she inevitably received was that marriage meant self-sacrifice and the end of one's own intellectual and spiritual identity. In essence, she learned the same lesson as Phelps: if you want to be a writer, which requires autonomy and individuality, do not marry.[80]

No doubt as a result of her experiences, Abigail Alcott instilled a strong desire for independence in her daughters. She once wrote, "I say to all dear girls keep up, be something in yourself. Let the world feel at some stage of this diurnal revolution that you are on its surface alive, not in its bowels a dead, decaying thing." Abby's own talents, untiring support, and expansive views about women's opportunities made her in many ways exactly the kind of mother the young Phelps longed for after losing her own. Abby provided not only encouragement but also a certain understanding of Louisa's nature that helped to legitimate her daughter's ambition. "People think I'm wild and queer; but Mother understands and helps me," Alcott wrote at the age of thirteen.[81] Abby also provided a model of women's abilities for her daughters. According to Charles Strickland, "Abigail provided her daughter both encouragement and a model for imitation. Abigail was a writer of considerable talent, and although she never wrote for publication, her letters and diaries possess a vigor of expression that is reflected in the best of Louisa's writing." Abby's literary talents were accessible to the young Louisa from a very early age. She wrote letters to Louisa as lessons on her behavior, rather than lecturing her, and, as Madelon Bedell writes, "the two wrote continually back and forth to each other, reading and annotating each other's diaries, composing poems in each other's honor."[82] While Abby possessed literary as well as musical and dramatic talents, the dreams she harbored of becoming a writer were left unfulfilled. Instead, she undoubtedly channeled her own ambitions into the young, headstrong Louisa, who showed both talent and determination. At the age of ten, Louisa wrote a poem titled "To Mother," which describes the intertwined artistic aspirations of mother and daughter:

> I hope that soon, dear mother,
>   You and I may be
> In the quiet room my fancy
>   Has so often made for thee —
>
> The pleasant, sunny chamber,
>   The cushioned easy-chair,
> The book laid for your reading,
>   The vase of flowers fair;
>
> The desk beside the window
>   Where the sun shines warm and bright:
> And there in ease and quiet
>   The promised book you write;
>
> While I sit close beside you,
>   Content at last to see
> That you can rest, dear mother,
>   And I can cherish thee.[83]

Abigail provided Louisa invaluable emotional support. At the age of eight, for example, Louisa produced her first poem, "The Robin," about which her mother was very proud, exclaiming, "You will grow up a Shakespeare!" And when Louisa was fourteen, her mother gave her a pen with the following poem: "Oh! may this Pen your muse inspire / When rapt in pure poetic fire / To write some sweet, some thrilling verse." Abby also predicted a brilliant future for her daughter. She told Louisa, "Lift up your soul then to meet the highest, for that alone can satisfy your great yearning nature. . . . believe me you are capable of ranking among the best." In 1863, after Alcott's first success with *Hospital Sketches*, Abigail wrote in her diary, "She will have no mean rank assigned her now. She is in the vestibule of the temple, but the high altar is not far off." And when her first novel, *Moods*, was published, Abigail believed that "Her powers are greater than she knows." Beneath this entry, she also pasted a clipping announcing the novel's publication and added that readers have found it "the finest American novel they have read, powerful, natural, and of the highest literary merit." This novel was dedicated to Abigail — "To Mother, my earliest patron, kindest critic, dearest reader" — as was her first book, *Flower Fables* (1855), about which Louisa wrote to her mother, "Whatever beauty or poetry is to be found in my little book is owing to your interest in and encouragement of all my efforts from the first to the last."[84]

Many of Alcott's biographers have noted the strong message she received to be a self-sacrificial daughter, the implication being that her parents stifled her creativity by demanding that she relinquish her ambitions to the service of her family. For instance, on Louisa's tenth birthday, Abigail gave her a picture of mother and daughter with a note that included the following lines: "I enclose a picture for you which I always liked very much, for I imagined that you might be just such an industrious daughter and I such a feeble but loving mother, looking to your labor for my daily bread."[85] But in her journals we find an evolving sense of self that closely mirrors the larger culture's liberal ideas about individuality. In other words, we see a dual emphasis on duty to family and a desire to discover and realize her own unique potential. At thirteen she confided to her journal, "I have at last got the little room I have wanted so long, and am very happy about it. It does me good to be alone. . . . I have made a plan for my life. . . . Now I'm going to *work really*, for I feel a true desire to improve, and be a help and comfort, not a care and sorrow, to my dear mother." This entry reveals the complex identity Alcott was creating, even at so young an age. With the help of her parents, who gave her a place to be alone and who nurtured her creative impulses, she saw herself as both a dutiful daughter who put her family's needs first and an individual who developed her God-given talents. Her family fostered her creative activity, and she thought of the times she spent alone as some of the most satisfying and free of her life, unlike Phelps's mother and other antebellum women, who felt they had to suppress any desire for solitude or creative endeavors. Alcott more closely resembled Dickinson, who said, "here is freedom" when she closed the door to her room.[86] But unlike Dickinson, Alcott did not feel the need to hide her writing from her family. Instead, her parents and sisters were her first and most appreciative audience, cheering her on to literary fame. Within a mutually supportive family one was supposed to reach his or her fullest potential. Alcott learned from her parents that by discovering and fulfilling her own destiny she would be the asset to her family that they desired. These two identities as dutiful daughter and self-reliant author, while they at times conflicted, also combined to make Alcott feel that she could aspire to be a "woman artist."

Undoubtedly, the fact that Alcott spent most of her formative years in Boston or Concord — the centers of Unitarianism and Transcendentalism, and the locale to which the nation looked for America's "culture" — contributed to her ability to feel that the development of her God-given talents was not only important but also imperative. As she would later write, Concord "is popularly believed to be the hot-bed of genius." The fame of its most illustrious inhabitants — Emerson, Hawthorne, Thoreau, and her own father — was firmly established by the time she began her writing career. Fuller had been a member of their circle and had taught under Bronson and visited his home, but she moved to New York in 1844, never to return. So while Fuller's memory loomed large over the young Louisa, most of the literary idols of her youth were male (although Child visited occasionally). These literary idols provided living examples to her, setting a standard of excellence at once tangible (because they were her neighbors) and remote (because they were men). So while Alcott grew up as the occasional playmate of Emerson's and Hawthorne's children and idolized their fathers and Thoreau, she also envisioned an eminent future for herself. Rather than feel stifled in their midst, she drew inspiration from their achievements. She wrote to her aunt in 1860 that she expected herself, "the great authoress," and her sister, the "artist," to add to the fame of "this famous land of Emerson Hawthorne Thoreau Alcott & Co."[87]

When the Civil War began the following year, Alcott felt as if her moment had arrived. With a strong desire to participate in the fighting, she capitalized directly on her experience during the war. When Alcott found a way to join the war, as a nurse in Washington, D.C., she wrote, "*must* let out my pent-up energy in some new way. . . . I want new experiences, and am sure to get 'em if I go." While getting new experiences was a way to release energy and discover a larger purpose for herself, it was also a way to become a writer. After publishing *Flower Fables*, Alcott wrote to her mother of her desire "to pass in time from fairies and fables to men and realities." The Civil War gave her the experiences and the material she needed to do just that. "I like to watch it all & am very glad I came as this is the sort of study I enjoy."[88] It was this watching, studying, and writing about all she saw that led to the publication of *Hospital Sketches*, from which she gained her first literary recognition. Thus, before she found her most lasting fame as a children's author, Alcott ventured far beyond the domestic sphere to discover herself as an author.

While Phelps and Alcott began their literary apprenticeships during childhood, Woolson and Stoddard, for the most part, developed their ambitions later in life and began their careers as adults. In Stoddard's case, it is easy to see why her powers remained latent for so long. She was born in 1823 in a remote village, perhaps too early and too far removed from the cultural centers to enjoy the opportunities for self-culture that New England was beginning to provide to its young women. She often lamented this fact later in life. "Of literature and the literary life, I and my tribe knew nothing; we had not discovered 'sermons in stones.'" In other words, the influence of Transcendentalist ideas had not reached the little coastal village of Mattapoisett, Massachusetts, where she grew up. In her first novel, *The Morgesons* (1862), she depicts her hometown as an isolated place, barren of any sort of culture and dominated by the sea trade. Perhaps because of the willful independence Stoddard exhibited even as a child, her family left her to pursue her own interests. That those interests tended more toward novel reading and walking by the sea than more appropriate pursuits like sewing and reading the Bible distressed her family. She later recorded that reading "had been laid up against me as a persistent fault, which was not profitable; I should peruse moral, and pious works, or take up sewing, — that interminable thing, 'white seam,' which filled the leisure moments of the right-minded."[89] But, like Phelps, she rejected the idea that domestic tasks should be her main occupation.

Stoddard stood out in her family and community as everything that other girls were not (and should not be). In his memoirs, her husband wrote, "Elizabeth Barstow was one of those irrepressible girls who are sometimes born in staid Puritan families, to puzzle their parents, and to be misunderstood. Her spirits were high, and her disposition wilful [*sic*]." Stoddard herself felt that there was no one to sympathize with her. While she was petted by her family, she nonetheless felt like an outsider. Her sister, for example, did not have "a particle of sympathy with or a knowledge of my mind," she wrote to a friend.[90]

Probably the most distinguishing characteristic of this "wilful" young woman in the religiously conservative community of Mattapoisett was her resistance to organized religion. She disdained the church her mother regularly attended and she refused to be converted when a revival swept up her fellow students at Wheaton, much like Dickinson did when she was away at school. This set her farther apart from her community. "When I was young, I was fed on the strong dish of New England polemics," she wrote in 1855. "God, my teachers said, did not reside in the natural heart of man, which fact I must learn through some process that my soul refused to understand." It was years before she would discover Thoreau, Emerson, and Transcendentalism. But in her effort to free herself from hollow tradition and conformity, she went farther than the early Transcendentalists and avowed something akin to atheism. Her pessimistic view of the cruel universe led her to look to the sea as a symbol of the alternating and arbitrary forces of good and evil. But despite her rejection of her family and community, she often returned to her childhood home to rest and write, looking to the sea for inspiration. The sea, her most personal connection to the nature that the Transcendentalists and romantics exhorted aspiring artists to study, fig-ures prominently in her fiction, representing the awesome force of nature and reflecting the inner turbulence of her heroines.[91]

Although Stoddard was sent to a number of female seminaries, including the well-known Wheaton in Norton, Massachusetts, she was not "studious." Rather than pursue a formal course of study, she preferred perusing the library of her minister, who fed her insatiable appetite for literature. Under his guidance she was able to seclude herself, wander through previously unknown worlds, and discover her love for books. According to her husband, she read "thousands of volumes," mostly eighteenth-century classics, constituting "the only education she ever had." In cultivating her literary tastes, she was also withdrawing from her family. In her later letters, she described her father as utterly uninterested and even antipathetic toward her literary endeavors. Her father, she wrote to a friend, "said to me utterly forgetting that I had ever written any — that he had no faith in novels, poor stuff—." In addition, he had loaned a copy of her first novel to a neighbor and forgotten to retrieve it for twenty years. Each time she returned home she felt as if she lost that part of herself that was so important to her — her writer self, whom no one at home would acknowledge. Her sister, she wrote, "has never given me a sign of recognition of my powers." Had Stoddard stayed at home she likely would not have developed her ambition to make her mark as an author.[92]

Stoddard's life at home effectively came to an end when one of her sisters and her mother died in 1848 and 1849. "Without these two deaths, Elizabeth might never have left Mattapoisett," James Matlack writes. These "sudden" deaths "cut her loose from the old moorings," and as her home broke up, she felt restless. Her brothers intended to go to California to make their fortune, and she had vague plans of accompanying them. However, while her brothers' restlessness found an object, hers could not. In 1852 she wrote to her friend Margaret Sweat that she also possessed "aspirations," but, "What is there for such women as you and me are? I have decided that an irresistible will compels me to some destiny, but vaguely shaped yet much desired."[93] The main problem, she suggested, was that she was a woman. Had she been a man, she could have gone to California like her brothers. When she began to visit New York in the early 1850s, she learned of another possibility. She attended literary gatherings and met many of the famous men and women who were in the business of making journals and books. She became a regular at literary parties where she rubbed elbows with publishers, editors, and famous writers like Bayard Taylor, George Boker, Caroline Kirkland, Phoebe and Alice Cary, and Richard Henry Stoddard.

When she first met Richard, they both possessed a "love of books," but while he had become a poet of some small fame, she, it appears, had not yet taken up her pen. However, the literary atmosphere of New York was beginning to have an influence on her. In the fall of 1851 she wrote to Sweat, "You are then living the life of books! . . . I have not fairly made a debut, but expect to in various ways be an admiring expectation of men & things." She went on to mention her literary friends in New York, indicating that their world enticed her. Indeed, she was beginning to think of the possibility of becoming an author by joining the circle of writers in New York, which included some women. But how would she establish herself there? "I am bitterly afraid I shall go to California," she wrote Sweat. "If I do, it upsets my theory of my destiny—I have arranged a different programme." At this point, she was torn between her love for her brother Wilson and her desire for independence. But a third element entered her life—Richard. He had confessed his love for her, but her feelings for him were uncertain. She had written to Sweat two months before, "Now I possess the quality of love for a man, . . . yet my self possession is indomitable. I am my own, I still hold to this devilish faculty of analyzation, still am actor & spectator, What shall I do?" She felt herself split in two—"actor & spectator"—but she also saw two potential identities for herself — wife and author — one defined by her love for a man, the other by her desire to be independent. In her letters to Sweat, she struggled (obliquely) with these two possibilities, attempting to resist Richard but never quite defining what her alternative was.[94] In October 1852, her father's financial failure set into motion the final breakup of her family. The house was sold and her brothers began to solidify their plans to go to California. In the following months, she wrote to Sweat of being in love, although she was reluctant to tell all. In fact, although she married Richard in early December 1852, she didn't tell Sweat of her plans to marry until December 23 and didn't admit to being married until early February, sure signs of her ambivalence about leaving her family and giving up her newfound independence.[95]

The "crisis of identity" that Stoddard felt during this period is a central theme of much of her early fiction, which depicts courtship as a "battle" between men and women. Often, as in her novel *The Morgesons* and the story "Tuberoses," the hero and heroine are both so willful and independent that romance requires a weakening of one or both parties, and their union is pictured as a "defeat." As part of her effort to maintain a sense of her individuality in marriage, Stoddard began to write. While Richard implied in his *Recollections* that she didn't start to write until after their marriage, she had written to Sweat, "In October [1852] I began to write, my first little sketch was published in the Lit World." She may have begun even earlier, considering that the sketch, "Phases," was published in the *Literary World* in October 1852. It is unclear what, if anything, Richard may have had to do with this first publication or her beginning to write. But she apparently did not publish another word for two years. In the meantime, she wrote to Sweat of her apprenticeship and her aspirations and doubts about writing. At first her expectations were low. "I fancy I shall never be much in a literary way anyway," she confided in May 1853. A month earlier she had claimed there were "moments . . . when I am ready to sacrifice an ambitious future to the most intensified form of love," and she anticipated that she would not be very "intellectual" anymore because "I must be in [a] clothes & housekeeping atmosphere." Again in May, she complained of the lack of mental stimulation in her life: "What shall I do to satisfy my intellect? The devices that fill our woman life are *nothing* to me. I chafe horribly when S. leaves me to go into the world of men. While I remain under cover waiting for him. But I am happy thank God as a wife." By September, however, she admitted that her lot as a wife was not enough for her. She had hoped "Love would prove Lethe," but she still felt "restless as a tiger. All others seem to me to be fulfilling their destiny; everybody has a way of labor but me."[96]

During her early marriage, then, she seems to have felt the two identities of wife and author to be at odds. But Richard may have encouraged her to try to combine the two. In his *Recollections*, he mused, "The habit of writing is sometimes catching, as my wife finally discovered when she caught herself penning little essays, and poems, and stories, which she brought to me in fear and trembling. She had a fine intellect, but it was untrained, and all that I could do for her was to show her how to train it." He does not account for her intense ambitions but sees her wanting to write as merely a form of emulation. However, what her family had not provided for her — a stimulating, supportive, literary atmosphere — her marriage in some ways did. Her husband gave her some encouragement, space, and time in which to practice her writing. He also tutored her, as she wrote to Sweat. "I go to school daily to my master-poet. . . . I play a very quiet part I assure you, and the most that I learn is my own insignificance." While she grew in her admiration of her husband's powers, she seemed to doubt her own. "I believe more & more in [Richard's] *genius*," she wrote to Sweat, adding, "You ask me about my *own* writing[.] Alas, laziness doth hedge about me as divinity about a king — or perhaps it is incapacity. [M]y desires or aspirations are above my creative powers. Sometimes a pang of belief shoots across my mind that it *is in me* but [it is] momentary. I relapse into the meager formulas of daily life & am no more than I seem to be." Although discouraged, she also revealed that her "desires or aspirations," which were more clearly defined versions of the vague aspirations that she had earlier felt, were still very much with her. Writing, then, was beginning to reveal itself as a way to fulfill her "destiny."[97]

The early years of Stoddard's marriage and her close association with the circle of poets to which her husband belonged threatened to stifle her ambitions, but these two circumstances also stimulated her to reach for the heights she perceived these poets to have attained. In 1901 she recalled how and why she first developed her ambitions as a writer:

> I had now come to live among those who made books, and were interested in all their material, for all was the glory of the whole. Prefaces, notes, indexes, were unnoticed by me. . . . I began to get glimpses of a profound ignorance, and did not like the position as an outside consideration. These mental productive adversities abased me. I was well enough in my way, but nothing was expected of me in their way, and when I beheld their ardor in composition, and its fine emulation, like a "sheep before her shearers," I was dumb. The environment pressed upon me, my pride was touched; my situation, though "tolerable, was not to be endured."[98]

She felt goaded on to prove to Richard and his friends that she was capable of the literary feats on which they so prided themselves. She was now in an atmosphere of intense aspiration, competition, and egos.

The circle of literary men to which her husband belonged was dominated principally by Bayard Taylor and George Boker. Later, Edmund Clarence Stedman and Thomas Bailey Aldrich would also join the inner circle. These men met in New York in the late 1840s and 1850s, and, as Richard Stoddard wrote of himself and Taylor, they shared "a love of poetry and a belief that we were poets. We may have doubted some things, but that supreme thing we did not and would not doubt." They gathered together in their rooms or at parties to discuss literature, art, beauty, and truth, those romantic ideals that linked them in brotherhood and helped give them strength in the face of a culture that did not appreciate its poets. They formed a mutual admiration society in which they hailed their powers as superior to others'. In 1856, Elizabeth Stoddard offered her humorous impression of their "literary visit[s]":

> A finds B writing a poem. A insists on B's reading it. B reads and A says "glorious." Then A takes a manuscript from his pocket, which B insists shall be read. A reads and B says "glorious." A asks if B has seen his last squib in Young America. B asks if A has seen his last review of that book by Muggins. Each man puts his feet on the sofa (no, literary people don't have sofas) — somewhere above his head — and then Tennyson, Browning, Longfellow, and their faults are discovered.[99]

As the wife of "A" or "B," however, Stoddard felt herself consigned to the margins of this literary fraternity, much as Abigail Alcott had been in the presence of her husband and his circle. But instead of allowing herself to be relegated to the role of bystander, she aspired to become a "C" in this chummy literary alphabet.

Although these men felt neglected by their society (especially Richard, who was less successful than Boker or Taylor), they drew strength from adversity and fashioned strong identities for themselves as poets, defining for Elizabeth what it meant to be a writer. They lionized the British romantics and admired the sages of Concord and Cambridge who were gaining the fame they hoped to achieve. Struggling to scrape together lives as men of letters, they had to work in editorial and political positions. Their belief in themselves and their strong egos as poets had two effects on Stoddard: they inspired her, but they also left her feeling ignorant and "dumb." They seemed to possess a secret, as she wrote in one of her early poems, "The Poet's Secret," that they would not share with her:

The poet's secret I must know,
If that will calm my restless mind.

.   .   .   .

In vain I watch the day and night,
In vain the world through space may roll;
I never see the mystic light,
Which fills the poet's happy soul.

.   .   .   .

The poet's secret I must know: —
By pain and patience shall I learn?[100]

This was essentially the primary question of her life as writer. The secret, one could say, was confidence, which they gained from each other, and which she satirized in her sketch of "A" and "B." Throughout her career, she looked to these men for the same kind of puffing up, but she often found that she would have to look elsewhere. Her husband and his friends were incapable of giving Stoddard the kind of confidence that Alcott's enthusiastic family circle gave her.

As she wrote, they expected "nothing" of her "in their way," so she had to fight to claim these poets' world as her own, to dare to ask for inclusion in their club, and to gain the respect of her husband and his peers. She once wrote to Stedman that she was "anxious" for him to see her new poem and that Richard "thinks it the best I have done — if I am right in my hope and aim, I shall prove to you males that I [am] your comrade." Although Richard encouraged her newly focused ambition, ultimately his support appears to have been ambiguous. At times, he thought very highly of her work and extended much-needed praise; at other times, his judgment was harsh and left her in tears. In 1854, she confided to Sweat that Richard was "a severe master and I get so discouraged that I cry dreadfully." After she had written her three novels, she wrote to William Dean Howells that Richard "had no interest in that art [novel-writing], he never cared for mine, in his heart never believed in them. When I gave him my first story to read, he had so little faith in it, in my prose talent, that he went off to read it by himself, and came back to say that it was good enough to offer." In contrast, his response to her poetry was "magnificently generous, and a wonderful help to me." One would expect that Elizabeth Stoddard chose to channel her energies primarily into fiction instead of poetry partly because of her desire not to compete with her husband and to establish her literary independence. Ironically, she received less support from him as a fiction writer than as a poet.[101]

Although Stoddard grew up in an isolated village and in a family that did not value literature, she had come "to live among those who made books," and their studiousness and enthusiasm about that art provided an environment that helped her begin to think of her own literary powers and ambitions. "Your literary patience, courage and conscience delight me," she wrote to Stedman, "for in my small way I possess them too—." But the close-knit, masculine community to which she belonged as a literary wife and hoped to enter on a more intimate basis as a "comrade" also left her feeling inadequate. Unlike Woolson, Phelps, and Alcott, Stoddard would give up her career, discouraged by the dismal sales and ambivalent critical reception of her work. Without a supportive family that could instill in her a strong sense of self-worth and provide her with models of creative and accomplished women, she was at a distinct disadvantage in her pursuit of the life of an artist.[102]

Alcott, Phelps, Stoddard, and Woolson all developed ambitions to be artists in the context of American individualism, Transcendentalism, the rise of the *Atlantic Monthly*, and their literary families. And they were inspired by the examples of illustrious women of genius in France and Britain. This cultural matrix explains the generational nature of their ambitions. Their generation of women, which Fuller anticipated, believed that they had something unique and important to say, not only in the formation of public opinion and not only as women or representatives of their sex, and yet not quite as individuals in a gender-neutral sense either. Their culture was too preoccupied with sexual difference to allow them to view themselves in a way that precluded gender. Rather, they believed that as *individuals among women* they had significant and extraordinary contributions to make to a national high literature, which seemed for the first time willing to grant provisional entrance to women writers. Such was the aspiration of these four women—to distinguish themselves as outstanding American women writers, as *women artists*—as difficult as the combination of those two identities would be.

CHAPTER TWO

"Prov[ing] Avis in the Wrong"

The Lives of Women Artists

Alcott, Phelps, Stoddard, and Woolson grew up in a middle-class culture that prized women who, like Lydia Maria Child's "frugal housewife" or Catharine Beecher's housewife in *A Treatise on Domestic Economy*, combined domesticity, housekeeping, and mothering with mental culture. Such women took a moment here or there from laundry or while the baby was sleeping to pen a letter, read a chapter in a novel, or even write a story to send off to *Godey's* or *Peterson's* as a contribution to the struggling family's income. This was the ideal woman (writer) that Phelps's mother and Harriet Beecher Stowe tried to be. The next generation of women who wanted to write professionally, while revering these women, did not feel capable of living up to this model. They no longer believed that a cultivated woman had enough energy to devote to both home and authorship. In 1867 Phelps declared, "As a general thing, it is next to impossible for a woman with the care of a family on her hands to be a successful writer." For these younger women, the literary life was as much a commitment as life with a husband and/or children. They often thought of their literary products as children and their careers as mates, as Alcott did when she wrote in her essay "Happy Women" (1868), "Literature is a fond and faithful spouse, and the little family that has sprung up around [me] . . . is a profitable source of satisfaction to [my] maternal heart."[1]

For most postbellum women writers, the roles of wife and literary artist were not compatible. They found it difficult if not impossible to envision being both. Emma Lazarus wrote, about a romantic disappointment, "so I have to resume my position of old maid *ad infinitum* — unless I inherit a fortune or turn out a genius like . . . George Eliot."[2] In Lazarus's construction, to be a "genius" is a full life in and of itself and poses an alternative to having a husband (or a fortune, which would provide its own kind of life). In fact, a woman of genius is no longer an old maid; she is already married, in a way, and therefore no longer seeks a mate. She has a purpose apart from her domestic status. The women of this study, who had discovered such a purpose in their lives, felt that they had to forgo marriage, and they struggled throughout their lives with their decisions. Stoddard, having made the difficult decision to marry, bravely tried to be mother, wife, and author, although she eventually gave up and devoted herself almost exclusively to her husband and son. Phelps married late in life, but her marriage did not end her career; rather, it could be said that her career ended the marriage. And even though Alcott and Woolson decided not to marry, this did not entirely free them from familial responsibilities.

The difficulty of reconciling or combining the seemingly contradictory identities of "woman" and "artist" became a main focus of some of the most compelling fiction produced by Alcott, Phelps, Stoddard, and Woolson. The same is true for Rebecca Harding Davis, and this tension was a central theme of some of Emily Dickinson's most engaging poetry. These writers were influenced by groundbreaking works about women artists that had established this theme as a powerful subject for women's art, particularly *Corinne*, by Madame de Staël, and *Aurora Leigh*, by Elizabeth Barrett Browning. In addition, marriage had become a chief concern for American women, particularly those of the middle class. Throughout the nineteenth century, as the issues of women's rights and duties were increasingly matters of public debate, so were questions about when, whether, and whom a woman should marry. And because such decisions were, as many commentators often reiterated, the most important ones a woman would ever make, it is not surprising that marriage was a popular topic for literature. However, while most novels about women before the Civil War focused on courtship and ended with either engagement or a wedding, after the war, many novels examined the aftermath of the decisions women made.

One such novel, Phelps's *Story of Avis* (1877), was one of the most widely read and debated works on the subject of marriage in nineteenth-century America. In depicting an artist heroine's attempt to combine marriage and art, this novel laid bare the difficult choices women had to make between living for themselves or living for others. Phelps's outlook was ultimately pessimistic; she was convinced that relations between men and women, as they then existed, precluded women's self-development and happiness. In her judgment, a woman was as yet incapable of being an artist while she was a wife and mother. Stoddard, Alcott, Woolson, and Davis came to similar conclusions in their fiction and in their lives. When Alcott's sister May (1840–79), an artist, was married, Alcott wrote to a friend, "May says — 'To combine art & matrimony is almost too much bliss.' I hope she will find it so & prove 'Avis' in the wrong."[3] The apprehension in this statement suggests that Alcott believed *Avis* was right, however. Phelps's *Avis* had become the emblem of the postbellum generation of women artists that Barrett Browning's *Aurora Leigh* had been for Phelps and her contemporaries as young women.

As Alcott, Phelps, Stoddard, and Woolson tried to figure out how to live their unprecedented and therefore unscripted lives as artists, they had to confront the age-old patterns of women's lives — domesticity, marriage, motherhood, and self-sacrifice. In spite of their many obligations as women, they tried to carve out spaces in their lives for the kind of solitude necessary to make art. And they dreamed of what life would be like in the future or in another place, particularly Europe, when and where solitude and freedom would be more possible. But difficult questions remained: would women ever be able to combine lives as artists with the love other women found in marriage and motherhood? Could they ever "prove 'Avis' in the wrong"? Would the woman artist forever have to choose between love and ambition? And was it true, as many had said, that only the woman who knew the love of a husband and children was capable of great art?

The Question of Marriage

Although the Civil War precipitated a period of decline in marriage rates and legitimated spinsterhood to a greater degree than ever before, the overwhelming majority of women continued to marry, and by the 1890s, marriage rates for women had returned to their norm of 90 percent. At midcentury, when Alcott, Phelps, Stoddard, and Woolson were still young and forming their opinions about marriage, discontent about the institution was growing, and it became the locus of cultural debates about women's status in American society. Women's rights advocates attacked the laws that made a woman's husband her representative in all public dealings, devolved her property and money to him, and made divorce difficult to obtain. Elizabeth Cady Stanton made marriage a prominent issue in "The Declaration of Sentiments," written for the first women's rights convention, at Seneca Falls, New York, in 1848: "In the covenant of marriage, she [woman] is compelled to promise obedience to her husband, he becoming, to all intents and purposes, her master — the law giving him power to deprive her of her liberty, and to administer chastisement."[4] As Stanton's language suggests, comparisons between marriage and slavery were rife during the early women's rights movement.

The loss of control over one's body and the menial drudgery most women experienced during marriage only amplified such comparisons. Women's rights leader Sarah Grimké promoted the right "of woman to decide *when* she shall become a mother, how often & under what circumstances." Too many women, she declared, discover once they are married that they are treated by their husbands as "legal prostitute[s]   Man seems to feel that Marriage gives him the control of Woman's person just as the Law gives him the control of her property." Methods of contraception and recipes for agents that would induce miscarriages can be found in nineteenth-century publications, although contraception and abortion (which some doctors and midwives practiced) were outlawed in many states as concerns increased about women's freedoms and the decline in birth rates, particularly among middle-class white women.[5] On the whole, once a woman married, she often had little agency in determining how many children she would bear. And of those pregnancies she did incur, a great number would end in miscarriage, stillbirth, or infant death.

In addition, the responsibilities of housework and child rearing were tremendously damaging to the health of American women. Even Catharine Beecher, a major spokeswoman for the cult of domesticity, claimed that for every healthy woman, three were sick. Women's household duties involved food preparation, including the continuous baking of bread and the laborious canning and preserving of fruits and vegetables; marketing on a daily or semidaily basis; tending fires for cooking and warming the house; cleaning floors, rugs, windows, furniture, and draperies; sewing, mending, laundering, and ironing clothes; knitting and all other needlework; caring for the sick; nursing infants and tending to small children; and instructing children in reading, writing, and math, as well as manners, morality, and religion. A woman might also have gardening added to her list of responsibilities, and if she lived on a farm, she could expect to participate in the tending and slaughtering of animals and perhaps to make many of the household's necessities, including soap, candles, cloth, and yarn. In addition to these daily duties, women also were expected to entertain and feed visitors, many of whom stayed for weeks or months at a time, and to care for the poor and underprivileged in their communities. Every woman of the household participated in each of these activities, so even unmarried women who stayed at home were rarely freed from housework. But when a woman married, she understood that all of these responsibilities, on top of the physical strain of childbirth, would comprise her daily existence. Is it any wonder, then, that few women had the time or strength to devote to literary or other pursuits? As Phelps asserted, "It is no easy matter to keep the 'holy fire burning in the holy place,' yet never be out of kindlings for the kitchen stove, nor forget to tell Bridget about the furnace dampers, nor let the baby have the match-box to play with." Women's myriad practical concerns crowded out virtually all other endeavors.[6]

In light of these responsibilities, marriage and motherhood were generally viewed as the endpoint of a woman's development. When de Tocqueville visited America in 1831–32, he astutely summed up the condition of women: "In America, the independence of women is irrevocably lost in the bonds of matrimony."[7] When young, a woman experienced a relatively great deal of freedom, but all that changed once she left her father's house to enter her husband's. As a wife and mother, she inherited duties that consumed her life and hindered any further growth. As Joanne Dobson has pointed out, nineteenth-century American women's poetry and fiction focused almost exclusively on "the girl" because social conventions kept women in a state of immaturity and dependence. The sense of selfhood and personal agency that come with mature adulthood were either silenced or killed off in marriage, and marriage itself signified a kind of death.[8] For the woman writer, this image of marriage was even more potent, for matrimony likely meant the end of her creative voice and aspirations. The woman writer who married was often more literally silenced than her nonartistic counterparts, and she probably experienced more palpably the death of a significant part of herself—the artist.

Despite the negative connotations of marriage for women, society, as de Tocqueville recognized, did not have to force women to accept this quasi death; instead they went willingly into matrimony, most of them convinced that they were not giving up all chance of happiness.[9] In fact, women were taught that they were entering the period of their lives in which they would realize the fulfillment and happiness that were supposed to be their destiny as wives and mothers. There were at least two reasons why women believed that the price they had to pay in marriage was not too great. The most prevalent one was the ideal of romantic love that had become prominent in the culture through novels, advice books, songs, and illustrations in periodicals and gift annuals. Grimké conveys the potency of this ideal: "Every man and woman feels a profound want . . . [a]n indescribable longing for, & yearning after a perfect absorption of [his or her] interests, feeling & being . . . into one kindred spirit."[10] According to the romantic ideal, no greater happiness could be found on earth than that of a true and lasting love between a man and a woman, except, of course, motherhood, which was the logical outcome of such a union. So the two greatest sources of happiness and tranquillity for women were believed to emanate from the marital union. A woman who did not marry, therefore, was deprived of love and earthly bliss. Hawthorne's Hepzibah (in *The House of Seven Gables*) and Zenobia (in *The Blithedale Romance*) are representative of how the spinster was usually perceived: as miserable and forlorn and as someone who had missed out on life's greatest pleasures. Secondly, the loss of independence in marriage could also be a great relief to women who, in Stephen Mintz's words, felt "anxieties about independence, the psychological consequences of individualism, and the longing for a marital union as an anchorage in a sea of doubts and a shelter from selfishness and despair."[11] Women who married could feel absolved from the guilt they felt about desiring freedom. Marriage was the ultimate self-sacrifice that allowed women to feel they were leading virtuous lives.

Rare was the spinster who felt free to live independently and was financially capable of doing so. Most devoted themselves to aging parents or to siblings who had families. Employment opportunities for women were also limited, and remuneration was often barely enough to support oneself. So to choose the single state did not automatically signal a declaration of independence. Not until the Civil War did young women begin to articulate and realize dreams of living on their own. But Alcott, Phelps, and Woolson, all of whom chose lives as "spinsters" while still young, still felt bound to their families, especially aging parents. It wasn't until 1880, at the age of forty-seven, that Alcott established "a home of [her] own," claiming, "as the other artistic and literary spinsters have a house, I am going to try the plan, for a winter at least."[12] But unlike Dickinson, who also deliberately chose a life of "single blessedness," they did not remain at home for the whole of their lives. They traveled, lived with other women, and lived by themselves on occasion.

So-called Boston marriages, in which two women lived together in committed relationships, were another solution to the need for companionship in light of many women's disdain for conventional marriage. None of the women discussed here formed Boston marriages, as Sarah Orne Jewett did with Annie Fields, but female friendships and support from other women were important to them as they strove to create lives as artists. In their fiction, they also depicted the significance of female community for single women. It is, in fact, quite possible that Alcott's, Phelps's, and Woolson's desires not to marry were due in part to their preference for the companionship of women. There are suggestions in their stories that this may have been the case. A few scholars have offered interpretations of some of their stories that suggest implicit lesbian themes, and stories by Woolson and Phelps have been included in an anthology of lesbian fiction by nineteenth-century women. For many women of this era, a life spent in intimate relationships with women allowed for more freedom and a greater potential for self-development than did heterosexual marriage. According to Lee Virginia Chambers-Schiller, "sisterly love provided opportunities to strengthen autonomy, support initiative, reinforce individual will, confirm vocational identity, and promote . . . aspirations."[13] The support of "sisterly love" helped encourage and sustain many women's literary ambitions.

Alcott, for example, longed for her sisters to remain unmarried, like her, so that they could live together and pursue similar goals of self-reliance and artistry. For brief periods she shared the artist's life with her sister May while they roomed in Boston and traveled in Europe. Most tellingly, Alcott told Louise Chandler Moulton that she was "half-persuaded that I am a man's soul, put by some freak of nature into a woman's body . . . because I have fallen in love in my life with so many pretty girls, and never once the least little bit with any man." The same certainly could be said of Jewett, and Dickinson is well known for her intimate relationship with Susan Gilbert Dickinson, which has been the source of much critical commentary.[14] Phelps was very close to Annie Fields, before the death of James Fields and long before Annie's Boston marriage with Jewett. Phelps also had an intimate friend, the doctor Mary Briggs Harris, with whom she lived off and on until the latter's death in 1886. Woolson's female traveling companions — her mother, sister, and niece — were important sources of support to her and preferable to a husband. Woolson, who appears never to have been in love with a man, once wrote in defense of a novel portraying "a woman's adoration of another woman[,] . . . I myself have seen tears of joy, the uttermost faith, and deep devotion, in mature, well-educated, and cultivated women, for some other woman whom they adored; have seen an absorption for months of every thought." Although these women went on to marry, she was sure that they still reflected fondly on "that old adoration which was so intense and so pure." As Woolson suggests here, such relationships were widely perceived as chaste and innocent girlhood fancies that eventually would be replaced with heterosexual marriages. As a young woman, Woolson had such a friendship that waned when the friend married. Similarly, Stoddard had an intimate friendship (most of it sustained via correspondence) with Margaret Sweat, which did not survive her marriage. But throughout her life, Stoddard continued to long for a close female friend and had many stormy relationships with women. She sought a deeper meeting of the minds and more mutual support than was possible with men, although she frequently complained that most women didn't understand her because she was so different from them. For many women, life outside of marriage or without men did not mean a life devoid of intimacy and love. But it is probably also true that Alcott, Phelps, Stoddard, and Woolson did not take advantage of the support and strength derived from the "female world of love and ritual" to the extent that other women, particularly Jewett and Fields, did.[15]

Of the four, Woolson was the most pessimistic about marriage. She respected the institution deeply, and later in life she seemed to envy women who experienced marital bliss, yet she was unable to envision a marriage that would not stifle a woman's artistic ambitions and talents. When her friend Arabella Carter married, Woolson tried to assure her that she approved of the match and her decision, using the romantic language of idealized love: "You don't know how I rejoice in your happiness, Belle. I am *so, so* glad for you. A man's true, earnest love is a great gift. If you do not accept it and enjoy it, I shall—shake you! . . . The glory of your life has come to you. Everything else is trivial compared to it. You and he are really alone in the world together. Two souls that love always are. Do give up your past life and duties and BE HAPPY!" In another letter after Carter's marriage, Woolson contrasted her own life as a "desolate spinster" with that of her friend, who has "the constant companionship of your husband." Woolson missed her close friend, although she assured her that "I highly approve of you in the character of Wife and Mother, but for all that I am none the less lonely."[16] At this point Woolson's sister Clara had also recently married and left home.

While her letters to Carter seem to indicate that Woolson felt marriage to be the greatest joy of a woman's life, and that she thought to be a "Wife and Mother" the holiest of a woman's identities, other letters indicate that she thought marriage was the greatest destiny for some women but not all, and that she did not regret her own decision to remain single. In another letter to Flora Payne, who was traveling in Europe, Woolson revealed that she felt herself more drawn to the life this friend was living than the one Arabella had chosen. "You are the most fortunate young lady I know, and ought to be the *happiest.* I envy you . . . , for although I am willing to settle down after thirty years are told, I do not care to be forced into quiescence yet awhile." Whereas she had told Carter that she ought to "BE HAPPY," suggesting that Woolson was perhaps trying to console Carter for what she was giving up, she frankly told Payne that she should be the *"happiest."* And Woolson never confessed to Carter, as she did to Payne, that she envied her. It was Payne's choice to travel, experience new things, and live an unsettled life (if only for a while) to which Woolson was most drawn. Later in life, she wanted her niece to have a similar opportunity. She wrote to her nephew, "I am extremely desirous that Clare should have happy years just at this time. Nothing can make up to a girl the free-from-care gay, lighthearted period after school is over, & before marriage." But she also believed that "[t]his period must not last too long, or it loses its charm."[17] At fifty-two years of age, Woolson felt, perhaps, that such a life without ties and a home had lost its appeal for her; but years earlier, when still young, she had not been willing to let it go. Despite her claim to Payne, she was hardly content to settle down when she was thirty. For it was then that she initiated her career as a writer and began to travel all over the South with her mother, and it would be another decade before she followed Payne to Europe.

Nonetheless, as Woolson pursued the kind of life Payne had embarked upon, she felt the loneliness of a single life and seemed at times to miss the love and intimacy that other people experienced. Yet she consistently believed that she had to sacrifice love for the kind of life she wanted as a committed artist. She also felt compelled to defend herself against the charge of selfishness for remaining single. In her notebooks appears the clearest expression of her feelings on this subject. To an overheard comment about single people — "They never seemed to think that they had any *duties.* They have always traveled about as they pleased." — she responded:

> Why should they not? They did not marry and have children; then let them have the pleasures of such a life, since they have not those of a family. Family people appear to think that unmarried people are very self-indulgent because they want to amuse themselves. It does not seem to occur to them that they (the married) gave themselves the pleasures which *they* preferred. Let them bear, then, the accompanying cares, and not criticize those who refrained from such ties.

In this defensive passage, Woolson also intimates, however, that "Family people" were the ones who were truly happy and "self-indulgent." George Eliot was a prime example of the happily married woman for Woolson (although Eliot was never legally married to George Henry Lewes), so much so that Woolson refused to pity Eliot for what appeared to be an otherwise hard life. After Eliot's death in 1880, Woolson wrote of her that "she had one of the easiest, most indulged and 'petted' lives that I have ever known or heard of." She had the "devoted love" of two men that most women never have from one. Although Eliot worked very hard, "she had the atmosphere she craved [of love and adoration] constantly round her. Thousands of women work as hard (in other ways) and finally die (as she did) of their toil, without it."[18] Rather than pity her, Woolson seemed to envy her.

Whether or not Woolson ever truly regretted her choice to remain single is not clear, although there is evidence that late in life her loneliness became over-whelming. While she earlier had reveled in the freedom that her solitary life offered, three years before her death she wrote to her nephew that family life was "the best thing in life; it's the only thing worth living for; this is the sincere belief — & the result of the observations — of one who has never had it!" For this reason, perhaps, she tried, while overseas, to maintain close relationships with her nieces and nephew, feeling that her identity as an "aunt" was important to her. But marriage appears to have been always out of the question. In her note-books, she expressed the importance of love: "You are afraid to love for fear of being duped, ill-treated, etc. But loving itself — the act of loving — is not only a pleasure, but a benefit. . . . ''Tis better to have loved,' (even if unloved in return) than never to know what loving is. Those who avoid it forever are dry, bitter, and sour."[19] It seems likely, therefore, that Woolson was no stranger to feelings of love, but to love from afar was preferable to becoming entangled in an actual relationship. Instead, she speculated in her fiction about what a union between a man and a woman who possessed ambition or predilections for self-development would be like, concluding time and again that while marriage meant the death of the soul and a silencing of the creative spirit for women, spinsterhood did not provide a particularly attractive alternative. In fact, the spinsters in her fiction are generally pathetic, isolated, misunderstood women,[20] although marriage is not always the blissful union of souls she portrayed to Carter. As Sharon Dean notes, "her short fiction presents a decidedly bleak view of marriage," although in her novels "the view of marriage is more complex and more positive," probably because she felt pressure to provide happier endings for her novels in order to appeal to a broader audience.[21]

Although Alcott appears to have been more comfortable than Woolson with her choice never to marry, her views on marriage were just as ambivalent and complex. Like most children, she played games of pretend marriages, but they taught her a decidedly different lesson than they did other girls. Years later she wrote, "I remember being married to Walter by Alfred Haskell with a white apron for a veil & the old wood shed for a church. We slapped one another soon after & parted, finding that our tempers didn't agree. I rather think my prejudices in favor of spinsterhood are founded upon that brief but tragical experience." Nonetheless, she was once tempted, at the age of twenty-five, to accept a marriage proposal from a man she did not love in order to provide for her family. Her mother dissuaded her from such a mistake.[22] Perhaps it was this experience coupled with the importance society placed on marriage for women that made matrimony such a thorny issue in Alcott's novels. Alcott particularly battled the conventional marriage plot in writing *Little Women* (1868). Having published the first part, depicting the adolescence of the four March sisters, she felt compelled to make the second volume, titled *Good Wives*, resolve their lives in happy marriages. Although she preferred to make Jo a "literary spinster," her readers and publishers demanded another outcome. "[P]ublishers are very *perwerse* [*sic*] & wont let authors have their way so my little women must grow up & be married off in a very stupid style," she lamented.[23] Although the genre of children's literature certainly demanded a more conventional plot, Alcott's serious novels for adults allowed her the freedom to subvert the idea that marriage was the apotheosis of a young woman's life. Her first novel, *Moods* (1864), tackled the issue of divorce and portrayed the consequences of a hasty marriage. And her novel *Work* (1872) depicted an idealized, companionate marriage, but it is only one episode in the varied life of the heroine, Christie Devon. Instead of ending in marriage, the novel concludes with Christie's discovery of her talent as a public speaker after the death of her husband.

In her autobiographical essay "Happy Women," Alcott penned one of the most forceful arguments of her generation in favor of a solitary life. She first pinpoints the cause of so many unhappy marriages: "One of the trials of woman-kind is the fear of being an old maid. To escape this dreadful doom, young girls rush into matrimony with a recklessness which astonishes the beholder; never pausing to remember that the loss of liberty, happiness, and self-respect is poorly repaid by the barren honor of being called 'Mrs.' instead of 'Miss.'" Then Alcott presents the life stories of four "superior women" who found happiness and fulfillment in their careers instead of empty marriages. They are a doctor, a music teacher, a philanthropist, and an author, the last modeled on Alcott herself, "who in the course of an unusually varied experience has seen so much of what a wise man has called 'the tragedy of modern married life,' that she is afraid to try it." In lieu of a husband and children, she has chosen a literary career, and she claims that she is "[n]ot lonely, for parents, brothers and sisters, friends and babies keep her heart full and warm."[24] Unlike Woolson living in exile, Alcott stayed close to home and had a large family, including nephews, who kept her from feeling isolated from loved ones. In fact, it is quite likely that she chose not to marry because her duties to this large family were already so demanding. Thus, she was very comfortable in her decision to remain single, convinced that her arrangement was the only one for someone who already had family responsibilities and ambitions as an author.

Phelps was also a vocal advocate of the single life, particularly during the first fifteen years of her career. "Because a woman hasn't a baby to rock," she proclaimed in 1867, "is no reason why she should be useless in her day and generation, a burden to herself and other people. One need not necessarily go to sleep while one is waiting for the Prince." Instead, she encouraged young women to "do something. Don't be afraid, ashamed, discouraged, deceived. Go to work." Many of her early works elaborate on this theme, denounce matrimony, or at least deflate the ideal of wedded bliss. She does this most explicitly in her novel *The Silent Partner* (1871). Both of the novel's chief female figures reject their suitors and become, instead of desolate, lovelorn spinsters, happy, useful women. Perley Kelso tells Stephen Garrick, "The fact is . . . that I have no time to think of love and marriage. . . . That is a business, a trade, by itself to women. I have too much else to do," namely devoting herself to the care of the poor. Her protégé, Sip Garth, in spite of her love for Dirk, vows never to marry for fear of bringing children into the world to work in the mills as she has done. Instead, she becomes a preacher and a "happy woman." The novel ends with Perley, after hearing Sip preach, walking through the streets, wanting nothing, "[l]ife brimm[ing] over" in her face.[25] Phelps portrays two women whose lives are full and complete without men. Any sacrifices they make by giving up heterosexual love are more than compensated for by the purpose they find in their work and their companionship with each other.

In addition to this argument in favor of women finding fulfillment outside of marriage, Phelps was also adamant in her belief that the time was not ripe for the kind of equal relationships between men and women that would allow women to fulfill their potential within the institution of marriage. Her article "The True

Woman" (1871) includes a powerful critique of marriage: "when marriage and motherhood no more complete a woman's mission to the world than marriage and fatherhood complete a man's; when important changes have swept and garnished the whole realm of household care; when men consent to share its minimum of burden with women," then the "true woman," rather than the cultural stereotype of woman, will reveal herself.[26] Men's selfishness required a corresponding selflessness from women, and only when men shared women's burdens, namely child care and housework, would women be fulfilled to the same measure that men were. In Phelps's ideal of domestic harmony, women would not find intellectual fulfillment through their husbands and only after all domestic duties were performed. But Phelps's message is essentially that because such conditions did not yet exist, those women who desired self-actualization should not marry. This was, of course, the path Phelps took herself, but over the years her single life became more and more of a burden to her.

Phelps lacked the close family relationships that Alcott had and sometimes regretted her isolation as a single woman, as revealed in a letter to the bachelor John Greenleaf Whittier, written eleven years after "The True Woman": "I write in my study alone . . . I think of you in yours. . . . These lonely lives are not right dear friend. God never meant them. We ought each of us to have married somebody when we were young. But as you say, it is too late now." In the same year, she published *Dr. Zay*, a novel that depicts the courtship of a woman doctor, who has devoted herself to a career and forsworn marriage, and a man who convinces her that their marriage will not interfere with her life as a doctor. This novel ends hopefully with their marriage. Although Phelps addressed many of the themes dear to her regarding women's independence, she allowed herself to gloss over the impracticality and even devastation of marriage for women who have strong commitments to their careers, which was a prominent theme in much of her other writings.[27]

At this time, Phelps, like Woolson, envied women (especially her friends Annie Fields and George Eliot) for their happy relationships with men. After the death of James T. Fields, she wrote his wife that she should thank God for her "exceptionally blessed life. — He was always my ideal of a husband." In Eliot's companionship with Lewes, Phelps saw even more to envy (despite the social isolation Eliot suffered), for not only did Eliot have domestic happiness, but she also had a mate who helped make her a complete artist. In a piece in *Harper's Weekly* (1885) she publicly echoed Woolson's private comments about Eliot's full life:

In the companion with whom she chose to spend her life, George Eliot had the most unbounded and unusual domestic sympathy. She was invigorated into doing her greatest work by a man who . . . appreciated her. . . . No half-riped life could have written *Romola* or *Adam Bede. Middlemarch* could not have sprung out of a famished heart. It needed a full woman's life, rich to the beaker's brim. . . . What glory, renunciation and loneliness may work in the human soul — and God grant they may! — it is not the glory of the great creative novelist.[28]

Eliot was complete as an artist because she did not have to sacrifice love, as the lonely spinster did. The support of her husband had enabled Eliot to accomplish more than any previous woman author, in Phelps's eyes. This belief in the inability of the single woman to achieve greatness without love would haunt Phelps and her contemporaries.

In 1888, at the age of forty-four, Phelps thought she had found a man who could make her life "full" in the way Eliot's had been. He was Henry Dickinson Ward, a writer seventeen years her junior. As Phelps got older, marriage became a more attractive proposition. She was not close to her father, her mother had died, her "favorite brother had died," she had no sisters, and her friend Mary Briggs Harris had also recently died. As Carol Farley Kessler suggests, "To maintain her unmarried status in a society valuing the married, Phelps would have needed friends or relatives emotionally closer to her than was the case by the mid-1880s." Phelps appeared to have felt much more alone in the world than Alcott or even Woolson, both of whom had close sisters. And she thought that marriage to a younger man held more promise of equality, having the examples of Madame de Staël, Charlotte Brontë, Fuller, and Eliot before her. It is clear that she intended to continue her career, and it is even possible that she was inspired by Eliot's example to try marriage, hoping that it would make her a happier woman and a better artist. But her marital bliss was short-lived. Phelps, who had appended Ward to her name, soon returned to publishing under her maiden name. Only five pages are devoted to Ward in her autobiography (1895). One of her few statements about her marriage is an ambivalent one: "A literary woman's best critic is her husband; and I cannot express in these few words the debt which I am proud to acknowledge to him who has never hindered my life's work by one hour of anything less than loyal delight in it, and who has never failed to urge me to my best, of which his ideal is higher than my own."[29]

Phelps's public assessment of her marriage echoes the idealized image she had of Eliot's relationship with Lewes. But, although Ward did not hinder her work, he certainly did not support her in the way Lewes did Eliot. By the time Phelps wrote her autobiography, she and Ward had been living apart and essentially estranged for many years. Phelps indicated on one occasion that marriage had changed her as an author. Although she found marriage to be a rich topic for literature, she also believed that "the married are unfairly hampered in what they can say. I remember that when I wrote 'Avis,' I said — 'Were I married, I could not write this book.' "[30] So although she portrayed Ward as urging her on to do her best, it is clear that she no longer felt free as an artist, certainly a precondition for the creation of one's best work.

As a married woman and mother, Stoddard had the most difficulty of the four writers in sustaining her career as an author. Her fears about giving up her independence in marriage led to the depiction of courtships as intense struggles between strong wills, with men trying to gain mastery over women who try to maintain their identity and liberty. In her fiction, marriage is often portrayed as a kind of death for one or both parties, with the domineering male often subdued to make him a more suitable mate for a strong-willed woman.[31] Although marriage to Richard Stoddard initially meant the opening of a new literary world, she still encountered difficulties in combining her life as a writer with her wifely duties. Having children, especially, seems to have interfered severely with her writing. Unlike Alcott, who during the late 1860s–1870s alternated between time at home caring for her family and time alone (or with her sister May) in Boston, where she kept rooms for the sole purpose of cultivating the solitude she needed to write, and Phelps, who found her escape in "a tiny cottage on Gloucester Harbor . . . where I keep old maids' Paradise,"[32] Stoddard had no room of her own. Nonetheless, she did make her own attempts at Thoreauvian solitude. While she found it difficult as a wife and mother to "worship" at the same "altar" of "[i]ndividuality" as Thoreau, she was nonetheless inspired by his experiment in solitude, for this is what was required to be an author. Somehow, she felt, she would have to carve out a space of solitude for herself in the midst of her home life. After her first son, Willy, was born, this proved increasingly difficult. Trying to work on her first novel, she wrote to her friend Edmund Clarence Stedman, "I pore over my Ms every day, struggle, fight, despair, and hope over it. I have a hundred and twenty-five pages done — not yet half completed. . . . I cannot work as fast as I am prepared in mind, on account of not being well, and the care of Willy. I have to do everything for him, wash, dress, feed, and watch him." But as her novel progressed, she was determined to find a release from her time-consuming duties. As she prepared to return home with her son from a visit to her family in Mattapoisett, she wrote to her husband, "At any rate have a woman there to help me. I am never going to do any more housework if I can help it, I am an AUTHOR."[33] To adopt this identity, she would have to be released from the domestic duties that were her responsibility alone. But simply finding hired help to perform those tasks did not ensure the freedom and free time to focus on one's art. And having a maid did not alleviate the feeling that as a wife and mother, one must be devoted to others first.

Stoddard's sense of commitment to self and resistance to domestic encumbrance were at odds with her belief that she should be content as a mother and wife. In the poem "Nameless Pain," the speaker admonishes herself: "I should be happy with my lot: / A wife and mother — is it not / Enough for me to be content? / What other blessing could be sent?" Although she had told her husband that she was an "AUTHOR," not a housekeeper, when Willy died only a few months later (December 1861), she experienced a crisis of identity. "I am perplexed as to what I shall do, my occupation is gone, the sweet anxious cares and observances that have filled my life for six years and a half have vanished. My brain is smaller than my heart and I can do nothing with the former."[34] She had already finished *The Morgesons*, but, despite her grief, she soon began work on another novel. Two years after Willy's death, she was once again a mother, having given birth to Lorry, a son, who would grow into adulthood and would increasingly occupy her time and define her life.

In the summer of 1866, when Lorry was only two and a half, Stoddard was still determined to make time and space for her writing. She moved into a beach house in Mattapoisett and attempted an experiment in solitude, going for long walks on the beach, exploring nature, reading and writing after the house was quiet, and keeping a journal that resounds with the lessons she learned from *Walden*. Her brother, Altol, and Lorry lived with her, her husband visited, and they entertained other guests. But after Lorry went to bed, Stoddard would shut herself up in her room with books, pen, and paper and relish her freedom in solitude. Although she had been grateful to Richard for rescuing her from the backwater of Mattapoisett, she also longed for the opportunities her hometown afforded for solitude and communion with nature as she tried to establish herself as an author. James Matlack explains her "ambiguous attitude toward Mattapoisett" in this way: "she sometimes paints the town as a tight-knit, backward, repressive society from which she joyfully escaped. At other times, it is the blessed rural retreat to which she (or her protagonist) gladly repairs from the din and dint of the metropolis."[35] While Richard found that the city and its literary society nourished his creative energies, Elizabeth associated true genius with nature and solitude. All of her novels, and most of her stories, take place in a rural setting reminiscent of Mattapoisett.

By keeping a journal, Stoddard hoped on this visit to devote herself to exploring her psyche and courting the creative power of nature. In her first entry, for April 22, 1866, she looks ahead to the joys and the difficulties she anticipates: "when the books are arranged, I shall be ready to write my book, and the method of my life will be tantalizing, unique, picturesque, unsocial, sad, incomplete." In the progression from positive to negative adjectives, she indicates how ambivalent she feels about the freedom of a writer's life and the solitude necessary for it. Throughout the rest of the journal, she vacillates between reveling in her retreat from the world and feeling oppressed by her loneliness. She also feels pulled in two directions — toward solitude, self-knowledge, self-reliance, and the power of creativity, on the one hand, and toward her family and wifely duties on the other. In her second entry, she laments, "Splendid spot to read & write in, but Lorry will not allow either." On April 25, she records, "My boy makes me love him so, and his exactions are so annoying and so winning that isolation seems impossible." The next day, she writes only two sentences, one reporting that "Lorry has been ill today." When her husband comes to visit, an even more troublesome distraction overtakes her. She enjoys his visit, but when he leaves she feels "lonesome" and must essentially start her whole project over. "The room here, does not seem the same — his coming and going have changed its tone, and I have got to fight myself back into the old channel."[36]

Within a couple of weeks she had fought her way back. As she sits in her room reading Wordsworth, she exclaims, "I shall never be *happier* than I am now. What makes me so? Because I am alone with *my own power!* It is the scene outside & the scene within." Discovering the creative power of nature, she feels at one with the universe, but this feeling won't last; transcendence is always temporary for her. Something — guilt, dedication, or fear of solitude — keeps pulling her back to her family, causing her to waver between moments of intense loneliness, frustration, and creative energy. And she enjoys taking care of the house and her family. On May 29, she writes, "There's too much chaos here for me to be laborious with the pen. It is too pleasant a life here — I love to loiter over all that pertains to my domestic affairs, parlor & kitchen." She also finds it difficult to be away from her husband. On June 1, she writes, "I feel dull, illish, and sad, homesick for Stod[dard]." However, at other times she sees her duties as "distractions" that keep her from her writing. But she manages to return to her work and find her creative fire again. "Dull & unhappy as I may have been through the day, I feel a change at night—when the door is bolted, and the family are abed. My papers are like life then." But the very next entry, written almost two weeks later, reveals that her husband has spent "several sick days with me. My novel lags, and so do I." By the end of the summer, as she looked over her journal and assessed what she had accomplished, she was disappointed. "I thought how I had failed to write out the power that has passed and repassed in my life since I came here," she wrote. She felt that her summer had been a busy one, but her journal did not show any intellectual achievement. She had lived much but had been unable to meditate on her experiences. In her last entry, she wrote, "I'll leave this ineffectual record behind me, and look at it next year, or will another do it for me, Stoddard perhaps."[37] Elizabeth Stoddard's life as a writer and a wife and mother, as revealed in this journal, was not exactly like the complete life Phelps had idealized for Eliot. It was, Stoddard undoubtedly felt, more akin to the "half-riped life" that Phelps suggested was lived by the unmarried woman writer. Of course, Eliot did not have children, and motherhood no doubt made Stoddard's life more complicated. But Stoddard seems to have felt fulfilled by neither her "woman"'s life nor her artist's life as each was to some degree neglected in her attempt to combine the two.

Temple House, the novel that Stoddard began during the summer of 1866, would be her last. Thereafter she gave up her ambitions to be recognized as a serious artist and devoted herself to her husband and son. Although she wrote some potboilers, articles, and a few serious stories, she never again devoted herself to the single-minded pursuit of writing a great novel that might ensure her a lasting reputation. Many factors contributed to her giving up her ambitions, such as her self-doubts about her abilities, the lack of popular success, and the critics' mixed responses to her novels, but the difficulty of combining domestic duties with writing played a major role. The last book she wrote, *Lolly Dink's Doings* (1874), a children's book that provides a telling look at how she viewed her home life, attacks her husband for leaving all of the parenting to her and devoting himself to his writing. It suggests that she felt, much as Alcott did about her father, that there was room for only one self-centered and self-committed author in their family.[38]

For Alcott, Phelps, Stoddard, and Woolson, marriage was decidedly not the blessed institution or the quintessential goal of a woman's life. In their own lives, they recognized that marriage, as it then existed, could not fulfill a woman who possessed artistic ambitions or other career goals. In their essays and fiction they tried to revise the notion that marriage was the *sine qua non* of a woman's existence in a way that earlier American women writers had rarely done, with the exception, of course, of Margaret Fuller. However, while Fuller envisioned a spiritual union of complementary equals as the ideal marriage, women writers of the Civil War and postwar years had a more difficult time confidently promoting such a revolution in gender relations. Whether married or not, women writers of this generation understood that the ideal promoted by Fuller, which theoretically would allow women to realize their creative potential side-by-side with their soul mates, was a long way from being realized.

Narratives of Marriage and Art

In their fiction, Alcott, Phelps, Stoddard, and Woolson approached the subject of marriage for women artists with a great degree of skepticism. Their narratives featuring women artists reject the formulation of the sentimental artist heroine promoted by their countrywomen in favor of the European romantic woman of genius. In both traditions, the question of the artist heroine's marital status was central to her characterization and the story's plot. For most nineteenth-century Europeans and Americans, this question boiled down to a tension between the essentially feminine nature of "woman" and the masculine conception of "artist." In their narratives of women artists, antebellum American women writers privileged the "woman" in the woman writer. Instead of the *Künstlerroman*, a novel of the artist's development, they wrote a type of female *Bildungsroman*, as the heroine learns to become a "true woman." However, in the European tradition of women artist narratives, the tension between "woman" and "artist" is not resolved in favor of "woman." Instead, the "artist" is privileged to a degree unseen in America before the Civil War. A significant marker of the postwar generation of women artists, then, is their break with their American predecessors in favor of engagement with the European women's *Künstlerroman* tradition.

The American sentimental artist heroine is best represented by Fanny Fern's Ruth Hall, in the novel of that name (1855), and Augusta Jane Evans's Edna Earl in *St. Elmo* (1866). Ruth Hall's story is one of repeated abandonment by the men in her life (through death or neglect). A widow with two children, Ruth must find a way to support her family. She eventually discovers that she can turn an exceptional ability for writing into a profitable vocation. Her talent is not integral to her identity, however, only a fortunate boon. She turns to writing only out of necessity and, even after her success, claims that she writes only to feed her children. As Linda Huf remarks, "Her 'sacred calling' . . . is not art but mother-hood. She writes not for glory but for her helpless children." The source of her drive to write, in fact, is her daughters. Fern writes of Ruth's self-sacrificial efforts at writing: "She had not the slightest idea, till long after, what an incredible amount of labor she accomplished, or how her *mother's heart* was goading her on." As a result, "ambition is . . . [a] hollow thing" to her in comparison with her role as a mother. Ruth represents the midcentury domestic woman writer whose identity as an author is subordinate to her identity as a mother. Edna, in Evans's novel, is in many ways Ruth's antithesis. She is neither mother nor wife and writes not for money but for fame. However, her ambition is clearly portrayed as de-structive to her happiness and health. Having rejected the role of "feminine" popular author, choosing instead to write "masculine," intellectual novels, she is first punished for her choice and then rescued from her fate by a suitor. First, however, she rejects the proposal of Mr. Manning, who tells her, "You must let me take care of you, and save you from the ceaseless toil in which you are rapidly wearing out your life." He offers her his home and the tutelage of his niece and tells her, "You are inordinately ambitious; I can lift you to a position that will satisfy you, and place you above the necessity of daily labour — a position of happiness and ease, where your genius can properly develop itself." Whether he, an influential editor, promises to further her career or not remains vague, but this point is not integral to Edna's decision. At first, she is tempted to accept for fear of becoming an old maid: "Either she must marry him, or live single, and work and die — alone." Far from the happy women of Alcott's and Phelps's writings, Edna views spinsterhood as a curse and her work as a burden too heavy to carry alone. But her real reason for turning him down is her persistent love for the rake St. Elmo. In the end, she accepts the proposal of a reformed St. Elmo, who liberates her from the oppression of her authorial career: "To-day I snap the fetters of your literary bondage. There shall be no more books written! . . . You belong solely to me now, and I shall take care of the life you have nearly destroyed in your inordinate ambition." Love conquers all and rescues Edna from a literary ambition that, Evans has been suggesting all along, would have killed her. Just as the novel Edna writes promotes women's domestic role, so does Evans's in the end, and the contradictions inherent in the real and the imagined novel are never resolved as the "artist" is buried and the "woman" takes her place.[39]

Ruth and Edna renounce or never even consider participating in the cult of genius, a realm that remains irrevocably male. Although both novels nonetheless participated in the legitimization of women's writing in the public sphere (*Ruth*

Hall by claiming authorship as a viable occupation for a woman and *St. Elmo* by depicting at length the intellectual achievement of a woman), neither novel allows women to be artists or blurs the boundary between high literature (associated with men) and middlebrow literature (the proper sphere of women, if they wrote at all). As a result, these works did not speak to Alcott, Phelps, Stoddard, and Woolson about the dilemmas that preoccupied them. Ruth and Edna were not role models for them or their heroines because these characters did not take their art seriously enough and did not confront the difficulty of combining the identities of "woman" and "artist." On the other hand, the artist narratives by European women, particularly de Staël's *Corinne, or Italy* (1807) and Barrett Browning's *Aurora Leigh* (1856), gave them the pre-texts they needed not only to envision themselves as artists but also to create their own works of art. For these two works not only helped to suggest the identities and life possibilities of the woman artist; they also represented the most highly regarded achievements of women writers. By participating in this tradition, implicitly or explicitly reworking these plots and modeling their heroines after Corinne, Aurora, and other similar types, postbellum women writers created some of their most accomplished works of art.

Corinne, de Staël's novel about a woman genius, was the first of its kind: an exploration of the special difficulties that faced the brilliant woman as she grew up and sought happiness and love. It depicted a gifted woman who was a poet, musician, singer, actress, dancer, artist, *improvisatrice* (improviser of poetry), and a national hero. In the opening scenes, Oswald Lord Nelvil travels from Scotland to Italy, where he stumbles upon a public ceremony paying tribute to the famous Corinne. The reader is therefore introduced to Corinne through the hero's eyes, suggesting the significance of male opinion regarding the woman artist. Just as he overcomes his prejudices and falls in love with her, so is the reader invited to accept her brilliance as an exceptional woman to whom "the ordinary rules for judging women cannot be applied."[40] In addition, as Oswald compares her to a work of art — her arms are "ravishingly beautiful," and her figure is "reminiscent of Greek statuary" (21) — the reader also is initially invited to view her as an art object. But Oswald watches her transformation from woman/object to artist/subject as the crown of myrtle and laurel is placed on her head: "No longer a fearful woman, she was an inspired priestess, joyously devoting herself to the cult of genius" (32).

Having begun at the high point of her life and career, however, the novel begins its descent as Corinne falls in love with Oswald. She resists at first, feeling "enslaved" by the emotion, and tells him, "Loving you as I do does me great harm: I need my talents, my mind, my imagination to sustain the brilliance of the life I have adopted." Only the domestic woman who has no other commitments can love freely because love "absorb[s] every other interest and every other idea" (90). But, as Corinne says, her commitment to her art is not easily discarded; it is necessary for her survival. Nonetheless, de Staël suggests that Corinne's life is not complete without love. This is the vicious circle that will become the defining quality of this tradition of the woman's *Künstlerroman*. As a nineteenth-century "woman," to be the object and the giver of love was one of life's basic necessities. But, as Corinne confesses, to love as a woman is not compatible with being an artist: "Talent requires inner independence that true love never allows" (301). However, the artist's life is not a career choice for Corinne, the woman of genius, as it is for Ruth or Edna; it is central to her identity. And, as the narrative goes on to show, to fall in love means the death of the artist. Here, both woman *and* artist die. First, Corinne loses her gift as she falls in love with Oswald, and then she slowly succumbs to a broken heart when he decides that he cannot accept her as a wife. Following his father's wishes, he rejects her because she is too much the artist and instead marries her half sister, the sheltered, simple, and good Lucille with no talents beyond her domestic role. Oswald has fallen in love with Corinne's opposite, "lost in a dream of the celestial purity of a young girl who, always at her mother's side, knows nothing of life but daughterly affection" (317), in other words, a woman who feels no conflict between love and art because she is the apotheosis of womanly love. The story is a tragic one, ending with Corinne's death, but not before she has taught the daughter of Lucille and Oswald to please him with the myriad talents Corinne herself possesses, a reminder of what he gave up and a complement to the sweet but talentless mother.

The contrast between the domestic Lucille and the genius Corinne is also manifested in their national affiliation. Corinne, with an Italian mother and English father, embraces her Italian heritage (representative of passion and the classical tradition of art and literature), while Lucille, who shares the same father, was raised by her English mother. After the death of her mother in Italy, Corinne spent her adolescence with Lucille's mother but later escaped a dismal domestic fate in England under her oppressive rule. Her stepmother believed that "women were made to watch over their husband's households and their children's health, that all other ambition was harmful" and advised Corinne to "hide any ambition [she] might have" (255). But in Italy, de Staël insists, she was free to realize her genius.

In many ways a response to *Corinne*, Barrett Browning's *Aurora Leigh*, a novel in blank verse, also depicts a woman of genius whose artist identity is central to her understanding of herself. Like Corinne, Aurora is born of an Italian mother and an English father and is brought to England after the death of her mother and father to be raised by a woman (her aunt) who "had lived / A sort of cage-bird life."[41] Aurora, who is "A wild bird scarcely fledged" (1.310), rebels against the traditional mold into which her aunt tries to put her: "We sew, sew, prick our fingers, dull our sight, / Producing what?" (1.457–458). Realizing that the domestic woman produces only slippers or cushions for her husband, she aspires to create something loftier for humanity, namely poetry, for poets are "the only truth-tellers now left to God, / The only speakers of essential truth" (1.859–860). Against the objections of her aunt "when she caught / My soul agaze in my eyes" (1.1030–1031) and "demurred / That souls were dangerous things to carry straight / Through all the spilt saltpetre of the world" (1.1033–1035), Aurora devotes herself to discovering the "Muse-Sphinx" (1.1020), or the source of poetic inspiration.

On her twentieth birthday, as she crowns herself with an ivy wreath, mimicking the similar ceremony at the beginning of *Corinne*, Aurora feels a tremendous faith in her future. "Woman and artist, — either incomplete" (2.4), she begins, in the famous phrase that neatly encapsulates the dilemma of *Corinne*. However, she continues, "Both credulous of completion. There I held / The whole creation in my little cup" (2.5–6). The purpose of *Aurora Leigh* is to solve the dilemma de Staël had established and to prove wrong the naysayers who claimed that a woman artist is neither a true woman nor a true artist. Her cousin Romney represents these voices, telling her, "The chances are that, being a woman, young / And pure, with such a pair of large, calm eyes, / You write as well . . . and ill . . . upon the whole, / As other women. If as well, what then? / If even a little better, . . . still, what then? / We want the Best in art now, or no art" (2.144–149; ellipses in original). When he asks her to instead join him in his social reform as his wife, she rejects his proposal because it shows he forgets that "every creature, female as the male, / Stands single in his responsible act and thought" (2.437–438). A woman can join a man in his "work and love" only if they "are good for her — the best / She was born for" (2.441–443). Here Aurora directly echoes Corinne's belief, "Is not every woman, as much as every man, obliged to make her way according to her own character and talents?" (255). Although Romney only sees her, a woman, as his "complement" (2.435), she informs him, "I too have my vocation, — work to do" (2.455).

Aurora's assertion of her duty to pursue her vocation rather than marry Romney undoubtedly comes more easily because she believes there is no true love on either side. Just as Corinne rejected three offers of marriage before meeting Oswald because none of them inspired true love, Aurora rejects the loveless marriage, admitting that, had he loved her, "I might have been a common woman now / And happier, less known and less left alone, / Perhaps a better woman after all" (2.513–515). This part of the narrative is written with the hindsight of the Aurora who has since left her home to pursue her literary career in London and has found only an empty fame. She comes to hear Romney's voice more loudly in her ears, telling her that she "played at art, made thrusts with a toy-sword" (3.240). "And yet," she laments, "I felt it in me where it burnt, / Like those hot fire-seeds of creation held / In Jove's clenched palm before the worlds were sown, — / But I — I was not Juno even! my hand / Was shut in weak convulsion, woman's ill" (3.251–255). Instead of Jove's powerful hand, she possesses a hand crippled by overwork. Like Edna Earl, she is in danger of losing her health to her work. But unlike Edna, rather than wither until rescued, she goes back to Italy, her birthplace, to recuperate and rejuvenate herself after completion of her book.

Although Aurora has gained a wide reputation for her verses, she has not been content with her lonely life. She leaves her solitary writer's existence to participate in the world again and first comes upon Marian, a poor woman whom Romney had almost married as part of his social vision of uniting upper and lower classes. When Marian was lured away by the villainous Lady Waldemar to a French brothel, she conceived a child through rape, but Aurora overcomes her socially instilled prejudices and brings Marian and her baby to live with her in Italy. Reawakened to her desires for love by the example of this mother and child — whom God has granted "the right to laugh" (8.25), while for Aurora "there's somewhat less" (8.27) — Aurora is now ready for Romney to reenter her life, which he does, blinded in a fire set by the people he was trying to help. Romney proves to be not only weakened, as the formerly arrogant suitor is in so many women's narratives, but also reformed. He has become inspired by Aurora's book and grants her the supreme ability of a poet: "You have shown me truths" (8.608), by which he means universal, spiritual truths. Their reconciliation, however, is effected over a deeper matter. For Romney had not only declared women incapable of being great poets; he had also proclaimed the poet's work inferior to that of the reformer. Having failed at his social reform efforts, however, he now declares Aurora's work of the soul as superior to his work of the material world.

On her side, she has come to acknowledge the importance of the poet's grounding in the real, tangible world through "love," that mysterious last word of her father: "Love, my child, love, love!" (1.212). In order to effect in herself this unity between the soul and the material through love, she must fulfill the vision that was yet incomplete on her twentieth birthday. Then "woman" and "artist" were still incomplete; now she tries to fuse the two: "Passioned to exalt / The artist's instinct in me at the cost / Of putting down the woman's, I forgot / No perfect artist is developed here / From any imperfect woman" (9.645–649). By discovering her love for Romney, she unites what had been separate, imperfect identities into one. And rather than find them incompatible, as de Staël had, Barrett Browning insists, through Aurora, that they enhance each other. For love is not a distraction from genius, it is the source of genius: "Art symbolizes heaven, but Love is God / And makes heaven" (9.658–659). Having formerly rejected the way of "A simple woman who believes in love" (9.661), she now tells Romney that if "you'd stoop so low to take my love / And use it roughly, without stint or spare, / As men use common things . . . / The joy would set me like a star, in heaven" (9.674–679). The path to heaven, that which art aims to represent, is through love, which Barrett Browning romantically describes as a union of equal souls. This is not the motivation of sacrificial mother-love that Ruth Hall feels; rather, it is the divine inspiration to see universal truths that only the poet who knows love here on earth can experience. But, as this passage suggests, love need not be returned in order to effect the completeness Aurora desires. The point is more for her to realize her capacity to love (her "womanhood") than to be loved in return. Of course, however, Romney does love her, and the poem ends with the two lovers united in purpose and declaring that "Our work shall still be better for our love, / And still our love be sweeter for our work" (9.925–926).

In the writings by American women of the Civil War and postbellum years, we see a tremendous debt to *Corinne* and *Aurora Leigh*, particularly in their depiction of women artists committed to the pursuit of genius. Corinne and Aurora made it possible for American women writers also to create autobiographical artist heroines who reject the path of ordinary women and develop masculine ambitions. However, these later writers shared neither the romantic fatalism of de Staël nor the passionate idealism of Barrett Browning. While they were drawn to the depiction of romantic genius in *Corinne* and *Aurora Leigh*, they were less inclined to adopt a romantic attitude toward love. In short, they were more realistic in their depiction of the woman artist's life choices. None of their artist heroines dies of the grief that killed Corinne, although there are plenty of deaths, real and metaphorical. Most importantly, though, none of their works envisions the unity of love and art in the woman artist's life the way *Aurora Leigh* does. Their fictions end time and again in the death of the "woman," the "artist," or both. Unable effectively to resolve this issue in their own lives, they wrote realistic narratives of how women writers and artists were forced to choose between their desire for expression and self-realization as artists and their desire for heterosexual love. None of them envisioned a female community supportive of the woman writer, as Jewett would to some extent much later in *The Country of the Pointed Firs* (1896). Instead, perhaps out of a desire to enter into a tradition of women's artist narratives and also motivated by autobiographical concerns, they engaged the dilemma presented by *Corinne* and seemingly, but unrealistically, solved by *Aurora Leigh*.

Stoddard's short story "Collected by a Valetudinarian" (1870) can be read as participating in this women's *Künstlerroman* tradition. Written at a time when Stoddard had given up writing novels herself and was essentially looking back on her own career, the story splits Stoddard's consciousness into two or three different female characters, suggesting the incompleteness she felt as a woman and an artist. The story's narrator is Eliza Sinclair, who possesses the same initials as Stoddard as well as a shortened form of her first name. Returning to a place familiar to her in her youth to recover from some unnamed grief, Eliza seeks solace in the past and in solitude. She is no longer known in this town, suggesting an absence of identity. Having established a romantic atmosphere by declaring her determination to "remain as long as the perturbed ghosts, my present rulers, would permit," she soon meets a romantic double, Helen, who is the cousin of a "woman of genius," Alicia Raymond.[42] All three women are linked in the story: Helen "bore a shadowy resemblance to myself" (288), Eliza claims, and Helen tells her that "Of all the persons I ever knew, you might have understood and aided [Alicia]" (289). The names Eliza and Alicia are also nearly homophonic. As Eliza and Helen, who have no past of their own ("Mrs. Hobson [Helen] never told me her history; I never asked it. Having no wish to reveal mine why should I demand hers?" [288]), dwell on Alicia's past, the three women merge. Reading Alicia's diary, Eliza thinks, "I was Alicia, or I was the dream of myself — which?" (296).

As Eliza and Alicia, in particular, melt together, they also become connected to a long line of earlier women of genius. In lamenting the obscurity of her cousin, Helen compares Alicia's life to that of the Brontë sisters: "I say, what a mockery the life of genius is! What half of a community knows it?" Fame is "all luck," Helen continues, using the example of the Brontës, who had "starved every way—most of all, starved for Beauty," and only after such a desolate life had found fame (289). Like them, Alicia had been deprived and isolated, but nonetheless, "this gifted woman, Alicia, discerned a world of beauty and truth that made an everlasting happiness for her great soul, as did Charlotte Brontë" (290). Alicia is also linked to George Sand, whose portrait she has on her wall and whose work she reads. She may also be linked, obliquely, to Corinne. Alicia's brother, Alton (named after Stoddard's brother Altol), punning on his own metaphor likening the creation of art to the formation of coral in the sea, calls her "Coralline" (294). The name is likely derivative of Corinne, or even of Corilla, an Italian *improvisatrice* who was "crowned with laurel at the Capitol . . . in 1776" and may herself have been a model for the fictional Corinne.[43] Alicia's name may also be linked to "Aurora," and her last name, Raymond, to "Romney." Alicia is therefore much more than an individual woman; she is an American manifestation of the woman of genius embodied by Brontë, Sand, Corinne, and Aurora. Alicia's fate, though, is quite different from Corinne's or Aurora's and suggests the ways in which American women writers found it difficult fully to envision the woman of genius.

Intertextualities with *Aurora Leigh* can be seen in the evocation of a young woman's discovery of her individuality through the symbol of birds and descriptions of nature. The landlord of the boardinghouse where Eliza and Helen are staying condescendingly tells them: "Birds of a feather flock together" (288), suggesting by this cliché that they are unusual women. Birds are a recurrent and potent metaphor for the woman writer (poet in particular) in *Aurora Leigh*, as they are in many women's writings, including *Jane Eyre*.[44] The bird sings beautifully but can also be silenced or domesticated and caged, its free flight restricted, making it a perfect symbol for the woman writer. In fact, it was so widely used that we could read the landlord's comment here as a not-so-veiled statement that Eliza and Helen are artist figures. In the beginning of *Aurora Leigh*, Aurora feels like "a nest-deserted bird" (1.43) when her mother dies. Then, as we have already seen, she contrasts her aunt's "cage-bird life" with her own free, "wild bird" nature. The "Muse-Sphinx" she invokes is also a kind of bird, as a Sphinx has wings. Before she finds her voice as a poet, the sun tells her, "I make the birds sing—listen! but, for you, / God never hears your voice, excepting when / You lie upon the bed at nights, and weep" (1.658–660). As she later prepares to crown herself, she describes her harmony with everything around her: "I was glad, that day; / The June was in me, with its multitudes / Of nightingales all singing in the dark" (2.9–11). She goes on to describe the "green trail across the lawn" that her gown makes and the "honeyed bees [that] keep humming to themselves" (2.21, 27). In "Collected," a nearly identical scene is described when Eliza visits Alicia's house to read her diary: "I was glad to be alone. The grass on the lawn waved me a welcome; butter-cups glistened in it; bees and butterflies hummed and hovered every where . . . and birds constantly twittered over my head" (296). It is at this point that she wonders if she is Alicia or is dreaming of herself, or, one could extrapolate, dreaming of Aurora Leigh. Clearly Stoddard was drawn to the early parts of Barrett Browning's *Künstlerroman*, particularly the description of Aurora's discovery of herself as a poet. Stoddard must have been less sure about the latter parts in which Barrett Browning expresses her idealism about the ability of Aurora to combine "woman" and "artist." Alicia attempts this fusion as well but with slightly different results.

Alicia's diary, which covers the span of one summer, borrows extensively from Stoddard's diary from the summer of 1866. However, condensed within one season's reflections we can see the course of a life that in significant ways mirrors the lives of previous women of genius, including Corinne, Aurora, and Charlotte Brontë. Alicia certainly resembles these women in her isolation and difference from other women. As in *Corinne*, this difference is brought into focus by contrasting the woman of genius with a so-called ordinary woman. Here the two are rivals not for a lover but for Alicia's brother, who is a kind of platonic lover to his sister and therefore does not present the same threats as a sexual lover. Julia is "the pretty creature" who does not understand Alicia's work, just as Lucille was incapable of comprehending art in general and Corinne's genius in particular. To Alicia she is a "child" who "has never suffered" (305), in stark contrast to Alicia's own life of suffering. The source of this suffering is the same as for earlier women artists: isolation, lack of understanding, and lovelessness. When a suitor comes to ask for her hand, she "wish[es she] could fall in love with him" (300) and thereby reconnect with human beings. But his ardor, expressed in his willingness to "mend your pens to my dying day" is finally not tempting: "what would become of my literary career? A strong man's love might interfere with my hero; and my heroine might interfere with him" (301). Her work comes first. It is clear, though, that Alicia is not rejecting the "true" romantic love that Corinne and Aurora found. After he leaves, however, she feels first "free" then "lonely," and her work suffers while the world is "Blank to me" (302). Memories of an earlier love, Arnold, also recur: "He had the best of [my soul], yet left me. Eternally my heart is his." This true love, although enshrined safely in the past, continues to threaten her work as she finds "No motive for writing" and doubts her abilities (300). By now, she is also making frequent references to her impending death. After having read Emerson and George Sand one evening, she felt "the walls of an invisible, fearful destiny . . . slowly closing round me" (299), bearing out the romantic imagery from the beginning of the story. It appears on the surface that Alicia is meeting the fate of so many women artists — mysterious death for lack of love and for committing herself to her art.

However, Alicia's life is not entirely loveless. Her brother provides her companionship, even if he doesn't share her literary tastes and appreciation for art and doesn't require of her the duty that a husband would. Also, his impending marriage to Julia provides her with the understanding of love that she needs to complete her novel. In fact, as Alicia slowly dies, Alton's and Julia's romance (the inspiration for her art) picks up. Sensing a "shadow" on their love because she is dying, she is convinced "that will pass. Love will have its way, George Sand says, upon the bones of the dead" (305). After she dies, their love will continue, as will her novel. By living vicariously through them, though, she discovers the love necessary for great art: "The drama here [between the two lovers] refreshes me. One way I see that I have failed in the story I am writing; that is, they teach me so" (305). Although she sees Julia as taking her place in Alton's heart, it is their love that teaches her how to finish her novel (she is at least on "the last chapters" [306]). Even Julia, who admits she does not "understand" the book, recognizes the "truth about us women" in it (306). The next diary entry, two weeks later, is Alicia's last.

This story's obvious reflection of Stoddard's life suggests that Alicia is, in part, the author's self-construction as a misunderstood artist. In trying to understand her isolation, Eliza sums up Stoddard's self-image at this time: "I dare say no one understood her. . . . What should drive one into solitude, if a lack of comprehension of one's sincerest feelings and motives can not?" (295). She claims here, through Eliza and Alicia, to have stopped writing because she was unappreciated. Others previously have read this story as one of compensation or wish fulfillment for Stoddard,[45] but even more significant is how she creates Alicia as simultaneously a representative of herself *and* a composite figure of the nineteenth-century woman of genius. Always anxious to distinguish herself from other American women writers, who she thought were inferior, Stoddard places Alicia, and by extension herself, into the tradition of European women artists. But Alicia, like her author, did not meet the same fate as those earlier idols and their creations. Without even reading her work, only the diary, Eliza decides to leave

Alicia's writings unpublished. Although Alicia seems to have briefly found completeness as an artist, and Eliza has told Alicia's story, the narrative ends with a closed circle of silence as Eliza tells Helen, "She had her world in Alton, in you, and will have in me. . . . That is enough" (307). She is therefore like Corinne, who is surrounded by Oswald, Lucille, and their daughter as she dies, but also unlike Corinne, who was simultaneously mourned by a nation, commemorated by a "funeral procession to Rome" (419). While Corinne remains as a symbol — warning or inspiration — to later generations, and Aurora looks into a future of prophetic art as a poet-wife, Alicia is buried and forgotten beyond a small circle. Such is the case for nearly all of the woman artists created by American women writers, who not only found it difficult to combine love and art but also found it nearly impossible to achieve the recognition that de Staël and Barrett Browning did.

What we have not yet seen in these narratives of women artists' lives is a woman's attempt to combine the life of a "wife" with the life of an "artist." Corinne loses her genius just by loving, and the implication is that if she did marry, her art would become purely domesticated. Aurora becomes "woman" and "artist," but we do not see her become a "wife." And Alicia feels compelled to choose one over the other, assuming that the two cannot coexist. It is in Phelps's magnum opus, *The Story of Avis*, that full consideration is given to this most complicated aspect of the woman artist's life. With a high regard for romantic genius but a stark realism in her portrayal of the married woman artist, Phelps created the most important novel of her generation about a woman artist. But before analyzing this novel in the context of the European women's *Künstlerroman*, we must consider two other works that had a profound impact on its creation.

The first of these, George Eliot's verse drama *Armgart* (1871), provides an epigraph to one of the chapters of *Avis* and serves as the basis for the proposal scene in chapter 7. *Armgart* was published one year after Stoddard's "Collected" and is a clear participant in the *Corinne–Aurora Leigh* debate about love for the woman artist. Armgart, a famous singer, soundly rejects the man in her life, Graf (Count) Dornberg, despite her apparent love for him. She feels like a "bride" when she sings and proudly relishes the recognition she receives from her audience. When "Graf," as Eliot refers to him, tries to tempt her with his audience of one and tells her that fame is fickle while love is lasting, she is not convinced. He wishes that she would subordinate her art to her womanhood: "Nay, purer glory reached, had you been throned / As woman only, . . . Concentrating your power in home delights / Which penetrate and purify the world." Resenting his suggestion that she "Sing in the chimney-corner to inspire / My husband reading news," she insists that nature has "willed" her to be an artist for the world. "I am an artist by my birth, — / By the same warrant that I am a woman : / Nay, in the added rarer gift I see / Supreme vocation." She refutes the implication that she is less a woman for being an artist and tells him that he has not learned, since he last proposed, how to win her: "As I remember, 'Twas not to speak save to the artist crowned, / Nor speak to her of casting off her crown." She tells him that he asks of her what he would never consider for himself: "one of us / Must yield that something else for which each lives / Besides the other." While he wants her to live for him alone, he will have both her and his vocation. She explains that her refusal is not due to lack of love for him: "it is her sorrow / That she may not love you." Knowing that "my kind is rare," she urges him to "seek the woman you deserve, / All grace, all goodness, who has not yet found / A meaning in her life, or any end / Beyond fulfilling yours. The type abounds." The suggestion is that Graf will go on to meet his Lucille, having been rejected by his Corinne. Meanwhile, like Alicia, Armgart feels complete without marriage: "O, I can live un-mated, but not live / Without the bliss of singing to the world, / And feeling all my world respond to me."[46]

In the remaining five pages, however, Armgart must learn how to do just that. She has lost her beautiful singing voice owing to an illness. Grief-stricken, she accuses her doctor of murdering her voice; she cries that his cures "hold me living in a deep, deep tomb, / Crying unheard forever!" This Gothic image is the most poignant expression of the pain associated with the death of the artist in any of these narratives. In a more conventional metaphor, she also calls herself "songless as a missel-thrush." Insisting that she would not marry Graf now, for "It would be pitying constancy, not love," she must find a new direction for her life. After complaining that her "lot" is now the old story of all ordinary women, "The Woman's Lot : a Tale of everyday," her lame cousin Fräulein Walpurga admonishes her for her selfishness. Brought down to Walpurga's level by her "[m]aim-[ing]," Armgart learns to have "a human heart." Walpurga shows up Armgart's hubris: "For what is it to you, that women, men, / Plod, faint, are weary, and espouse despair / Of aught but fellowship? Save that you spurn / To be among them?" In the end, Armgart vows to "take humble work and do it well, — / Teach music, singing, what I can" and to return Walpurga to her home, which she had left to support Armgart in her career.[47] Armgart therefore seems to embrace the worldly purpose of Aurora and Romney, but she finds it through homosocial kinship and bonding instead of heterosexual love. In addition, she had to lose her gift in order to sympathize with the lives of others. Although Eliot addresses the same kinds of issues that are integral to the woman artist's narrative, she appears to be the least approving of women's commitment to art. Armgart is presented as selfish and self-centered, and the main impetus of the story is to teach her to feel for others rather than be absorbed in her own career or the pain that results from losing it. Unlike *Ruth Hall* and *St. Elmo*, *Armgart* does not promote motherhood or marriage as superior to art; however, it clearly portrays self-sacrifice as the proper aim of a woman's life.

The renunciation of the selfishness of artistry is also the main theme of another pre-text of Phelps's novel, her mother's story "The Husband of a Blue" (1853). In this story, however, the message is about the superiority of domesticity, and therefore it has more in common with *Ruth Hall* and *St. Elmo*. Shortly after her mother's death, Phelps's father published a collection of her mother's stories, including "The Husband of a Blue," a work that, like *The Story of Avis*, focuses on the complications of marriage for a woman committed to her work. The heroine, Marion Gray, is a young woman who accepts a marriage proposal even though she is more devoted to her studies and her intellectual development than to being a wife and mother. Her name recalls Phelps's given name, Mary Gray Phelps, making it plausible that this story was the mother's lesson to her daughter about the decisions that would confront her one day. Marion has no mother, just as Mary Gray Phelps soon would have no mother to guide her through her young adulthood. Unfortunately, Marion makes a bad decision about marriage. The problem is not whom to marry, as is usually the case in female *Bildungsromane* like *St. Elmo*, but marrying without any idea of the pitfalls that await her. When Marion tells her lover that she is not cut out for housekeeping and that she is committed to "her books," he responds, "A housekeeper he could hire, but where could he find another woman like Marion Gray?"[48] Yet shortly after their marriage, the misfortune begins. Marion is "selfish" and locks herself up in her study, "apparently forgetful of her husband's comfort," while he, in contrast, is "generous" and "indulgen[t]" of her moods (101–102). The narrator claims that she is incapable of the "self-sacrificing devotion" necessary in a wife (103), while he appears more willing to sacrifice his needs. Soon she descends into a deep depression. "How utterly unfitted did she find herself for domestic life; how unfortunate that her passion for literary pursuits should have been so strong! But, then, ought she to be blamed for the domestic discomfort which resulted from it? Did she not give her husband full warning of what he might expect?" (106). She even accuses him of "deceiv[ing]" her, to which he replies that he believes no woman, "married or unmarried," would be happy if she was wholly without domestic duties (107–108). After they have children, the situation worsens. Mr. Ashton must sacrifice his own work in order to care for the children, whom Marion neglects. When her aunt comes for a visit, she makes their house a *"home"* (113), and Mr. Ashton finds that he prefers her company to his wife's, which Marion interprets as evidence that "he did value domestic accomplishments more than much learning." Despite his earlier admiration of the intellectual stimulation she offered him, it becomes clear that what he really wants in a wife is *"recreation,"* a peaceful haven from his "great pursuits" (115).

Perhaps the most important message of "Husband," however, is not about the domestic disharmony that results when a wife has her own "great pursuits," but that those pursuits are necessarily in vain. The narrator suggests that Marion's efforts and "aspirations" will not bear fruit because she has developed only one part of herself: "just in the ratio in which her intellect was cultivated, her heart was neglected" (116). She only begins to comprehend her mistake when she meets Mrs. Graves, the model of the perfect woman, as intelligent as Marion but more accomplished, but whose name suggests once again the death of the woman artist.[49] "I love my books," Mrs. Graves informs her, "but . . . I never open my writing desk until every domestic duty is performed. I do not neglect [my husband], or his house, for my studies. I think a woman loses more than she gains by such a course" (123). Mrs. Graves is the model woman writer of the antebellum years who, like Ruth Hall, always puts her family first. Faced with this model, "Marion felt reproved and humbled. Might it not, after all, prove true, that there was some such mysterious connection between a woman's intellect and her heart that the one could never develop its full vigor unless the heart grew strong with it; and that in the charmed duties of a *home* must it exercise its best affection?" (123). Here we see a construction similar to the combination of "woman" and "artist" in *Aurora Leigh:* love is the key to completing the woman artist. But, Barrett Browning did not take this argument to its logical conclusion for most nineteenth-century women: as Mrs. Graves says, art, even reading, must take second place to her "duty" to loved ones. However, perhaps more concerned with the idea that by taking second place, her work will suffer, Marion quickly dismisses Mrs. Graves's implicit advice and returns to her "selfish" ways. As a result, the narrator suggests, she fails to fully mature as a writer. "[G]enius" leaves as quickly as it appears, sending her "back to earth" (125). Meanwhile, her husband, in spite of his many cares, writes a profound article for the "North American" (126).

Although Phelps (the mother) found it difficult, if not impossible, to cultivate her mind while running a household, in "Husband" it is the husband who is stretched so thin that his intellectual endeavors are threatened. When Marion grows ill and demands his constant attention, he wonders, "What could be accomplished, with such broken time?" (127). *He* must juggle domestic responsibilities with his writing, but the outcome is very different for him than it is for the first Phelps's married woman writer in *The Angel over the Right Shoulder* (1852), who must compromise her intellectual development, devoting only stolen hours now and then to her study and never able to write productively. Mr. Ashton, by contrast, successfully completes his work and gains recognition for it. Meanwhile, Marion self-destructs, succumbing to her "nervousness" (128). The husband, who, as the title implies, has been the real focus of this story, is the martyr who triumphs despite his wife's "criminal neglect" (133). While she gains nothing more than "the reputation of a '*deep Blue*,'" he, "made strong by nobly enduring suffering, became, at length, one of the great men of his day" (133). Interestingly, there is never any mention of the fruits of Marion's seemingly ceaseless literary endeavors. Apparently, she toils away at no tangible product. By trying to be what she cannot and should not be, she fails. The narrator confides in the last lines that only by uniting her intellect with her husband's and by joining in his work could she "have ascended the meridian with her husband" (134). This is similar to the lesson graciously learned by Mrs. James in *The Angel over the Right Shoulder*, namely, that if she is to receive her heavenly reward for a life well lived, she must be equally committed to "cultivat[ing] her own mind and heart" and "perform[ing] faithfully all those little household cares and duties on which the comfort and virtue of her family depended."[50] "Husband" suggests that a woman is incomplete without love and domestic happiness, that she could not be the kind of intellectual light that a married woman could be. Marion's failing is that she tries to continue living her life as if she were a single woman, implying that even if a woman remains unmarried, she cannot hope to achieve what men achieve.

Retelling her mother's "Husband of a Blue" from the wife's perspective in *The Story of Avis*, Phelps takes a similar heroine and puts her to the same test as Marion, although Avis is allowed a long period of self-development and dedication to art (including six years of study alone in Europe) before she is wooed. The outcome is different for her but tragic nonetheless. In the daughter's portrayal of the problem, it is the wife, not the husband, who is the martyr. Unlike Marion, Avis rises to the occasion and sacrifices herself and her art rather than neglect her husband and children for selfish ends. However, the blissful union of two strong souls, which her mother held up as the ideal at the end of "Husband," is not possible in the daughter's story because, she implies, men are not ready for such a relationship with women. Like *Corinne*, *Avis* blames a man for the woman artist's decline. But in *Corinne*, Oswald is only responsible for killing the "woman"; the death of the "artist" is deemed inevitable. In *Avis*, however, the man kills the "artist," luring her, as in "Husband," with unrealistic promises.

Avis is deeply intertextual with these earlier women's artist narratives, particularly *Aurora Leigh*, *Armgart*, and her mother's works, but also, by extension, *Corinne* and "Collected." As in each of these previous works, the heroine is autobiographical and decidedly different from ordinary women. Avis is also contrasted with her friends, the conventional Coy and Barbara, who possess the usual feminine attractions and have no other ambition than to be wives and mothers. Instead, Avis, like her fictional predecessors, is devoted to her career and sees herself first and foremost as an artist. Additionally, just as earlier artist heroines had, she falls in love and has to confront the dilemma of whether to mix love and art. However, by combining the female *Künstlerroman*'s valorization of romantic genius for women with her mother's focus on the aftermath of the woman artist's choice to marry, Phelps created the most realistic narrative of the woman artist's dilemma. Rather than idealize romantic love or the artist's isolation, Phelps wrote a stark critique of the pressures that still made it impossible for her generation of women to achieve the ideal unions promoted in either *Aurora Leigh* or her mother's works. For Phelps, men were not capable of granting women the necessary equality in marriage, and the woman artist could not so easily renounce her ambition.

The novel begins with Avis at the height of her powers, before she has fallen in love. Like *Corinne*, then, this is perhaps less a *Künstlerroman* than a novel of the woman artist's decline. For the story of her youth and her development as an artist is brief, told in only two chapters. As a young girl, Avis asks her mother, "what shall I be?"[51] In contrast to Barbara, who wants to marry, and Coy, who wants to be a "lady," Avis prefers the boys' aspirations: college president or even dog-store owner (23). In this conversation, Avis discovers that her mother had desired to be an actress and senses the depth of the pain associated with the renunciation of her ambitions when she married Avis's father. The lesson to the young Avis is that marriage is not full compensation for the lost opportunity to develop one's unique talent. But Avis's mother, as in the case of Phelps's own mother, wastes away under an unknown illness, leaving the young daughter, like

Mary Gray and Marion Gray, to make her way in the world without any guidance. Although Corinne's and Aurora's mothers also died when they were young, here the loss is portrayed as even more inauspicious. The lack of a supportive maternal guide and kindred spirit seems to ensure Avis's downfall, as she succumbs to the same lure of love that her mother did and suffers the same grief over the loss of her art.

After her mother's death, Avis, like Corinne and Aurora, is raised by a surrogate mother (an aunt) who tries to instill the domestic, feminine virtues in her. Avis's rebellion is more thorough, however. Avis tells her father, "I hate to make my bed; and I hate, hate, to sew chemises; and I hate, hate, *hate*, to go cooking round the kitchen. . . . mama never cooked about the kitchen" (27). Avis identifies more with her deceased mother than with her Aunt Chloe, who epitomizes the traditional woman. This section of the book very closely mirrors *Aurora Leigh*, which Avis reads at the age of sixteen, discovering her ambition to be an artist. In addition, the symbol of the bird is utilized throughout the novel to an even greater extent than in Barrett Browning's work. Avis's name, in fact, means bird, and suggests the common phrase *rara avis*, highlighting her uniqueness. Her mother was "bird-like" (23), and Avis is likened to birds throughout the novel. This relationship is established in the opening chapter, when the narrator initiates one of the ruling metaphors of the book. Seating herself where she will be placed against a bold color, "Avis went to it as straight as a bird to a lighthouse on a dark night. She would have beaten herself against that color, like those very birds against the glowing glass, and been happy, even if she had beaten her soul out with it as they did" (6–7). Later, Avis gets caught in a storm trying to rescue birds flying into the lighthouse, and as she falls in love, she is described again by the same metaphor. By choosing to fly instead of nest, Avis is headed for destruction because she flies toward an ideal—a light that calls her and that she instinctively obeys, even though it will kill her. This metaphor, more than any direct statement in the novel, suggests the inevitability of her capitulation to romantic love. Whereas, in *Aurora Leigh*, the symbol of the bird is used to signify artistic aims as well as strength (Aurora is likened to a falcon and an eagle, among other birds), in *Avis*, the bird is a decidedly ominous symbol encapsulating the tragic fate of the woman artist, as in the following passage describing her mother's thwarted ambitions: "The sparrow on her nest under your terrace broods meekly; but the centuries have not wrung from one such pretty prisoner a breath of longing for the freedom of the summer-day. Do her delicate, cramped muscles ache for flight?" (23).

Aurora Leigh is also overtly invoked in the novel when Avis reads the epic in a scene reminiscent of the same one that inspired Stoddard's description of Eliza reading Alicia's diary. Taken together, these three scenes link the reading of a woman artist's life story to the inspiration of the romantic genius through nature, the power that Aurora first felt on that June day. In this scene is expressed all of the hope of the young woman finding her voice and discovering that her purpose in life is to be an artist. The month is again June, and "In the meadow the long grass rioted; and black and brown and yellow bees made love to crimson clovers" (30). Avis has picked up the book to check the quote she used that day to explain to Aunt Chloe her impatience with housework: *"carpet-dusting, though a pretty trade, was not the imperative labor after all"* (31). She senses that her life is intended for something more, but she is not yet sure what that is. In her reading that day, seeking to "solve the problem of her whole long life before that robin yonder should cease singing," she discovers, like Aurora, that "purpose and poetry were . . . one." Rushing in to tell her father that "It had come to her now . . . why she was alive; what God meant by making her" (32), she declares, "Other women might make puddings," but she was going "to be an artist." She decides she will study and "paint pictures all my life" (33). Again quoting *Aurora Leigh*, she insists upon the seriousness of her commitment to art: *"I who love my art would never wish it lower to suit my stature"* (34).

After her father agrees to send her to Europe as part of the education of a refined young lady, Avis surprises him by requesting to stay on after the traditional year of travel. He reluctantly agrees, and she devotes herself to six long years of serious study. Like Aurora in London, she dedicates herself with "ungirlish doggedness" to the task of acquiring "a disciplined imagination" (37). When she finally succeeds in gaining her teacher's endorsement, she is ill for two days from the shock of success and feels like a woman who has won a proposal, the man of her dreams "kneel[ing] at her feet" (38). Shortly afterward, she ventures into the streets of Paris where she first encounters the young man Philip, who will try to replace artistic achievement as her lover.

After they both return home, Philip, a tutor at the town's college, ingratiates himself by rescuing Avis from a storm and sitting for a portrait. His conquest of her is very gradual and is drawn out over many chapters. While her time in Europe was described in a mere three pages, this episode is clearly the most important to Phelps and requires a much more detailed explanation. The chapter in which Philip first proposes to Avis begins with an epigraph from *Armgart:*

ARMGART: *I accept the peril;*
I choose to walk high with sublimer dread
Rather than crawl in safety.
GRAF: *Armgart, I would with all my soul I knew*
The man so rare, that he could make your life
As woman sweet to you, as artist safe. (66)

Phelps juxtaposes passages from two different parts in scene 3, in which Graf
renews his proposal to Armgart, and she claims her high ambitions as an artist,
accepting the dangers of failure. Graf's comment comes later in the scene, after
Armgart has made it clear that she will not marry him. By uniting these two
passages, Phelps invokes the beginning and the end of the conflict — Armgart /
Avis is an artist first, and in the end, no lover's reasoning will obscure the fact that
she requires a man who can accept her as "artist" and "woman." That Philip is
not such a man becomes clear, however, very quickly, for he plays the role of Graf
to Avis's Armgart in this chapter. And, as Graf also indicates, he is not the man
who can be everything a woman artist needs. By first rejecting Philip, Avis willingly makes the same sacrifice of love for art that Armgart does. Although she has
never loved before, she thinks to herself but does not admit to him, "I am human,
I am woman! I have had dreams of love like other women!" But she decides that
"God gave her the power to make a picture before he gave her the power to love a
man." Feeling the pain of this loss, Avis "almost wished that she could have
loved like other women" (69). But she holds fast to her ideals of art while Philip
confronts her with the same arguments as Graf confronted Armgart: "But suppose . . . that your future should fail to fulfill its — present promise. . . . You dare
the loss of what nineteen centuries of womanhood has held as the life of its life;
you dare the loss of home and love" (71–72). Echoing Armgart's claim that Graf
is the man she refuses to love, Avis tells Philip, "For your soul's sake and mine,
you are the man I *will* not love" (73).

Nonetheless, Avis is beginning to love for the first time, against her will. This
awakening love is not portrayed with that romantic combination of anguish and
bliss that we see in *Corinne*. Instead, Phelps begins to employ death imagery,
allowing the reader to feel no joy in Avis's discovery of love. As Philip walks away
defeated, Avis lies down: "She thrust her cheek down into the cool, clean earth,
and let the grass close over her young head with a dull wish that it were closing for
the last time" (72). From the moment that Philip saved her from a snowstorm but
was unable to rescue the bird she had endangered herself to save (the bird dies in

his coat pocket on his heart), it is clear that Philip will kill part of Avis, namely her artist self. And sure enough, soon after Philip's proposal, the war between the "artist" and the "woman" begins in earnest, and her art suffers. Having heard of Philip's enlistment in the Civil War, Avis goes back to her studio but finds that her powers have left her: "she found the lips of her visions muttering in a foreign tongue. She sat entire days before an untouched canvas. She stared entire nights upon untapestried darkness. Her father found her one day, burning the sketches in her studio in a fever of self-despair" (76–77). Here Phelps obviously borrows from *Armgart*, but even more, perhaps, from *Corinne*. For it is the wars going on within and without, both of which are related to her dawning love for Philip, that distract her from her work and rob her of her genius. The power that she had felt upon first returning home to "[t]he elemental loves of kin and country" is lost. She had discovered in her home the inspiration of the "afternoon sun in her father's study," which "thrilled her as no glory or story of Vatican, Pitti, or Louvre, had ever done" (77). In other words, she found close to home the supportive place she needed to be inspired, the contact with the "real" that Aurora finds in Romney. But here we see Phelps's departure from Barrett Browning in her insistence that however important home and love may be to the artist, the woman artist should not look for that support in the context of heterosexual love. While before, "Every sense in her [had] quivered to homely and unobtrusive influences" (77), Philip's love is anything but unobtrusive.

As Avis confronts this supreme crisis presented by Philip's love, she makes a desperate attempt to invoke inspiration: "She had fallen into one of the syncopes of the imagination in which men have periled their souls to stimulate a paralyzed inspiration. By any cost — 'by virtue or by vice, by friend or by fiend, by prayer or by wine' — the dumb artist courts the miracle of speech" (78). Summoning vision with a liqueur, she takes a Faustian plunge and discovers a series of images, holy and profane, ending with the supreme symbol whose vision is both the beginning and the end of her full realization as an artist: the Sphinx. The dilemma of the woman artist narrative is here given more levels of symbolic signification through the metaphor of the Sphinx, the subject of Avis's most ambitious painting. Just as Phelps channeled her highest aspirations into *Avis*, Avis invests her greatest energy and inspiration in this work. Phelps may have derived this symbol from *Aurora Leigh*, where Aurora invokes the "Muse-Sphinx" (1.1020) as the source of poetic genius. But in order to discover it, Aurora believes, "The melancholy desert must sweep round, / Behind you as before" (1.1021–1022). This is, of course, at the beginning of the epic, before Aurora learns the true source of inspiration, namely love. In *Aurora Leigh*, therefore, the "Muse-Sphinx" becomes a symbol of the older ideal of poetic genius that Barrett Browning is trying to replace with a new ideal of the poet inspired by the world in which she lives. Phelps takes this symbol and, recognizing that the Sphinx as muse is also, historically, female and a winged creature, gives it multiple levels of meaning.[52] On one hand, it represents, as it did in Barrett Browning's work, the mysterious origins of romantic genius, which has traditionally been more accessible to men. On the other hand, it represents the woman as muse, either an awesome force that has the power to destroy men or that is locked into the role of the male artist's helpmeet (the role in which Romney tried to cast Aurora), a sort of divine but decidedly domestic muse, such as Phoebe in Hawthorne's *House of Seven Gables*. In this role, then, the Sphinx represents the legions of women from which Armgart tries selfishly to disassociate herself. Phelps describes them as "the silent army of the unknown" (82). These are, once again, Phelps's "unhappy girls," who have no agency or vocation of their own and are therefore the objects of man's art, power, and scorn. Finally, the Sphinx represents the dilemma of the woman artist, "[t]he riddle of ages" (83): how to discover the source of ancient, mysterious, divine inspiration, or romantic genius, when one is also a woman.

But Phelps makes it clear that she believes the dilemma is not simply socially imposed but is inherent in woman's nature. Whereas de Staël understood romantic love as absorbing a woman's interests and therefore replacing a woman's genius once she discovered it, and Barrett Browning saw love as the key to a woman's poetic genius, and Stoddard and Eliot portrayed women artists who believed romantic love and art to be incompatible and therefore chose art over heterosexual love, Phelps's novel makes the dilemma overtly irreconcilable. She portrays a figure in whom the two identities of woman and artist do not harmonize, as they do in Aurora Leigh. Avis tells Philip that God "has set two natures in me, warring against each other. He has made me a law unto myself — *He* made me so. How can I help that?" (107). As Karen Tracey argues, Avis tries to "reconcile her warring natures by giving the Sphinx a voice" through her painting.[53] In this paradox is perhaps Phelps's most devastating message: Avis's great work is born out of Avis's recognition of love and the war between woman and artist, but the war itself means that the woman artist will not survive. Picking up where *Aurora Leigh* left off, *Avis* goes on to show how the woman artist who loves — not platonically like Armgart or vicariously like Alicia but heterosexually — is doomed as both a woman and an artist. For Avis's painting of the Sphinx remains unfinished and her marriage to Philip is a failure.

As many have noted, Phelps takes a page out of *Aurora Leigh* and *Jane Eyre* by wounding Philip before having Avis "surrender" to him (111). In addition, Avis is won by his claims that he will support her art and is not asking her "to be my housekeeper!" (110), echoing the suitor's promises in "Husband of a Blue." Not long into her marriage, they both realize the folly they have committed. Her studio becomes completely neglected as she is forced by a series of incompetent servants to take on household duties for which she is unprepared. Eventually the care of two children is added to her list of responsibilities, and, she realizes, her hopes for artistic accomplishments have been effectively extinguished. The narrator points out the common nature of Avis's sacrifice:

> Women understand — only women altogether — what a dreary will-o-the-wisp is this old, common, I had almost said commonplace experience, "When the fall sewing is done," "When the baby can walk," "When house-cleaning is over," "When the company has gone," "When we have got through with the whooping-cough," "When I am a little stronger," then I will write the poem, or learn the language, or study the great charity, or master the symphony; then I will act, dare, dream, become. (149)

As Avis's responsibilities accumulate, she begins to falter under the heavy burdens she carries, and Philip also begins to falter in his appointed role as breadwinner and husband. First he loses his position at the college; then Avis discovers his infidelity with her rival, Barbara. As she gains in strength after a near mortal illness, his health worsens, and he travels to Europe to recuperate. During his absence, their son becomes ill and dies. After Philip returns, Avis resumes her wifely role, taking him to Florida for the winter, where they are gradually able to rekindle their love for each other shortly before he dies.

Nonetheless, despite the fact that after Philip's death she has fewer responsibilities and more time for her art, Avis's talent has been extinguished. When she was in need of money to pay one of Philip's debts during his absence, she had hastily finished the Sphinx, putting a child with its finger to its lips in the foreground to silence the Sphinx. Unable to fully realize the vision she had once had of revealing its secret, she "struck the great sphinx dumb" (205) in an hour and sent it off. She has been reduced to the status of a painter who, like Ruth Hall, works for money to support her family rather than the inspired romantic genius she once aspired to be. However, the painting was immediately sold and won her instant fame: "New York has gone wild over you in one week's time!" her old teacher tells her (204). But she soon discovered that this would be her one and only great work. Like the Sphinx in the painting, she herself is silenced. Unable to paint with her previous energy and talent, she tells her father that "the stiffness runs deeper than the fingers" (244). Looking back on her marriage, she wonders if the dream she had during their engagement of combining love and art had ever been possible. When Philip had encouraged her work and told her, "I think you would make a greater picture of it [the Sphinx] after we are married," the implication is that love and a home would enable her to fulfill her ambition (121). She wove herself from these words a beautiful vision, which serves as an ironic comment on the idealism of *Aurora Leigh:* "Down through the years she suddenly saw herself transfigured by happiness. She saw her whole nature deepening, . . . herself idealized, by love. . . . [T]his man brought her, she thought, that transcendent experience which is so often given to a man, but alas! so unknown to women, . . . in which love shall be found more a stimulus to than a sacrifice of the higher elements of the nature" (121–122).

Men had found support and inspiration in the context of family; why not women as well? But, as we have seen, daily cares and Philip's inconstancy made love a bitter thing to her and sapped her desire to make art. "She was stunned to find how her aspiration had emaciated during her married life. Household care had fed upon it like a disease" (206). Even when they later reconcile and rediscover their love for each other, Phelps is less than sanguine: "She did not cheat her clear nature by telling herself or him that she found in her married lot vicarious atonement for what she had missed. A human gift is a rebellious prisoner, and she was made human before she was made woman." However, Phelps seems to tone down this depressing admission by continuing, "But *she thought* it mattered less to her than it did once, — all this lost and unquelled life. They had saved the life of life, they had saved their wedded love: the rest could be borne" (234; italics added). Phelps does not say categorically that it now matters less, but that she thought it did, suggesting that Avis is still learning to cope with the situation. Even if love is "the life of life," Avis is barely living. Love can never make her a better artist, even after Philip's and her son's deaths. Her life now is simply about survival as she tries to provide for herself and her child by giving art lessons. Knowing that she still loves Philip simply makes it easier for her to keep on living, even in the absence of creating. Now, in spite of her earlier image of a life and art enriched by love, "She did not know how to express distinctly, even to her own consciousness, her conviction that she might have painted better pictures — not worse — for loving Philip and the children; that this was what God meant for her, for all of them, once, long ago. She had not done it. It was too late now" (244). Although Jack H. Wilson argues that the novel ostensibly indicts society but really implies "that it was not God's intention to make [her] an artist at this time,"[54] this passage suggests that God's plan had been for Avis to become a better artist. This is not simply the author's vision, she claims, but God's ideal vision as well.

Phelps can't let Avis's ambition materialize even now because a happy ending would undercut the seriousness of her warning to her female readers. However, Phelps softens the blow of this tragic ending by having Avis focus her energies on her daughter, who is, significantly, named Wait. Avis, therefore, does not fail, for, like her own (and Phelps's) mother, she will help her daughter to become what Avis herself cannot. As Carol Farley Kessler explains, "Avis [is] a pivotal link in the change from constrained womanhood of her mother to liberated possibility for her daughter."[55] Avis took an important step forward, but Wait must complete God's plan. Phelps herself, in the voice of the narrator, argues that the process to make "A WOMAN" must span over three generations, and only then will "such a creature" arise who "is competent to the terrible task of adjusting the sacred individuality of her life to her supreme capacity of love and the supreme burden and perils which it imposes upon her" (246). Sensing the promise of the future, Avis wonders, "Had the stone lips of the sphinx begun to mutter?" Avis can live on through Wait, for she realizes it will "be easier for her daughter to be alive, and be a woman, than it had for her" (247).

Wait provides a kind of hope, therefore, that was not present at the end of the romantically tragic *Corinne*. Corinne did not pass on her talents to Oswald's and Lucille's daughter to create a tradition of women's art but in order to keep her own memory alive. For the daughter's talents are not her own and do not represent the future but the past. And whereas *Armgart* renounces an artistic vocation as essentially selfish, Phelps never has Avis renounce her former ambitions. Likewise, the narrator never undercuts the significance of the woman artist's vocation, as the narrator in *St. Elmo* does. *Avis*'s ending is also more hopeful than that of Stoddard's "Collected" because even though Avis is silenced, her daughter will not be. Alicia, by contrast, has left no legacy for future generations. As is the case in "Collected," however, the autobiographical nature of Phelps's book suggests the author's own desire to see not only her work but also her life in the chain of great women writers beginning with de Staël and including Barrett Browning and Eliot. The novel itself, therefore, like "Collected," seeks to establish a legacy of artistry for American women writers.

European Possibilities

A significant component of the American woman artist's narrative was the opportunities provided by travel to Europe. *Corinne* and *Aurora Leigh* had depicted Italy as the place where women artists could both realize their genius and gain recognition. At the end of "Collected" we learn that Alicia has died abroad. Stoddard probably thought it fitting that her artist heroine should end her days in Europe — "the Old World, cities whose legends enchant you, . . . the birth-place of genius you worship, the cradle of the arts you revere," as Alicia's suitor tells her. "Oh, the pictures that flashed across my soul as he spoke the glowing vision of life without being aware of it!" Alicia responds in her journal (301). Again, Stoddard was writing out a fantasy of her own. She longed to go to Europe for her "development" and hoped her brother would get a post abroad and take her with him. But Stoddard was never able to make the pilgrimage to the Old World of which many nineteenth-century American artists dreamed.[56]

Phelps also longed to go to Europe, but, like Stoddard, she was not able to because she had no one to accompany her. She wrote to Annie Fields in 1882, "Yes; of course I ought to be in Europe, and I would gladly dare the experiment if I had anyone to dare it with me."[57] She was now thirty-eight years old, yet even grown women felt they needed companions, if not chaperones, to venture the long and dangerous trip. When Avis traveled to Europe, Phelps sent her over with friends for the first year. Thereafter Avis stayed on alone for five more years. She started out among the circles of American artists in Italy, some of whom were women, and she lived in a high tower like Aurora (and Hilda in Hawthorne's *Marble Faun*). Finally, she made her way to Paris, where she studied diligently with the most prominent masters, proving that she possessed true genius. A great future was predicted for her. Returning to America was, in a sense, Avis's downfall. Only in Europe could she truly succeed as an artist. It is the place of her greatest opportunities, while America is her tomb.

For Alcott, the idea of the freedom provided in Europe inspired her to begin to write a woman artist's novel that also engages the female *Künstlerroman* tradition. It is, like the others, autobiographical, as she based it on her and her sister's experiences in Europe. By the time Alcott and her sister May (and later, Woolson, who lived abroad even longer) made their respective journeys to the Old World, the American literary market had already been flooded by European travel narratives depicting travel abroad as full of adventure, freedom, and never-ending encounters with the magnificent and the picturesque. Europe held a special importance for nineteenth-century American artists and writers who sought there the kind of rich, tradition-laden culture they believed the United States lacked. In their desire to create for the New World a high culture to rival that of the Old, many felt that a European education (formal or informal) was essential. Almost all of the century's influential American male writers, painters, and sculptors had traveled to or lived in Europe. Many published accounts of their excursions or residences abroad, and some made Europe a subject of serious literature, as in Hawthorne's *Marble Faun* (1860) and James's *Roderick Hudson* (1875) and *The American* (1877). In such books, Europe emerged as the world's art gallery, as the repository of the highest accomplishments in art, and as the sublime and picturesque subject that had inspired the master geniuses of Western civilization. For American men, travel abroad also meant escape from a utilitarian, materialistic society that thwarted their development as artists and writers. As James Buzard argues, "Insofar as domestic society appeared to stultify feelings and imagination, touring seemed to offer opportunities for the exercise of thwarted human potential."[58] This was, of course, even more so the case for women, whose desires to pursue lives as serious artists also were hindered by a patriarchal society. Yet the dream of artistic fulfillment for these women in Europe became less tenable by the 1880s as the scrutiny of American women abroad intensified.

Margaret Fuller and Julia Ward Howe initiated the exodus of American women writers and artists to Italy in the 1840s and early 1850s. Following them, other American women writers and artists established the foreign sojourn as an important part of a woman artist's development, just as it had been for men. Actress Charlotte Cushman traveled abroad with writer Grace Greenwood and sculptor Harriet Hosmer in 1852, and Harriet Beecher Stowe went on a tour of England in 1852 after the success of *Uncle Tom's Cabin*. Many of the experiences of these early pioneers were published for American consumption in Fuller's columns for the *New York Tribune*, Greenwood's *Haps and Mishaps of a Tour in Europe* (1854), and Stowe's *Sunny Memories of Foreign Lands* (1854). In addition to Hosmer, the sculptors Vinnie Ream and Emma Stebbins became associated with Italy, drawn there by the examples of de Staël's Corinne and Barrett Browning's Aurora Leigh. These women found an independence there that they could never gain at home. As Leonardo Buonomo has written about Howe, in Italy, "She was confronted with the prospect of uncontrolled social and intellectual experimentation." For her, Italy was "associated with the idea of unhampered movement and expression, while home [Boston] gradually came to stand for stifling rigidity of manners and feelings." Hosmer shared her view, writing home to a friend in 1853, "I wouldn't live anywhere else but in Rome, if you would give me the Gates of Paradise and all the Apostles thrown in. I can learn more and do more here, in one year, than I could in America in ten." Hosmer's success was widely publicized in America. She stood out in Rome because of her gender, and her example was carefully watched by all. As Lydia Maria Child observed in 1858, "the cause of woman-kind had so much at stake in her progress." Eventually, she proved herself worthy of the title "genius." Having met Hosmer, Hawthorne was inspired to write about her and her sister artists in Rome in *The Marble Faun*, where he described his heroine, Hilda, as "an example of the freedom of life which it is possible for a female artist to enjoy at Rome. . . . all alone, perfectly independent . . . doing what she liked. . . . The customs of artist life bestow such liberty upon the sex, which is elsewhere restricted within so much narrower limits."[59]

Before the Civil War, few American women traveled to Europe on their own and for their own purposes. While men crisscrossed the Continent, often by themselves, or went abroad to take up diplomatic posts, as Hawthorne and Howells did, women were most often dependent on the support of others to get them abroad and to show them around. But by the late 1860s, with the advent of the "luxurious 'steam palaces,'" foreign travel had become more comfortable and accessible to (well-to-do) women, and, as Mary Suzanne Schriber writes, "American women began to journey to foreign lands in significant numbers, for their own reasons and independent of men."[60] The numbers of American women who fled a constrictive home life and found their destiny in Europe quickly increased, and their European ventures were widely publicized. As a result, Europe became in women's minds a kind of otherworldly place where they could enjoy more freedom than in America. Leo Hamalian sums up their fantasy: "For most women, immobilized as they were by the iron hoops of convention, the term 'abroad' had a dreamlike, talismanic quality. It conjured up a vision composed of a whole cluster of myths, half-myths, and truths — of sunlight, of liberty, of innocence, of sexual freedom, of the fantastic and the healing, of the unknown and mysterious — all those concepts that stood in direct confrontation to domesticity."[61] Going abroad was first and foremost a release from duties at home, freedom from the sacrifice of self to others that marked women's lives.

For the exposure to art and the opportunities for freedom that Europe offered, it was natural that Alcott would want to go to there. When she first went, in 1865, she confided to her journal, "I could not realize that my long desired dream was coming true." While life at home was reality, even drudgery, life abroad was magical, an opportunity for fulfillment that seemed almost too good to be true. In London, she wrote, "I felt as if I'd got into a novel while going about in the places I'd read so much of."[62] Unfortunately, she went as the companion of an invalid and her brother, an arrangement that prevented Alcott from experiencing the freedom she desired, although she was exposed to many of the cities and sights considered essential for a cultured American's trip abroad. After her year-long trip, she was anxious for May to see them as well.

Louisa, eight years older than May, viewed her younger sibling as a sort of surrogate daughter. She hoped to help May achieve the kind of life that she felt was slipping through her fingers, much as Avis hoped that her daughter would have an easier time of it than she had. May represented to her the future for women artists, and Louisa watched over her with maternal eyes, trying to keep May on the straight and narrow path of becoming an artist. They had both started out with the same encouragement and aspirations — May was referred to as "Little Raphael," while Louisa was the family's "Little Shakespeare."[63] But by the 1870s Louisa felt that her own time had already come and gone. Her health was failing (largely due to overwork and the aftereffects of the mercury treatments she had received during the war), and her attempts at gaining a serious reputation with *Hospital Sketches* and her novel *Moods* had failed. Although Louisa sometimes resented the advantages that May so easily received, she also was May's greatest benefactor. Her success with *Little Women* in 1868–69 enabled her to provide an artist's life for May in Europe, which she did until May's death in 1879. When the two of them went abroad in 1870, with a friend of May's, Louisa went for rest, she said, for she was worn out from the heavy burden of caring for her family and trying to satisfy the publishers' demands for new work, whereas May was embarking on her life as a professional artist.

May had also dreamed for years about going to Europe. She wrote home, "You ask if after dreaming of foreign parts for so many years I am not a little disappointed in the reality. But I can say that everything so far has been quite as picturesque, new, and lovely as I expected." May exemplified the adventurous American woman who relished her freedom from duties at home and the opportunity to flout convention. She bragged to her family about her exploits, including a daring hike to the pass of St. Bernard in a potentially deadly storm and a ride atop the "coupé" with the luggage in order to better view the Italian countryside, while crowds of Italians jeered at them and Louisa sat inside, "begg[ing] us to come down."[64]

Louisa capitalized on their trip abroad by publishing *Aunt Jo's Scrap-Bag. Shawl-Straps* (1872), in which she portrays herself as Lavinia, a "poor, used-up, old invalid" who is reluctant to go to Europe but is lured by the prospect of "no spring cleaning," a much-needed release from domestic duties. Lavinia is predisposed not to enjoy herself or experience much but merely to chaperone her younger sister, Matilda, and her friend, Amanda, while she also tries to regain her health. These "infants," as Lavinia calls them, refer to her as "Granny." In the preface, Alcott apologizes for focusing so much on Lavinia's views (which provide the book's humor), suggesting that the book should be about "the younger and more interesting shawl-strapists."[65] The three single women, making "the last Declaration of American Independence," relish their freedom from men and traveling in foreign lands, although Alcott is quick to point out that they do so within the bounds of propriety.

> No lord and master, in the shape of brother, spouse, or courier, ordered their outgoings and incomings; but liberty the most entire was theirs, and they enjoyed it heartily. Wisely and well too; for, though off the grand route, they behaved themselves in public as decorously as if the eyes of all prim Boston were upon them, and proved by their triumphant success, that the unprotected might go where they liked, if they conducted themselves with the courtesy and discretion of gentlewomen.

Lavinia, as narrator and chaperone, is careful to check the younger women's independence, expressing her discomfort with the new freedom all three are experiencing. By the same token, however, she also resents intrusions on their independence. Throughout the book, she is on the lookout for men who threaten their liberty. Above all, romance with a European man must be avoided. When the three witness a young French girl married off to a French colonel whom they believe to be a "fiend," they cry "Spinsters for ever!" Later, they meet an American girl who is going to marry a Russian and feel "much pity . . . for the feeble girl doomed to go to Russia with a husband who had 'tyrant' written in every line of his bad, *blasé* little face and figure." Matilda is in the greatest danger because of her sociable nature. When she flirts with a French count on the train, Lavinia thinks, "If the man don't get out soon, I'll tie her up in my shawl, and tell him she is mad." Lavinia also prevents Matilda from throwing away her good name by not allowing the soldiers of Albano, Italy, to lure her into "gambading away for a ride *sans* duenna, *sans* habit, *sans* propriety, *sans* every thing."[66] So the freedom Europe represents to these women is a fragile one. Lavinia is sending a clear message to her female readers to beware of the romantic traps that Europe also represents. But at the end of the book, Lavinia argues for women's freedom not only to travel in Europe but also to live there, not as wives of European tyrants but as independent women artists. She is now ready to leave Matilda alone in London to "enjoy the liberty with which American girls may be trusted when they have a purpose or a profession to keep them steady." Alcott encourages other young women "to strap up their bundles in light marching order, and push boldly off. . . . Wait for no man."[67]

For May, going abroad was about more than new sights and daring adventures; it was also about being someone new. She wrote to her mother on her second trip, "As soon as I land on this side [of the ocean] it always seems as if I were someone else . . . and in a measure I lose my identity and feel like a heroine in some novel."[68] Arriving in Europe brought new possibilities of selfhood. Once there, she could exchange the identity of daughter for that of artist, a transformation that felt unreal. She went abroad to "[gather] up the advantages of the Old World" in the form of exposure to the greatest works of art the world had produced. She also found a new mode of life that suited her immensely: "[A]rt life abroad is very charming and after my day among the Turners [paintings in the National Gallery she was copying], I heartily enjoy wandering through London, taking a trip to Hampton Court, Kew, or Richmond, a row on the river, a brisk canter in the park, or a ten-mile tramp to see the May-Pole Inn. So free, so busy, so happy am I that I envy no one, and find life infinitely rich and full."[69]

This trip inspired May to write *An Artist's Holiday* (1877–78), a work part autobiographical travel narrative and part fiction that was never published in full. In it, she characterizes herself as intent on experiencing England to the fullest without heed to conventions or restrictions: "[A] great advantage of being among strangers in a foreign land is that one may do just as one pleases." With this feeling to embolden her, she follows her impulse to row down the Thames, ignoring the shock of her friends and the shouts of men on the shore, and she "play[s] vagabond" by roaming the countryside alone, experiencing "the most charming episode of my life." She felt so free during her solo residence in London that she even recorded her desire to join her male friend in smoking a cigarette, although someone later crossed out this apparently scandalous passage in the manuscript.[70]

Although May came home twice, on her third trip to Europe she began a new life, never to return to America. Over the next two years, Louisa followed May's adventures closely, anxiously hopeful that May would devote herself to her career and wishing she could join her. Paris had become the mecca for painters who wanted to make a name for themselves, so May made Paris her destination. The American artist Mary Cassatt lived there and was a member of the burgeoning Impressionist school, greatly impressing her French counterparts. Young women, eager to follow in her footsteps and those of the French painter Rosa Bonheur, filled the studios of respected teachers like Couture, Julien, and Müller. May had already gained the attention of John Ruskin, the famous art critic, who had praised her copies of Turner as the best he had ever seen. Now, at thirty-six years of age, she regretted that she had not been able to devote herself sooner to serious art study and felt that this was her last opportunity to make her mark. Early on she decided that she would have to stay for a lengthy period, and she explained to her mother, "This is what I think my life must be . . . for I am awfully in earnest now and can do nothing at home for some time to come." She went on to study under two famous art teachers (both men) and launch a very promising career, exhibiting twice at the Salon, the pinnacle of achievement for an artist.[71]

But when May married the Swiss Ernest Nieriker in 1878, settling permanently in France, she embarked on a new adventure, that of attempting to combine marriage and an art career. May continued to find life in France the "ideal" one for a woman artist, because, as she wrote, "We mean to live our own life free from conventionalities." A year after she married, her life there still seemed no more real than when she had first come abroad. She wrote home to her family, "*Here* it is possible for a woman to pursue art with sufficient diligence to achieve success, & at the same time be faithful to her domestic duties. . . . In America this can not be done, but foreign life is so simple so free. [W]e can live for comfort not for company." She was able to shut out the world and worry only about her art and her new home. As an expatriate, she occupied a unique position; she was a member of neither American nor French society, so she was essentially free to define for herself what her life would be. In fact, she could no longer imagine any other way. She told her family, "This foreign life is so satisfactory so full of the picturesque, so independent & charming that Concord or Boston would be like a prison to me, & home could never seem the same."[72]

How Louisa, sitting at home, must have felt reading this, we can only imagine. May had come to the realization that she could never return home, and Louisa would have to learn to accept that she could never experience the European life that May was leading. In April 1878, Louisa had contrasted her life with May's new one: "How different our lives are just now! — I so lonely, sad, and sick, she so happy, well and blest. She always had the cream of things, and deserved it. My time is yet to come somewhere else, when I am ready for it." The following month, she wrote, "I plan and hope to go to them [May and Ernest], if I am ever well enough, and find new inspiration in a new life. . . . I doubt if I ever find time to lead my own life, or health to try it." May's new life in Europe inspired Louisa to view Europe differently, as not just a place for her recuperation and May's art study but a place where she could start her life over, free from the care and duties at home. But as the months wore on, she had to give up her plan. She remained at home, caring for her widowed father and sister. To make up for her lost dream, she began to write *Diana and Persis*, a *Künstlerroman* about May's life and what her own life abroad might have been like.[73] Because she herself could not return to Europe, she imagined in *Diana and Persis* joining May in her pursuit of artistic excellence and fame in Europe. Apart from the autobiographical reason for the double heroines, the split also suggests, as in "Collected," the incompleteness of the woman artist's life and her divided psyche. With these two artist figures, Alcott explores two different life paths, trying to resolve the dilemma posed by earlier women artist narratives.

While it is impossible to confirm Alcott's ultimate intentions for this un-finished work, it is clear that she was inspired by May's example to try to fictional-ize more fully than Phelps was capable of doing how women could achieve the "full" life that Eliot seemed to have led but that no woman writer had yet com-pletely imagined in verse or prose. This story is much more than an autobio-graphical catharsis of her "jealousy" toward May and her resentment that "May Alcott's self-realization depended upon Louisa's self-abnegation," as Natania Rosenfeld argues.[74] Rather, it is Alcott's attempt to work through in fiction, if not in life, the choices between love and art confronting women artists. By respond-ing directly to *Avis*, hoping to prove that novel "wrong," she also thereby invokes a long tradition of women's *Künstlerromane*. While Avis could not realize the possibility of becoming a better artist by combining love and art, Alcott's artist heroines, Percy and Diana, seem on their way to doing so. Unfortunately, they don't reach that goal because Alcott had completed only four chapters when she stopped writing, grief-stricken by May's death in childbirth.

Persis (Percy) is closely modeled on May, but Diana is like Louisa only in her personality and relationship to Persis/May. Like Louisa, Diana is firmly com-mitted to spinsterhood, but unlike Louisa, she is young, healthy, and a sculptor, suggesting Harriet Hosmer as a model as well. Her most significant difference from Louisa is that she has no family and hence no obligations to anyone but herself and her work. She is even more solitary than Alicia Raymond because she has no brother or cousin, only her friend Percy, another artist. While Percy and Diana possess the same aim in life ("success and happiness"),[75] Diana is more firmly committed to the pursuit of art in the absence of "happiness," or the joys of conventional womanhood, namely marriage and family. Like Alicia and Armgart, Diana does not believe that combining the two is possible, and so she chooses her art, sacrificing the love of a family. She also tries to hold Percy to the same commitment. "Diana, devoutly believing that 'Success is impossible, unless the passion for art overcomes all desultory passions,' held Percy to her ideal with stern vigor, always hoping that the time would come when her friend would give all to art and let love go, as she herself had done" (393). When Percy decides to pursue her painting in France, Diana applauds the idea, believing the trip will free Percy of her suitors' distractions. Like the other women artist narratives, this one sets up a striking contrast between female characters, but this time it is between two types of women artists rather than the artist and her typical foil, the ordinary, domestic woman. Having set up this contrast, it seems likely that Alcott will take the two heroines on journeys that allow both of them to learn to combine love and art and thereby become "full" women artists. Diana must learn to love, and Percy must learn to devote herself more to her art.

The second chapter shows Percy's growing commitment to her art. It is comprised of letters from France, taken, in large part, from May's letters home. Here we see the narrative of a woman artist's development, which Phelps only briefly alluded to in *Avis*. Percy lives with other young women and attends art classes and has a painting accepted at the Paris Salon. There is no mention of a romance. But suddenly, in the next chapter, Percy has married and given birth to a child, and Diana decides to visit her to "see how well Percy's experiment succeeds. If she can combine art and domestic life harmoniously she will be a more remarkable woman than even *I* think her" (410). Diana is obviously not optimistic about this experiment, and later Diana jests with Percy's husband, August, about the situation. "But you know," she declares, "the wiseacres say we women cannot have all, and must decide between love and fame, so I am curious to see which of us [Percy or me] will fare the best" (423–424). His response is very revealing: "Pardon, I believe a woman can and ought to have both if she has the power and courage to win them. A man expects them, achieves them, why is not a woman's life to be as full and free as his? . . . I not only cherish this belief but I hope to see it beautifully realized by the success of this splendid wife of mine, who is to be the greater artist for being a happy woman, please God!" (424). The idea, a further take on Graf's wish for Armgart and Phelps's hope at the end of *Avis*, is given even more force by the fact that it is expressed by a man. Like Phelps, Alcott allows for the possibility that marriage and motherhood can make women superior artists, although Phelps puts that possibility off until future generations. Therefore, contrary to Rosenfeld's argument that "Persis/May . . . is quickly going the way of Phelps's Avis,"[76] it seems possible that with such an enlightened husband Persis will "prove 'Avis' in the wrong." However, while the author may be suggesting as much, Diana is more skeptical. She does not respond to August's optimistic speech; instead she "bowed gravely, charmed with his warmth but not one whit convinced by it" (424).

Throughout Diana's visit she sees signs that make her uneasy. When she first arrives, she notices that Percy's easel is dusty and the paint on the palette is dry, indicating a long period without use, just as Avis's studio gathered dust during her long absences when familial duty called. She also sees Percy looking into the "unknown future of [her] child" (413) rather than her own bright future as an artist. But Percy endeavors to reassure her: "it has been such a rich and perfect year. . . . [I] only wonder how I ever lived so long alone" (414). Percy is clearly adjusting to the situation much more easily than Avis did, another suggestion that it will not crush her artist's spirit in the long run. For Avis's loss of talent was due not only to household cares but to a negligent husband and many family illnesses, including her own. There is no ominous sign that such despair is around the corner for Percy. However, August's progressive attitude is cast in doubt. When Diana and Percy get the studio back in order and take the baby as their model, August perhaps shows his true colors by bursting in upon what he calls their "painting frenzy" and declaring, "Unnatural mother! Would you sacrifice your child at the altar of your insatiable art?" (421). Percy immediately whisks the baby up and wraps a blanket around her. The optimism that Alcott had allowed for earlier in this chapter is muted by the end. But it is not at all certain that Percy won't, once the child is older, be able to return to her art. She is not weighed down with cares and stifled to the extent that Avis was. In contrast to Avis, Percy has a capable husband and it seems likely that Alcott, had she concluded the book, would have made her a better artist for her love of family, rather than worse. For this is the direction in which she takes Diana in the last chapter she completed.

In this final chapter, Diana travels to Rome, where she is prolific, alone once again, and immersed in her art. However, she is not fulfilled. Like Aurora, she increasingly discovers that her life is incomplete without human relationships. One day, while observing the "gay throng" of visitors to the tourist spot of Pincio, she reflects on "her own life, so high and lonely, its ever growing ambition, and the sense of power that strengthened every year. Yet at times she was conscious of a deeper want, an unconquerable yearning, a bittersweet regret for something lost or never found." As if in response to her thoughts, a young boy, Nino, solicits her attention, "evidently hungry for the fostering tenderness mothers alone can give" (428). Diana responds, surprised at her own capacity for affection. Touching the boy "thrilled her sensitive hands chilled by long contact with cold marble and damp clay. . . . all the pent-up tenderness of her nature seemed to gush out" (429). She has not had time to notice children or to lament their absence in her life until this moment. As it turns out, the boy's father is the famous sculptor Stafford, who is a widower. He meets Diana, and it is through him that she discovers the support a man is capable of giving to a woman artist. He praises her sculpture of Saul for its "virile force," a compliment that impresses her, for "[f]ew men would say that to a woman" (438). His response reveals that he is willing to accept women as comrades and does not want their talents restricted to "womanly" art and domestic subjects. Instead, he invites women to take on "masculine" subjects and blur gender distinctions. In a sense, then, he is Alcott's improvement on Romney. Stafford is not weakened in order to bring him down to Diana's level. Instead, the equal relationship is created by his lifting her up to his level — or allowing her to ascend on her own.

Inspired by her new friends, Diana has begun work on a head of Nino, revealing a motherly tenderness that touches Stafford. Diana, in his eyes, possesses the capacity to be both mother and artist. And given the fact that Nino is not an infant like Percy's child and does not demand as much care, the prospects for Diana's successfully being mother and artist, at least in the short term, seem more promising. One senses the possibility of a union between the two sculptors, but the issue is not broached by Alcott. The final paragraph of the unfinished novel reads: " 'One feels as if there was a fine man and a fine woman working there together [in Diana], and one scarcely knows which to admire most,' [Stafford] thought to himself as he went away, leaving Diana to work with enthusiasm on the arched head of the boy, to which she added a pair of winged shoulders and called it Puck" (441).[77] Stafford's parting thoughts reveal that Diana is complete in herself, not "half a person" but whole, capable of realizing the capacities traditionally accorded to both man and woman, which might indicate that she has no need for a husband. At the same time, though, Stafford appears to have integrated his male and female sides as well, as revealed in his role as affectionate father and in his appreciation of Diana's work, both the Saul and the Puck, which represent masculine and feminine artistic sensibilities. Charles Strickland notes that Alcott sought to "portray men who possessed what sentimentalists might have regarded as feminine sensitivity to the needs of others."[78] For Alcott, Stafford represents the possibility of a new man who is the only possible heterosexual companion to the woman artist, unlike Phelps's pessimistic portrayal of Philip's failure to appreciate his wife's ambitions. This chapter could also be about Diana's learning that to be a great artist she must recognize and develop her feminine as well as her masculine side. That a man and a child awaken her femininity leads one to suspect that Alcott was trying to understand the "happiness" that May had found, and that she was speculating about the effect it would have on a woman artist who, like herself, had renounced any such relationship. Diana seems to be discovering that August was right: when women did find such happiness, they became more complete, and hence better, artists.

We will never know if Alcott intended for Stafford and Diana to marry.[79] One cannot even tell if Alcott herself knew how Diana's and Persis's "experiments" would end. While Diana's seems more likely to suceed, I would argue that Alcott most likely was trying to envision a way for both women to achieve the union of love and art. That Alcott ultimately failed to do so probably has as much to do with her own disbelief in the possibility than with her grief over May's death. As she intimated to a friend in 1880, women had to choose one role or the other. May's desire for love had cost her the very life she had always hoped for and had so recently found: " 'All for love,' seems a mistake to my eyes, but those who have tried it say the world is well lost if even a short taste of the divine madness is all that is gained. So I try to think my brave bright sister did not give her life in vain, & was satisfied with two years of happiness instead of many as an artist."[80] After May's death, Alcott's life was taken up with caring for Lulu, May's daughter, whom Louisa now called "my daughter." Echoing Avis's desires for Wait's future, Alcott wrote in 1881, "I hope I may live to see May's child as brave & bright & talented as [May] was, & much happier in her fate."[81]

Like the Alcott sisters, Woolson was drawn to the opportunities for travel and freedom that Europe offered; however, as she would discover during her stay from 1879 until her death in 1894, the kind of liberty May had found was increasingly tempered by the serious scrutiny American women abroad were beginning to receive. The idea that American women were cavorting all over Europe without appropriate protection or restraint captured the popular imagination in America. Louisa and May were aware of the criticisms directed at American women abroad, who were portrayed in the press as lacking any seriousness of purpose beyond catching a duke or a count for a husband. In 1876, May wrote that she wanted the "brave" American women who had gained entrance to the foremost art schools in Paris to be remembered over "the indiscreet, husband-hunting butterfly" who most commonly represented "the typical American girl abroad."[82] But those May preferred to represent American womanhood in Europe were also ridiculed by the popular press as too independent and ambitious. Girls in America, commentators agreed, were already more independent and "indulged" than in any other country. As they ventured abroad, watchful eyes recorded the stir they made. In her "American Women Abroad" (1876), Lucy Hooper condemned "the fast girls" who were "loudly uproarious and boldly self-asserting" and, worst of all, who flirted with foreign men and went to balls with them unchaperoned. It was these girls, she lamented, who were making a bad name for all American women in Europe. A year later Albert Rhodes asked, "Shall the American Girl Be Chaperoned?" His answer was a resounding yes. "Our girls are the boldest of all," he wrote, as he recounted many disastrous incidents which could have been avoided had the girl in question been properly chaperoned.[83]

Therefore, when James's "Daisy Miller" was published in 1878, all eyes were already on the "American Girl." Daisy's main sins were a flirtation with a courier and an excursion with an Italian man, alone, to see the Coliseum in the moonlight. James's story hit a nerve at the right cultural moment and created an uproar in America, where many felt offended that James had portrayed "our girls" in this way. Others rose to James's defense and were eager to castigate the "Daisies" they had met abroad. Among James's defenders was a close friend of his and Woolson's, John Hay, who, in the *Atlantic*'s "Contributors' Club," declared James's story a "truth[ful]" portrayal and an important "lesson" to women not to exercise their "freedom" abroad if they were to avoid serious consequences. After the publication of Hay's piece, Woolson wrote to him, "I am glad you said what you did about 'Daisy Miller'; it was needed. . . . As the 'Daisies' are what they are through pure ignorance, Mr. James's work—, and yours in calling attention to it—, is a sort of 'Tract for the Times' which will do good." When she wrote this letter, Woolson had not yet been to Europe, but as she prepared for her voyage overseas eight months later, she must have had these warnings to American women travelers on her mind, desiring to distance herself from such admonitions.[84] The intense scrutiny of women abroad made Woolson and others more cautious and self-conscious than emboldened by the possibilities of self-transformation in Europe. The many portrayals of American women in Europe criticized not only their indiscretions but also their desires for self-improvement. Hooper had taken aim not only at the "fast" girls but also at the "strong-minded *Americaine*" who was "middle-aged, energetic, and undaunted by fatigues or obstacles." Indeed, she lamented that this "ubiquitous and indefatigable" type of American womanhood, who "c[a]me abroad to improve her mind," was so visible in Europe. The best examples of American women abroad were those who "come and go amid the sights and salons of Europe, and who leave no trace behind, . . . pass[ing] by unnoticed and unknown," which certainly was not the case with the many women writers and artists traversing the Continent.[85]

Woolson's dreams of going abroad had always been strong, but her duty to her mother after her father's death kept her in America. She had to "give up again my plan for going abroad," she wrote in 1876. "So much for myself."[86] In November 1879, following her mother's death, she finally made the trip with her sister and niece, who over the next fourteen years would be her frequent companions, although she often preferred to live and travel on her own. In the late 1870s, Woolson had become an admirer of the writing of Henry James, most certainly reading about his European travels in the articles he wrote for the *Atlantic Monthly*. By the time Woolson embarked on her own European experiment, she was eager to meet James, to explore the places he and others were writing about, and to join their ranks by publishing European sketches and stories in the *Atlantic* and other prominent magazines. Some of her first publications after going abroad were "A Florentine Experiment," "The Roman May, and a Walk," and "In Venice," two of which were published in the *Atlantic*.[87]

In late April 1880, Woolson finally met James, something she had been trying to do since she first arrived in England. His friendship had a profound impact on her experience abroad. He showed her around the many galleries and shared his love of the masters she was trying to learn to appreciate. And it was primarily through him that she came to know many other Americans of artistic temperament, most importantly Francis Boott and his daughter Lizzie, who was an artist. With them, and James himself, she felt, for a while, part of a community of like-minded and mutually supportive artists. But she ordinarily shunned society and preferred to have her days "serenely free" to write. Like May Alcott, she felt that her life in Europe freed her from the obligations of visiting.[88] But she also found the comfort and strength to live a solitary writer's life abroad in the company of James and his friends. After Lizzie Boott's marriage to the artist Frank Duveneck, she shared a villa in Florence with the newlyweds and Mr. Boott. She wrote Mary Mapes Dodge, "I have made a temporary home for myself in a villa (Aurora Leigh's) at Bellosguardo." She also wrote to many of her friends about the joy she felt at living in the villa where Barrett Browning had written *Aurora Leigh*, and from where she could see "Hawthorne's tower," a reference to Hilda's abode in *The Marble Faun*. She was fulfilling all of her dreams about coming to Europe, and she was excited at the prospect of living in a sort of artist's colony with the inspiration of Barrett Browning and Hawthorne to spur her on. As she anticipated moving in, she wrote about sharing the villa with her friends: "They too, have a garden — in which they Paint! And I shall write in mine!" In another letter she confided, "I was so happy to be here that it was almost wickedness!"[89]

Italy, especially, possessed a dreamlike quality for Woolson. From Florence she wrote, "here I have attained that old-world feeling I used to dream about, a sort of enthusiasm made up of history, mythology, old churches, pictures, statues, . . . vineyards, the Italian sky, dark-eyed peasants, opera-music, Raphael and old Michael, 'Childe Harold,' the 'Marble Faun,' 'Romola,' and ever so many more ingredients." And in Rome, she wrote that she was "stirred . . . by the thought that I was really and actually in '*Rome*'! the city I have dreamed about since childhood with a real, and sometimes, very intense longing." Now that she was finally there, she didn't plan to leave anytime soon. She felt she belonged in Europe, much like May had. From Venice, she wrote to James (who was temporarily in America), that she "wonder[ed] . . . whether the end of the riddle of my existence may not be, after all, to live here, and die here."[90]

Beholden to none, Woolson was experiencing total independence for the first time in her life. She wrote to her friend Edmund Clarence Stedman that the greatest "advantage" of her new life was "liberty. If I were to take a fancy to go to China, or the North Cape, tomorrow morning at ten precisely — there is absolutely nothing in the world to prevent it!" Ironically, though, she did not grant her female protagonists the same kind of freedom in Europe that she herself experienced. For example, "In Sloane Street" (1892) portrays a sensitive, cultured single woman whose trip to Europe is determined not by her own desires but by those of her companions, who neither understand nor appreciate her. And "A Florentine Experiment" (1880) depicts the life abroad of Miss Margaret Stowe, who is tied to her invalid aunt, while the American expatriate Mr. Morgan heads off to a new destination whenever he feels the urge to do so. He is the one, not Margaret, who experiences the kind of "liberty" Woolson claimed for herself.[91] Perhaps eager to keep her distance from the ridicule showered on the Daisies and female artists abroad, she shied away from portraying the liberating potential of Europe for American women.

It is also notable that in her stories of women writers and artists in Europe,

Woolson depicted Europe as lacking opportunities for women to develop their creative potential. They do not discover the supportive environment or the artistic fulfillment that Corinne and Aurora do. Instead, they meet their literal or figurative deaths. In "'Miss Grief'" (1880), a woman of genius dies, penniless and friendless, and is buried with her unpublished manuscripts in Rome. In "The Street of the Hyacinth" (1882), an ambitious woman artist's marriage to an arrogant art critic is called a "great downfall" and likened to the demolition of the street on which she lives.[92] But "At the Château of Corinne" (1887), as the title suggests, is particularly intertextual with *Corinne* and *Aurora Leigh* and comments specifically on the failure of Europe to liberate the woman artist. In this story, Woolson, even more disturbingly than Stoddard, suggests that the legacy of the woman of genius, which Corinne and de Staël represent, is no longer available to women writers. In many ways, it represents an endpoint to the nineteenth-century women's *Künstlerroman* tradition. If Alcott could see no way to complete her optimistic contribution to this tradition, Woolson's "Château" sounds the death knell of the woman artist's development and the tradition that began with *Corinne*.

Woolson first wrote the story in 1880, shortly after her arrival in Europe and about the time she visited Coppet, Switzerland, de Staël's home in exile. Woolson also immersed herself in the writings of de Staël and her friend Madame Récamier, who is also invoked in the story. But she laid aside "Château" for seven years until, during her stay in Bellosguardo, in Florence, she remembered the story. As Cheryl Torsney argues, she probably recollected it owing to her new villa's associations with *Aurora Leigh*. But unlike the rebirth that both of these earlier artist heroines experience in Europe, Woolson's protagonist is robbed of her independence and, hence, her voice. The story is pervaded with images of death. "Château" begins in late August, rather than the June of *Aurora Leigh*. It ends even later in the fall, the end of October, as winter is about to set in. And the story is centered around four visits to Coppet, the home and the final resting place of de Staël. The château shows "not a sign of life," and the famous author's burial there becomes a metaphor for the death of the artist as well as the death of the tradition of women of genius.[93]

"Château" suggests many corollaries to de Staël's and Barrett Browning's texts. Katherine, whose name is reminiscent of Corinne, is a composite figure of the two earlier artist heroines. She is widely admired for her beauty and literary talent. And, like Corinne, she has her own money, having inherited it from her dead husband. She is a "very complete, woman of the world" (215). Her chosen art form is poetry, aligning her with Aurora. Most importantly, though, she is a devotee of de Staël and visits her château frequently. Like de Staël, she is in exile, enjoying the freedom of being away from home and feeling a kinship with this woman of genius from the previous century. She wonders, though, if her life here is a product of her "imagination only, her longing dream" (215). She voices Woolson's own feelings about Europe as a kind of fantasy, but as the story progresses, we learn that her freedom is a dream and that de Staël and the legacy of the woman of genius is "something from fairy-land" (215).

The other significant characters are also figures inherited from the tradition of women artist narratives. The American John Ford is reminiscent of both Oswald and the young Romney. Like Oswald, Ford represents a more traditional, rigid culture that refuses to grant women the right of independence or artistic ambitions. Upon his arrival, he also discovers a woman of considerable talents who is the center of attention, but unlike Oswald, he refuses to participate in the universal admiration of de Staël or Katherine. He declares de Staël "eager and voracious" and delights in recalling how Goethe and Schiller objected to her forwardness (229). And although Katherine's book of poetry "received a good deal of praise" (231), he cannot share the world's opinion. It becomes clear, however, that his aversion to de Staël and Katherine's poetry is the result of his disdain for women with ambition. "[W]hat is the very term [women of genius] but a stigma?" he asks. "No woman is so proclaimed by the great brazen tongue of the Public unless she has thrown away her birthright of womanly seclusion for the miserable mess of pottage called 'fame' " (229–230). Although he proclaims to be no "critic," Katherine forces him to judge her poetry. When he finally does, he objects foremost to its "daring," or ambition. Echoing the Romney of book 2 of *Aurora Leigh*, he tells her, "We do not expect great poems from women any more than we expect great pictures." By trying to create great poems, she has committed an "unpardonable sin. . . . For a woman should not dare in that way" (233). But Katherine soundly rejects his characterization, secure in the love of another man who appreciates her talent.

Lorimer Percival, Katherine's fiancé, is a sincere admirer of de Staël and of Katherine, but he proves to be a sham, like Oswald. His relationship with Katherine is a literary romance, as they close themselves up in the library and make visits to Coppet. On a visit to de Staël's home, Percival pays homage to de Staël and other "[f]air vanished ladies of the past" and suggests that "the more rigid customes of our modern age" have been responsible for their decline in reputation (226). However, Percival makes the same choice as did Oswald, selecting a

younger, simpler, more conventional woman over Katherine. In fact, his supposed regard for Katherine is put into question when we learn that his broken
engagement with her was a "great sacrifice" because his new wife has no fortune
(246). The imputation is that Percival, who has already squandered his own
inheritance, was more interested in Katherine's money than her genius.

"Château," therefore, enacts the female doubling we saw in *Corinne*, "Collected," and *Avis*, casting Mrs. Percival and Sylvia Pitcher as conventional women
in contrast to Katherine. Sylvia, who is Ford's aunt and Katherine's cousin, plays
the role of the traditional, domestic woman, similar to Corinne's and Aurora's
aunts. She takes a decidedly maternal attitude toward Ford, suggesting her essential womanliness. She also lacks a true appreciation for art. Although Sylvia
admires de Staël and reads Byron, she secretly prefers Charlotte Yonge — who is
meant to represent the conventional, feminine writer — and her favorite hobby is
making wax flowers, a feminine, domestic art form. She is everything that Katherine is not, as is Mrs. Percival. As Ford tells her, Percival's wife reminds him of his
aunt because these two ideal women are "very lovely and very lovable" (238). The
seventeen-year-old girl also "cannot in the least appreciate the true depth of
[Percival's] poetry" (237), a skill neither necessary nor desirable. She cannot be
the kind of literary soul mate that Katherine would have been. But Ford understands her appeal to Percival and wishes that Katherine were more like her. She is
a "beautiful young girl, with a face like a wild flower in the woods," Ford tells her.
"She has . . . an expression of sweet and simple goodness, and gentle confiding
trust." In response to his gushing adoration, Katherine recommends that he find a
woman like her. Not in the least offended at his preference for this Lucille-like
woman, Katherine must, however, be stung by Percival's decision, although the
narrator never tells us she is. Instead, the reader, like Ford, continues to see only
her pride, which he believes is a "barrier" between them (243).

Like other woman artist narratives, this story is focused on the conflict between "woman" and "artist," represented by opposing characters and contained
within the artist heroine herself. Katherine seems to believe that she can combine
the two in a literary marriage with the poet Percival. However, when Percival
rejects her, she does not begin her slow march toward death, as Corinne does.
Instead, she remains independent and defiant of Ford, who has made his wishes
clear. He will not admire her as a poet, and he cannot love her as a woman until
she gives up her writing and shows him "the sweet side of your nature, the gentle,
womanly side" (234). Rejecting this "condition," however, she mocks his devotion to the ideal woman. To win his love, she tells him, "I need not have been in

earnest. I had only to pretend a little, to pretend to be the acquiescent creature you admire, and I could have turned you round my little finger" (235). In other words, he is not interested in real love, the union of souls that Aurora and Romney or even Corinne and Oswald have. He is only interested in the image of the devoted, dependent woman who reflects his own worth and possesses none of her own. It is clear that Katherine can never love this man. On the one hand, he cannot appreciate her art, and, on the other, she cannot willingly give up her art for the bliss of love. His efforts to "rival the printed page" (227) — to take the place of literature in her life — must fail, until she loses her fortune and, hence, her independence.

Just as in so many of these women's texts about marriage, the courtship be-tween these two is portrayed as a power struggle. When Katherine shows Ford her poetry, he believes she is trying to make him her "victim" (234) or make him fall in love with her. Although she believes him impervious to her tactics, artless though they may be, he responds, "perhaps I conceal my wounds" (232). Ford is never literally wounded as Romney and Philip are, nor is he appreciably weak-ened. Even though he finally wins her hand by going down on his knees and getting tears in his eyes, he is kneeling before his image of a dependent woman, not Katherine. As he had told her before, when woman "is her true self she is so far above us that we can only be humble" (235). What finally humbles him in the end is not her tremendous talent, as is the case in *Aurora Leigh*, but her weakness. She is the one who is wounded — by the loss of her fortune. Now she is reduced to playing the role of the "acquiescent creature" he desires. When he tells her, "It will be very hard for you to give up your independence, your control of things," her reaction clearly conveys that she has decided to adopt the mask of his ideal woman: "she turned towards him with a very sweet expression in her eyes. 'You will do it all for me,' she answered" (245). This response is so unlike every other thing she has said in the story that clearly she has made a conscious decision to wrap him around her finger by playing to his only weakness — the cult of ide-alized femininity. However much we may wish to find some sign of strength in her manipulation of him, though, the conquest is clearly his. He lights a fire and produces a meal, turning the château of Corinne into a domestic space and signaling Katherine's transformation from artist to wife. The loss of her indepen-dence and her repudiation of her poetry make her lovable to Ford, like Sylvia and Mrs. Percival. He promises to "forget" her book or that she ever wrote poetry (246) and wins from her the promise never to write again, essentially burying her artist self beside Madame de Staël in Coppet.

As Ford proposed to her, a "wet and bedraggled little bird . . . in the tree above" sang one last note and then began to "arrange his soaked feathers" (241). This image, suggestive of Katherine's loss of voice, conveys the extent to which this story, like *Avis*, is about the demise of the woman artist. Here, as in Phelps's novel, the bird is rendered flightless and is silenced. Although this little bird will survive, like Katherine (her marriage being a survival strategy more than anything), the ending of the story provides no ray of hope. There is no faith in a future generation, as in *Avis*. Instead, the gardens at Coppet are "a picture of desolation; all the bright leaves, faded and brown, were lying on the ground in heaps so sodden that the wind could not lift them, strongly as it blew." The château rises "among the bare trees, cold, naked, and yellow, seeming to have already begun its long winter shiver." To Katherine, this place is "the end of the world" (240). And although Ford enters and rescues her from her desolation, this is no victory, as the marriage at the end of *St. Elmo* is for the nearly destroyed woman writer. For there is no indication that Katherine has ever loved Ford. Although *Avis* was widely considered the most pessimistic depiction of the woman artist's fate, Woolson's story is much darker. Avis was at least allowed to love and could hope that her daughter would be able to fulfill her potential. But Woolson suggests that it is not the ravages of love that destroy the woman artist, as in *Corinne*, or the pressures of domesticity, as in *Avis*. Instead, it is men's rejection of women's genius, which makes the combination of love and art impossible, and the lack of money, which makes an independent life as an artist impossible. Of course, Woolson herself was able to lead such a life without a great fortune. But she was something that Katherine was not—a professional artist. Having lost her money, Katherine possesses neither the strength nor the vision to turn down the support of the chauvinist suitor as Aurora Leigh did when she chose to be a poor, struggling poet rather than marry Romney or accept his money. By modeling herself after Corinne, an "antique" (247) ideal of the woman artist who was supported by the admiration of her friends, Katherine has adhered to an outmoded form of the woman artist's life. She gives into Ford precisely because she cannot imagine her writing as a moneymaking activity. Like Alicia Raymond, her refusal to enter the literary marketplace is what truly silences her.

In the end, Ford returns Katherine to a conventional life in America and irrevocably consigns de Staël to the past: "Here's to you all, charming vanished ladies of the past, . . . may you each have every honor in the picturesque, powdered, unorthographic age to which you belong, and never by any possibility step over into ours!" (243). Tellingly, Katherine has no dialogue in the final scene of the story. She is seen but not heard. In each of Woolson's European artist stories, Europe fails to offer new opportunities for self-creation. Instead, the promise it had held is a thing of the past, what only Corinne and Aurora Leigh could achieve. After "Château" sat for seven years in a drawer, Woolson remembered the story upon hearing the lyrics "le temps s'en va, le temps s'en va, ma belle," which Ford repeats in the story (219).[94] The days of Corinne are over, and whatever recognition and happiness she was able to achieve are not available to Woolson's generation.

The fantasy of Europe as a place where women could experience the freedom and independence they were denied at home and as a place where they could more fully develop their artistic abilities, even in marriage (as Eliot and Barrett Browning had done), seems to have given way for American women artists and writers in the 1880s and 1890s. The reality was that even in Europe they could entirely escape neither the bounds of women's lives nor the watchful eyes of a society that tried to keep their ambitions in check. Furthermore, financial security was as elusive abroad as it was at home. Ultimately, Alcott, Phelps, Stoddard, and Woolson were unable and unwilling to "prove 'Avis' in the wrong." Combining love and art, even in the haven of European exile, was still beyond the grasp of the new generation of serious women writers, whether love took the form of a romantic alliance or a supportive community. Nevertheless, none of these four authors suffered the fate of Avis, or Alicia, or Katherine—silence. They were all at least partially successful at making room in their lives to pursue their art seriously and to complete important works of art that reflect their high ambitions to be remembered alongside European women writers.

CHAPTER THREE

"The crown and the thorn of gifted life"

Imagining the Woman Artist

When Rebecca Harding Davis first met Alcott in 1862, at the home of James and Annie Fields, she found Alcott "a tall, thin young woman standing in a corner. She . . . had that watchful, defiant air with which the woman whose youth is slipping away is apt to face the world which has offered no place to her."[1] As Davis's words suggest, she was describing not only Alcott but a type of the suffering, neglected, marginalized woman author, a type that she knew from personal experience. Phelps also took notice of the ambitious female author relegated to the sidelines of the literary world in her article "A Plea for Immortality" (1880), written on the occasion of the *Atlantic Monthly*'s Birthday Breakfast for Oliver Wendell Holmes. At the hub of the *Atlantic* event are the old, "well-nourished lives," including a male and female author revered for their literary and social standing, although "Mrs. Jones" clearly ranks below "Mr. Smith." But Phelps's greatest attention is devoted to the young, struggling authors, particularly a woman in the corner. Cut off from the literary world of Boston, this wallflower nonetheless has high ambitions and has shown much promise, but her life hangs precariously in the balance between fame and a death brought on by rejection and discouragement.

In her description of this nameless woman, Phelps incorporates many of the hardships that plagued writers who (like herself, Alcott, Stoddard, and Woolson) looked up to "[t]he prophets, the priests, the kings of our tribe" and felt "nervous, . . . unrestful, insistent, . . . full of the stir of ambitions satisfied or thwarted, of aspirations nurtured or famished, of the jar of *doing*, not the calm of *done!*" Under her simple black dress the starving writer "hides impatient, crippled life enough to stir the world. . . . Her story in The Atlantic commands attention. She is young. Life is before her. She is ambitious. She has power; she knows it, and so do we. All the sibyl in her chafes." But she must also care for her invalid mother in a town sixty miles from Boston. The final blow is a rejected manuscript returned from an editor. "A literary life seems as impossible to the poor girl as a dragoon's or a drayman's." Phelps tries to offer her encouragement but asks, "How shall we tell her to be patient, — how bid her to go to her Goethe and read what he said of the power that developed best by long suppression?" In other words, how can we tell her to patiently wait for her moment of glory when we know she is so discouraged that she is ready to give up altogether? "It needs a greater than Goethe to help that woman," Phelps writes, "to teach her that the lesson learned in endurance may be the one which the world wants."[2] This is small consolation, she knows, but it is all the hope she has to offer. It is, in fact, the hope that sustained many postbellum women writers: that all of their suffering, if patiently endured, would lead to great art and eventually help them to achieve the recognition they longed for.

At the party for Holmes, Phelps witnessed "the success . . . and the struggle, the hope, and the dismay, the crown and the thorn of gifted life."[3] In this phrase, she sums up the artist's life as one of ecstasy and agony, of great ambition and hope mingled with the deepest despair and discouragement. The efforts of writers who arduously plied their trade for profit could not compare to the deep commitment of artists who experienced the full range of emotions necessary for the creation of art. As this generation of women writers began to identify themselves as artists, they adopted the tortured life of the individual who sacrificed herself and her happiness for her art. Like the romantic genius, they saw themselves as driven by forces beyond their control, as suffering from physical maladies that attended their great exertions, and as struggling to gain the attention of a society that did not value their abilities. A significant part of their claim to artistry, then, was their experience of suffering that in some ways mirrored the Christlike martyrdom of womanhood in general. For the struggling woman writer is hampered not only by her society's lack of appreciation for genius (the main obstacle of the romantic artist) but also by her special burdens as a woman and her society's disbelief in woman's genius. Nonetheless, Phelps's struggling woman writer still publishes in the *Atlantic* and therefore has hopes that the American democracy of genius may extend to her. Women writers' attempts to reconcile their trespass on the male realm of "art" with their desires for literary fame often resulted in an effort to combine the identities of the tortured romantic artist-outcast and the self-sacrificing ideal woman, a fusion embodied in Phelps's anonymous woman writer. Alcott, Phelps, Stoddard, and Woolson believed that only through great suffering and patience could they achieve immortality.

Just as Emerson, Hawthorne, and the British romantics were preoccupied with the identity of the poet/artist/hero/scholar in a society that privileged other vocations for men, so were Alcott, Phelps, Stoddard, and Woolson deeply concerned with the identity of the woman artist. Their private writings and published narratives reflect their engagement with the same concerns raised in the artist narratives of Madame de Staël, Elizabeth Barrett Browning, and George Eliot and reflect the turmoil they felt as they wrestled with the competing ideas of genius that existed in American and European culture: the romantic genius that was gendered masculine or combined masculine and feminine qualities, the feminine genius as morally superior and a higher ideal than masculine genius, the genius as rare and unappreciated, the genius as communicative and embraced by the culture, genius as innate, genius as divinely inspired, and the emerging idea that genius (if it even exists) is the result of patience and hard work, not otherworldly inspiration or God-given abilities. Ever-present also was the taboo against ambition in women, which remained quite strong despite new opportunities for self-development for women. Ultimately, however, Alcott, Phelps, Stoddard, and Woolson found a way to reconcile their desires for serious recognition with their shame about possessing such high ambitions, a way that differed significantly from the "solutions" offered by *Corinne*, *Aurora Leigh*, and *Armgart*. In the absence of privileges like those that many male writers enjoyed (extensive education and social networks), they felt that they could achieve immortality only through great hardships. They could not reach the immortal crown of glory until they had suffered the earthly crown of thorns.

Women and Genius

As the four women of this study wondered about their capacity for genius and struggled to have faith in their own powers, they confronted the most basic of obstacles: the related questions of whether women's minds were inferior to men's, whether women were capable of genius at all, and whether women possessed a special brand of genius. Such questions had been raised time and again throughout the nineteenth century as women entered the public sphere of authorship. The message women writers received from reviewers was that women were not expected to produce literature worthy of serious attention because women simply lacked the ability to make "art," largely because, as Nina Baym explains, women were deemed incapable of "the individuality that is the foundation of genius." Women were expected to write as exemplars of their sex, not as individuals.[4] Forever lumped together in a separate class, women were deemed inferior from the outset.

Although tensions between elitist and democratic views of the American genius helped to create the possibility for women to envision themselves as potential geniuses, a competing cultural discourse about women's incapacity for genius also influenced how Alcott, Phelps, Stoddard, and Woolson viewed themselves as artists. The very idea of "genius" had, since the Greeks, denied women access to that privileged sphere. The etymology of the term itself reveals a masculine bias, derived in part from the Latin word for male procreativity and paternity. Arguments against the possibility of genius in women, commonplace throughout the Western world, were rooted in assumptions about women's sexuality and mental abilities. The nature of creative genius was understood as analogous to male sexuality, which was powerful, explosive, procreative. Female sexuality and, hence, female nature were seen as receptive and nurturing. The power to create new life was entirely the function of the male's "seed." A woman could not be the creator or the actor; she was, instead, acted upon or was, perhaps, the muse who inspired the male creator. Woman's role was that of an intermediary, an assistant to the godlike male creator.

For a woman to create art was to mimic male procreative power, making her, in the eyes of many, monstrous, an aberration of nature, no longer a woman. According to William Duff in 1807, "A woman can have a powerful imagination only by being unsexed: by being a freak of nature." Similarly, Cesare Lombroso claimed in 1863, "There are no women of genius; the women of genius are men." Immanuel Kant, one of the foremost theorizers of art and genius in the eighteenth century, believed that "for a woman to aim at the sublime makes her merely ridiculous . . . and even worse, '*ekelhaft*' (loathsome). She is an unbeautiful, unnatural freak who is disobeying nature and aping the genius of the male — who is her (and nature's) lord and master." When Avis tells her father she wants to be an artist, he uses similar language, telling her, as he holds a copy of Kant's *Critique of Pure Reason*, "Nonsense, nonsense! . . . I can't have you filling your head with any of these womanish apings of a man's affairs, like a monkey playing tunes on a hand-organ."[5] By declaring her desire to create art, then, a woman made herself as unnatural and ridiculous as the monkey who mimicked man by playing a musical instrument.

In addition, while the artist as creator was sexually powerful and free, the nineteenth-century ideal "woman" was sexually inhibited and controlled. Hence, the woman who tried to be an artist unsexed herself not only by engaging in "man's affairs" but by implicitly claiming a degree of sexual freedom. As Deborah Barker has shown, fears about women's creativity were linked to men's desire to control women's sexuality: "Women's independent ability to create original works could be construed as an allegory for the circumvention of the male role in procreation." As the male artist's creativity was viewed as an extension of his libido, the woman who desired to create art was perceived as not only sexually independent but potentially a sexual aggressor, hence another reason to fear her. The woman artist was therefore likened to that most shameful of outcasts, the fallen woman. In *Corinne*, Count d'Erfeuil suggests that the woman artist has forfeited her respectability as a virtuous woman and is therefore fair game for a man's sexual advances: "A woman alone, independent, and who lives almost an artist's life should not be hard to win," he tells Oswald. Corinne, therefore, is not marriage material, the count claims, and Oswald eventually agrees with him. In addition, the woman artist whose genius extended beyond the domestic sphere was claimed by an adoring public that threatened to sexualize her. Oswald continually desires to rescue Corinne from her public role and make her a respectable woman. The example of George Sand is also instructive here because her daring as an artist was frequently associated with her donning of men's attire and her extramarital affairs. As Justin McCarthy explained in *Galaxy* magazine, Sand was considered a "feminine fiend, endowed with a hideous power for the destruction of souls and an inextinguishable thirst for the slaughter of virtuous beliefs." This image of her was largely "due to the fearful reports wafted across the seas, that this terrible woman had not merely repudiated the marriage bond, but had actually put off the garments sacred to womanhood." As one of the foremost women of genius the world had ever known, Sand represented the ultimate deviation from the innocent, virtuous woman.[6]

However, such women would remain rarities, it was believed, because women's biology made them intellectually inferior and incapable of artistic greatness.

Elizabeth Stoddard's portrait, from William Dean Howells, *Literary Friends and Acquaintance; a Personal Retrospect of American Authorship* (New York: Harper & Bros., 1900)

Constance Fenimore Woolson. Date unknown. Courtesy of the Western Reserve Historical Society, Cleveland, OH.

Louisa M. Alcott, pen in hand. Date unknown. Courtesy of Concord Free Public Library, Concord, MA.

Elizabeth Stuart Phelps, from her autobiography, *Chapters from a Life* (Boston: Houghton, Mifflin, 1895)

"An Incident in the Life of Elizabeth Stuart Phelps. — 'Thimble or paint brush, which?'" Illustration from *Our Famous Women* (Hartford, CT: Hartford Publishing Co., 1888). This scene illustrates the choice Phelps believed she had to make between the pursuit of art and her domestic duties. The two could not be equally fulfilled. (Before Phelps settled on writing, she tried her hand at painting.)

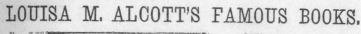

JO IN A VORTEX. — Every few weeks she would shut herself up in her room, put on her scribbling suit, and "fall into a vortex," as she expressed it. — PAGE 44.

LITTLE WOMEN; OR, MEG, JO, BETH, AND AMY.   Parts
First and Second.   Price of each, $1.50.

ROBERTS BROTHERS, *Publishers, Boston.*

"Jo in a Vortex," advertisement for *Little Women*, from Louisa May Alcott, *Silver Pitchers: and Independence, a Centennial Love Story* (Boston: Roberts Bros., 1877). In *Little Women* Alcott lovingly described the way her writing pulled her into a "vortex," suggesting complete absorption in one's work and the pursuit of genius. Courtesy of General Research Division, New York Public Library, Astor, Lenox, and Tilden Foundations.

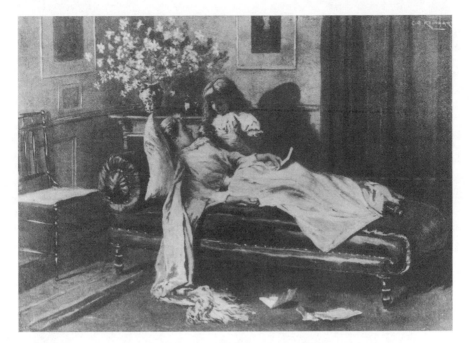

Illustration from Elizabeth Stuart Phelps, "The Rejected Manuscript," *Harper's New Monthly* 86 (Jan. 1893): 293. Mary Hathorne, suffering from the type of illnesses common among late-nineteenth-century women, especially those with ambitions, is overcome with the news that her book will be published by a prestigious publisher after months of rejection and years of toiling for her family.

"The Children's Friend," from Ednah Dow Littlehale Cheney, *Louisa May Alcott, the Children's Friend* (Boston: L. Prang, 1888). This image of Alcott as a beloved storyteller for children would be her most lasting legacy despite her early ambitions and recognition as a serious artist.

The medical establishment of the eighteenth and nineteenth centuries insisted that the mental exertion necessary for serious scholarship and creative genius was a physical impossibility for women owing to their weaker frames and biological makeup. A woman's energy and blood were believed to be pulled away from her brain by her uterus, making sustained intellectual concentration either impossible or physically and psychologically dangerous. Young women, especially, needed to refrain from all mental and physical exertion to ensure the proper development of their reproductive organs. The message women received from their doctors and families, Christine Battersby writes, was that "[n]ature had provided women with a physique that would punish them with madness or disease if they attempted to rival the males" in the areas of scholarship or art.[7]

It also was widely believed that when women did think, they did so differently from men. In Western culture, women were aligned with emotions and intuitive thinking and men with intellect and reason, again largely due to their different procreative functions. As a result of their different mental capacities, C. C. Everett expounded in the *North American Review*, men were the superior artists. "There is perhaps no more general distinction between the mind of man and that of woman, than that, where the former requires something to mediate between itself and the object of its contemplation, the latter approaches this object directly, without any such mediation." The difficulty for woman was gaining enough distance from "the ordinary concerns of life" and her emotions to become the "artist." Everett explained, "[N]ot only is it required by the highest art that outward objects shall not be exhibited in their direct connection with ourselves; the feelings also must be represented as something without the mind, which can be contemplated by it. The direct utterance of feeling is not poetry, or at least not the highest. . . . The artist must hold himself aloof, in some degree. . . . The artist must feel deeply; but he must not be under the dominion of his feelings." Thus, her proclivity toward feeling rather than analysis made woman incapable of creating "the highest art." Ironically, Everett's argument prefaces his positive review of *Aurora Leigh*, in which Barrett Browning shows up the chauvinism of Romney, who believes in the beginning that women cannot be great poets because "You generalize / Oh, nothing, — not even grief! Your quick-breathed hearts, / So sympathetic to the personal pang, . . . incapable / Of deepening, widening a large lap of life / To hold the world-full woe." By the end, however, Romney declares Aurora a "poet" because "in this last book, / You showed to me something separate from yourself, / Beyond you, . . . You have shown me truths, . . . truths not yours."[8] In addition to becoming a superior poet by uniting the spiritual and the social in her art, Aurora has also proved herself capable of rising above her sex, as her contemporaries would have seen it, by moving beyond the personal to the universal.

Taking a similar but slightly different tack than Everett's or the early Romney's, the *North British Review* declared women incapable of the highest order of thinking, imagination, which, in European romantic terms, was the instrument of divine creative ability, akin to genius. "[T]he main deficiency of feminine genius," according to the writer, was that "[i]t can observe, it can recombine, it can delineate, but it cannot trust itself farther; it cannot . . . imagine." The presumably unalterable logic that women's minds were not capable of the highest, masculine form of genius was used time and again to dissuade women from even trying to use their imaginations. As John Ford, in Woolson's "At the Château of Corinne," tells Katherine Winthrop, "a woman should not dare in that way. Thinking to soar, she invariably descends. Her mental realm is not the same as that of man; lower, on the same level, or far above, it is at least different." While men had distinguished themselves as great artists, poets, and writers and would continue to do so, women's supposed innate difference from men meant that these highest achievements must be beyond them.[9]

The net result of such reasoning was to allocate women to a different and decidedly inferior type of artistic production. Deemed unable to create from the imagination, women were relegated to the role of copyist or genteel amateur. As visual artists, Barker explains, women were "often limited to feminine subjects — flowers, still lifes, genre painting, portraits." This is certainly true of Corinne's fair cousin and foil, Lucille, who tells Oswald, "absolutely the only thing I can do is copy flowers, and even then, only the very simplest." Her lack of imagination is a crucial part of her identity as the perfect "woman." The same is true of Sylvia, in Woolson's "Château," who makes wax flowers. In contrast, Avis signals her high ambition by declaring that she will do more than paint copies and portraits: "I do not mean to paint portraits. . . . I have different plans: at least I have different hopes."[10] As the result of those plans, her Sphinx suggests the highest imagination, her insight gained through reverie and intoxication. In the realm of literature, women were deemed to be most capable of writing that required little or no imagination or analysis, namely sketches of domestic subjects or works that were effusions of the feelings, namely sentimental poetry or novels. Women, therefore, were supposed to possess their own brand of genius, which excelled at the sentimental and the quotidian but went no farther.

The nineteenth century, however, did witness some serious challenges to the doctrine of women's intellectual inferiority and inability to produce great art. Some claimed that genius itself was sexless, drawing on Enlightenment theory of sexual equality and the romantic idea that genius was androgynous. But these theories did little to alter the pervasive belief that actual, individual women could not possess genius. Enlightenment philosophy posited a split between mind and body that could sever the supposed link between women's biology and mental capacity, allowing for their access to masculine logocentrism. However, this idea of intellectual equality between the sexes could not legitimate a public role as authors because women were still bound by their bodies to their families and the home. Likewise, the romantic idea that genius was produced from a fusion between masculine and feminine traits did not necessarily extend to real women. As Susan Wolfson points out about Coleridge's famous association of genius with androgyny, "he was thinking only of male minds with feminine qualities."[11] While Fuller tried to appropriate this notion of genius for women in her argument about Minerva and the Muse in *Woman in the Nineteenth Century*, it remained for her an ideal. Women were not yet free to acquire the masculine traits of energy and power embodied by Minerva. Women were still perceived as defined by their bodies, their emotions inextricably linked to biology and their relations to others.

Another line of attack was to redefine "genius" to make it compatible with then-current ideas of a woman's nature, a popular approach among midcentury American women writers. "[T]he Victorian ideology of women's intellect," Baym explains, "rejects the sexless mind, elevates the value of spirituality over intellect, and associates women with spirituality." The next step, then, was to equate genius with spirituality, not a difficult task given its origins in the concept of divine inspiration. For example, Sarah Josepha Hale, who was especially instrumental in redefining feminine genius, declared in 1852, "Those who hold the doctrine of equality will be no doubt shocked to hear that I am convinced the difference between the constructive genius of man and woman is the result of an organic difference in the operations of their minds." But while critics previously had labeled feminine genius as inferior, Hale viewed it as superior to the masculine form of genius owing to its moral purity: "Is not moral power better than mechanical invention?" she asked. "Why should women wish to be or to do or to write like men? Is not the feminine genius the most angel-like?"[12] An interesting expression of this view of feminine genius as "angel-like" and therefore superior can be found in Sarah E. Henshaw's essay "Are We Inferior?" (1869). Championing the idea of sexual difference, Henshaw declares that "woman's faculty is akin to genius" because of its intuitive nature, while man's is practical and prosaic. "Her faculty was meant for reference, consultation, for prophetic perception, which should point the way of the world. It is of a higher order than his — not lower. Its divine flight is crippled now, but is gradually gaining in strength and certainty." This superior faculty, though, will not be used to usurp men. She concludes, "He will . . . find himself undisputed king of the world, and will administer un-challenged the affairs of the kingdom, while she will be its priestess — she will consult for him the oracle — she will keep the sacred fire."[13] In this utopian vision, men and women will gain equality through their difference, and they will reign as partners, utilizing their equally valued, complementary abilities.

The strategy of feminizing genius was a powerful counter to the taboo against ambition under which antebellum women struggled to define themselves. Their culture discouraged them from desiring recognition outside the home by warn-ing them that ambition and pride were unwomanly. Women who discovered that they possessed abilities at writing (or even sanctioned feminine activities like sewing), and who actually enjoyed developing and displaying these talents, wres-tled with self-doubt and even self-hatred. Women often referred to their desires to exhibit their talents as "temptations," as if it were a sin to crave recognition. And ambition was deemed a vulgar thing to be either suppressed or disavowed altogether. The twenty-year-old Charlotte Forten Grimké wrote in her diary, in 1857, "I have constantly a longing for something higher and nobler, than I have known. Constantly I ask myself 'what shall I do to be forever known?' This is ambition, I know. It is selfish, it is wrong. But oh! how very hard it is to do and feel what is right."[14] Grimké was likely one of a large number of young women who were beginning to crave such fame and achievement, most of whom would never realize their dreams.

One such woman, S. E. Wallace, published a revealing essay in *Harper's* in 1867, titled "Another Weak-Minded Woman. A Confession." This woman's sin was attempting to become a published author. Feeling guilty for the ambitions she harbored, she hid herself in the attic when she wrote. "No deed of shame was ever hidden with more anxious care," she confided. When she sent out a poem to be published, she felt like a criminal. "Had I been caught stealing I could not have felt more guilty." But when her poem appeared in *Harper's*, she briefly basked in the glow of her fame. "For one transcendent hour," she wrote, "I wore the robes of prophecy, and looked from shining heights into a glory yet to come." From that point on, her real sin began, she felt, as she invested most of her energy in seeking her future glory rather than in catering to the needs of her husband and children. When a "jury" of twelve editors handed her their "sentence" that her writings were "worth nothing," she burned the evidence of her crime, and once again "[p]eace descended upon our house." Her confession concludes with the advice to women that they "[f]ling away ambition, or invest it in your sons" because pursuing glory as an author is not only a sinful neglect of duty but also futile. "I do not believe the world will ever produce a feminine Shakespeare or Milton, or a woman's hand write grand oratorios or create beauty like Apollo," she opined. "We will vote before a great while; we may hold office; we may be angels; but we can never be men." This silenced writer reiterated the view of her culture that women would never be able to compete with men for literary laurels, so they should remain in their appropriate sphere, living out their ambitions through their sons, inspiring them to achieve what they, as women, could not.[15]

Alcott, Phelps, Stoddard, and Woolson shared Grimké's and Wallace's discomfort about possessing high ambitions, as did Jewett, Dickinson, Davis, and virtually all women writers of this generation. As a result, they modified their ambitions, modestly denied that they possessed any, or even claimed that they possessed no talent as writers. But their subterfuge should not conceal their belief in women's right to pursue artistry and, with the removal of obstacles, their capability of achieving it. They never fully believed that by trying to be artists they were trying to be men. So they never disavowed ambition altogether, the way Wallace did. Instead, they found ways to incorporate their ambitions into their lives as women, as Grimké did when she wrote in her journal, "My earnest longings [*sic*] to do *something* for the good of others. I know that I am very selfish. Always the thought of *self-culture* presents itself *first*. With that, I think I can accomplish something more noble, more enduring, I will try not to forget that, while striving to improve myself, I may at least *commence* to work for others." She tried to overcome her sense of guilt by combining her ambitious desire for "self-culture" with a more noble (and feminine) duty to others. For many women writers, as for Jewett, the way to assuage one's guilt for "growing ambitious" was to fall back on the argument that it was her duty to develop her God-given talent.[16] As we have seen, Elizabeth Stuart Phelps's mother also legitimated her writing in this way.

The main barrier to these women's expression of their ambitions and their belief in themselves as writers was the charge of vanity or egotism, and their feelings in this respect reveal the basic difficulty they had in striving to be artists: they feared the accusation that they lacked femininity. Vanity was one of the primary characteristics associated with that dreaded epithet, "bluestocking," and another way that reviewers tried to shame women writers (and other women who sought recognition or demanded equal rights) into silence was to accuse them of writing only for their own selfish gratification or for praise. In her essay "Women in Literature" (1891), Davis accused men and women of seeking "the possible crown to be won" from a literary career: "a chance of gratification for that desire for personal notoriety with which the American soul, both male and female, seems of late to be so fatally tainted." What she hoped to see instead were men and woman who wrote "simply because there is in them a message to be given, and they cannot die until they have spoken it. . . . [who wrote with] noble purpose, and who will help themselves and the world by so writing." Again, Davis appeals to the idea of an innate compulsion beyond one's control, the message that must come out, as if it came from God. This argument is reminiscent of Harriet Beecher Stowe's well-known claim that "God wrote" *Uncle Tom's Cabin* and is also commensurate with the ideal of genius. But whereas Stowe, in essence, used the idea of divine inspiration to deflect recognition of her talents and to absolve herself from the charge of being ambitious for herself, Davis, as did many other women of her generation, used the argument of God-given talent or genius to justify her ambitions. As Davis goes on to write, having already established the "noble purpose" that should guide the writer, she hopes women will "be stirred by ambition to leave something more permanent behind them than reports of Sanitary or Archeological clubs, and will paint as they only can do, for the next generation, the inner life and history of their time with a power which shall make that time alive for future ages."[17] With this noble purpose, a special ability to depict one's age, and a message that must be spoken, Davis believed, women could legitimately pursue their ambition to make their mark in the literary world.

At the same time that many American women writers were feminizing genius and ambition, the successes of de Staël, Sand, Brontë, Barrett Browning, and Eliot became the centerpiece of another powerful argument for women's access to genius. Instead of the feminized genius promoted by Hale and Henshaw, these women writers were deemed capable of what Fuller had dreamed about: combining the "Minerva" and the "Muse." The most common explanation for their genius, however, was that they were exceptions among women, rather than representative of what women were capable of, a defense that the writers themselves seem to have embraced. As we have seen, they portrayed their autobiographical artist heroines as unlike other women. And the masculine pseudonyms adopted by Eliot, Sand, and the Brontë sisters are indicative of their desire to distinguish themselves from the disparaged mass of authoresses and to be regarded as men, who were accorded more freedom in subject matter and more respect from their peers. But as each was found out to be a woman, the critics' discomfort with their literary independence and "masculine" style and/or subject matter overwhelmed much of the discussion of their works.

In each case, however, as the passage of time allowed for greater reflection on the quality of their literary achievements, these authors were deemed by many to have accomplished what other women had not: they had risen above their sex by writing as well as men. They gained respect as artists by proving themselves capable of the masculine creation of art that was strong, powerful, and truthful. Rather than write as women, or merely ape men, or even become men, they combined the virtues of both sexes in their works. For example, Theophilus Parsons wrote of de Staël that no woman "had done so much to vindicate the intellectual equality of woman with man. . . . The character of her mind was formed by a combination of qualities which rarely meet together. With an imagination luxuriant to excess, she reasoned acutely and sometimes profoundly; and while her understanding acted with such rapidity and promptness that it almost seemed instinct, its grasp was wide and strong." Her imagination combined (feminine) excesses and instinct with (masculine) reasoning and strength. In a similar vein, Everett declared Barrett Browning superior to other women writers for her "great learning, rich experiences, and powerful genius, uniting to her woman's nature the strength which is sometimes thought peculiar to a man." Likewise, McCarthy claimed of Sand, "Her soul, her brain, her style may be described . . . as exuberantly and splendidly feminine; yet no other woman has ever shown the same power of understanding and entering into the nature of a man. . . . [I]f ever a single human being could have the soul of a man and soul of a woman at once, George Sand might be described as that physical and psychological phenomenon." A similar assessment of Eliot appeared in the *Southern Review*: she "truly possesses an intellect which is so far above ordinary womanhood as to include strength and grasp, the critical acumen and large outlook of a man, with the tenderness and purity of a woman."[18] Ultimately, these women were perceived as exceptional examples, although some believed that their achievements were a sign that the time had arrived when "woman" would fulfill her greatest potential. Their achievements, however, provided both inspiration and difficulty for the Civil War and postbellum generation of women writers, who desired to follow in their footsteps but also feared the charge of unwomanliness that was often associated with the reputations of these women of genius.

However, just as some women had laid claim to genius, even redefining it to associate it with feminine spirituality and moral superiority, and others had been deemed possessors of the genius that combines masculine and feminine qualities, "genius" in its traditional sense as divine inspiration began to lose ground. As realism gradually came into vogue, not otherworldly inspiration but experience, hard work, and "scientific" observation became the hallmarks of literary excellence. In the 1880s and 1890s, realists and neoromantics waged war in the periodicals over the term "genius," although the seeds of these voluble debates had been sown in the decades of Alcott's, Phelps's, Stoddard's, and Woolson's literary productivity. Neoromantics felt that genius was the instigator of human progress and the source of true "art," whereas realists associated genius with "egoism," "moral deterioration," "elitism," and "hero-worship."[19] Women's claims to romantic genius, which some American women were beginning to adopt in the 1860s, were therefore cut short. As realist aesthetics closed off one avenue to genius for women, it seemed, though, to open up another in its emphasis on the writer as observer and professional. For if the attainment of otherworldly inspiration was deemed impossible for women, then certainly the observation of common people in everyday settings was something at which women could excel, and they already had shown their capacity for professionalism. However, with the rise of realism's more scientific approach to literature also came so-called scientific studies once again proclaiming the inferiority of women's mental capacities.[20]

Writing the Woman of Genius

In their private and published accounts of their identities as artists and in their artist narratives, Alcott, Phelps, Stoddard, and Woolson employed various strategies to mask their ambitions and/or their gender. We see these strategies most visibly in their stories about women artists. Although they did not adopt masculine or androgynous pseudonyms (except in the case of Alcott's sensational stories, which she covertly wrote for money, not for recognition), they sometimes did adopt masculine or asexual narrators. Similarly, they valued "virility" and "strength" as qualities that distinguished high from low art. However, we also see in their depictions of women artists and in their personal writings attempts to find a theory of art with which they were comfortable and which fit with their understanding of themselves as women. Engaging cultural debates about women's special genius, they explained their art as alternately spontaneous, the product of divine inspiration, or the result of hard work. And, as they did so, they engaged in contemporary debates about whether "genius" itself *was* the source of "art."

Of the four writers, Stoddard was the most explicit about her courting of genius. This is not surprising, considering that she began her career slightly earlier when the cult of romantic genius was at its peak in America. And her husband and their friend Edmund Clarence Stedman were two of the major proponents of "genius" during the debates in the 1880s and 1890s. Stoddard used the term "genius" in the romantic sense of the word, having been heavily influenced by the European romantic ideals of poetry professed by her husband and his friends. As a result, her allusions to creativity usually took on a masculine cast. For example, in discussing her novel *Two Men* with a (female) friend who reviewed it, she wrote, "I must have failed where Balzac would have succeeded in a masterly delineation of the cause and effect of emotion. . . . Oh why was I not given that genius whose insight teaches and makes the mysteries of the human heart understood." Although she understood "genius" as exemplified by "masterly" powers, her statement nonetheless reveals her ambition to acquire this same type of power possessed by Balzac. She does not seem to believe that her lack of it is due to her sex. By comparing herself to him, she casts herself in the role of a gender-neutral "author" instead of as a "female author," something that was incredibly difficult for American women writers to do. Elsewhere, Stoddard also associated creativity with "viril[ity]" and wrote of discovering the "kingly power" within herself, reflecting her belief that "art" was masculine and a woman must eschew the feminine in order to create it. She described her admiration for *Jane Eyre* in these terms, calling it "a daring and masculine work." Brontë was a model for Stoddard because she "possess[ed] more moral strength than the government and gun-powder heroes of the day."[21]

In keeping with her romantic ideals of the artist, Stoddard also equated genius with alienation and ostracism. In her story "The Chimneys" (1865), she declared, in clear reference to herself, "Some people never discover genius even, when it is born in the same town with themselves. I am told that one of our noted authoresses is considered a miserable housekeeper in her town." The town, presumably her hometown, Mattapoisett, has no appreciation for genius, especially when exhibited in a woman. It is only interested in her domestic skills. After her three novels failed to gain her a wide readership, her sense of alienation became more acute and perhaps even a defensive badge of pride, as it was for authors like Hawthorne and her husband's circle of discontented poets. By the time she wrote her essay "A Literary Whim" (1871), she clearly still understood geniuses as otherworldly and hoped to be recognized as one of their number. "Genius 'cometh from afar,' and its 'trailing clouds of glory' are not for us to grasp while we are in the prison-house of the commonplace." But like "the great men buried in Westminster Abbey," she also expected to "die an impenetrable secret," as inexplicable to her contemporaries, who thought her "abnormal" and a sort of " 'Learned Pig.' "[22]

Stoddard's private correspondence reveals alternating moments of belief in her own genius and periods of tremendous doubt. Possessing such a masculine and high ideal of genius, it is not surprising that she had difficulty maintaining her faith in her capability of possessing it. When her works were reprinted late in her life and met with some very high acclaim, she more openly discussed her genius than she had in the 1860s. In 1889, basking in the showers of praise from reviewers, she wrote to Lillian Whiting, "Stoddard [her husband] said . . . there is more genius in *The Morgesons*[,] more art in *Two Men*, more power in *Temple House* — and I guess he is right." When the republished version of her second novel reached the third edition (decades after the first version had been released), she was elated. "Now if I can but be noticed in England, it will be the 'hall mark' — I shall go up like a kite, and hover over the top of Parnassus!" She also directly confronted her husband, asking him to confirm whether or not she possessed "genius," as she wrote to Stedman.[23] She was no longer shy about what had been, in her early years, a more taboo subject.

During her apprenticeship, Stoddard had wrestled extensively with her doubts about her own abilities. She came to believe, though, that lack of education, the absence of encouragement, and women's duties were the real reasons women had been unable to fully realize their genius and that she herself might not succeed in doing so. In 1852, while she was beginning her apprenticeship and confronting her intense self-doubts about her abilities, she believed that inspiration, the hallmark of romantic genius, was accessible to women. But divine inspiration, she soon realized, was not enough. She wrote to her friend Margaret Sweat, who was also struggling with her writing: "I understand the condition of mind you speak of, . . . you perceive but you have not yet acquired the analytical power enough to reflect them into method, method indeed is what the minds of women lack, . . . their minds are crowded, confused[.] Women depend too much on inspiration, inspiration avails little. [I]t is only the laborious process of human reason that can resolve the mind into clearness & truth."[24] Here Stoddard is critiquing the kind of feminine definition of genius promoted by Hale and Henshaw. While women were capable of possessing inspiration or genius, she believed them largely incapable of the hard work and intellectual capacity to give it shape. Unable to apply (masculine) reason to their flashes of (feminine) inspiration, women lacked the

discipline to do what Emerson understood as the final stage of genius — to translate the moment of insight into an enduring and communicable "truth." Stoddard therefore suggests that while she feels creative power momentarily, she feels
incapable of bringing it to fruition. This is, in fact, the kind of frustration we also
saw in her 1866 journal. (It is also similar to Fuller's complaints that she found it
difficult to translate the power of her conversations into literature.) But Stoddard's letter does not recognize this condition as innate in women. Instead, like
Fuller, she believed that although women "have not yet acquired the analytical
power," they can and one day will, with hard work. Throughout her career,
though, Stoddard would bemoan her lack of training to cultivate such a power.
"I am aware of a basis of thought which requires time and patience only to
bring it up into some perfect structure," she insisted. However, she continued,
"My radical defect in *form* is hard to struggle with — but so much the more labor
that's all."[25]

In addition to her want of education and training, Stoddard also confronted
other obstacles, namely prejudices against women's literary abilities. In the 1850s,
as she stretched her literary wings in columns for the San Francisco *Daily Alta
California,* Stoddard was "anxious to discover the innate inferiority [of woman's
mind] to the mind masculine, or its equality with it," an indication that she
questioned assumptions about women's mental weaknesses. But she could come
to no concrete conclusion about the matter, she insisted, because she believed that
women of true ability were unable to flourish in the literary marketplace, which
was overrun with inferior women writers. "The eight books in ten are written
without genius; all show industry and a few talent," she wrote. But the examples of
successful women, who tread on "the domain appropriated by men to themselves" despite the "disadvantage" of babies and men's lack of support, showed
that "a parity of circumstances would bring about a parity of intelligence between
[women] and our good lords and patrons."[26] Women had not gained "parity" with
men purely because, weighed down with women's burdens, they could not adequately develop their minds. The issue was not whether women's minds were
innately inferior but how their different duties and the messages they received
from men stifled their potential.

In the article "Woman and Art" (1870), most likely written by Stoddard, she
more fully explored the subject of women's supposed mental inferiority. But her
husband's advice to publish it anonymously suggests its inflammatory nature. In
this piece, she wrote to Whitelaw Reid, she endeavored to explain why "no
supremacy of intellect has yet been shown in the creative arts by any woman."

She ridicules the "foolish virgins" who exasperate critics by dabbling in what men take seriously. For while men search for the work of art that will be the "Light of the World," the artistic woman sketches at picnics, seeing in art only the "practical purposes" of socializing and of attracting mates. "Were she, indeed, once to forget them, she might become . . . a George Sand. In other words, she might find herself an artist, loving and studying art for its own sake, solitary, despised, eccentric and blue. From such a destiny aesthetic woman turns scornfully away." While seeming to criticize women harshly for their lack of seriousness, she ends by suggesting that women are kept down by their culture and the very critics who ridicule them. The main reason women "leave [serious painting] comfortably to Academicians and rough-bearded creatures" is that they fear ostracism from men. Being an artist like George Sand would make one "despised" by her society for daring to tread on man's realm of serious art. Can anyone blame women for their frivolous approach to art? she seems to ask.[27] In another article she took the next step of celebrating a woman artist who gave her the example she needed to prove women's minds were not inferior. In "Woman in Art. — Rosa Bonheur" (1872), this time published under a pseudonym, she came to the conclusion that with encouragement and education women's abilities could be equal to those of men. "There are many who believe," she wrote, "that no advantages of training and culture will ever give women, as artists, rank in the profession by the side of men. Out upon such folly!" She offered Rosa Bonheur (the French painter) as "proof . . . of woman's capacity in art. . . . Woman though she is, none will deny her the possession of genius."[28] To Stoddard, women were quite capable of genius; they simply needed the requisite intellectual training and the serious support of men, both of which she felt she had been denied.

But because American women writers had been denied these necessary conditions, which Phelps's unnamed struggling author in "A Plea for Immortality" also clearly lacked, they had produced, in Stoddard's eyes, only inferior writing. In her *Daily Alta California* columns, she scoffed at the popular women's novels of the day. She agreed with "[a] critic in *Putnam's* [who] says that the women-novels contain puppets, instead of characters." She read one such novel, *Juno Clifford*, "with scorn and derision." In another column, she objected to the ideal of womanhood promoted by Caroline Chesebro's *Victoria, or The World Overcome:*

> Miss Chesebro's dogmatic and pious ideal of a woman assails me in reading her
> book. I object to the position she takes in regard to the reader — that of a teacher.
> The morality is not agreeable, and quite impossible. . . . Why will writers, espe-

cially female writers, make their heroines indifferent to good eating, so careless about taking cold, and so impervious to all the creature comforts? The absence of these treats compose their good women, with an external preachment about self-denial, moral self-denial. Is goodness, then, incompatible with the enjoyment of the senses?

In this passage Stoddard attacked two basic characteristics of American women's fiction at midcentury: didacticism and the moral imperative of self-denial. She added that Chesebro' took on the position of a teacher in respect to the reader, which is to say, condescended to the student/reader. What Stoddard objected to, then, was the reader's being treated like a child. In addition to the author's didactic mentoring, Stoddard also objected to the lesson Chesebro' was teaching, namely that young women should forgo the pleasures that Stoddard believed they were entitled to. Self-denial, she implies, was not the virtue so many women novelists would claim; rather, it precluded self-development and maturity. She continued,

In reading such books I am reminded of what I have thought my mission was: a crusade against Duty — not the duty that is revealed to every man and woman of us by the circumstances of daily life, but that which is cut and fashioned for us by minds totally ignorant of our idiosyncrasies and necessities. The world has long been in a polemical fog. I am afraid we shall never get into plain sailing.[29]

The "polemical fog" of advice that poured forth from the press and the pulpit, promoting good citizenship in the form of ideal Christian womanhood, among other virtues, clearly distressed Stoddard. Such preaching stifled women and men, sapping them of their individuality (and by extension the originality required to create art), hence the "crusade against Duty" that informed all of her serious work. This crusade, more than anything else, allowed her to develop an original voice in the midst of pressure to conform to ideals of womanhood that did not suit her, and in the midst of a literary book market dominated by formulaic women's fiction that allowed little room for experiment or individuality of vision and expression. Two of Stoddard's stories about artists, "Me and My Son" and "Collected by a Valetudinarian" (both published in 1870), reveal her efforts to express such individuality and her ambivalence about how much artistic self-discovery was allowed women.

"Me and My Son" dramatizes Stoddard's critique in her early *Alta* columns and her later *Aldine* articles of the cultural forces that stifle women's potential. In this story, she portrays a variation on her favorite (autobiographical) heroine — the stifled, unconventional young woman from a remote small town with vague desires and ambitions but no outlet for her energies. In the opening paragraph, Laura Calton mocks the "[m]echanical piety" and the "cheerful heroine" in the novel she is reading. She dismisses what appears to be a typical midcentury woman's novel, in which the heroine "is driven from all material happiness with a sharp stick."[30] Her disdain for the novel reflects Stoddard's attitude toward most women's novels expressed in her critique of Chesebro' fourteen years earlier. By beginning the story with these views, she signals both her heroine's and the story's departure from such conventional works. But Laura's individuality is cut short and will not lead to her becoming an artist but rather to marrying one.

The description of Laura as a girl clearly marks her as a potential artist in the vein of Corinne, Aurora Leigh, and Avis. She was "a girl of some force and originality, [who] kicked in the orthodox walking-stool provided for her by her guardians and friends," leading "even her good mother [to think] her queer, and no example to follow." Her difference led to her "[o]stracization" and to repression by her community. "She was never allowed to be a law unto herself," the narrator explains, using the same language Avis used to explain herself to Philip. Instead, she had an unhappy girlhood, and, like Stoddard, Alcott, and many of their heroines, "she was a child of 'ups and downs,' possessed by Satan." As a result of her isolation and lack of opportunity to discover her unique nature, "[n]o inner life was developed, and her outward life was cold and empty." When she turns twenty, the age at which Aurora Leigh crowned herself on a June day, Laura is "possessed" by "ennui," despite the "midsummer" season "when Nature promises all to the senses." But unlike Aurora, she is uninspired by the blooming world around her: "[The] child of nature, Thoreau or Emerson, would have delighted in the season and the scene; but Laura had no soul for nature, . . . no dream of that relation between the seen and the unseen, which brings us glimpses of 'that immortal sea which brought us thither.'" Laura's repressive upbringing has made her incapable of realizing the promise of genius offered by Emerson. She probably has never even heard of Emerson. As the narrator points out, "Full of latent abilities, not a single one had been called into play" (214). Then one day, she meets a Mr. Calton, who will rescue her from boredom. Thus ends the narrative of the potential artist and begins the story of the wife.

However, Stoddard complicates what would be a typical plot of a willful young woman subdued and placed into the appropriate channel of matrimony. She does this by embedding the narrative of her courtship and married life in the middle of a story about her overall awakening. After two years, Laura loses her only child, and after five years, her husband dies, leaving her the widow Mrs. Calton. This was where we first found her at the beginning of the story, an older and wiser woman, yet still dissatisfied and bored with the conventional narratives of women's lives. "Her liberty [remained] restricted because she was a woman, because of Mr. Calton's [will], and because her fortune was small" (217). But her life begins to change with the arrival of her husband's cousin, Martha, who has received money from his estate on the stipulation that she live with Laura. Martha's son, Lester, is "a genius, an artist," who has achieved some success. His sculpture "stands behind the Speaker's chair in the hall of Congress." More importantly, the statue looks like Laura. When Lester saw her photograph, he "thought your brow was regal," Martha tells her. It also becomes clear that Laura is "not heartbroken" by the loss of her husband, and "that there was some lack in Laura's nature. . . . it might be repressed, undeveloped, or shallow" (218). The question is whether this "lack" is love or art. Her potential as an artist, however, has been extinguished long ago, and instead she is transformed by Lester into an art object and, eventually, a wife. At first, of course, she resists the charms of both "the artist life" (which she would live through him) and Lester. She has "always thought artists were queer" (219), she tells Martha, using the same word her mother used to describe her and that Martha will use as well in reference to her in the final line of the story.

The final pages throw Laura and Lester together in scenes reminiscent of Stoddard's other depictions of courtship as "a sort of guerrilla warfare" (220). But Laura finally relents, realizing that her life has been "a crude waste. All the ordinary experiences of womanhood bringing her to this result!" She wonders, "Was the right way before her at last?" (221). Life as Lester's wife will be anything but the "ordinary" life of a woman, but it is still far from the life of an artist. That is reserved for Lester, who clearly has had the supportive mother, community, and education that allowed him to awaken his potential and pursue his career, none of which were granted to Laura. Her access to the world of art will be through him. But her question of whether this was the "right" way undercuts the romantic ending. Laura has found a way to live an unconventional life, but has she found an outlet for her "latent abilities"? This story powerfully conveys the ambivalence that Stoddard herself felt about her own ebbing career. By conceiving of no way for Laura to discover her relation to nature and hence her individuality and her potential as an artist, "Me and My Son" (the very title of which excludes Laura) is a paradigmatic story of the failure of the woman artist.

While many such stories, such as *Armgart* and *Avis*, depict the withering of the woman artist's talent, Laura's talent remains dormant from the beginning.

At the same time, however, "Me and My Son" demonstrates Stoddard's continued efforts to produce high-quality work. Despite its contrived ending (the happy ending being the most difficult narrative convention to subvert), this is a serious story that clearly positions itself in opposition to the women's novels that she lampooned in her *Alta* columns. Just as Laura objects to the way the sanguine heroine of the novel she is reading puts off happiness until the afterlife and, presumably, resigns herself to an unsatisfactory life in the here and now, Stoddard's story works against such a moral and such easy, "[m]echanical piety." Her heroine, by contrast, does not blithely resign herself to unhappiness; instead she slowly dies inside, only to be rescued by Lester from a living death. The author surprises us not only with her unconventional heroine but also with abrupt prose meant to reflect Laura's individuality. For example, after Laura examines Lester for the first time and admits that "he was undeniably handsome," the narrator interrupts the description of him to tell us, "She felt like having a fight with him, and made up her mind to avail herself of the first opportunity" (220). Such a passage is characteristic of Stoddard's liveliest prose, which, although not always appreciated by her contemporaries, was a conscious effort on her part to break with the angelic didacticism of her sister novelists and to align herself with the "gunpowder" of Charlotte Brontë.

Published later the same year, "Collected," as we have already seen, clearly allows the artist heroine to develop her abilities, although it does so in a kind of a vacuum. Alicia is still no Lester. She has no supportive community (apart from the love of her brother, who understands her mind but not her writing), and although she has corresponded with other writers, she is more like Emily Dickinson in her seclusion. Additionally, her success is validated only within her family circle. She is not recognized by the nation, as Lester is with his statue in the hall of Congress. However, we can read "Collected," a sort of companion piece to "Me and My Son," as the fulfillment of the woman artist's (Laura's) potential. In fact, an autobiographical reading of the two stories would suggest that they represent the two selves — wife and artist — that Stoddard had been struggling to resolve. Shortly after the publication of these two works, Stoddard would essentially give up that fight, while her husband, like Lester, pursued his career largely unfettered.

The heroine of "Collected," Alicia, is twenty-eight years old and unmarried, and therefore is past the crisis points depicted in the earlier story. She has already loved and lost and rejects a second suitor in favor of her own development. This is not the story of a restless young woman seeking her purpose in life but the story of a more mature woman whose purpose has been found. There is no mention of Alicia's family, beyond an "unhappy mother," who must be dead, and her brother.[31] Stoddard has erased any discontented, stifling childhood. As a result, Alicia is allowed to embrace her idiosyncrasies and explore nature for its hidden depths of meaning. While the sea "stirred no mental echo in Laura's spirit" (214), Alicia takes frequent, "perfect" "woodland walks" (299) and writes after one such walk, "Full-blooded summer swells the sea and is in my veins" (300). These walks clearly fuel her creative energy, the growth of which Alicia's journal documents.

Alicia's diary makes many references to her courting of masculine "genius." In the first entry, Alicia writes that "in rummaging my brain today I believe that I thanked God for suddenly feeling virile; I mean that I emerged from my fog" (294). The first part of this sentence, taken from Stoddard's 1866 journal, suggests that Alicia associates her creative powers with male sexual energy. Also, emerging from a fog, she is now able to see clearly. This "virile" energy, which results in the power to see clearly, is suggestive of the gaze of the "artist," which penetrates into the secret meanings of things not available to the ordinary person. As Everett wrote in his review of *Aurora Leigh*, unlike the average individual, the artist sees "objects as existing for the eye alone. . . . Before they can be transferred to his canvas, they must be to him transmuted into color only." Emerson, influenced by Coleridge, also stressed the ocular ability of the artist. He wrote in *Nature*, "There is a property in the horizon which no man has but he whose eye can integrate all the parts, that is, the poet." And, of course, there is his infamous metaphor of the "transparent eyeball. I am nothing. I see all."[32] Laura, significantly, possesses no such ability to "see": "The brilliant July sky was a tiresome spectacle to her; she watched it from vacancy" (214). Her empty eyes are matched by an empty soul, which has to be filled up by an artist husband. But Alicia writes that she is "[s]pying inside and outside of myself for the fashion of my novel" (295). Possessing the power to see both internally and externally, she is preparing to create great art.

However, as we have seen, Alicia experiences a period of frustration. At one point, she writes in desperation, "Let me sew a womanly seam. Who am I to summon giants?" (300), suggesting that her doubts about her abilities stem from her gender. She knows that she is supposed to be sewing rather than creating art. But having rejected her lover in order to devote herself to her writing, she finds her strength again as an artist. At the same time, however, her body begins its decline toward death. With her body failing, her eyesight takes over, suggesting that she is becoming now the consummate artist, the bodiless transparent eyeball, who has no corporeal presence in the world. Reclaiming the artist's power of vision, she declares, "Who has ever looked thoroughly into the lining of things?" (303). Here she most emphatically adopts the penetrating, masculine gaze of the artist, who looks beyond the surface into the mysterious depths. She has refused the role of wife, and presumably mother, both of which would mean a physical, sexual existence. Instead, she recommits herself to the role of observer/artist, who takes possession of nature and begins to watch her brother's courtship of Julia develop. Rather than become a participant in romance, a subjective role, she maintains the distance of the observer. Here we see the most common claim made by Alcott, Phelps, Stoddard, and Woolson about the woman artist—in order to create art, she must remain distant and aloof. Once she has entangled herself in intimate relationships, she has lost her capacity for insight.

This situation presents a paradox, however. When Julia reads Alicia's novel and declares, "I did not know that one could create without experience," she alludes to cultural arguments against women's capacity to create because of their secluded lives. The implications are even more damaging for the unmarried woman artist: without a subjective knowledge of love, how can one write about it? However, Alicia takes her powers as an artist beyond the realm of women's ordinary experiences by claiming the perceptive power of the transcendent artist. She tells Julia, "like Ulysses, I am a part of all that I have seen" (306). In these allusions to Alicia's ability to see "into the lining" of things and to merge her consciousness into those things outside of herself through creative perception, Stoddard allows Alicia to realize the "virile" power of the artist that she often felt was beyond herself. Alicia becomes, like Charlotte Brontë, a "self-contained" artist (292). As Stoddard wrote about Brontë, "Fame and money were not her incentives, she wrote, she says, because she felt it 'needful to speak,' and what she experienced in her own life, or what she saw in the life of others she expressed."[33] Like Davis's ideal author, Alicia writes from such pure motives, but she is not allowed, like Brontë or Davis's female writers, to speak to or for her age. As a result, Alicia does not complete the stages of Emersonian genius. With this story, Stoddard seemed to give up on the ideal of genius as communicative, as embraced by the nation. Such a symbiotic relationship between genius and audience is available only to Lester, the male artist. Alicia, then, although allowed to sprout and grow well beyond Laura, remains incomplete, killed off before full fruition of her genius.

Woolson's artist heroines, in contrast to Alicia's remarkable access to the vision of the artist, are denied the masculine power of the objective gaze necessary to the creation of "art," in addition to the voice of Emersonian genius. The silencing of Woolson's female artists is blatant—Katherine loses her voice at the end of "Château"; Miss Elisabetha's voice is usurped by that of a prima donna who steals the affection of her ward; Margaret Harold in *East Angels*, who is described as "a combination of our own Margaret Fuller and Madame de Staël," is denied a voice: "she is a Corinne Mute, a Margaret dumb."[34] Like Armgart, these women are buried alive by their voicelessness. What has been less noticed, however, is the way Woolson robs her female artists of the ability not only to speak but also to see. Her most fascinating woman artist narratives—"The Street of the Hyacinth," "'Miss Grief,'" and "At the Château of Corinne"—are told through the perspective of male or male-identified narrators. These stories subject women artists to the male gaze, reducing them to the status of object, or "woman," foreclosing from the outset the possibility of their developing, within the gendered hierarchy of the narrative, the status of subject or "artist."

Woolson, who did not have as thorough a commitment to romantic ideals of art and genius as Stoddard did, nonetheless shared her understanding of women writers' need to acquire "masterly" powers in order to create art. Woolson tended to use the term "genius" in the masculine, romantic sense of otherworldly, innate energies, and as a result, she was conflicted on the question of whether women could possess genius. Our understanding of Woolson's views on the subject is complicated by her profession to her friends Edmund Clarence Stedman and Henry James that women were incapable of genius. She wrote to Stedman that in his essay on Elizabeth Barrett Browning in *Victorian Poets*, "you have veiled your entire disbelief in the possibility of true fiery genius in woman. . . . You have no objection to a woman's soaring to lofty heights in the realm of space allotted to her; the only thing you wish understood is that it *is* in her allotted space. . . . I do not quarrel with you about this; and the reason is—that I fully agree with you!" As Sharon Dean writes in regard to this letter, "For a writer who pushed herself to be the best literary artist she could be and who created fictional characters with similar goals, the statement appears problematic." Dean resolves the contradiction by arguing that "Woolson believed that 'true fiery genius in woman' was unavailable because the definition of genius was a male-based construct." There is much in Woolson's writings to support Dean's conclusion that Woolson felt women "had not been given access to the education or life experiences necessary to cultivate genius in themselves or to recognize genius in others." Most tellingly,

Woolson once wrote that she believed more education was all women needed to develop their minds. She did not think the "feminine mind inferior," she claimed. "But it has been kept back, and enfeebled, and limited, by ages of ignorance, and almost servitude." If we contrast the letter to Stedman with Woolson's marginal notes in her copy of *Victorian Poets*, we can see that what she wrote to the author was not necessarily all she felt. Next to the section on Elizabeth Barrett Browning, Woolson commented, "Mr. Stedman does not really believe in woman's genius. His disbelief peeps through every line of the criticism below, whose essence is — 'She did wonderfully well for a woman.' "[35] Her tone here is so visibly different that one must question the opinions she professed to Stedman. In the privacy of her own copy, she implicitly challenges his disbelief in women's genius by ridiculing chauvinism.

Woolson herself, so far as I have been able to determine, did not discuss genius in connection with herself in her correspondence. When her childhood friend apparently praised her skill as a writer, Woolson characteristically denied possessing any extraordinary powers: "I have but little ability of the kind you mention; all I have is immense perseverance and determination."[36] Disavowing talent, she nonetheless revealed her ambition and her ethic of hard work, which is more in line with the realist conception of the writer. She clearly felt more comfortable adhering to this new professionalism than to romantic ideals of genius. By doing so, she was also able to sustain her ambitions much longer than Stoddard, whose desire to be recognized as a "genius" apparently created more anxiety than Woolson's ambition to achieve recognition for literary excellence with talent and much "perseverance." Woolson also felt more squeamish than Stoddard about women's advancing on the male sphere of "true fiery genius." In fact, of the four women examined in this study, she appears to have had the most difficulty in even venturing a public career as a writer. But as she overcame that fear, she did not so easily overcome the fear of challenging men in the realm of genius. Her letters to Henry James reveal the pains she took to appear nonthreatening to one she considered the highest genius. And his abilities, she intimated, would always be superior to a woman's, even George Eliot's, because "A woman, after all, can never be a complete artist."[37] However, it is clear from her stories about women artists that it is not a lack of innate ability but the male domination of Western art that hinders their development. By adopting the male perspective in these stories, filtering her portrayal of women artists through the views of Stedman, James, and other male critics of women's writing, she shows most vividly the impossibility of women's becoming "complete artist[s]."

The decisions of the Brontës, Sand, and Eliot to adopt male pseudonyms, and the way Sand and Eliot in particular established male authorial identities (Eliot even separated her public male persona from her private, female self, "Marian Evans" or "Mrs. Lewes"), can be likened to a woman writer's adoption of the male or androgynous narrator in her works. As we have seen, Lydia Maria Child used this strategy in her first novel, but few American women writers of the antebellum years did so. Instead, they claimed the sentimental authority of maternal narrators, as Stowe did in *Uncle Tom's Cabin*, expanding the realm of their influence through humor or social critique. But it was not until the Civil War and postbellum years that women writers began using male personas or androgynous narrators to claim the authority of the artist. For example, Davis deliberately obscures the gender of her narrator in "Life in the Iron Mills," most probably in an effort to ease her entrance into the high cultural pages of the *Atlantic Monthly*. To express her ideas about art, Emma Lazarus also used male artist figures, through which, Bette Roth Young suggests, she may "have been living vicariously." Apparently believing, as she wrote in her poem "Echoes," that "woman-souled I dare not hope, / . . . the might / Of manly, modern passion shall alight / Upon the Muse's lips," she instead chose to write about the artistic issues that concerned her through the voices of male artists. Stoddard also wrote her novels *Two Men* and *Temple House* from the perspectives of male characters and used the male voice in her poem "Mercedes," about which Paula Bennett writes, "She has used her pen not to record the pure and delicate intuitions of her heart, but to invade literary, sexual, and emotional territories that, according to domestic ideologists such as Sarah Josepha Hale, the 'lords of creation' had reserved for themselves."[38] Adopting a male persona was one way to make a clear break with sentimental, domestic literature and ideology and to write about taboo subjects for women. Certainly, the ambition of the woman artist was one such subject.

In an idea for a story Woolson recorded in her notebooks, we can see how she used the male critical perspective to critique feminine genius:

> The case of Mrs. B, unable to read any tongue but her own, and having read herself but very little even in her own language — but who can yet produce works that touch all hearts — carry people away. A man of real critical talents (like Arnold) and the widest culture, thrown with such a gifted ignoramus. His wonder. At first, he simply despises her. But when he sees and hears the great admiration her works excite, he is stupefied. He follows her about, and listens to her. She betrays her ignorance every time she opens her mouth. Yet she produces the creations that are utterly beyond

him. Possibly he tries — having made vast preparations. And while he is studying and preparing, *she* has done it![39]

As Woolson's italics imply, the gender of the two authors here is not accidental. An author of great learning and "critical talents" must be a man. And the writer without any formal training who "touch[es] all hearts" must be a woman. Mrs. B. appears to have been born with almost magical gifts that are at once superior and inferior to the male writer's acquired abilities. Although Woolson does not use the words here, her contemporaries would have recognized the distinction she was making between the innate "genius" of the female writer and the learned "talent" of the male writer. Mrs. B. is, in part, reminiscent of Corinne, whose highest genius was expressed through improvisation, suggesting the association of women's genius with spontaneity. In mid-nineteenth-century America, however, the distinction between woman's heart and man's intellect was often used to denigrate women's artistic abilities, but here Woolson's male writer realizes that his intellectualized idea of literature is inferior and cannot duplicate the power of the woman's gifts of the heart. She touches people and gains more "admiration" than he ever could, and this is the seal of genius as many understood it in nineteenth-century America. Without the masculine creative powers of Alicia, then, she is able to reach an audience and gain the appreciation that is the ideal culmination of genius. However, Mrs. B. is still incomplete as a writer because she lacks the education and "culture" of the male writer. Barred from the training necessary to create great art, she could never gain the respect of the male critical elite, the goal of Woolson, Stoddard, and many of their female contemporaries.

This lack of knowledge about literature is a significant aspect of the story idea because it is told from the male critic's perspective, echoing the views of Stedman, James, and Woolson herself. That Mrs. B. is an "ignoramus" is, of course, the Arnoldian critic's view. So we, as readers, if the story were written, would probably have little way to ascertain for ourselves whether or not she was such an inferior writer. The contrasts drawn between the two, therefore, are not objective. They are the male writer's way of understanding himself, his abilities, and his failure, much in the way Henry James's narrator of "Greville Fane" (1892) contrasts his own failed literary career with the successes of a popular woman writer. What make this story idea so compelling, however, is the way that the female author of the story (Woolson) adopts a male authority's perspective to describe another female writer. In this fragment, such a move is less problematic than it is in "Street," " 'Miss Grief,' " or "Château," because it is safe to say that Woolson's sympathies lie, for the most part, in this case, with the male critic. She distances herself from the popular woman writer who possesses a feminine version of genius, "inspiration" without "reason," as Stoddard would have put it. Rather than valorize this form of genius, as Hale or Henshaw would have done, Woolson looks through the male writer's eyes and senses both superiority and envy, which she herself probably would feel toward such a woman writer who wrote effortlessly, won admiration, and appeared to be unconscious of her ignorance.

Like Stoddard, Woolson was particularly critical of popular women writers like Mrs. B. and advocated another form of literature that she knew was both less feminine and less popular. In her notebooks, Woolson derided women's taste for pleasant stories and romances: "Oh, her idea of literature is 'pretty and pleasant' stories — not too long. Not having feelings herself, she cannot in the least appreciate the tragedy of deep feelings in others. . . . One would like to plough up such persons and *make* them suffer! 'Pretty and pleasant stories,' indeed!" In another entry she wrote, "Many women, good women, think scenes in certain novels and plays, 'So untrue to nature!' These are the women who live always in illusion! They believe in all sorts of romances which have never had the least actual existence. . . . they go swimming through life in a mist of romantic illusion." Naturally, such readers preferred the popular writers, whom Mrs. B. likely represents.[40]

In her ambition to be an artist, Woolson endeavored, therefore, to write against these "pretty and pleasant" works, as she explained to her childhood friend: "I have taken (within the last year) a new departure in my writing. I have gone back to nature and exact reality. I have such a horror of 'pretty,' 'sweet' writing that I should almost prefer a style that was ugly and bitter, provided it was also *strong*." In another letter, she insisted, "whatever one does must be done with one's might and I would rather be strong than beautiful, or even good, provided the 'good' must be dull."[41] Here, in addition to an incipient realist aesthetic, we can see Woolson's effort to align herself with the kind of genius accorded to European women writers that combined the masculine (strength) with the feminine (beauty), even privileging the former over the latter. In fact, it was this mixture that Woolson particularly admired in Eliot, as we see in her poem "To George Eliot." Like Stoddard, Woolson also engaged in a "crusade against duty" and the piety of sentimental fiction, and she often went farther than Stoddard by refusing to tack on happy endings, particularly happy marriages. As a result, she often felt, like the male writer in her idea for a story, left out in the cold compared to popular women writers. Woolson similarly expected that most readers would not approve of her writing because they favored an "exaggerated . . . style" characteristic of women novelists. "I generally throw half across the room all the new novels of the day," she wrote to a friend before she had written her first novel. "Now *these* novels the *Public* like! Moral: will they not be likely to throw mine *entirely* across the room? I fear so."[42]

It is interesting that Woolson never drafted the story about Mrs. B., as it would have been her only one featuring a successful female artist figure, at least in terms of public acceptance. It is likely that she chose not to write it because the woman possessing feminine genius did not represent the complicated dilemma presented by the woman who tries to access masculine powers, a more compelling issue to her. However, the stories she did complete and publish were not written from the perspective of the autobiographical artist heroine, as "Collected" was. This does not mean, however, that Woolson's artist stories are more muted or less powerful than those told from the woman artist's perspective. On the contrary, they convey the anger and the pain of the woman artist, seething just below the surface, to a greater extent than any of the other works, with the exception of Phelps's *Avis*. This is probably, why, in fact, Woolson distances herself from her artist heroine's psyches. To allow them to speak directly, or to speak directly herself, even if through her characters, either would necessitate the muting of their anger or would result in an unfeminine expression of their rage. It would also reduce the effect, as she perhaps saw it, of the artistry of the story. For to be a considered an artist, the woman writer had to forgo the personal and adopt a distanced, objective perspective. Eliot is well known for such a strategy, and Woolson also used it to great effect. However frustrated today's feminist reader may feel by the distance she creates between her narrators and her female artists, this was one way Woolson distanced herself from the "pretty," "sweet" qualities of much women's writings. But when Woolson uses a male persona to depict a woman artist, the issue becomes much more complicated than simply trying to establish one's authority as a (masculine) artist against feminine writing. For as in "The Street of the Hyacinth," Woolson subjects her woman artist to the gaze of men who try to neutralize the threat she poses as a woman and an artist.

The power of the male gaze has been a popular topic of feminist literary and film critics. Using the theories of Jacques Lacan and Michel Foucault, they have constructed a feminist understanding of how men historically, particularly as artists, have objectified women and robbed them of their capacity to develop individual identities and to create art.[43] We can see the destructive power of the male gaze in Phelps's *Avis* as Philip gains control over Avis by neutralizing her ability to see as an artist. The first time they see each other in Europe, Avis, still an artist, notices "a remarkable face, . . . certainly, in the impressive background of the dim-lit church, it blazed like an amber intaglio." Avis also "liked the shape of his head, which her artist's glance had caught simultaneously with the color and character of his eyes." The narrator is clear that the impression he makes on her is not personal: "The artist's world is peopled with the vanishing of such mute and unknown friends; and the artist's eye is privileged to take their passports as they come and go." However, the way he looks at her in return disrupts her calm, distant observation of him and causes her to feel "a great tidal wave of color surge across her face," suggesting her transformation from observer (artist) to observed (woman). "If the eye of that amber god across the Madeleine had caught an artist, it had held a woman," the narrator explains. "Avis became aware of this with a scorching, maidenly self-scorn. She dropped her veil, and hurried from the church." This initial encounter is only a microcosm of their relationship as Philip, over the course of weeks, catches her and lays claim to her. Back in America, as Avis paints his portrait, she regards him as if she were a "physician"; Philip "hoped some sudden, abashed consciousness would overtake her calm, professional scrutiny," and she would blush again as a result. What he does not know is "the intricate strife of the artist with the woman" that is simultaneously going on inside her. She tells him that she has always been "color-blind" to the attractiveness of men — "my eyes were made with different lenses" — but she eventually learns to see like other women.[44] This transformation from seeing subject to observed/desired object is central to Avis's decline, as it is for the artist heroine's "downfall" in Woolson's "Street."

As in the Mrs. B. fragment, "Street" sets up a contrast between a male and a female artist. The "literary artist" Mr. Noel, who is also a well-regarded art critic, has the knowledge of the Arnoldian figure but also the success that he lacked.[45] His superiority is without question. His exact opposite is the young, naive artist Ettie Macks, who has come to Rome expressly to meet and study with Noel, whom she knows only through his writings. But he is shocked by her boldness in demanding his instruction and guidance and is unwilling to share his knowledge with the untutored artist. The most salient contrast between the two figures is Noel's worldliness and Ettie's innocence, which is manifested not only in her lack of awareness that she has imposed herself on a strange man but also in her lack of embarrassment about her designs to become a great artist. She frankly declares, "I have always had a great deal of ambition; . . . It seemed to me that the point was — just determination. And then, of course, I always had the talent. . . . All sorts of things are prophesied [at home in Tuscolee] about my future. . . . they like to think they have discovered a genius at their own doors. My telling you all this sounds, I know conceited" (173), but she clearly does not care about making such an impression on Noel. Instead, she naively expects that he will overlook her impertinence once he has discerned both her drive and her considerable talents. Raised to believe that she is a "genius," she expects him to feel the same way about her.

The most surprising thing about Ettie, therefore, is not simply her innocence but her belief in herself. For, as we have seen, the shame that women felt about their ambitions was born out of the cultural assumption that such grand designs were futile and therefore merely vain. But for Ettie, her talent is simply a given, making her ambitions natural. Her innocence, then, is not merely of social convention, as Noel suggests, but of cultural stereotypes about women and genius. She simply doesn't realize that she is supposed to limit herself to caring for her mother or, at most, making pretty copies. Least of all is she supposed to be approaching famous art critics to solicit their aid in developing her genius. In her innocence and crudeness, Ettie is one of Woolson's most pathetic artist figures, even more so than Mrs. B. Although Mrs. B. is also ignorant, at least she does not dare to succeed in the male critic's realm. She stays within her "allotted space." Ettie's ignorance, however, is due not only to her sex but also to her origins in the American West. She knows so little of society or the culture of the Old World that, as she later discovers, "she made a fool of herself" (202).

Because the limited omniscient narrator tells the story from Noel's perspective, we are allowed to see her only as he does. His perspective is so powerful that Ettie eventually comes to see herself as he does, losing her faith in her talent. In this story, Woolson adopts the perspective of the Jamesian male critic and narrator, drawing most explicitly on "Daisy Miller." Similarly, she adapts scenes from Eliot's *Middlemarch*, in which the heroine is also subjected to the male gaze of the artist. The relationship between male authority and naive aspirant in "Street" mirrors those between Winterbourne and Daisy, and Ladislaw and Dorothea. As Patricia E. Johnson shows, the effect of the gaze of the narrator and the male characters on their heroines is a major characteristic of James's and Eliot's works.[46]

There are numerous signs of "Daisy Miller"'s influence on "Street." Both Ettie and Daisy are unrestrained American girls who are ignorant of European customs and whose mothers fail to chaperone them. The more worldly Noel and Winterbourne both live in exile and are having affairs with elusive European women. In both stories, voices of respectable society, to which the girls are oblivious, are audible only to the men. And both stories are set in Rome. But I wish to focus on how the limited omniscient narrators of both stories focus the portrayal of the young women through the elder men's eyes.[47] Both stories are preoccupied with these men's alternating attraction to and aversion to these women. Their fascination stems from the frank, open manner of Ettie and Daisy, and their difficulties in reading the two women's behavior are central to understanding their relationships with them.

The governing question in James's story is, is Daisy a virtuous (i.e., innocent) girl or simply an amoral flirt? Noel confronts a similar question about Ettie, which is complicated by her artistic ambition. He wonders if her behavior is a result of her ignorance or is the sign of a sexually aggressive woman. As an American girl from the West, Ettie, like Daisy, fails to adhere to social norms for young ladies. But, as an artist, the deviance from gender expectations is even more pronounced. In a rare departure from Noel's perspective, the narrator records the comments of Ettie's fellow passengers "on the voyage over, . . . 'If that girl had more color, and if she was graceful, and if she was a little more womanly — that is, if she would not look at everything in such a direct, calm, impartial sort of way — she would be almost pretty'" (175–176). Her "direct" and "impartial" gaze in particular marks her as unwomanly. In other words, she has the eyes of an artist rather than the veiled or downcast glance of a woman. Barker's comments about nineteenth-century norms of gender and artistry apply perfectly to Woolson's portayal of Ettie's unfeminine behavior: "The ability to gaze openly and to move about town freely . . . was a masculine prerogative that implied the sexual freedom to pursue, purchase, or paint the object of the unfettered gaze."[48] In other words, such an open gaze makes Ettie unfeminine precisely because it betokens sexual aggressiveness. Furthermore, whereas a woman was supposed to have a personal interest in the people and things she looked at, owing to her emotional nature, an artist looked impartially, showing no particular favor, recognizing little or no relationship between the object and oneself. The artist's personality and corporeal presence dissolve as the artist observes and transforms objects into art. Rather than feel an emotional bond with or interest in the people or things around her, Ettie objectifies them, as the artist does.

This direct, impersonal way of looking at things exemplifies her bold manner and confuses Noel, who briefly questions her sexual innocence. When he first meets her, he thinks he would have been even more repelled "if she had betrayed the smallest sign of a desire to secure his attention as Raymond Noel personally, and not simply the art authority" (177). When he tries to put her off, however, her appeals become more aggressive: "Mr. Noel, I am absolutely at your feet!"

she pleads. Noel is "startled" by this outburst and wonders, "was she, after all, going to — But no; her sentence had been as impersonal as those which had preceded it" (179). He is relieved that she is not appealing to him personally and therefore poses no sexual threat. The implication, as in "Daisy Miller," is that he wonders if her seemingly innocent advance is actually a game of manipulation played by a very cunning woman masquerading as a virginal, ignorant girl. As an unconventional woman artist who breaks all rules of propriety, she is, potentially, the stereotypical George Sand figure, who is a sexual predator. But Noel and the narrator decide (much more quickly than Winterbourne does about Daisy) that Ettie is indeed innocent. In fact, the narrator explains her direct gaze as a sign of her naiveté: "Her gray eyes had a clear directness in their glance, which, combined with the other expressions of her face, told the experienced observer at once that she knew little of what is called 'the world.' For, although calm, it was a deeply confident glance; it showed that the girl was sure that she could take care of herself" (175). And, of course, she must be deluding herself because the "experienced observer," as Noel no doubt believes himself to be, knows that a girl cannot take care of herself. While the reader may quickly brush by this passage, upon closer inspection we can see Woolson perhaps calling into question the narrator's and Noel's authority as "experienced observer[s]." While they believe a woman must need a protector, someone to care for her, as Oswald believes Corinne does, and Alicia Raymond's suitor believes she does, Woolson most likely did not believe this, given her own single life traveling in Europe. Ettie's naive confidence also extends to her belief in herself as an artist. Just as the narrator and Noel believe that she cannot take care of herself, so do they believe that she cannot be an artist. Therefore, Noel never takes her ambitions seriously. And, unlike Daisy, who is allowed, in a manner, to escape the power of Winterbourne's gaze (through death), Ettie succumbs to Noel's attempts to confine her in the role of a conventional woman, or wife. In other words, the pattern of *Avis*, "Château," and "Me and My Son" is repeated here.

Noel destroys Ettie's artist identity by refusing to treat her as an artist and instead objectifying her. Through the narrator, he comments on the "color" in her face and how it changes her appearance (184, 186). Noel's primary interest in her is for the "contrast" she poses to his lover, "Madame B — —," who "was art itself." The narrator explains, "Raymond Noel had a highly artistic nature. He admired art. This did not prevent him from taking up occasionally, as a contrast to this lady, the society of [Ettie]" (188). Here we can see Ettie's transformation from artist to art object, in the eyes of the narrator and the consciousness of Noel.

Noel, as he later reflects on "the canvas of his Roman impressions," sees "the figure of Miss Macks" (193) and then decides to go visit her. She is a "figure," an aesthetic object, to him and operates as such in the story. She is not given the agency of the artist. Any ability that Ettie may possess to "see" as an artist is, in fact, doomed from the beginning, as the story focuses on Noel's perceptions of her. Ettie's vision is never conveyed to the reader. There is no description of her paintings, nor is she allowed to voice any of her impressions. When Noel meets her in the street, he sees her as "a novelty, . . . with her earnest eyes, and her basket on her arm" and decides to walk with her, "curious to see whether she would notice the colors and outlines that made their picturesqueness." However, "She noticed nothing but the vegetable-stalls, and talked of nothing but her pictures" (180). Ettie was on an errand to buy food for her invalid mother, so it is likely that she was too preoccupied with her duties as a daughter to play the role of the artist at this moment, as Cheryl Torsney suggests.[49] Nonetheless, how do we know Ettie didn't notice the colors? Noel doesn't believe that she does, but what does he base this on? The only way he would have known was if Ettie had not only seen but spoken of the colors. And this, it is clear, Ettie is not capable of doing. She does not have the vocabulary to discuss art, as Noel does.

Ettie's lack of knowledge about art and the language to express her perceptions about art is highlighted in the scenes where Noel acts as her guide in the galleries. In these scenes we can see the influence of chapters 21 and 22 of *Middlemarch*, where Dorothea is educated by Ladislaw in the significance and meaning of art. In "Street" and *Middlemarch*, the young women, who were brought up very far from the centers of the art world, are initiated into the wonders of art in Rome, "the city which," as Johnson writes, "represents Western Art." Both women fail to appreciate these works or understand the significance they hold for their male guides. For Dorothea, "there is so much I don't know the reason of—so much that seems to me a consecration of ugliness rather than beauty." Ettie also proclaims the paintings "very ugly," and about two in particular she says, "There isn't any reality or meaning in them" (185). But, as Johnson argues, Dorothea's lack of appreciation may "have more to do with [her] discomfort with her culture's view of women than with her esthetic immaturity." Dorothea, who is placed in the roles of romantic object by Ladislaw and aesthetic object by his artist friend, cannot appreciate a male-dominated tradition of Western art because she has not been trained to see as the male artist sees. She tells Ladislaw, concerning her lack of appreciation for art, "It is painful to be told that anything is very fine and not be able to feel that it is fine—something like being blind, while people talk of the sky."[50] As a woman, she is left out of the conversation and feels "blind," lacking the sight of the male critic who appreciates art through the objectifying gaze.

Ettie is similarly blind and placed in the role of aesthetic and, eventually, romantic object. With no education in Western art beyond Noel's essays (which are part of the conversation from which she and Dorothea are excluded), she cannot understand his views because they don't include her in the role of observer or subject. Western art has no "reason" or "meaning" for a woman who is not trained to see as a man does. But this is precisely what Woolson is trying to do in the story, to look through male eyes, which means she must distance or even divorce herself from the object of that gaze, the woman. However, while Eliot, at the very end of *Middlemarch*, allows Dorothea to escape from her position as object and to imagine a kind of vision that "move[s] beyond power, surveillance, or a narrowly-gendered subjectivity," as Johnson argues,[51] Woolson launches her attack from another route. By adopting the gaze herself and critiquing it from within, she demonstrates the "downfall" of the woman artist who internalizes the male artist's gaze and becomes the subject rather than a creator of Western art.

Ultimately Woolson undercuts Noel's and the narrator's authority and manages to portray Noel's conquest of Ettie in an unsympathetic light, encouraging the reader to take Ettie's side rather than Noel's. Noel begins his destruction of her artist identity by refusing to pass judgment on her work. Although he finds her paintings "all extremely and essentially bad," he does not tell her this, convinced that "where women were concerned, a certain amount of falsity was sometimes indispensable. There were occasions when a man could no more tell the bare truth to a woman than he would strike her" (181). This is the gallantry of the critics that prevented them from taking women writers seriously. Assuming that Ettie cannot take serious criticism and that to give her such would be a violation of gender codes, Noel refrains from responding at all to her work. The narrator follows suit, giving no description of her paintings. As Torsney argues, "we are asked to have faith that Ettie's painting is bad when we are offered no evidence except reaction from a patriarchal establishment that would be seriously threatened by revolutionary work from a woman."[52] This lack of evidence suggests, however, the potential unreliability not only of Noel but the narrator as well. Just before Noel declares her work inferior, the narrator explains, "There was not one chance in five hundred that her work was worth anything" (181), suggesting that the deck was stacked against her from the beginning. But Noel later confesses to another character that Ettie possessed "intelligence without cultivation," and when he sends her to an art teacher, Mr. Jackson, he is surprised to hear this alternative authority say that she has "talent." Jackson tells him that "[h]er work was very crude, of course; she had been brutally taught." In an effort to retrain her, "[h]e had turned her back to the alphabet; and in time, they — would see what she could do" (183). This conflicting opinion certainly casts doubt on Noel's judgment of her work and suggests that she may indeed possess the spark of genius but lacks the technical training to develop it. By going "back to the alphabet," she may yet be able to realize that genius. This is, in fact, what Avis did when she studied in Europe. She was told she had to go back to the basics, and after years of hard work, she succeeded in realizing her talent.

Ettie, however, is not allowed to develop in this way. But the fault lies squarely with her teachers. When Noel later looks at "some of the work she had done under Mr. Jackson's instruction," he sees right away that the teacher "had not kept his word, . . . he had soon released her [from serious study], and allowed her to pursue her own way again. The original faults were as marked as ever. In his opinion all was essentially bad." But Ettie tells Noel that Mr. Jackson thinks "my strongest point is originality" in subject; "my execution is not much yet." Ettie believes, contrary to Noel, that "the idea is the important thing; the execution is secondary" (190). Ettie takes what would have been considered at the time as a very feminine approach to her art. She is more concerned with inspiration. As Stoddard believed, though, "inspiration avails little"; the technical aspects of form and style, "method . . . is what the minds of women lack." So when Noel condemns her art as "bad," he is the voice of the critics who belittle the efforts of women artists and writers who try to advance on the realm of "art" without rigorous training. For Noel, as for the male critic in the Mrs. B. sketch, there can be no spontaneous genius. Even if the inspiration is divinely granted, it must be shaped by education, rules, forms, which only the masculine mind can comprehend. But Ettie is not allowed to receive this serious training and is not taught the necessity of it. At every turn, Noel avoids being the guide and mentor she asks him to be. Instead, he talks to her as if she were a "child" (184) or as if he were her "uncle" (189), but never as an equal. And her teacher falls in love with her and therefore, blinded by love or more concerned with winning her, Jackson does not give her the serious criticism she requires. How can she improve if she has no idea what her shortcomings are? This is precisely the complaint that Stoddard had about the male critics. They coddled female writers, instead of treating them like equals. And, as a result, women continued to produce mediocre work while no one ever told them how to improve.

Whereas Mrs. B. remains ignorant of her deficiencies, Ettie loses her innocence, but not in a way that allows her to identify her faults and improve. Instead, she comes to understand that her belief in herself was foolish, adopting Noel's view of her. While he travels about Europe, Noel sends Ettie some unnamed books that are intended to tell her what he cannot, namely that "as an artist, [she] would never do anything worth the materials she used" (192). Upon his return, he discovers that the books have done their duty. He notices that "[t]he expression of her face had greatly altered. The old, direct, wide glance was gone; gone also [was] *what he had called* her over-confidence" (194; emphasis added). The gaze of the artist, which Noel interpreted as naive "over-confidence" but which the narrator allows could be something else (perhaps a genuine power), has disappeared because Ettie no longer has "faith" in herself. Noel even calls her by her middle name, "Faith," implying that in the absence of any real talent, she could be identified by a misguided faith in her own abilities. The subject of the books, which finally show her the futility of her ambition, is never mentioned. They may contain the rules and forms of art appreciation. Or they may be philosophical treatises by Kant or Schopenhauer that aimed to define art as a masculine realm. Or they could simply be intended to represent Western culture itself, from which Ettie has been sheltered. Once she is exposed to it, she becomes convinced that she does not belong there. Rejections from two other art teachers also persuade her of the "truth" (197). One told her "that I had better throw away my brushes and take up sewing" (196). It is the old choice between thimble or brush that was imposed upon the young Phelps. But Ettie explains that if she didn't need to provide for her ailing mother, she might have held out longer in her pursuit of artistry. This suggests that, in the end, duty won out over ambition, as, no doubt, Noel's books told her it should.

In this second half of the story, after Noel's return, Ettie now plays the role of "woman" rather than "artist." One of the first changes Noel notices about her, in addition to her gaze, is her altered hairstyle. Whereas before she was too preoccupied with her art to care about the old-fashioned style of her hair, now her hair is arranged "in the prevalent style" (194), suggesting the transition from seer to the object of others' perception. She also becomes embroiled in various romantic plots. First, when Ettie tells Noel that Jackson had proposed to her, he constructs a story to explain Jackson's former belief in her talent. Noel muses, "Of course he [Jackson] saw to[o] the full imperfection of her work, the utter lack of the artist's conception, the artist's eye and touch; but probably he had loved her from the beginning, and had gone on hoping to win her love in return" (195).

Jackson believed that he could replace her ambition with love. For the rest of the story, her ambitions are forgotten and the romance narrative takes over. Having rejected Jackson, she is first courted by a count, whom she also rejects, and then, finally, by Noel himself. As a struggling teacher and governess, unable to support herself and her mother, Ettie eventually succumbs to Noel. As he falls in love with her, he descends from his position of superiority and confesses, "You are worth a hundred of me. . . . You are true and sincere; I am a dilettante in everything. But, dilettante as I am, in one way I have always appreciated you," namely as a woman rather than as an artist (202). It seems as if Noel has come to realize, through his relationship with Ettie, that he possesses only a superficial appreciation for art, whereas her heart was always in it. Over the course of the story, Ettie has learned, though, that she only has value as a woman, a romantic object. In the end, she must settle, like Stoddard's Laura, for being the wife of an artist. But having already tasted the life of an artist for herself, this marriage can only be a "downfall" for her (209). "But," Noel tells Ettie, "the heights upon which you placed yourself, my dear, were too superhuman" (209). This is Ettie's greatest lesson, that to strive for genius as an artist is, for a woman, to reach well beyond her grasp, to try to be above all other women, hence "superhuman."

By taking on the male critic's perspective and reducing Ettie to the role of aesthetic and romantic object, Woolson both replicated the stereotypes of gender and artistry and critiqued them. Her critique is embedded in Noel's infantilization, objectification, and, ultimately, romanticization of the female artist and in her undercutting of the narrator, particularly as she calls Noel's opinion of Ettie's art into question. In her adoption of this gendered perspective, Woolson most vividly displays the challenges of the woman author who strove to achieve the masculine ideal of genius or artist. But her works also transcend the discomfort that her artist heroines exhibit about their ambitions. Woolson manages to distance herself from her failed artist heroines by asserting with ease the control of the realist narrator — analyzing, observing, pointing up contrasts, and refusing to sentimentalize. As a result, her artist heroine stories, although they deny her protagonists agency as artists, allowed her to exhibit precisely such agency for herself.

The Taboo against Ambition

Whereas Stoddard's and Woolson's writings about women and art reveal the complications involved in pursuing "masculine" artistry, those of Phelps and

Alcott wrestle more vividly with the taboo against ambition. Phelps, in particular, registered the discomfort that this generation of women writers felt about possessing high ambitions, let alone sharing them with others. In her autobiography, where she describes how she hid her writing from her family, she echoes the language of S. E. Wallace, the "weak-minded woman," who equated her writing with "stealing." "Indeed, I carried on the writer's profession for many years as if it had been a burglar's," Phelps admitted. She told her family nothing about her first story or her first novel until they were already published and she could no longer hide her crime. Even in retrospect, she seemed to feel that her family was just in their neglect of her need for privacy or quiet. Why should they have supported her writing, she asked, and why should they have thought that it would amount to anything? "The girl who is never 'domestic' is trial enough." Her regret about not being the kind of (domestic) daughter her family wanted her to be led to her shame about writing.[53]

As Phelps looked back on her early writing career, she still appeared conflicted about what it meant to her then. When she wrote her first novel, she claimed, she possessed no ambitions. "Literary ambition is a good thing to possess; and I do not at all suggest that I was superior to it, but simply apart from it." Insisting at first that ambition is "good," she then implies that it is something base and inferior and one might feel above it. She also disclaims ever having had any faith in her abilities or even interest in the question of whether she possessed any literary ability: "There was nothing of the stuff that heroines and geniuses are made of in a shy and self-distrustful girl, who had no faith in her own capabilities, and, indeed, at that time the smallest possible amount of interest in the subject." Long after she had established her reputation, she wrote to her friend John Greenleaf Whittier, one of the country's most beloved poets, that she had "thought nothing" about "recognition" until she had it, "for I don't think I had what can be called ambition; only a fierce and unmanageable aspiration." To desire recognition and actively seek it out—in other words, to possess ambition— would be presumptuous. Instead, Phelps felt more comfortable claiming only "aspiration," a word that suggests a more passive hope that recognition may come one's way and even implies that it is beyond one's grasp. She objected to the word "ambition," making sure Whittier didn't think she had any. In her autobiography, she also preferred the word "aspiration," considering "ambition too low a word," presumably because "ambition" implies eagerness, competitiveness, even aggressiveness, qualities associated with men. That Phelps called her aspiration "fierce," though, indicates how strong her desire was for the recognition that

Whittier and other literary men gave her. Clearly, she did possess what we would now call ambition (a drive to succeed and gain admiration), although she was loath to be labeled an ambitious woman. Nonetheless, once her first novel, *The Gates Ajar*, became a sensation, she did admit to possessing "now, at last, . . . ambitions." By disclaiming ambition when she started writing, she portrayed herself as a kind of innocent writer who had no sense of her own worth. But once she was discovered by the critics and male authorities, she could feel more confident acknowledging her desire to succeed. Driven not by her own vanity but supported by literary men, she could retain her femininity. Without ambition, she claimed, she was simply invited into the men's club. Once there, she could work hard to maintain her place without fearing the charge of unwomanliness.[54]

Alcott also wrestled with her ambitions, which were prodigious. Alcott often depicted autobiographical women artists who struggled consciously to discover the best way to realize their considerable talents. "A Modern Cinderella" and "Psyche's Art" are two stories into which Alcott projected many of her own struggles to overcome the taboo against ambition. She did this by convincing herself that her writing was part of her role as a dutiful daughter. But it is important to understand how and why she came to view her writing in this way. Alcott scholars have often noted the extraordinary way in which she fused her ambitions and her duties as a daughter. Veronica Bassil, for instance, describes Alcott's "dilemma as a woman torn between the desire to create and the desire to serve, one who channeled the dangerous and potentially immoral energies of the artist into the apparent safety of the home." Richard Brodhead offers a similar interpretation of Alcott's view of herself as an author. Writing for children in the " 'heavy moral' mode" appealed to her, he argues, because "for an author who needed to demonstrate that she had overcome her selfish will, this writing style had the paradoxical attraction that it signified self-sacrifice, signaled that she had set aside personal pleasure for specifically useful work." However, if examined within the context of other women writers of her generation struggling to overcome the anxiety of trespassing on the male realm of ambition and genius, Alcott's evolving perception of herself as an author reveals more than a transformation from ambitious young writer courting the literary elite into successful, popular children's writer who, in Brodhead's words, has "shut down a level of ambition."[55] We can also see that she was finding a way to be both artist and woman in a culture that obliquely suggested but often overtly denied the possibility of combining the two identities and in a family that was already burdened with supporting one "genius" (her father).

Alcott was learning to be both a dutiful daughter *and* an ambitious writer, and her family assisted her efforts to combine the two identities. The kind of prolonged "fits" of writing she engaged in could only be supported by others. In February 1861 she described one such fit: "Another turn at 'Moods,' which I remodelled [*sic*]. From the 2d to the 25th I sat writing, with a run at dusk; could not sleep, and for three days was so full of it I could not stop to get up. . . . Mother wandered in and out with cordial cups of tea, . . . Father thought it fine, and brought his reddest apples. . . . It was very pleasant and queer while it lasted; but after three weeks of it I found that my mind was too rampant for my body, as my head was dizzy, legs shaky, and no sleep would come." A year later, while teaching away from home, she wrote that she "often longed for a crust in a garret with freedom and a pen." Even though she was not always able to retreat from her responsibilities and go into her "vortex," as she called it, she looked forward to those times as the ultimate "freedom." In 1864, after the success of *Hospital Sketches*, she was able to focus more exclusively on her writing. This complete abandonment of the rest of the world is lovingly described in *Little Women*:

> She [Jo] did not think herself a genius by any means; but when the writing fit came on, she gave herself up to it with entire abandon, and led a blissful life, unconscious of want, care, or bad weather, while she sat safe and happy in an imaginary world full of friends almost as real and dear to her as any in the flesh. . . . The divine afflatus usually lasted a week or two, and then she emerged from her "vortex," hungry, sleepy, cross, or despondent.

The "vortex" into which Jo descends is, as Susan Naomi Bernstein writes, "a celebration of the inner life."[56] It is also, despite Alcott's protestations, something akin to the romantic understanding of genius. The "divine afflatus" overtakes Jo, and she gives herself up to its power. But Alcott is sure to mention that Jo does not think of herself as a genius, lest she be seen as vain. This depiction of Jo, though, is the adult author's revision of what she had actually felt as a young woman. In Alcott's youthful journals we see so many expressions of her desire to make her mark that it is clear there is much more to her pursuit of a literary career than a desire to support her family. In 1858, she wrote, "I feel as if I could write better now, — more truly of things I have felt and therefore *know*. I hope I shall yet do my great book, for that seems to be my work, and I am growing up to it." During these early years she was "living for immortality," as her sister told her.[57]

As an adult, Alcott felt much less comfortable owning up to what she thought of as her childish and youthful dreams. An especially telling alteration of her earlier expression of ambition can be found in her mother's journal. On Christmas Day, 1854, when Alcott's first book, *Flower Fables*, a collection of stories for children, was published, she gave a copy to her mother with the following note: "Into your Christmas stocking I have placed the first fruits of my genius." Such, at least, is the wording her mother copied into her own journal on that day. But a later hand, which appears to be Louisa's, struck out the word "genius" in Abigail's journal and replaced it with "little talent." Apparently embarrassed by her frankness, or afraid that future readers of her mother's diary would condemn her youthful vanity, Louisa revised her exuberant faith in herself so that she would appear a more modest young writer. When the letter Louisa had written to her mother was published in Alcott's biography after her death, it had been revised again (undoubtedly by Alcott herself): "Into your Christmas stocking I have put my 'first-born,'" the published version of the letter reads. The messy talk of "genius" and "talent" had been completely erased.[58] Here we can see most clearly the kind of masking of ambition in which this generation of women writers engaged.

Six years after the publication of her first book, Alcott embarked on an even more ambitious project: a serious novel. At the time, she unselfconsciously recorded in her journal, "Genius burned so fiercely that for four weeks I wrote all day and planned nearly all night, being quite possessed by my work." Later that same year, she wrote to a friend about her belief that she and her sister (a visual artist) would be "'an honor to our country & a terror to the foe.'" But this youthful exuberance had worn off by the time she published *Moods* in 1864. To her publisher she wrote, "I'll try not to be 'spoilt,' . . . but people mustn't talk about 'genius'—for I drove that idea away years ago & dont [*sic*] want it back again. The inspiration of necessity is all I've had, & it is a safer help than any other."[59] Modest aims are "safer" because they keep her ambition in check. At first glance it seems that Alcott abandoned her desires for recognition and genius. But if we look more closely at her adult perception of her career, we see that she tried to transform her desire for genius and fame into motivations with which she felt more comfortable. She rejected the romantic notion of "genius" as detached from everyday life and concerned only with immortal fame. Such a self-absorbed inspiration, she learned, was unproductive. While her father may have felt comfortable sacrificing his family's welfare to such an idea of "genius," Alcott wanted to find another, healthier reason to write, and, not uncoincidentally, one that might help her achieve the kind of recognition and self-sufficiency that had eluded her father. She had deviated greatly from the conventional path of womanhood by developing her literary talents and descending into the "vortex" of inspired creativity. But she also paid for that self-absorption with a growing feeling of guilt. On one level, this guilt certainly stemmed from her gender. Other women, such as Phelps and Jewett, felt it as well. Jewett complained that "I don't like to shut myself up half of every day and say nobody must interfere with me, when there are dozens of things that I might do. . . . I'm afraid of being selfish."[60] But Alcott's fear of selfishness also had another source: she saw in her father the great burden such self-absorption could place on the shoulders of others. She felt guilty for abandoning her duties and leaving them to her mother and sisters. She did not wish to repeat her father's exploitation of his family.

In her autobiographical story "A Modern Cinderella" (1860), Alcott portrays how two sisters, Di (modeled on herself) and Laura (modeled on May, the visual artist), leave the household chores to their less talented and less ambitious sister, Nan (modeled on Anna, her oldest sister), whenever the " 'divine afflatus' descends upon [them]." Just like her father's abandonment of his family when genius called, these two sisters enact the same kind of desertion. But when the girls notice the physical toll that their selfish neglect of duty takes on Nan, they put away brush and pen to devote themselves to her and the household. In this lesson, Di learns how to become an artist by gaining her inspiration from her family and writing to support it, her father having died. Di tells her sister's fiancé, "I'll turn my books and pen to some account, and write stories full of dear old souls like you and Nan; and some one, I know, will like and buy them, though they are not 'works of Shakespeare.' I've thought of this before, have felt I had the power in me; *now* I have the motive, and *now* I'll do it."[61] Having discovered a nobler reason to write than self-gratification, she is ready to channel her "power" into a worthy form of art. Like Alcott, Di learns to push the inspiration of genius into the back of her mind and replace it with "the inspiration of necessity," a move that will allow her to express her real talent and bring her fame. Modestly claiming that her work is not as good as Shakespeare's, she nonetheless feels the artist's "power" and is confident that "some one . . . will like and buy" her art. The someone who liked and bought this story of a young woman writer's lesson in modifying her ambition was the prestigious *Atlantic Monthly*, which published Alcott's work in the company of Emerson, Longfellow, and Stowe. In her coming of age as an artist, Alcott believed that she would find success and recognition from the likes of the *Atlantic* by learning to write not for the gratification of her ambition but for others. But the goal of receiving fame as an artist remained. So the "shut[ting] down [of] a level of ambition" that Brodhead identifies was a more complex transformation. What also made it so was the *Atlantic*'s specific advice to Alcott about how to get the recognition she craved.

Before she wrote "A Modern Cinderella," Alcott had submitted an antislavery story, but Howard Ticknor, an editorial assistant at the magazine, advised Alcott to submit a shorter "story or sketch of a decided *local* flavor — more after the manner of 'Elkanah Brewster's Temptation.' " This story, published in the *Atlantic* by Charles Nordhoff in December 1859, blended regionalism with a moral message. In the story, a young man from a fishing village on Cape Cod possesses the ambition to become an artist. He forsakes mother, father, and fiancée in order to pursue his dream in New York. After years of neglecting them and living for his own selfish aims, he learns of the death of his future father-in-law and returns to marry his intended. To support her, he reluctantly returns to shoemaking and fishing. Although he gives up the career of an artist, in his hometown and the sea he eventually discovers the true subject matter he was made to paint, and he creates the best work of his life. As a collector of his work moralizes at the end, "The highest genius lives above the littleness of making a career. This man needs no Academy prizes or praises. To my mind, his is the noblest, happiest life of all." By living for others, rather than for himself, Elkanah Brewster became a "genius."[62]

By asking Alcott to write a story like this one, Ticknor was also passing along a lesson that Alcott certainly did not miss, one that applied to male as well as female artists. Ticknor essentially advised her to stick to themes closer to home and to be less ambitious. In response, she wrote a female version of "Elkanah Brewster's Temptation," her updated Cinderella story. Also set in a small New England town, it incorporates the advice Ticknor was suggesting. Given this editorial direction, it is tempting to read Alcott's story as an ironic attempt to appease the *Atlantic*'s editors rather than simply an expression of her true convictions. "A Modern Cinderella" brought her praise from Emerson and other "people [who] wrote to me about it and patted me on the head," she wrote in her journal, suggesting that she resented the paternal approach these men were taking to her work.[63] However, we also can see Alcott taking to heart this lesson of success through duty rather than ambition and applying it to male writers and artists as well as to female. After Alcott had achieved fame (not in the *Atlantic*, but as a children's writer), she explained to the young, aspiring author Maggie Lukens how she came to understand her motivations as a writer: "As a poor, proud, struggling girl I held to the belief that if I *deserved* success it would surely come so long as my ambition was not for selfish ends but for my dear family." This idea, reminiscent of "Elkanah Brewster's Temptation," also closely mirrors the definition of the "genius" in her story "The Freak of a Genius" (1866). The genius is "one, who possessing a rich gift, regards it with reverence, uses it nobly and lets neither ambitions, indolence nor neglect degrade or lessen the worth of the beautiful power given them for their own and others' good." Furthermore, "true genius is always humble," the noble character Margaret explains to a male character who does not understand the lesson of success through self-sacrifice. This was the kind of author Alcott wanted to be. She never abandoned the ideal of genius. But she believed that she would only be found worthy of the name if she didn't actively pursue that goal. She must patiently "work & wait."[64]

As Alcott struggled to live up to her modified idea of the humble artist, she worked through her feelings in stories about young women who come to conclusions similar to those of Di in "A Modern Cinderella." In these stories women learn that the path to success for women who desire recognition from the male-dominated worlds of art and literature is one of patience, endurance, and hardship. But their path is often more difficult than men's, in keeping with her belief that the focus must remain on the task of self-transformation. The rewards are seldom discussed. Yet the implication is that the crown of recognition will eventually come. Like Phelps's young woman author in "A Plea for Immortality," Alcott's heroines have to learn to toil patiently and wait for fame.

Alcott's "Psyche's Art" (1868) most fully explores her views on how women can develop their genius. In this story, women's path to artistry is differentiated from men's, suggesting that women have an even greater imperative to squelch ambitions than men do. Like Woolson, Alcott uses the technique of contrasting male and female artists to highlight how gender complicates the pursuit of genius. The story's protagonist, Psyche, has caught the "new disease called the Art fever" raging among young women.[65] But Psyche's commitment to her art is portrayed as higher and nobler than that of her fellow students, who seem more interested in finding beaus than discovering their latent genius. Although she is lauded by one of the other students as a "genius," she feels frustrated by her apparent inability to create something great. Echoing Alcott's letter to Redpath, she retorts, "never tell people they are geniuses unless you want to spoil them" (209). Psyche's humility deepens when she views a sculpture of Adam by a male student, Paul Gage, and finds in it "the indescribable charm of something higher than beauty." "If I could do a thing like that I'd die happy!" she exclaims (212). Again, as in "Street" and Stoddard's poem "The Poet's Secret," the female artist recognizes that the male artist knows a "secret" that she does not, the secret of how to make powerful art, and she asks him to share it with her. Paul gives her the only "receipt for genius" he can, which is, "Work and wait, and meantime feed heart, soul, and imagination with the best food one can get," to which Psyche responds that she doesn't know where to find this "food" (213). He can only share with her the general recipe for genius. He cannot help her find it in herself because her path will be different than his.

While Ettie tried and failed to work hard for artistic achievement in the way Paul Gage or other male artists did — by studying in a studio with a master — Psyche learns that, as a woman artist, she must take a different route. Paul tells her that each person must find his or her own source of inspiration. She wants to be able to possess "the art of reproducing [beauty] with truth," she tells him. "I have tried very hard to do it, but something is wanting; and in spite of my intense desire I never get on" (213). She receives her answer in the form of a poem by Ellen Sturgis Hooper, which happens to lie on the table next to her:

> I slept, and dreamed that life was beauty;
> I woke, and found that life was duty.
> Was thy dream then a shadowy lie?
> Toil on, sad heart, courageously,
> And thou shalt find thy dream to be
> A noonday light and truth to thee. (214)

Psyche decides that "doing one's duty [is] a good way to feed heart, soul, and imagination." The implication here is that although Paul's greatness in art may be the result of "the rich gift bestowed upon him" and his hard work in the studio (214), hers will be accomplished only through hard work at home, diligently serving her family. Free of the overwhelming cares at home that preoccupy her, he benefits from an art education, while she must leave school and learn her lessons from life. When she returns to her studio, she smashes her bust of Venus, a symbol of her failed attempt to enter the Western classical tradition of art, which is also off-limits to Ettie Macks. Psyche announces to her fellow female students that she is "going to work at home hereafter" (215). But more than simply choosing duty over beauty, she is accepting the former as a means of achieving the latter.

Once at home, Psyche "shut[s] herself into her little studio" and asks not to be disturbed, yet her duties distract her from her art (215). As the summer wears on, she accomplishes little, but Alcott explains that "this was the teaching she most needed, and in time she came to see it" (219). Whereas Psyche starts out seeing her performance of duty as "a means toward an end" (215), or the means by which she could become a great artist, she learns, because of her sister May's illness and pain, to give herself "heart and soul to duty, never thinking of reward." A miraculous transformation takes place at this point: "All turned to Sy [Psyche] for help and consolation, and her strength seemed to increase with the demand upon it. Patience and cheerfulness, courage and skill, came at her call like good fairies who had bided their time. House-keeping ceased to be hateful, and peace reigned in parlor and kitchen" (219). After May dies, the family begs Psyche to make a bust of the child. She responds, "I'm afraid I've lost the little skill I ever had." But "she tried, and with great wonder and delight discovered that she could work as she had never done before." The genius she had so long courted came to her when she ceased to ask for it, and her "newly found power . . . grew like magic" (220). Finally, she creates something worthy of the term "great." Unlike Ettie, who needed to learn the skills necessary to give shape to her inspiration, Psyche has to give up her study of method and even abandon her pursuit of art altogether to unleash her genius. She has to return to the state of the unconscious, even untrained artist, in order to produce something of value. Her art, though, is not meant for the world. It is a tribute to her sister and, as a gift to her family, it is placed on display in a prominent place in the home.

Meanwhile, Paul has achieved fame with his statue of Adam, and he seeks out Psyche to discover the results of her experiment. At Psyche's home, her mother tells Paul that she thinks "ambition isn't good for women; I mean that sort that makes 'em known by coming before the public in any way. But Sy deserves some reward, I'm sure, and I know she'll have it, for a better daughter never lived" (223). If a daughter does her duty well and possesses great talent, the reward will come of its own accord. What kind of reward, though, is unclear. When Psyche tells Paul that she has "been working and waiting," he tells her that she also has been "succeeding," his praise serving as a form of reward. But Psyche still seems to have higher aspirations. She reveals to him that she will "Never!" relinquish all of her dreams of achieving greatness as an artist although she is not concerned with recognition. She explains, "I thought at first that I could not serve two masters; but in trying to be faithful to one [duty] I find I am nearer and dearer to the other [art]. . . . when my leisure does come I shall know how to use it, for my head is full of ambitious plans, and I feel that I can do something *now*." Paul is convinced that she has learned the "secret" (225).

But the story ends on an ambiguous note. The narrator resists ending her story by marrying off the two artists, undoubtedly feeling, like Woolson, that it would mean the woman artist's "downfall":

Now . . . we will stop here, and leave our readers to finish the story as they like. Those who prefer the good old fashion may believe that the hero and heroine fell in love, were married and lived happily ever afterward. But those who can conceive of a world outside of a wedding-ring may believe that the friends remained faithful friends all their lives, while Paul won fame and fortune, and Psyche grew beautiful with the beauty of a serene and sunny nature, happy in duties which became pleasures, rich in the art which made life lovely to herself and others. (226)

We are left with two unreconciled images of Psyche as artist and Psyche as dutiful daughter. Alcott does not allow Psyche completely to fulfill her potential as an artist. While Paul is allowed to develop his, both Psyche and her art become "beautiful" and exist to make others happy. So although Alcott resists turning this narrative of a woman artist into a romance story, as Woolson did with "Street," she also does not allow Psyche to develop the masculine power of the artist that Stoddard accords Alicia in "Collected."

By the time Alcott began work on her novel *Diana and Persis* (1879), as we have seen, she could more concretely envision the kind of devotion to art and masculine strength of the woman artist that Alicia Raymond represents. In this work, the woman artists, like Alicia, possess no responsibilities to family. Instead, "the tie between them [was] artistic ambition and a sincere respect for each other's powers. Both were unusually gifted, not only with talent but with the courage and patience which are the wings of genius; and after ten years of steady upward climbing they were now ready for the flight out of the world of effort into the region of achievement, that promised land which so many sigh for and never see."[66] Diana and Persis strive for perfection as Paul Gage does — by studying art and devoting themselves to hard work for many years. And, as we have seen, Diana gains the respect of a male peer for her ability to portray strength as well as beauty in her art. However, this story remained unfinished, as Psyche's essentially did as well. Like Phelps, Stoddard, and Woolson, Alcott was unable to imagine the complete achievement of the woman artist.

The Grief of Genius

Another key quality that unites the disparate portrayals of artist heroines in the writings of Alcott, Phelps, Stoddard, and Woolson is their grief. Time and again, the four writers returned to the figure of the suffering woman (artist) who is deprived of the fulfillment of her genius, which was also a prominent theme of

Davis's fiction. Although it may appear that arguments against women's ability to possess genius and the cultural taboos against women's ambitions prevented Alcott, Phelps, Stoddard, and Woolson from fully envisioning themselves or their heroines as artists, they nonetheless found one way out of the impasse: the grief of genius. The one constant in these four women's reflections on women and genius was the belief that, as Woolson wrote, "only the unhappy women took to writing." Echoing the heroine's exclamation in Fanny Fern's *Ruth Hall* that "no happy woman ever writes," Woolson suggests that women who were happy identified themselves by their relations to men and children. She explained, "The happiest women I have known belonged to two classes; the devoted wives and mothers, and the successful flirts, whether married or single; such women never write." These thoughts were precipitated by news she had received of Stoddard's poor health from their mutual friend Edmund Clarence Stedman. "I am grieved to hear that Mrs. Stoddard is ill," she commiserated; "why do literary women break down so?" She also mentioned Phelps (asking Stedman if he liked her poetry) directly after her comments on how happy women never write, implying that her thoughts about women's "grief of artistry," as Cheryl Torsney calls it, led her from Stoddard to Phelps, and, presumably, to herself.[67] In fact, all four writers perceived their lives as literary women to be burdened by an inordinate amount of pain, illness, and grief.

Certainly earlier American women writers had also perceived the woman writer's life as a painful one, even cornering the market on sentimental literature that explored sadness and suffering. Cheryl Walker has noted that many nineteenth-century American women poets employed the "motif [of] 'the secret sorrow,'" which gave them a singular identity as women poets. By composing the poetry of pain, they carefully avoided "lay[ing] claim to the kinds of power jealously guarded by the patriarchy."[68] But Alcott, Phelps, Stoddard, and Woolson combined the sentimental self-sacrifice of the prototypical woman writer with the suffering of romantic genius, thereby reenvisioning the unhappy woman writer who sacrifices her health toiling for her family, like Ruth Hall, or whose pain as a mother is her chief motivation to write, as it was initially for Helen Hunt Jackson and Harriet Beecher Stowe. The unhappy women writers envisioned by Alcott, Phelps, Stoddard, and Woolson are not burdened by a woman's or a mother's pain but by the pain of the stifled artist. And because they are women as well as aspiring artists, their pain is more acute than that of the male genius and its transformation into art is more often thwarted by familial responsibilities or the interference of men. For Avis, Alicia, Ettie, Psyche, and their sister artist heroines, the source of their suffering is their attempt to be artists.

The same is true for the protagonist of Phelps's story "The Rejected Manuscript" (1893), written near the end of her career. The name of the artist heroine, significantly, is Mary Hathorne. Phelps was a great admirer of Nathaniel Hawthorne (who added the "w" to his family name) and no doubt carefully selected her heroine's name to suggest both Mary's tremendous talent and her isolation as a neglected genius who suffers repeated rejection before belated recognition — the romantic form of genius that Hawthorne had come to represent. In making her heroine a female version of Hawthorne, however, Phelps posits a special path to genius for the woman writer. In addition, Phelps seems, in part, to be reflecting back on her own early ambitions. Mary Hathorne "had stumbled upon literary success. . . . She had written a book, and people had read it. That was all she knew about it. Editors had fought upon it, women had cried over it, and men smoked over it; libraries took twenty copies of it; her dearest poet wrote her about it, and her most dreaded critic recognized her for it all these facts had puzzled her as much as they pleased her."[69] Using these incidents from her own early career (specifically the publication of *The Gates Ajar*), Phelps portrays a woman writer whose first success was unanticipated, much like Mrs. B.'s in Woolson's story idea, and much like Phelps's own as she described it in her autobiography. In addition, Mary "was too modest, too naïve, too spontaneous a woman to analyze or train herself" (286), aligning her with the tradition of untutored women writers who stumble upon their fame without ambition. But she cannot go on writing in this way. Phelps suggests that such power cannot be sustained: "She had flashed and puffed out. She was threatened with the fate that meets the gift which has no sustaining power" (286). Relying on instinct, as Stoddard and Woolson's Ettie Macks discovered, can only take an artist so far.

Long after the success of her first novel has faded, Mary Hathorne is attempting to get her second book published. She is working hard on various literary projects, all the while tending to her home and family, for she is married and has two children. Her health fails steadily over the course of the story, as she suffers through poverty, hard work, and a pregnancy that ends in the premature delivery of a stillborn baby. But just as, if not more, important is the fact that she is also suffering through repeated rejections from publishers. Her very life seems to depend upon the successful publication of her novel. After one rejection, her daughter finds her "lay[ing] unconscious upon the rude lounge" and believes

"Mummer's dead" (289). After enduring several such rejections, she decides to approach the "prince of American publishers" (who seems to be modeled on James T. Fields, the publisher of Hawthorne and Phelps herself). The narrator explains, however, "Her courage was born of her despair. She had never dared to approach him before. Her own publishers [of her first book], selected with her natural timidity and in youth, had been but second-rate folk; and of the firms that had rebuffed her since, not one presumed to compete with the distinguished house to which, at last, so to speak, she crawled" (289). Not deliberately seeking fame or high recognition, she goes to the publisher with the highest reputation only as a last resort. This kind publisher perceives that she "is a dying woman" and encourages her to "Believe in yourself—for the public believes in you; and so do I" (290). However, lacking faith in herself, and waiting so long for the publisher's reply that she assumes his answer will be no, she gives up her will to live. She tells her husband, "My work is over. . . . My day is done. I've run my race, and I'm not fashionable anymore. I don't suppose I write after the new style. And I haven't been very strong, you know" (291). Her breakdown after childbirth clearly has as much to do with the death of her career as the death of her child. Her husband realizes that "she was sinking for lack of a stimulant which he could not give," presumably literary recognition. Seeming about to breathe her last breath, she tells him, "Don't let Popsy [their daughter] take to writing" (291). The next day, however, the letter of acceptance comes from the distinguished publisher, telling her that her novel is "a story of a high order" and enclosing a check for a thousand dollars. The accompanying illustration depicts Mary laid out on a lounge as if she were in a coffin. Her daughter stands over her, admonishing her for having dropped her "good-luck letter." Rather than portray her recovery, which the letter will shortly effect, the illustration emphasizes her physical and emotional decline. Even her eyes are closed, giving the impression that she has died and her daughter is grieving over her. This potent image of the lifeless woman writer, killed by neglect and the exhaustion of motherhood, remains the dominant one of the story.

However, Mary is nonetheless revived by her unexpected success. The publisher's praise and the money bring Mary back to life. "Hope had done its hearty work. The wine of success sprang to her head and bounded in her veins" (292). But the success of Mary's novel is not accidental this time. It has everything to do with the grief she has suffered. Just as her baby was born prematurely, so was her career. Time, experience, and much suffering were required to ripen her talents and turn them into the "wine of success." She discovers that great art is produced not by keeping up with the current style but by creating works that grow out of her experience of suffering. When she was young, the narrator explains, she knew little of what she wrote about: "Poverty she had read about. Poverty—with the assurance of ignorance and youth—she had written about; . . . but personal poverty, biting, blinding poverty, such as comes to the rich in mind and spirit," she knew little of, until her marriage to a poor scholar (285). Now, having "come to desperate straits" (284), she has been forced to write for money, but she also continues to strive for recognition. In addition to the "little Sunday-school book, written over a year ago to meet the doctor's bill" (286), she is writing a "novelette for the *Pacific*" (287), undoubtedly another name for the *Atlantic*. But the goal, of course, is that financial and literary success will come together, as they eventually do with the publication of her novel. Although the narrator gives few clues about her novel, it is titled *"Love's Daily Bread,"* and is called by one publisher "too 'earnest'" to be popular (289). These small details suggest that the novel has grown directly out of Mary's life, in which she is trying desperately to keep her family from the brink of despair and starvation, and that the intensity of her feelings has gone into it. In this more mature work, therefore, has been poured the toil, suffering, and grief that alone (rather than instinct or inspiration) can grant the woman author success and serious recognition.

The woman writer's path to genius and respect, Alcott, Phelps, Woolson, and Stoddard believed, was not the one that seemed to be reserved for the male romantic genius—selfish devotion to the Muses—but hard work, humility, self-sacrifice, and much suffering. Success would not come easily. Looking forward to the publication of *Moods*, Alcott hoped it would be well received, and she claimed that "ten or fifteen years of snubbing [was] rather good training for an ambitious body." Her pride had been stepped on by editors, publishers, and critics, making her ready for success. But the financial success that Alcott also needed would not come until the publication of *Little Women* in 1868. By then years of struggling and ambition had taken their toll on her, much like the "sick, tired, and too early old" woman writer Kate King in Alcott's *Old-Fashioned Girl* (1870), the impoverished women writers in Phelps's "Plea for Immortality" and "A Rejected Manuscript," and Davis's artist figures.[70] Physical and psychological suffering were closely intertwined with Alcott's, Phelps's, Stoddard's, and Woolson's lives as writers, and it was a badge they wore somewhat proudly, couching their claims to genius within a rhetoric of sacrificial womanhood. In essence, they found a space, somewhere at the convergence of the sentimental ideal of the Christlike suffering of woman and the agony of the romantic genius, where they could define themselves as artists. As Gustavus Stadler explains, "The victim, the martyr, the consumptive: in these figures the discourses of romanticism and the literary phenomenon we have come to define as American women's sentimentalism meet."[71] While the figure of the woman artist as victim or martyr may appear to be a veil behind which to hide their ambitions, it is, ironically, through this veil that we see their highest ambitions to gain serious recognition.

Historians have noted the powerful and enigmatic role that illness and depression played in women's lives in nineteenth-century Britain and America. And many contemporary observers recorded the prevalence of nervous disorders among women, especially in America. As Elaine Showalter notes in *The Female Malady*, the numerous nervous illnesses experienced by women in the nineteenth century were linked by doctors to women's growing "ambition" and desire "to compete with men instead of serving them."[72] One of the most tragic and well-known such cases was that of Alice James, sister of Henry and William. She might easily have been a writer herself, as her diaries reveal much talent, but her family's severe repression of women's ambitions outside of domesticity caused her to find the only acceptable "career" that she could, namely invalidism.[73] The repressed ambition of the woman writer who could find no way to become an artist often turned into severe illness, as in James's case.

For Alcott, Phelps, Stoddard, and Woolson, although they did not adopt the role of the invalid, as Alice James did, illness was nonetheless part of their identities as women artists. All four complained of the kinds of ailments that were prevalent among women in the nineteenth century—insomnia, nervous attacks, brain fever, depression, neuralgia, writer's cramp—and they tried many of the new medicines and cures available. Alcott also suffered from the prolonged effects of poisoning from mercury prescribed when she had typhus during her stint as a Civil War nurse. Growing deafness plagued Woolson during the last fifteen years of her life. At one time, she wore "artificial drums" to aid her hearing, causing her severe discomfort. A doctor claimed that the pain she experienced was the result of "neuralgia." " 'Neurotic' was his word," she wrote, suggesting how common it was for doctors to diagnose women's illnesses as nervous disorders.[74] Phelps and Alcott were proponents of homeopathy, and Alcott unsuccessfully tried the mind cure. Both women also took opium to help them sleep, as Woolson and Stoddard likely did as well. Their physical ailments and the treatments they tried were prominent parts of their lives. As a result, Alcott and Phelps developed close friendships with their doctors, and Woolson and Stoddard were also on familiar terms with doctors they visited frequently. Doctors also appear in their fiction. Stoddard's story "The Prescription" is specifically about a doctor's treatment of a woman with a vague illness. And Phelps's novel *Dr. Zay* promotes homeopathy and female doctors for female patients.

The maladies these women suffered should not simply be labeled psychosomatic. But it is clear that their suffering was more than physical; it was often attended by deep depression. Woolson conveyed this when she criticized a man who "hasn't the slightest conception of either grief, or illness. I really think he believes that *I* cd. have got better soon, if I had only *tried!* He has never in his life had any real sorrows, or any illness — I mean the illness that hangs on, & baffles effort, & takes heart out of a man." Alcott, Phelps, Stoddard, and Woolson all lived with illnesses that hung on and sapped their energies, causing prolonged periods of depression and even breakdowns. But they wrote through the pain and viewed their suffering as an emblem of the writer's life, male or female. However, read together in the context of the grief experienced by so many stifled women at that time, we can link their illnesses to their culture's messages about the taboo against ambition in women. The same is probably true for Jewett, Davis, and Grimké, who also suffered from depression.[75]

As these writers achieved success, they reminded themselves and others of the hardships they endured and thus assured themselves and others that they would not be "spoilt,'" as Alcott said. To their families, friends, and readers they insisted that writing was a laborious task, and they often associated creativity and genius with the ailments they experienced. Their frequent illnesses therefore contributed to their self-image as writers. In her autobiography, Phelps referred to herself and other authors as "fevered by the creative faculty." Similarly, Woolson wrote, "I get nervous *mentally*, when very hard at work, and little things wear on me." To her family, she often made a point of how difficult it was to write. "I don't suppose any of you realize the amount of time and thought I give to each page of my novels," she wrote to her niece. "It takes such entire possession of me that when, at last, a book is done, I am pretty nearly done myself." Phelps's and Woolson's depiction of the writing process as "fevered" and taking "possession" of one recalls Alcott's "vortex" and suggests links to romantic conceptions of authorship and genius.[76]

They also often attributed their ailments not only to the draining nature of creative endeavor but to overwork. Alcott wrote of her father's stroke as the result of "overwork and taxation of the brain" and admitted that she was "doing the same thing myself" and could be "stricken down as he is," despite the fact that she was thirty-three years younger. Her earlier fits of intense writing were also accompanied by illness. After one such instance, in 1867, she wrote, "Sick from too hard work. Did nothing all the month but sit in a dark room & ache. Head and eyes full of neuralgia." Phelps complained that she was forbidden to write because overwork had made her ill. Alcott, Phelps, and Woolson also recorded breakdowns after they completed novels. And Woolson, who for years had suffered from inherited depression, apparently committed suicide shortly after she finished her final novel, *Horace Chase.* Her suicide during a prolonged illness was undoubtedly the result of her failing health and her disturbed mental state.[77]

In their emphasis on the hard work and mental energy they put into their creations, which they described as extremely draining, they ostensibly disavowed the divine inspiration of genius. Echoing Alcott's protestations about talk of genius and Woolson's claim that she possessed only "immense perseverance and determination," Phelps tried to disabuse people of the notion that the writer's life was an easy one. In her autobiography she explained to aspiring writers,

> Emerson's phrase was, "toiling terribly." Nothing less will hint at the grinding drudgery of a life spent in living "by your brains."
>
> Inspiration is all very well; but "genius is the infinite capacity of taking pains."
>
> Living? It is more likely to be dying by your pen; despairing by your pen; burying hope and heart and youth and courage in your inkstand. . . .
>
> There are privileges in [a writing career], but there are [also] heart-ache, mortification, discouragement, and eternal doubt.

Phelps drew on the authority of Emerson here to claim her ethic of hard work as the highest aim of the artist. Objecting to the assumption of a friend ("a learned man, accustomed to study from fourteen to eighteen hours a day at his own profession") that she could dash off a short story in a couple of hours, Phelps described at length the arduous, weeks-long process of writing one. But it was precisely because composing a short story required such hard work that she thought its status should be elevated to that of a "work of art."[78]

That pain and suffering were particularly emblematic of the woman writer's life was simply assumed by all four authors. Sympathizing with her friend John Hay on his recovery from completing a book, Woolson essentially told him that any strain he had experienced did not compare to what she endured. "For my own part, one novel takes *my* entire strength, & robs me of almost life itself! I am months-recovering. A man, however, is stronger." Of her mother, Phelps wrote, "She lived one of those rich and piteous lives such as only gifted women know; torn by the civil war of the dual nature which can be given to women only." After the success of *Little Women*, Alcott wrote to her publisher, "After toiling so many years along the up-hill road, always a hard one to women writers, it is peculiarly grateful to me to find the way growing easier at last."[79] They had learned from de Staël's *Corinne*, Barrett Browning's *Aurora Leigh*, and the biographies of Barrett Browning, Charlotte Brontë, and Eliot that the woman writer's life was marked by special hardships. Upon the posthumous publication of Eliot's letters and journals, Woolson wrote to a female friend that she felt their tone was the result of "the bodily weariness of such constant literary toil; and (alas!) the melancholy which seems to me to belong to all creative work in literature, or most all." Alcott's and Stoddard's comments on Brontë's hard life have already been noted. Stoddard's warrant repetition here: "Patience and pain ruled her [Brontë's] life, and brought to perfection her wonderful genius." Alcott's *Life, Letters, and Journals*, published shortly after her death, also placed her in this lineage. Woolson read her life story and was "greatly impressed" by Alcott's "heroic, brave struggles" peculiar to the woman artist.[80]

But as these women preached the virtues of perseverance and a strong work ethic and seemed to disavow otherworldly inspiration or genius, they also equated the suffering they experienced from their hard work and the unhappiness of their lives with genius, betraying a belief in their powers. By doing so, they aligned themselves with the great male geniuses whose lives were a sublime mixture of ecstasy and despair. In Woolson's story "A Florentine Experiment" (1880), a character describing the view of life embodied by Michael Angelo's sculptures concludes, "genius, I suppose, must always be sad. People with that endowment, I have noticed, are almost always very unhappy." Read in the context of Woolson's many references to her own depression and her claim that only unhappy women write, it is probable that she saw her sufferings as the burden she must endure and, perhaps, as evidence of at least latent genius, which she would never overtly admit to. Stoddard was the most forthright about her depression and genius. Musing upon death, suffering, and insanity, she confided to a friend, "Sometimes a cloud falls on me and I am so alone in its blackness that I am appalled. You foolish girl, genius is misery — Think of that noble misused creature Byron," she insisted, associating her own misery with that of the quintessential tortured romantic genius. In her autobiography, Phelps also explicitly equated the suffering she experienced with the maladies experienced by other great writers. In regard to her insomnia, she referred to de Quincey's similar agonies and wrote that his "Opium-Eater . . . stands for all time [as] one of the greatest pathological contributions of genius and of suffering to literature." She also recorded that

Longfellow once told her, "No truly sensitive man . . . can be perfectly well." In that vein she mused, "I would rather be well than be Shakespeare. . . . But would I? How can one tell?"[81] Illness was simply the price one paid for genius.

These four writers also linked their illnesses with their claims to the grief of genius by commiserating with male writers they admired. As Woolson wrote to John Hay about the illnesses they experienced after finishing a book, "Having just come out of a condition that had some resemblance . . . with yours, as you describe it, I can fully sympathize with you." Phelps carried on an extensive correspondence with both Longfellow and Whittier about their shared illnesses, especially insomnia. She sent powders to Longfellow and shared his pain. By equating suffering with the genius's life and showing these men that they shared their ailments, Woolson and Phelps covertly revealed a conviction that they shared their ambitions and abilities.[82]

Woolson's letters to another male writer with whom she commiserated about the tortured writer's existence most vividly suggest the complex web of pain, ambition, and self-assurance that marked genius. To Paul Hamilton Hayne, she counseled, "I beg you to fight against 'Depression,' that evil spirit that haunts all creative minds. . . . Think of yourself . . . as well, as highly as you can; be just as 'conceited' as possible. It will buoy you up; and [take] my word for it, even then you will probably estimate yourself lower than you ought to." This last sentence reveals the difficulties she had in taking her own advice. No matter how much she, Alcott, Phelps, and Stoddard tried to bolster themselves with a belief in their abilities, they were confronted with their society's taboos against such convictions in women. Woolson continued,

> You may laugh at my preaching self conceit as a *virtue;* but I have long thought that a good dose of self conceit was the best medicine for the creative mind. And I think you will find that the great artists are nerved to their greatest works by a sublime consciousness of & belief in *their own great powers.* And if a creative mind can only be surrounded and buoyed up by the close appreciative warm belief & praise of his own family, *then* he has reached the highest place this world can give him; he is *inspired* to do great things. Alas; few, few are so surrounded.[83]

Woolson seems to speak here from personal experience. That she preaches such self-assurance is a bold step for her, indeed for any woman of the time. She was acutely aware of how important it was for the development of one's full potential. Underneath the constant endurance of pain, as she reveals, women writers also had to maintain a belief in their powers. The only way they could do so, it seems, was by covertly comparing their suffering to that of the great male writers. The romantic equation of genius and misery helped them to persevere by fueling their belief in their own ailments as a sign of creative powers. And through their suffering, they felt they might earn the right to recognition. Afraid to ask for it boldly, they would "work and wait," in Alcott's phrase. They preferred to see themselves essentially as martyrs rather than as vain, ambitious authors. Only thus could they avoid being "despised," the fate, Stoddard claimed, of women who pursued art seriously.

In their musings about women's and men's mental and artistic abilities, their fears of appearing ambitious, and their covert admissions of genius in their complaints of ill health and depression, these four writers negotiated their age's prejudices against women as artists. In the process, they articulated their ambitions to be women artists, combining the masculine with the feminine and trying to find a way to strive for genius without becoming "unwomanly." Just as the male romantics adopted the pose of alienated artists, and antebellum women writers often adopted the pose of "scribblers," so did Alcott, Phelps, Stoddard, and Woolson adopt poses that helped them find authorial identities with which they were comfortable. The pose of the unambitious author has, particularly in the case of Alcott, been misunderstood as the whole of their authorial identities. But this squelching or disavowal of ambitions was not the complete story. The fact that the theme of artistry recurs in their works reflects their desire to contribute to the emerging high literary culture in America. As their female artist characters devote themselves to literature or art, so did these authors understand their work in a new, high cultural sense. Mary, Alicia, Ettie, and Psyche, as well as Avis, Diana, Persis, and Katherine, all aspire to the creation of high art. In fact, the authors' high aims are reflected in what their female artist figures are capable of achieving, such as Katherine's book of poetry, Alicia's or Mary's novels, Avis's painting, or Diana's sculpture. Each of these is regarded as a serious work of art by either the narrator or male authorities referred to in the texts. By creating such heroines, Alcott, Phelps, Stoddard, and Woolson circumvented, to some degree, the impasse facing the woman artist. However pessimistically they portrayed the outcomes of their female artists' careers, the authors' successes in these compositions and their identification with the grief of genius and ambition experienced by their artist heroines are testaments to their own ambitions and achievements.

CHAPTER FOUR

"Recognition is the thing"

Seeking the Status of Artist

In her essay "A Literary Whim" (1871), Elizabeth Stoddard described herself as "a member of the literary race," craving acclaim and appreciation from peers and critics. "*Recognition* is the thing; for praise I labor as well as money," she wrote. "The crumbs which fall from my pampered critic's table I swallow thankfully, even though I gain a dreadful indigestion thereby. It inflates my pride when I meet the distinguished of my class, and hear them say I am not unknown to them." The serious attention and appreciation proffered by esteemed and powerful critics and writers was central to her understanding of herself as an author. As she explained in a private letter, she wanted the "respect of the intellectuals . . . — common praise I do not care a copper for — . . . I want that which gives me faith in myself."[1]

For Stoddard and her sister authors, the ultimate evidence of artistic achievement was receiving the respect of the literary elite. They measured success not only in terms of sales but also in terms of critical praise. Acceptance by the reading public (made up mostly of middle- and upper-class women who possessed the leisure to read fiction) was not enough. Like their artist heroines, they also wanted acceptance by the men who ruled and policed the emerging realm of "high" literature. Rather than consider themselves part of a separate literary sphere for women, they befriended powerful literary men, enlisted their aid, and hoped that these associations would open the door to literary recognition. They understood that these men exerted a powerful influence over what Americans believed was serious, important literature worthy of being added to the cultural treasury.

In the eyes of Alcott, Phelps, Stoddard, and Woolson, serious recognition did not necessarily preclude acceptance by the reading public and the financial security that accompanied it. Success still entailed the attainment of modest popularity among the reading public *and* the approbation of the critics. As Nina Baym argues, "the realms of high, low, and middle culture" were not "distinct . . . for most of the nineteenth century . . . [and a] writer, especially a novelist, might realistically hope for conjoint critical and popular success."[2] However, by the 1850s and 1860s, critics were beginning to establish themselves as authorities who would have the final say on what authors and books comprised "American literature." Literary critics often revealed their confusion over the public's preference for books like Susan Warner's *Wide, Wide World* and began to announce their disdain for the literary tastes of the masses. Richard Stoddard displayed such antagonism when he wrote to his friend Edmund Clarence Stedman that he would look anxiously for Stedman's review of his wife's *Morgesons* (1862), "not on my own account, for I have no doubt of its merit, but for its influence on that eternal Donkey, the Public."[3] In addition, high cultural magazines, such as the *Atlantic Monthly* (founded in 1857), were beginning to establish themselves with the express purpose of publishing literature of a higher rank than the popular novels of the day. Alcott, Stoddard, Phelps, and Woolson came of age as authors during the period in which "the *Atlantic* group" was solidifying the delineation between literature for "the 'masses'" and literature for "the 'classes.'"[4] They were greatly influenced by the authority of these magazines, and they witnessed the birth of a high American literature in their pages and longed to be a part of it.

But as they made their bid for inclusion in the emerging high literary culture, they encountered serious obstacles. One of the most significant problems was that the critics, almost all men, tended not to take women writers seriously. Critics increasingly came to understand themselves as a class threatened by the popularity of female authors. Their efforts to lay claim to literary authority, therefore, often took on a gendered cast. But Alcott, Phelps, Stoddard, and Woolson tried to prove themselves to be exceptions — woman authors capable of genius. However, their attempts to form friendships with powerful literary men, to break into the pages of the nation's most esteemed literary magazines, and to gain critical favor from reviewers who tended to disdain women's literary efforts were met with limited encouragement, resistance, and even at times hostility. While Alcott, Phelps, Stoddard, and Woolson received enough encouragement early on from powerful literary men to raise their hopes and expectations and fuel their ambitions as artists, all of them eventually suffered disabling discouragement as they gradually discovered that the men controlling the emerging high literary culture could see them only as writers ineluctably marked by their gender and therefore as part of a separate class.

Making Friends with the Male Literary Elite

Alcott, Phelps, Stoddard, and Woolson each hoped to gain from their friendships with literary men varying degrees of advice, encouragement, help in getting published, favorable reviews, assistance with payments from publishers, camaraderie, and a less tangible quality—a sense of belonging to "the literary race." They wanted above all to be taken seriously. One way to achieve this was to befriend some of the nation's foremost male literary figures, as many women writers of their generation did. The most famous example, of course, is Emily Dickinson's relationship with Thomas Wentworth Higginson, whose *Atlantic* essay "Letters to a Young Contributor" conveyed his willingness to help unknown women writers. His generous encouragement in his position as an editorial assistant at the magazine and as a key figure in the emerging high literary culture was extended to Alcott, Phelps, Harriet Prescott Spofford, Helen Hunt Jackson, and many others. Jackson called him "my mentor—my teacher—the one man to whom & to whose style, I chiefly owe what little I have done in literature." It was also not uncommon for women writers to view their male mentors as father figures. John Greenleaf Whittier, who also used his ties to the *Atlantic* hierarchy to help young women writers get published and to give them the confidence they needed to pursue serious literary careers, was a fatherly mentor to Phelps, Sarah Orne Jewett, Lucy Larcom, and Celia Thaxter. Jewett, for instance, thought of herself as Whittier's "honorary daughter,"[5] just as Emma Lazarus and Alcott thought of themselves as Emerson's. Likewise, Henry Wadsworth Longfellow was an advocate of many talented women writers, including Phelps and Sherwood Bonner, and Stedman proved to be one of the literary men most generous in lending his aid to struggling women writers, providing inestimable encouragement and aid to Stoddard and Woolson, as well as Lazarus.

Most often, these literary friendships originated in the men's overtures, but on occasion they were initiated by the women themselves, who approached their idols in the hopes of finding a literary mentor or companion. Such was the case not only between Dickinson and Higginson but also between Bonner and Longfellow, Woolson and Henry James, and Lazarus and Emerson. It also was not unheard of for women writers to send their publications to the most esteemed male writers, just as Walt Whitman famously had done when he sent his *Leaves of Grass* to Emerson. Lazarus sent her first book of poems to Emerson, Stoddard sent *The Morgesons* to Nathaniel Hawthorne, and Rebecca Harding Davis sent her first story, "Life in the Iron Mills," to Hawthorne as well.

Despite the tremendous encouragement that many struggling women writers received from established literary men, their relationships reveal that they were always on unequal footing. Many women writers stood in awe of the more experienced and more successful male authors and editors whose attention they courted. They often approached such men with servile gratitude for any notice they received and with self-deprecating comments about their own meager abilities. An example of this attitude of inferiority is visible in a letter that Alcott wrote to Higginson's wife: "Please give him my hearty thanks for the compliment; also for the many helpful & encouraging words which his busy & gifted pen finds time to write so kindly to the young beginners who sit on the lowest seats in the great school where he is one of the best & friendliest teachers." As Alcott's words indicate, the relationships between male and female writers were likely to be that of teacher and pupil. Dickinson, who frequently sought out male "Masters," "preceptors," and "tutors," wrote letters to Higginson, which also convey the self-abasement of the student:

> Would you have the time to be the "friend" you should think I need? I have a little shape — it would not crowd your desk — nor make much racket as the Mouse, that dents your Galleries —
>
> If I might bring you what I do — not so frequent to trouble you — and ask you if I told it clear — 'twould be control, to me– . . .
>
> But, will you be my Preceptor, Mr. Higginson?[6]

Phelps's many relationships with powerful literary men particularly illuminate the support based on the implicit barriers to equality that marked most of these friendships. Early in her career, Phelps received letters of congratulations from Higginson and Whittier for her first story in the *Atlantic Monthly*, signaling a new beginning for her as a serious author. She went on to become a member of the circle of *Atlantic* authors who congregated at James and Annie Fields's house on Charles Street in Boston, where she cultivated friendships with many of the preeminent writers she admired. Chief among them were Whittier, Longfellow, and Oliver Wendell Holmes, all older men who essentially served as paternal substitutes. She carried on a long-term correspondence with each of these men that reveals her great admiration for them. Because they were older and already recognized as foremost among America's poets, it was inevitable that her relationships with them would be unequal. She often sent her work to them and solicited their advice, many times receiving well-meaning but nonetheless condescending responses. Longfellow, for example, told her that a poem she sent him was "simple and sweet," and Holmes wrote to her that her collection of stories (probably *Men, Women, and Ghosts*) was written from "your true woman's heart," describing "emotional complications" that only women could understand, suggesting his inability to appreciate her stories. Often he and Longfellow drew attention to her sex when addressing her or responding to her work, offering comments that pointed out the barrier between them. In her letters to them, as well, the inequality was palpable, as her following comment to Longfellow reveals: "It was more than kind in you [to write] — with your lame arm; which is almost as antagonistic to letter-writing as my lame brain."[7]

Phelps's relationship with Whittier, however, was more equitable. "Dr. Holmes and Mr. Longfellow have been very kind to me," she once wrote to him. "But no one is just like you." His appreciation of her work meant more to her than anyone else's, "except my father." His praise for one of her books "made me feel as if I hadn't lived or worked in vain." But Phelps at times also wrote to him in tones suggesting that he could never be a comrade or peer. When she asked him for his picture and sent hers to him, she wrote, "My picture will be of small interest to you, but yours will be an inspiration to me, like the measure of a Hebrew prophet. . . . that especial picture of you that I [request] looks as if 'you could not sin' — 'because you were born of God.' Forgive me for saying so much about it."[8]

Despite her humility and deference to Holmes, Longfellow, and Whittier, Phelps was not shy about telling the world she was friends with these luminaries. Chapter 8 of her autobiography focuses on her reminiscences about them. "Of our great pentarchy of poets, one — Lowell — I never met; and of another — Emerson — my personal knowledge, as I have said, was but of the slightest." But, she exulted in writing, "With the remaining three I had differing degrees of friendship; and to speak of them is still a privilege full of affectionate sadness."

She recalled a luncheon with Holmes and Whittier at which she was so awed she was unable to open her mouth. "[M]y speech seemed a piece of intrusion on the society of larger planets, or a higher race than ours," she claimed, indicating the extent of the disparity she felt between their world and hers. Phelps also publicized her relationships with these men in magazine articles, perhaps at least partially out of a desire to gain recognition by connecting herself in the public's mind with some of America's leading authors, as Susan Coultrap-McQuin has argued.[9]

Interestingly, Phelps had no such reverence for her male contemporaries, as is evidenced by the critique of William Dean Howells's theories of literature in her autobiography and the scathing attack on Henry James's biography of Hawthorne that she wrote for the *Independent*. In this latter piece, she charged that "[t]o defend our great novelist against our little teller of tales were a Quixotic waste of knight-errantry. The critic's imperfect appreciation of a nature and a work so foreign in h[e]ight, breadth, and depth to his own, is a small matter."[10] It is rare, indeed, to see a woman writer of this period venting such vituperation on a male writer. In her relationships with three of America's already canonized poets and in her defense of Hawthorne, we can see Phelps's reverence for the "select few" who had established America's high literature. But as her generation came of age as authors, Phelps was ready to compete in the marketplace and in the critical realm with younger male writers. Howells and James were not established masters but peers with whom she felt emboldened to do battle.

In stark contrast to Phelps's distinction between towering older masters and younger rivals, Woolson sought out and nourished relationships with the up-and-coming male writers of her day, particularly Stedman, Howells, and James. Her highest esteem was reserved for James, with whom she had a notoriously complicated relationship. While Woolson admired James as ardently as Phelps did Whittier, she also, at least initially, hoped for a literary friendship based on mutual respect and equality. Her deep reverence for him, however, did not preclude feelings of competitiveness. Her three stories that grew out of her relationship with James—"Street of the Hyacinth," "At the Château of Corinne," and " 'Miss Grief' "—offer the most striking literary exploration by any woman writer of this period of the obstacles women faced as they sought men's acceptance as peers in the literary world.

Woolson and James met in late April 1880 and remained friends until her death in 1894. Unfortunately, from what may have been a voluminous correspondence, only four letters have survived, all written by Woolson. As a result, efforts to understand the nature of their friendship have been largely speculative. For decades, the most popular depiction of the James-Woolson relationship came from James's foremost biographer, Leon Edel, who argued that Woolson harbored a deep desire for intimacy with James that was not reciprocated. Edel portrays Woolson as a "flirt" who "clung to [James] in a kind of pathetic dependency" and as someone who competed with him, possessing "a certain exalted notion of her own literary powers."[11] Recent feminist scholars have objected to Edel's portrayal of Woolson as a love-starved spinster pursuing the reluctant James all over Europe, insisting instead that she possessed a strong sense of herself as an author and sought out James for literary companionship and support, not love. " 'Miss Grief' " (1880) offers a particularly rich fund of evidence to support the latter view. And if read in light of the time in which it was written, the story strongly suggests that Woolson had serious doubts about the ability of James, a writer whom she admired above all others, to provide the literary and personal support she craved at a pivotal point in her life as she moved to Europe, alone after her mother's death. In addition, the story reveals that even before they became friends she felt compelled to challenge his critically acclaimed constructions of women.

Having spent a decade perfecting the regional sketch and writing her first novel, in 1879 Woolson was ready to take on an international project, perhaps inspired by the European writing of Henry James. She had written two anonymous reviews of James's *Europeans* for the *Atlantic* in 1879, one of which declared: "There is a great satisfaction in seeing a thing well done, and both in the substance and in the style of his books, Mr. James always offers an intellectual treat to appreciative readers; of course it is obvious that he writes only for the cultivated minority." In her review, Woolson claims membership in this minority, granting herself the status of an authoritative reader of James.[12] Their subsequent personal relationship, mirroring those between many other male and female writers, was marked by her attempts to prove herself one of the "cultivated minority" for whom James was writing.

Less than a week after she arrived (with her sister and niece) in London, this relatively reclusive woman went to Henry James's door with a letter of introduction from his cousin. But James was in Paris, and he returned just as Woolson left for the Riviera in search of a warmer climate. They would not meet until five months later (late April 1880), in Florence. It is very possible that Woolson wrote " 'Miss Grief' " during this interval between her first attempt to introduce herself to James and their eventual meeting, but she may have written it even before she left for Europe. In either case, the characters and subject matter make clear that the story was written in anticipation of meeting the great writer.

Although the story must have been written before Woolson met James (it appeared in the May 1880 issue of *Lippincott's*, two or three weeks after they first met), there are unmistakable similarities between James and the male writer who is the narrator of the story. The unnamed male author has inherited money as James had and does not need to depend solely on income from his writings; he writes "delightful little studies of society," as James did; and he claims, "I model myself a little on Balzac," as James's 1875 essay "Honoré de Balzac" indicated James did. Moreover, the male writer mentions two of his stories, "Old Gold" and "The Buried God," which featured antiquities and artifacts, as did James's "Last of the Valerii" (1874). And in the opening sentences of " 'Miss Grief' " the male narrator describes himself as a "literary success," which James had recently become with the sensational publication of "Daisy Miller." But these are all qualities that Woolson could have known from James's works and reputation as well as from their mutual friends Howells and John Hay.[13]

The fact that the narrator is not based on the actual James she personally came to know becomes even clearer when this earlier Jamesian character is contrasted with those versions Woolson created afterward in "Street" and "Château." In these later stories we are introduced to male figures who more closely resemble the kind of cool, detached, even arrogant personality James appears to have possessed. Raymond Noel and John Ford, who convince Ettie and Katherine that they have neither talent nor the right to pursue careers as artists, were modeled on the man with whom she had developed an intense relationship and who, she learned, had a more inflexible position on women writers than she had imagined. In contrast, the male writer featured in " 'Miss Grief,' " while reluctant to admit an "authoress" into his home, nonetheless admires her genius; he may be wary, but he never denies her talent or insists on the incompatibility of womanhood and art.

Although there are also similarities between the woman writer in the story and Woolson, there are also important differences. Chief among them is that Aaronna Moncrief, who goes by Miss Crief, is impoverished and unpublished and needs the narrator's assistance in launching her career, whereas Woolson had become well known in America as a writer of short stories and poetry and had just finished writing her first novel, slated for publication by Harper and Brothers. Therefore, rather than being simply an autobiographical projection, this story allowed Woolson to experiment with themes that reflect her anxiety about meeting James. More than anything else, Miss Crief represents Woolson's ideas about James's biases toward "authoresses."

In "'Miss Grief,'" Woolson depicts the efforts of a forlorn female author to gain the help of a successful male writer in publishing her work. As in "Street" and "Château," his perspective is privileged, but here it dominates to an even greater extent, for he is the narrator, speaking directly to the reader without the intervention of a limited omniscient narrator as in the other two stories. However, Woolson still finds ways to undercut his authority. The title itself, "'Miss Grief,'" is the name the male writer chooses for her. But the quotation marks Woolson places around the name call his perspective into question. This story is clearly his version of events, which may be distorted. The fact that the story is told through his eyes again distances the reader from the woman's experience and neutralizes her anger. As many critics have noted, this story in particular points a damning finger at the male literary world for its neglect of women writers. For Woolson to raise her voice and point that finger directly would have been too provocative, especially as she prepared to meet James, the current darling of the literary world. So, instead of directly telling her story of betrayal and exclusion, Miss Crief remains relatively silent. We experience her grief primarily through the male narrator, who at virtually every turn belittles and ridicules her in his own mind.

Initially, the male writer is put off by Miss Crief's tenacity in seeking an interview. But her ragged, impoverished appearance gains his pity. From the beginning, he believes she is "mad" (254) and insists on calling her "Miss Grief," using the name to suggest the grief she seems to cause him; however, the name most potently conveys the grief that she herself is experiencing, for her suffering pales in comparison to his. Contributing to her grief is his inability to recognize her as a peer. Instead of accepting her as a fellow writer, he constantly contrasts her with Isabel Abercrombie, the highly desirable, conventional woman he is courting. Whereas Isabel is young and attractive, Miss Crief is her exact opposite: "shabby, unattractive, and more than middle-aged" (251). When Miss Crief seeks entrance to the house, the narrator suspects she is some sort of saleswoman who wants to sell him antiques. But she slowly reveals that she has come for another purpose. "I am your friend," she insists. "I have read every word you have written." And she begins to demonstrate her admiration for him by reciting a passage from his work that happens to be the narrator's favorite. Here, like Woolson herself, she displays a deeper understanding and appreciation for his work than did the general public, who "had never noticed the higher purpose of this little shaft, aimed not at the balconies and lighted windows of society, but straight up toward the distant stars." Indeed, he admits that she "understood me almost better than I had understood myself" (252). By showing a genuine appreciation for his work, she gains his attention, and he agrees to read some of her work, including a drama, "Armor," the title of which signifies her need to protect herself from the blows of the male-dominated literary world and, by extension, perhaps even his own response to her work. Fortunately, he admires the drama and agrees to help her.

When he delivers his judgment of her work as "full of original power," Miss Crief begins to cry, "her whole frame shaken by the strength of her emotion" (257). Hanging over the side of the chair, she seems to have nearly lost consciousness, and the narrator fortifies her with wine and biscuit. What truly revives her, however, is his continued praise. Like Mary Hathorne in Phelps's "Rejected Manuscript," Miss Crief has been, essentially, dying of critical neglect. With no one to appreciate her work, she has lost the will and the means to live. As she tells the narrator, "My life was at a low ebb: if your sentence had been against me, it would have been my end. . . . I should have destroyed myself" (258). His praise alone, however, proves to be insufficient to sustain her. She will receive no thousand-dollar check, as Mary does, another key to the woman writer's survival. For her works prove to be unpublishable. Despite "the divine spark of genius" that he believes her works possess (257), he sees "faults" that must be corrected to gain the acceptance of an editor or publisher (258). "To me originality and force are everything," he tells her, echoing Ettie Macks in "Street," "but the world at large will not overlook as I do your absolutely barbarous shortcomings on account of them" (259). The "world at large," namely the male literary elite, demands the kind of training and adherence to forms and rules that also prohibit Ettie from entering the art world.

However, Miss Crief refuses to acknowledge any faults in her work or allow the narrator to make any changes. Exasperated by her "obstinacy," he gives up and decides to pass her works on to some of his friends in publishing, convinced that, flaws notwithstanding, they possess "originality and force" (259). But the pieces are rejected. The writer, therefore, decides on his own to revise them, but he soon discovers he cannot " 'improve' Miss Grief" (265). Shortly thereafter, he learns that she is dying of poverty and starvation. Her aunt, a powerless protector, expresses the anger that Miss Crief is herself incapable of voicing: "Your patronizing face shows that you have no good news," the aunt tells him, "and you shall not rack and stab her any more on *this* earth." He is confused and wonders of whom she is speaking. "I say you, *you*, — YOU literary men!" she replies. "Vampires! you take her ideas and fatten on them, and leave her to starve" (265–266). After this speech, the male writer's guilt compels him to tell Miss Crief that some of her work has been accepted for publication. Thus deluded, she makes the writer her literary executor and asks him to bury the rest of her unpublished work with her, which he does. Before she dies, she tells him, "Did you wonder why I came to you? It was the contrast. You were young — strong — rich — praised — loved — successful: all that I was not. I wanted to look at you — and imagine how it would feel. You had success — but I had the greater power" (268). As the story closes, he reflects on his own "good fortune," for he has succeeded not only in his career but in his personal life by winning Isabel as his wife.

Why was the injustice done to women writers at the hands of the male literary world on Woolson's mind as she anticipated meeting James for the first time? For one, she knew that James received favors and recognition that women writers rarely did. As she wrote to Paul Hamilton Hayne, "Mr Hurd, of Hurd & Houghton [the publishers of the *Atlantic*] . . . has let out that Howells [editor of the *Atlantic*] has 'favorites.' Chief among them at present, Henry James, Jr. I suspect there is a strong current of favoritism up there." More telling is what she wrote many years later to James himself: "I don't think you appreciated, over there, among the chimney pots, the laudation your books received in America as they came out one by one. (We little fish did! We little fish became worn to skeletons owing to the constant admonitions we received to regard the beauty, the grace, the incomparable perfection of all sorts and kinds of the proud salmon of the pond; we ended by hating that salmon.)"[14] There is an unmistakable strain of envy in this passage, as there is in " 'Miss Grief.' " These comments and Miss Crief's insistence that she possessed "the greater power" also suggest that the envy arose from the feeling that she was eclipsed by more established but not necessarily more talented male writers.

Edel's argument that as Woolson began her friendship with James she "felt herself, on some strange deep level, to be competing" with him is on the mark, although Edel fails to understand the context for this competition. It is likely that Woolson detected the rivalry in James's own writings before she ever met him. As Alfred Habegger points out in *Henry James and the "Woman Business,"* James was himself competing with women writers in general by adopting the themes of women's fiction and in a sense "correct[ing]" and "answer[ing]" them. As Habegger puts it, "James's own narratives have all along professed great authority on the subject of women." In a letter to James in 1882, Woolson accused him of treading on her literary territory. "How did you ever dare write a portrait of a lady," she remonstrated. "Fancy any woman's attempting a portrait of a gentleman! Wouldn't there be a storm of ridicule!"[15] At this time her first novel, *Anne*, and James's novel, *The Portrait of a Lady*, were being issued as books, both having been published serially in periodicals almost simultaneously from the late 1880 through 1881, and both dealing with the attempts of young women to find their place in the world.

But even when she wrote " 'Miss Grief,' " Woolson seems to have felt that James's work was competing with, perhaps even exploiting, women's fiction, including her own, and achieving recognition at the expense of women authors. To her, the failure of women writers like herself to achieve James's stature was primarily due to the contemporary conventional attitudes toward women writers and not the quality or subjects of their work. For example, James had recently become wildly popular in both Britain and the United States as the author of "Daisy Miller." Edel reflects the prevailing nineteenth-century response to the story when he writes, "James had discovered nothing less than 'the American girl' — as a social phenomenon, a fact, a type."[16] No doubt Woolson was aware that a generation of women writers before James, legitimate claimants to this achievement, never received the recognition that he now did. The aunt's accusation to the male narrator that he, as a male writer, is part of a class of "vampires" that "take her [Miss Crief's] ideas and fatten on them, and leave her to starve" (266) makes more sense when read in this context.

On the other hand, Woolson also indicated her deep appreciation for James's writings: "they voice for me — as nothing else ever has — my own feelings; those that are so deep — so a part of me, that I cannot express them, and do not try to. . . . they are my true country, my real home," she wrote to him in 1883.[17] Her sentiment that James possessed a greater power than herself to voice her own emotions is reminiscent of the male narrator's view in " 'Miss Grief' " that Miss Crief understood his work better than he himself did. Woolson felt such a deep affinity for James's writing that she seemed to have hoped for some reciprocity of understanding, a sort of meeting of the minds hinted at, indeed longed for, by Miss Crief. But Woolson's male narrator, while recognizing Miss Crief's "greater power," fails to comprehend the nature of her achievement, hoping instead to fix her work. The male writer's desire to "improve" Miss Crief indicates the real doubts Woolson had about James's ability to view her as an intellectual equal deserving of respect and admiration rather than paternalistic correction.

This lack of appreciation is revealed in the narrator's prejudices against women writers and his constant comparison of Miss Crief to Isabel Abercrombie. From the beginning of the story, he tries to make Miss Crief conform to his preconceptions of her, fearing that she may possess a supernatural power to control him. But this irrational fear is undercut by his own observations of her. Shortly after she reveals that she is an author looking for his assistance, he begins to perceive her as a threat: " 'She is mad,' I thought. *But she did not look so, and she had spoken quietly, even gently.* 'Sit down,' I said, moving away from her. I felt as if I had been magnetized; *but it was only the nearness of her eyes to mine, and their intensity*" (254; italics added). Just as he forms an opinion of her, he contradicts himself, suggesting that his impressions are based on prejudice rather than on facts. This passage reveals not only the narrator's unwarranted fear of the power the mysterious woman might have over him but also his inability to overcome his preconceived notions of women. Shortly thereafter, when confronted by Isabel's unpredictability, he is incapable of comprehending her as well, and he comes home confused about himself and her: "it was foggy without, and very foggy within. What Isabel really was, now that she had broken through my elaborately built theories, I was not able to decide" (255). Furthermore, he has already found a scapegoat as his excuse: when he sees Miss Crief's name on her manuscript, "A. Crief," he thinks, "A Grief . . . and so she is. I positively believe she has brought all this trouble upon me: she has the evil eye" (253). She too is part of his "elaborately built theories." To his relief, though, his temporary uncertainty about Isabel's true nature wanes, and he sees her again as the "sweet" (269), simple woman who knows her place.

The narrator of " 'Miss Grief' " here strongly resembles some of James's early male characters, most notably Winterbourne in "Daisy Miller" and Rowland Mallet in *Roderick Hudson*. For these men, as Priscilla L. Walton says about *Roderick Hudson*, "women function as the Other, the 'unknowable.' " All try, without much success, to understand enigmatic young American women. Just as Winterbourne in "Daisy Miller" is irritated when he learns that Daisy is spending much time with an Italian would-be suitor, so the male writer in " 'Miss Grief' " is upset when Isabel presumably flirts with "a certain young Englishman" (255). At issue are the "true" feelings of these women. The same is the case in *Roderick Hudson*, as Rowland attempts to deduce Christina's intentions with respect to his friend Roderick. Are these women displaying their "real" selves, or are they, as Christina is accused of being, merely superb actresses? Are they displaying, as Rowland muses about Christina, "touching sincerity or unfathomable coquetry?" The answer to this question was of the utmost importance be-

cause it indicated on which side of the fault line between angel and prostitute —
between "safe and unsafe," as Rowland says — these women would come down.[18]
Understanding these mysterious women, therefore, was a way of classifying and
containing them. Once they were understood, they could be controlled.

Drawing on Victorian conventions, James often had his heroes classify light
and dark women: the former asexual and a potential wife, the latter sexual and not
marriageable. The female sex, therefore, is divided into those who can be married
and those who must be shunned.[19] The narrator of " 'Miss Grief' " clearly evalu-
ates Aaronna in these terms and is confused by her: "A woman — yes, a lady — but
shabby, unattractive, and more than middle-aged" (251). In other words, she is
not marriageable, but she is respectable. The problem the narrator faces is how to
understand this woman who nonetheless has "sacrificed her womanly claims" by
persistently coming to see him (250). He confronts the same kind of problem that
Noel will in the later "Street" in trying to understand the motives of the forward
Ettie. As in that work, Woolson was aware that forward women forfeited men's
esteem. The task for the woman writer was to stake out a new territory, to be
taken for neither prospective wife nor sexually free woman, rather as fellow
author. Woolson critiques the angel/whore dichotomy by creating a heroine who
fits in neither category despite the narrator's attempts to classify her as a dangerous, "evil" woman. By portraying Aaronna with nothing to offer the man who
is drawn to women for their ornamental function, Woolson declares that the
woman writer does not desire the kind of attention beautiful young women
receive. She tries to get the male writer to accept her as a *writer*, not as a *woman*.
For if he views her as a woman, then any understanding between the two as
writers is forever lost, as Noel's insistence on viewing Ettie as a woman precludes
any relationship between them as artists.

Even more indicative of the narrator's unwillingness to accept women as writers is his clear preference for Isabel Abercrombie and the type of womanhood she
assumes in his imagination. For instance, he is "glad" that Isabel neither likes nor
understands Miss Crief's poetry, because it points to the contrast between the
two women. Miss Crief's poetry is "unrestrained, large, vast, like the skies or the
wind. Isabel was bounded on all sides, like a violet in a garden bed. And I liked her
so" (265). Interestingly, his description of Miss Crief's poems resembles the
ambition he had harbored for his own sketch that Miss Crief admiringly recited
to him on her first visit. Like the narrator, Miss Crief's writing indicates that she
too is reaching for "the distant stars" rather than the general public (252), a
sign of their competition with each other. Such an ambition, he assumes, is not

desirable in a woman. Instead, he prefers the woman happy in the "bounded" world Isabel inhabits, the woman who neither competes with him nor challenges his perception of her, just as Oswald preferred Lucille to Corinne and John Ford preferred Sylvia to Katherine.

Most male authors, Woolson perceived, were probably not ready to accept someone like her as an equal, in terms of ambition and serious devotion to literature. She would have to tread carefully, then, as she approached James. Indeed, she did not, as she later wrote to him, "come in as a literary woman at all, but as a sort of—of admiring aunt," despite being only three years older than he.[20] Having by then apparently given up on the possibility of a mutually supportive literary friendship with him, she limited herself to trying to be his ideal reader. But Woolson allowed Miss Crief to be what she did not dare herself: Miss Crief did not humble herself before the master, and she refused to let him correct or appropriate her art. In this way, then, she resembles Dickinson, who would not let Higginson alter her verse, no matter how much she admired his expertise. Ultimately, though, Miss Crief fails to interest the narrator in herself as a writer, displaying the deep ambivalence Woolson harbored about James's ability to look past her gender and receive her as a literary companion and equal. For while the male writer senses Miss Crief's "greater power," he also perceives her presence in his life as a "grief," and he is more than happy to bury her work with her when she dies, indicating how dangerous he thinks her writings are. Isabel's inability to understand Miss Crief's poetry is a great relief, and he hides the rest of her works from view, eager to extinguish the latent power that lurks within them.

In contrast to Edel's depictions of Woolson's amorous motives for seeking out a friendship with James, "'Miss Grief'" suggests that Woolson hoped for (although she did not expect) his understanding of and respect for her literary work and perhaps even some recognition of her genius. In 1884, Woolson wrote to the writer John Hay of her eagerness to find a kindred literary spirit and how rare such an occurrence had been in her life: "I shd. be so glad to have some talks with you . . . I am terribly alone in my literary work. There seems to be no one for me to turn to. It is true that there are only two or three to whom I wd. turn!" That Henry James was by that time one of the few with whom she would have liked to form a literary friendship is certain, but the meaning of the sentence is clear: he was not what she had hoped he would be; there is "no one" with whom to share her literary life. Even more telling are her 1883 letters to James in which she admonishes him for his inability to respond directly to her questions and carry on a real conversation, even about his work. She does not bother to ask him to respond to her work. Her August 30, 1882, letter to him remarks that in his brief replies to her very long letters there is "no allusion to anything I have said," indicating that her involved, carefully crafted responses to *The Portrait of a Lady* in her previous letter have gone unnoticed by him and, therefore, that James refused to reply to her as an appreciative and discerning reader. He would not allow theirs to be a writers' friendship based on the free exchange of opinions concerning their art, despite her clear desire to establish such a relationship.[21]

Woolson's predictions in " 'Miss Grief' " of how James would view her as a woman writer were correct. His destruction of many of her personal effects and letters after her death is eerily anticipated by the male narrator's burial of Miss Grief's writings, indicating that Woolson was aware of how dangerous men perceived the woman writer's words to be. Her extant letters to him and his essay "Miss Woolson," in which he assesses her work as "essentially conservative," indicate that she was correct in doubting his ability to accept her as a writer and a woman.[22] In her depictions of Jamesian men in "Street" and "Château," she wrestled with the problem of his potential power to extinguish her creative life. That she was able to overcome his judgment of women authors is a testament to her strong identity as a writer. Nevertheless, it is fair to say that the lack of appreciation and understanding she received from him contributed not only to her own personal and vocational grief but also to her marginalization at a time when the canon of American literature was taking shape. In " 'Miss Grief' " she uncannily forecast her fate and those of her female contemporaries: misunderstanding by male writers and rejection by the cultural forces of posterity. In addition, " 'Miss Grief' " expresses the anxiety that many women writers of her generation felt about approaching and befriending their male cohorts as well as their disbelief in men's ability to consider them equals in the literary world.

While Woolson seems largely to have accepted the terms James offered her in order to remain his friend, Stoddard was much more demanding of her male author friends; she was not afraid even to break off relationships with them when they refused to acknowledge her worth as a peer. It was primarily from the circle of her husband's friends that she sought appreciation and help, believing that these men would be her passport to a significant literary reputation. As she later wrote, "*I* have been made the little that I am, by my association with literary men." These associations introduced her to the ideal of the sanctity of the author's profession, and she was inspired by their seriousness. This is probably why she dedicated her first novel to "My Three Friends, the three poets, Richard, Bayard, George" (her husband, Bayard Taylor, and George Boker). Her desire to "prove to you males that I [am] your comrade" drove much of her early ambition.[23] She yearned for the fellowship of an experienced and successful author whom she could admire and from whom she could learn. But most of the male authors she met did not live up to her expectations.

At the beginning of Stoddard's writing career, two of the chief obstacles to her success, she felt, were "the contemptuous silence of [my] husband [and] the incredulity of all [my] male acquaintances." She had particularly rocky relationships with Boker and Taylor. She wanted their help in building up her reputation, and she asked them to write reviews for her, but she was not always happy with the results. And while they initially tried to support her budding "genius," her lack of respect for them and their condescending criticisms of her work led to great conflicts. When Taylor criticized *The Morgesons* (in a private letter to her), and she wrote to him scathingly in return, he protested that he was "a friend who loves you, who appreciates your genius." Nonetheless, he and Taylor resented her strong-willed, outspoken nature, and they made her gender an integral part of their attacks on her, calling her behind her back "the Pythoness" and "the Sybil," and in one dispute with her and Richard assuming that "E.D.B.S is at the bottom of this witches [*sic*] cauldron, stirring up her old hell-broth."[24]

Taylor, especially, tried to put Stoddard in her place: "[I now see] the intensely *feminine* character of your mind," he wrote her. "With all your power and daring—with an intimate knowledge of the nature of men which few women attain—you are *woman* to the smallest fibre of your brain." In this attack, Taylor gave her the greatest insult he could muster. Knowing that she was desperately trying to distinguish herself as an exceptional woman writer, he told her that she would always be beneath him and all other men, that she could never escape her sex and hence her inferiority. By doing so, he denied her any individuality and any distinction as an author. As she later wrote to Stedman, "He said what Caliban might have said, had he been an American author, to Miranda, when he got mad with her, and had the male vanity of wishing to crush her. . . . All I ever did against him—was to decry his immense vanity—to say that he was not a great writer." Years later she would confide to a friend that "[n]o person in this world has ever hurt and wounded us [her and her husband] individually as BT."[25]

The writer she most admired, Nathaniel Hawthorne, died shortly after the publication of her first novel. She had dared to send him a copy of *The Morgesons* and was delighted to receive an approving letter in return. He told her that he was "very glad to hear that you are writing another novel, and [I] do not doubt that something good and true will come of it." This letter was the "one immortal feather in my cap," she later wrote, the one sign of recognition that she had received from the powers on high. To prove her worth to her fellows who so neglected her, she included portions of the letter in her preface to *The Morgesons* when it was republished in 1901. However, Hawthorne had not lived long enough to be a sustaining influence on her career.[26]

In the 1870s and after it was Stedman who proved to be Stoddard's greatest supporter. He was a poet, critic, and editor who was coming into his own during this decade. He went on to become a very influential force in the New York literary world. It was to him that Stoddard owed "it all," she believed, when her reputation was recuperated in the 1890s. Although Stedman participated in some of the sniping about Elizabeth behind her back, and although she was unhappy with an early review he wrote of *The Morgesons*, she grew to feel that he believed in her more than any of her other peers. She also respected him as an author more than the other men she met and had a strong "ambition to please" him in verse, which she did. He wrote in his diary, "Read Mrs. Stoddard's poems. Have seen nothing so good from an American woman." He also felt strongly about her novels, writing to James Russell Lowell that he thought *Two Men* "artistic and powerful" and full of "genius." Most importantly, though, he did not belittle her or condescend to her. He respected her ambition, and she informed him, "it is a true comfort to have you understand and appreciate me as *no other has.*" While Richard had given "up hope," Stedman's faith in her never waned, she believed.[27] In the late 1880s and the 1890s, when Stedman helped her to republish her novels, he proved to be the kind of friend and mentor Miss Crief had looked for. He wrote a laudatory introduction to the republication of *Two Men* in 1888, which helped bring it to the attention of reviewers. And when he published *An American Anthology, 1787–1900* (1900), he included eight of Stoddard's poems, representing her prominently among the important American poets.[28]

Alcott, Phelps, Stoddard, and Woolson all felt that they needed the help of powerful men to advance their careers and reputations. But just as Alcott's *Diana and Persis* leaves the question open of whether Diana and her new supporter, Stafford, develop a romantic relationship, the issue of romance was always the subtext in friendships between single male and female writers. Woolson knew this in her relationship with James, and she tried to defuse the issue by assuring him that she felt herself to be a "sort of . . . admiring aunt" to him, and nothing more. This may also be why Phelps felt most comfortable approaching older men who would be surrogate fathers rather than potential husbands. As the only married woman, Stoddard probably was more successful at gaining the support of one of her male peers because personal intimacy was less of an issue. Because he was a friend of her husband as well, Stedman could give her advice, praise her writing, and work on her behalf without the appearance of impropriety.

Gaining Entrance to the *Atlantic Monthly*

One of the main goals of Alcott, Phelps, Stoddard, and Woolson in their friendships with literary men was not simply comradeship but, as in the case of Miss Crief, help gaining entrance to the literary world those men controlled. These women often asked for men's help or advice with publishers and editors, always conscious of the varying degrees of prestige associated with certain publishing houses and magazines. At the top of the ladder was the *Atlantic Monthly*. Gaining entrance to its pages was their dearest goal. As Ellery Sedgwick writes, the magazine was associated with "cultural accomplishment" for subscribers in remote areas cut off from the eastern centers of culture. For Howells as a young man in Ohio, "[r]eading the magazine and discussing it with friends led [him] to begin imagining a literary career."[29] The same was true for women writers, who even if they did live in the East, felt particularly removed from the centers of culture and privilege. Alcott, Phelps, Stoddard, and Woolson were all far outside the Hub of Boston and the elite literary circles (Woolson perhaps to the greatest degree). But the *Atlantic* connected them to that world, and, like Howells, they felt they could be a part of it by publishing in its pages, which all four did early in their careers.

When they saw their stories in the *Atlantic* next to works by such illustrious authors as Emerson, Hawthorne, Longfellow, Holmes, Stowe, and Whittier, they felt that they had arrived as authors. Phelps wrote in her autobiography about her early career: "I shared the general awe of the magazine at that time prevailing in New England, and, having, possibly, more than my share of personal pride, did not very early venture to intrude my little risk upon that fearful lottery." When her first story was accepted by the *Atlantic* in 1868, her friends voiced for her the amazement she felt at being placed in the company of established writers she so admired: "What! Has she got into the '*Atlantic*'?" Her welcome reception at the magazine awakened new ambitions in her, as it did in Alcott, who wrote in her journal in 1858, as she was beginning to feel confidence as a writer, "I even think of trying the 'Atlantic.' There's ambition for you! . . . If Mr. L. [James Russell Lowell, the editor] takes the one Father carried him, I shall think I can do something." Lowell did accept her story, giving her the encouragement she needed to devote herself to literature, a service he also provided for Stoddard. When he gave Stoddard advice and finally published one of her first stories in 1860, he "saved me," she later wrote. "[B]ut for him I should probably never have written prose again." Voicing the feelings of many women writers of her generation, Woolson wrote to editor Thomas Bailey Aldrich, "I have always had an especial regard for the magazine, — in fact I have never outgrown the reverential respect with which I used to read it when I lived in Ohio. And those of my sketches which have come out in its pages since then, have always had the air to me of having been presented at court." Valuing recognition from the literary elite over the larger payments made by other magazines, women writers time and again chose to publish in the *Atlantic*. Davis accepted less pay to appear in the *Atlantic* because, as she wrote to James T. Fields, "I am *in earnest* when I write and I find the audience I like in the Atlantic readers." Jackson insisted, "I am always glad to have papers in the Atlantic at less rate of pay than I get elsewhere, because I consider having them read by the Atlantic audience part of the pay." Like male writers, these women were "eager to ally their names with the great memories and presences on its roll of fame" and to be recognized by their peers, who were a significant part of the magazine's audience.[30]

The *Atlantic Monthly* offered a tremendous opportunity for women writers, giving them the impression that the realm of serious literature would not be off-limits to them, but from the beginning it also was clear that they would not be granted the same status as the men affiliated with the magazine. The Saturday Club, which started the magazine, was an exclusively male club (and remained so well into the twentieth century), as was its offshoot, the *Atlantic* Club. In fact, as Joan Hedrick writes, "Boston society was organized around a series of overlapping men's clubs, and the *Atlantic* was grafted onto this structure." Well after the magazine's formation in 1857, the decisions that charted its course continued to be made at club dinners from which women were excluded. As early as 1859, one disastrous attempt was made to include women at one of the *Atlantic*'s dinners. Although four women (Stowe, Spofford, Rose Terry Cooke, and Julia Ward Howe, the most valued female contributors in the early years) were invited, only Stowe and Spofford attended. Stowe, concerned about "the character of the gathering," requested that no wine be served. This created tension among the men, who felt that their genial gathering was being transformed by the presence of women. The men ended up drinking anyway. Spofford, who had only recently received attention after her first stories were published in the magazine, appears to have felt exceedingly awkward at the dinner. In letters to his mother,

Higginson mused paternalistically about his affiliation with "men and women of the 'Atlantic Monthly' " who "will one day be regarded as demi-gods" and about his induction of "little Harriet Prescott [Spofford] into that high company." He contemplated how Spofford must have felt as one of the two women in attendance: "Nothing would have tempted my little damsel into such a position, I knew; but now she was in for it." She was even seated next to the formidable Oliver Wendell Holmes — "think of the ordeal for a humble maiden at her first dinner party!"[31] Apparently, few of the other men in attendance shared Higginson's delight in the company of women at these hallowed events, for women were never again invited to an *Atlantic* Club dinner.

When the *Atlantic* commemorated its twentieth year in 1877 and honored one of its chief male contributors, Whittier, it invited not a single woman (contributor or otherwise) to the celebration. Fifty-seven men attended, including the illustrious Boston Brahmins who had started the magazine and a younger generation of men who, it was hoped, would carry on their legacy — Howells, Twain, Stedman, and Higginson, among others. As the after-dinner speeches commenced, "the women who were staying in the hotel filled the entrances and were favored with seats even between the tables," according to a newspaper account. Who these women were is not clear, but none had been formally invited. Within the next few days, angry responses from excluded women writers were published in eastern and western newspapers. In a letter that appeared in the *Boston Daily Advertiser*, the writer contrasted the equality of women and men in "the republic of Letters," where, she believed, "woman is a citizen," with the scene at the *Atlantic* dinner, where the "brilliant women" who contributed to the *Atlantic* were "conspicuous only for their absence!" Most upsetting to this letter writer, however, was the complete lack of any mention of the magazine's female contributors. She clearly recognized the fact that women's exclusion from the event meant that women writers could just as easily be exiled from the "republic of Letters." For, as Richard Lowry makes clear, the Whittier dinner was more than a chummy gathering of club men; it was a highly publicized step toward canonizing the principal (male) contributors to the *Atlantic*. In the words of the *New York Evening Post*, this very public neglect of women writers reminded many

that the Atlantic Monthly's staff of writers is much more largely masculine than is that of any other magazine in the country. It is, in a certain sense, our masculine magazine, and has always been so. A bigoted bachelor insists that this is because the Atlantic Monthly confines itself more wholly than any other magazine does to literature in the strict sense of the term, neglecting all the little prettinesses of household interests and all the gushing sentimentality which . . . women mistake for literature.

Although, as the *Post* writer notes, "there are women contributors named in its index whose fame is country wide," the *Atlantic*, as the fountainhead of America's "literature," was seen by many to be essentially a man's magazine.[32]

Two years later, when Holmes was honored on his seventieth birthday, one hundred guests attended the event, and this time women were among them. "The presence of ladies was something to be accounted for," Arthur Gilman noted in his reminiscences on the *Atlantic* dinners, "and Mr. Houghton said that they had always been wanted, but that the publishers had been 'too bashful' to invite them up to that time." The failed attempt in 1859 to include women in *Atlantic* dinners suggests, however, that the primary motivation for excluding them was not bashfulness but the feeling that the events themselves would be restricted, diluted, even ruined by the presence of women. Gilman lamented the changed quality of the later dinners to which women were invited: "The enlargement of the borders was like adding water to a cup of tea. There was a suggestion of the old times, but the strength of comradeship had been weakened."[33] In other words, the elite male club meetings, with their "intimacies," alcoholic drinks, and prestigious exclusivity had been transformed into more formal gatherings in order to accommodate women, who could not be "comrades." In 1882, Stowe became the first and only woman to receive the honor of an *Atlantic* party, this time a luncheon, to celebrate her seventieth birthday.

Despite these very public exclusions, women writers were quite visible in the pages of the magazine. More important, however, is the fact that their work was often viewed in a way that distinguished it from the serious literature the magazine supported. While the magazine's editors were known for cultivating an impressive list of female contributors and encouraging some of them to write fiction of a more "serious" bent, the publication of many of their works was viewed as a lowering of standards by some readers as well as the editors themselves. Stowe, the magazine's foremost female contributor, was never granted the kind of respect that the magazine's highest-ranked male contributors were. While she is occasionally cited among the inner circle of those authors who "made" the magazine in its early years, and although she was the only woman author to receive the recognition of a birthday party, it is clear that she was not accepted as one of the magazine's literary greats. Nor did she see herself that way.

In her biography of Stowe, Hedrick suggests that the *Atlantic*'s hegemony had the power to make women writers invisible to themselves, convincing even the most highly respected and prominent American female author that she did not belong in the male canon the magazine would consecrate.[34]

Lowell, editor of the *Atlantic* from 1857 to 1861, seems to have valued women's writing for its popularity with the reading public. He encouraged women such as Stoddard and Alcott and gave them the confidence they needed to take themselves seriously as authors.[35] Nonetheless, he and his assistant, Howard Ticknor, knew that the magazine depended on light stories of romance and domestic concerns, primarily contributed by women, to keep its subscription rates at an economically viable level, and Lowell received criticism from the Boston intellectual elite for publishing such stories. "The contemptuous Thoreau and the scholarly [Charles Eliot] Norton had their doubts about *Atlantic* fiction, especially that written by women," according to Ellery Sedgwick in his history of the magazine. "Norton warned Lowell that he heard the *Atlantic* roundly abused in some academic circles for publishing second-rate love stories." The male literary elite's opinions about such stories often influenced its perception of women writers as a whole. These men believed that the economically expedient decision to include women among the *Atlantic*'s contributors and readership compromised the magazine's mission to provide a belletristic, intellectual forum that could be found nowhere else in America, except in the *North American Review*, which was struggling to stay afloat.[36]

It was essentially these two groups — scholarly, elite men and the general (female) reader — that the *Atlantic* tried, in a delicate balancing act, to please over the years. The magazine's blatant attempts to attract female readers with work that it considered below its standards indicate that from the outset writing by and for women (most of it fiction) was viewed as a separate category from the magazine's primary content — the writings of the Fireside poets and essays by Boston scholars. And by publishing and perhaps even soliciting this kind of work from women, editors made it more difficult for women writers to be viewed as serious artists by the magazine's readers, reviewers, and editors, who were inclined to view such stories as typical of women's fiction in general. Alcott's and Stoddard's reception at the magazine was very much colored by Lowell's and Ticknor's perceptions about what type of women's fiction they wished to publish. Lowell was responsible for bringing both Stoddard and Alcott on board, but his encouragement did not lead to lasting relationships with the magazine for either writer.

Stoddard approached Lowell when the magazine was still in its infancy. Although she had published one of her early poems in the *Atlantic*, in 1858 she was eager to establish herself as a fiction writer. Her husband sent to Lowell, who had published many of his own poems, one of her first stories, "My Own Story." When Lowell did not respond in a timely manner, Stoddard took over the correspondence, asking for his advice and telling him, "although I am an old woman I am a young writer," signaling her willingness to play pupil to his tutor. When Lowell responded with suggestions for making the story more "respectable," Stoddard, as she reported in her next letter, followed his advice in hopes of pleasing him with her revisions. When the story was published in May 1860, she thanked Lowell for his "setting up of my story, and for the name also." What pleased her most was, "My friends speak well of the story, and say they think I am 'promising.'" With Lowell's guidance, she had gained entrance into the hallowed halls of high literature, and people were taking notice of her as a serious author for the first time. She also hoped to fulfill her "promise" by cementing her relationship with the magazine. "I hope that when I come along side with my small stores you will have stourage [*sic*] for me," she told Lowell.[37]

After the publication of her story, Stoddard continued to seek out Lowell's mentorship, although he clearly did not understand or fully appreciate her writing. At this time, though, she was less sure of herself and looked to him as an authority whose judgment must be sound. "Your warning strikes me seriously," she wrote to him, "am I indeed all wrong, and are you all right about 'going too near the edge' business? Must I create from whose, on what standard? . . . Do I disturb your artistic sense by my want of refinement?" She challenged his judgment that she "failed utterly" in a sketch she had published in the *Saturday Press*, but she could not help desiring to please him. "Your kindness and interest surprise me. You seem so much farther along in work than the men I know best — your experience and readiness give your works so firm a resistance, that I feel all you say very much." She also felt the inequity of their relationship, as disclosed in comments such as, "I hope I have not bored you." And she hoped that her next story "will not have the faults you have spoken of."[38] Undoubtedly, she wanted to send him this story for the *Atlantic*, but no other story of hers appeared in its pages.

In the spring of 1861, Lowell turned over the editorship to Fields. It is likely that Fields was not as indulgent toward Stoddard's frankness and that he was not receptive to her work. He hoped to keep the magazine genteel and respectable, two adjectives that, as perceived by the literary establishment at that time, did not characterize Stoddard's writing, which tended to be more romantic and passionate. When *The Morgesons* was published the following year, she ardently desired to have it noticed in the *Atlantic*, but Fields would not print the review that E. P. Whipple had offered to write because, Stoddard later wrote, "I had slandered one of the most respectable families in Essex County," a family related to both herself and Nathaniel Hawthorne. Although Hawthorne wrote to her personally of his admiration for her novel, it is possible that Fields, who, as his publisher, had made him famous, wanted to protect the author's reputation. Stoddard had (perhaps unwittingly) trodden on the sacred preserve of the male literary elite by portraying the Forresters of Salem as degenerate drunkards. What Whipple thought and perhaps wrote of the novel has not survived. And the *Atlantic* did not review her other two novels when they were first published. Only when her reputation was resuscitated decades later did the magazine take notice of her. In 1889, when all three of her novels were republished, a review of *Temple House*, considered representative of her work, appeared. The reviewer found the novel descriptive of "only a single dimension" and "intense, provoking, startling, and nightmarish." Despite some praise for certain "vigorous" passages, the critic found the book enigmatic and the author not "human" enough. Stoddard was very unsatisfied with this review and undoubtedly disappointed that her newfound recognition by other critics did not extend to the esteem of the *Atlantic*. But in 1901, when her novels were again republished, a more appreciative review appeared. The critic called her books "truly remarkable, though never widely read" and "strange and powerful." But the review is mostly an attempt to explain the strain of New England anti-Puritanism in her novels. There is little actual criticism. Nonetheless, Stoddard wrote then-editor Bliss Perry, "It was a sort of aged triumph, that review in the *Atlantic*."[39] This belated recognition, however, coming only one year before her death, did not reverse her earlier failure to be established as one of America's foremost female authors.

When Alcott broke into the early *Atlantic* with Lowell's help, she got the same kind of response from her friends and acquaintances as Stoddard had. "Hurrah!" she wrote in her journal in November 1859. "My story was accepted; and Lowell asked if it was not a translation from the German, it was so unlike most tales. I felt much set up." Like Spofford, whose first *Atlantic* story was so original and unusual for a woman writer that the editors assumed it must be a translation, Alcott received the ultimate compliment of being deemed above ordinary women writers. It was as if, after "pegging away all these years," she had finally arrived as an author. "People seem to think it is a great thing to get into the 'Atlantic,' " she wrote, and she foresaw having "books and publishers and a fortune of my own" as a result of her first "[s]uccess." In the "Notes and Memoranda" in her journal, she marked her *Atlantic* stories with a plus sign, denoting their importance to her not simply for their remuneration but for their prestige. As her mother wrote in her own diary when "Love and Self-Love," Alcott's first story in the *Atlantic*, was published, "She has reason to be encouraged for the Censorship of the 'Atlantic' is of no mean order."[40]

The *Atlantic* published two of Alcott's stories in 1860, although it also rejected an antislavery tale, "M.L.," which she had submitted shortly after the acceptance of "Love and Self-Love," a Gothic tale about a self-absorbed man who learns to love selflessly from his angelic young ward, who becomes his wife. Howard Ticknor, the assistant editor, wrote to Alcott that he was "disappointed" by "M.L.," which was not "pleasant." Furthermore, "the higher powers think that the majority of our hundred thousand readers wouldn't fancy it, either." He was referring to the antislavery stance of the piece. As Alcott wrote in her journal, she believed that the editors rejected the story because "the dear South must not be offended." To her, this was a great disappointment. For a magazine that was founded on antislavery principles and that had published many essays criticizing the southern institution, this decision appeared to be hypocritical. Instead of stories that addressed such unpleasant themes, Ticknor tried to steer Alcott in a different, more appropriate direction, presumably because the fiction needed to be lighter than the essays. His advice resulted in her writing of "A Modern Cinderella," as discussed in Chapter 3. After this, Alcott began to emphasize in her journal the money she received from the magazine and her ability to pay her bills rather than her high ambitions.[41] Instead of being raised up to a new level in America's literary landscape, Alcott found that the price for recognition she received for her *Atlantic* stories was being relegated to a proper sphere of domestic writing.

Significantly, her opinion of the *Atlantic* fell precipitously after the approbation she received for "A Modern Cinderella." The next story she submitted, "Debby's Début," was accepted in December 1860. In April of the following year, she wrote to a friend, "being sure of my $75 or 100 I fold my hands & wait, thinking meantime as you will do when you read it that it dont [sic] take much brains to satisfy the Atlantic critics. They like that flat sort of tale so I send it as I should a blood & thunder one if they ordered it for money is my end & aim just now." Gone were the pride and ambition she had felt when her first story was accepted. After her initial enthusiasm for having an original story like "Love and Self-Love" accepted and mistaken for a German translation, and her disillusionment when the *Atlantic* didn't accept "M.L.," she faced the fact that the magazine didn't want inventive and powerful stories from her after all. When the editors then lost her "Debby's Début," Alcott became even more discouraged, because, "I cant [*sic*] send another till [it] is well out of the way." In December, Ticknor wrote to Alcott that he had found the story but that he was "led to believe that the tale should have been returned to you long ago." Alcott had to remind him that he had already accepted it and paid her for it, upon which he agreed to "send the MS to the printer." It wasn't published until August 1863, almost three years later.[42]

When Fields took over the editorship in 1861, he, as both publisher and editor, was eager to bolster the magazine's subscription rates. The way to do this, he believed, was by shortening the length of the heavy essays and by providing short, light pieces — such as stories and articles from popular women writers like Stowe and Gail Hamilton — which would counterbalance the magazine's more serious offerings. Under his editorship, fiction, much of it by women, briefly became a more prominent feature of the magazine. However, in the mid-1860s, the percentage of contributions of fiction by women dropped significantly from 90–100 percent of the total fiction featured in the first seven years of the magazine to only 30–40 percent. A growing number of men were moving into the area of fiction, and by the time Fields's editorship ended in 1871, men virtually dominated this department. Richard Brodhead claims that the *Atlantic* "underwent a palpable stiffening of its selection criteria" during this period, and Kenneth Lynn notes that the magazine "was in a state of transition in the mid-1860s." Lynn attributes the shift to the changing literary marketplace: "the New England literary wave had actually crested a decade before and was now beginning to break," and the *Atlantic* "had begun to feel the hot breath of the New York competition," primarily from *Harper's Weekly*.[43] In addition, two new competitors arrived on the scene: the *Galaxy*, which began publishing in 1866, and *Lippincott's*, which began in 1868.

This competition created an even more pressing need for Fields to differentiate the *Atlantic* from the new upstarts, and its stiffening of standards, most likely a reaction to a diversifying market, had a profound effect on the presence of female authors in the magazine's pages. It seems that, fearing the scales had tipped too far in the direction of the mass-market magazines, the *Atlantic* strengthened its elitist position in part by publishing less fiction by women. Thus, the magazine cultivated a niche for itself in the market based on its reputation as the home of the most respected American authors: Emerson, Longfellow, Lowell, Holmes,

Hawthorne, and Whittier. Fields began the intense promotion of these authors, advertising their association with the magazine and marketing their portraits as special incentives to new subscribers. Whereas fiction in general had previously been relegated to an inferior position vis-à-vis serious prose, the *Atlantic* now began to distinguish between high and low fiction, favoring work by Henry James and John W. DeForest to the stories of romance and domestic concerns by women, work that had been popular in the late 1850s and early 1860s.[44] As literary tastes tended more toward realism, the kind of stories that many women were contributing were deemed less important. Stoddard's stories, which were intensely romantic in their depiction of passion and the female psyche, were not wanted. Whereas Lowell "object[ed] strongly to the realistic tone of our present literature," Stoddard informed Stedman, Fields would become a proponent of the new school. But even Davis's stories, which were early examples of realism, were turned down by Fields. Despite the success of "Life in the Iron Mills" and her novel *Margaret Howth*, Fields dropped her from the list of contributors in 1868 when she published her novel *Waiting for the Verdict* in the *Galaxy*.[45]

In 1862, Fields had given Alcott the message that she was no longer welcome at the *Atlantic*, giving her the biggest blow of her career. Despite the fact that he and his wife, Annie, who was a distant cousin of Alcott's, had taken her into their home, Fields made it clear to Alcott that he did not think her worthy of induction into the exclusive club to which Lowell had admitted her. "Debby's Début" had been accepted while the *Atlantic* was still under Lowell's watch, and as soon as Fields took over, the story was no longer wanted. In January 1862, Fields gave her forty dollars to start a kindergarten and told her, according to Alcott, "Stick to your teaching; you can't write." Alcott accepted his bargain and perhaps his opinion as well, but she didn't last long as a teacher. "I went back to my writing," she wrote in her journal, "which pays much better. . . . Being wilful [*sic*], I said, 'I won't teach; and I can write, and I'll prove it.' "[46] It is quite likely that Fields based his opinion of Alcott's worth on the two stories Lowell had encouraged her to write and that she herself felt were inferior. Had he read "M.L.," his opinion might have been different, for the story foreshadows some of her Civil War stories, which Fields would later praise.

During her stint as a teacher, Alcott stayed in Boston with the Fieldses and met many of the *Atlantic*'s luminaries, including Stowe, Holmes, and Longfellow. This must have been a painful period for her. But she did get the opportunity to prove to Fields that he was wrong. In 1863 she had her big break with "Hospital Sketches," which was published in the *Commonwealth*. She received universal praise for her depiction of her wartime experience as a nurse and managed to catch Fields's attention. As the sketches first began to appear, Fields accepted her poem "Thoreau's Flute," which commemorated the man she had grown up admiring. It was not she, however, who had approached Fields with the poem. Bronson Alcott had brought the verses to Sophia Hawthorne, who, Louisa wrote, "without telling me their destination sent them to sit in high places where they hardly belong." Annie Fields also helped Alcott edit the poem, and it was with this support that she was brought back into the fold. When the poem was published, it was "praised & glorified," and she was bestowed "the honor of being 'a new star' & 'a literary celebrity.' "[47]

In August 1863, Alcott ventured to send a new story to Fields, this time a story about the war, "The Brothers." Fields's acceptance of the story appears to have been predicated on the newfound respect he had for her because of "Hospital Sketches." The story features a nurse reminiscent of the narrator of "Hospital Sketches," establishing a clear link between this tale and the sketches. But Alcott remained skeptical about the *Atlantic*. She wrote to James Redpath, who published "Hospital Sketches" in book form, that she planned to publish more stories in the *Atlantic* and she hoped to collect them in a volume, "when a good variety has stood the Atlantic test (which by the way I dont [*sic*] value two straws except as far as others are influenced)." No longer holding the illusion that the *Atlantic* was the ultimate measure of a writer's worth, she nonetheless knew that most people perceived it that way, and she still wanted to make a name for herself as an important author.[48]

At this time, Fields proposed to Alcott that she go to Port Royal, North Carolina, "to teach contrabands" and that she write about her experiences for the *Atlantic*. Clearly, Fields wanted something along the lines of her "Hospital Sketches." According to Bronson Alcott, they were to be called "Plantation Sketches." Alcott desired greatly to go, but as a young, single woman, she was forbidden to by "Mr Philbrey," presumably the director of the enterprise.[49] In the meantime, Fields asked if she didn't have a book that he might be interested in publishing. She wrote in her journal, "Father spoke of 'Moods' & the great James desired to see it. So I fell to work & finished it off, thinking the world must be coming to an end & all my dreams getting fulfilled in a most amazing way. . . . There is a sudden hoist for a meek and lowly scribbler who was told to 'stick to her teaching,' & never had a literary friend to lend a helping hand!" It appeared as if she would finally become the successful and well-respected author she dreamed of becoming through her association with the *Atlantic* and the house of Ticknor and Fields, the most respected publishing firm. But it was not to be. She discovered that "it would be a breach of contract to give [*Moods*] to Fields," so she had to give it to Redpath. Subsequently, Fields rejected her new story, "On Picket Duty," and a year later, in November 1864, Ticknor rejected "An Hour." "As I thought it good," she confided in her journal, "was pretty sure they would n't [*sic*] take it." (Alcott promptly sent it to the *Commonwealth*, where "it was considered *excellent.*") She was also convinced that the *Atlantic* rejected both stories because they were about slavery.[50] But the former was a war story, and it appears that Fields's interest in such timely fiction was now tempered by the need to provide a distraction for readers from news of the war.

Alcott never again published a story in the *Atlantic*. At the time Ticknor rejected "An Hour," however, he also accepted a "fairy tale," "Nelly's Hospital," for Ticknor and Fields's children's magazine, *Our Young Folks*. He also asked for more, which she gave him. Ticknor wanted to publish the new fairy tale as a book, but then he began to hedge, reminiscent of how he had treated "Debby's Début." He told Alcott the manuscript was lost, initiating a protracted negotiation between author and editor that was never resolved to Alcott's satisfaction. Meanwhile, he also rejected a volume of verses. Two years later, in 1867, he paid Alcott for what had been the anticipated sales of the book and closed the matter. In 1869, Alcott wrote to Lucy Larcom, coeditor of *Our Young Folks*, hoping still to recover the manuscript. She indicated that Ticknor lost the manuscript twice (the second time after she had rewritten it) and the blocks as well. "I shall be very grateful for the kindness," she wrote Larcom, "as my own researches only end in wrath & vexation of spirit." With these words one could sum up Alcott's relationship with the *Atlantic*.[51]

When Alcott's first novel, *Moods*, appeared in 1864, the *Atlantic* did not review it, even though Fields had recently been so interested in her work. In the years that followed, her career went in the direction that Ticknor had suggested. Instead of becoming an author known for her realistic stories of slavery or women's experiences of war, with the publication of *Little Women* in 1868 she became a children's author. This was how the *Atlantic* would view her ever after. In 1870, it condescendingly reviewed her children's book *An Old-Fashioned Girl*, opining that it possessed "some poor writing, and some bad grammar," but "pleasing the little book remains . . . and nobody can be the worse for it." In 1878, the "Contributors' Club," in a column on "the real secret of literary hits," commented on "Miss Alcott's books," referring only to her children's books but citing them as among the age's most popular. Little did the *Atlantic* know that it had in the previous year very favorably reviewed her adult novel, *A Modern Mephistopheles*, which was published anonymously. George P. Lathrop was convinced that it came from the pen of Julian Hawthorne, an assumption deemed a "compliment to his powers." In stark contrast to the belittling tone the magazine took toward *An Old-Fashioned Girl*, it saw this novel as possessing "signal force" and "vigorous and clear" language.[52] The Alcott who had been pigeonholed by the *Atlantic* as a children's writer had continued to exercise her inventiveness and considerable creative abilities, albeit anonymously.

After her death, the *Atlantic* reviewed the volume of her letters and journals published by Ednah Cheney, concluding that "[h]ere was a strong, affectionate nature with powers half understood, restlessly beating against the cage, . . . the power was used recklessly, and yet it was a power." Especially noteworthy is the reviewer's conclusion: "One cannot escape the conviction that great possibilities were lost in Miss Alcott's career."[53] This writer apparently knew nothing of the disappointments and rejections she had suffered at the hands of Ticknor and Fields that shut off the very "possibilities" that might have given her a very different legacy. The *Atlantic* certainly had the power and opportunities to make a name for Alcott as one of its foremost contributors. Instead, it pushed her in the direction of children's literature, for which it afforded her little respect.

Phelps was much more warmly received by Fields than Alcott was, leading to a lifelong relationship with the *Atlantic* and its publishers, even though her reputation with the magazine's editors declined steadily over the years. Her status rested primarily on her popularity with the reading public rather than on the magazine's critical approval. On Annie Fields's advice, James Fields published Phelps's first novel, *The Gates Ajar* (1868). Owing to its success, Phelps became one of the publishing house's most prominent authors. Throughout her career, the same firms that published the *Atlantic* published all of her books. But it was her contributions to the magazine that had critical currency. Although *The Gates Ajar* had made her a household name, it was "The Tenth of January" (1868), one of her first stories in the *Atlantic*, that "distinctly marked for me the first recognition I received from literary people," she wrote in her autobiography. Higginson and Whittier sent her letters of praise, giving her faith in herself. "Both these distinguished men," she explained, "said the pleasant thing which goes so far towards keeping the courage of young writers above the sinking point, and which, to a self-distrustful nature, may be little less than a life-preserver." It is to these two men that Phelps credited her courage to strive for artistry and serious recognition, just as Stoddard had claimed that Lowell's acceptance had "saved" her. Phelps also recalled "the pleasant, the hopeful, the appreciative words with which [Fields] stimulated my courage and my work." James and Annie Fields made Phelps feel welcome at the *Atlantic* and in their home when she was still "a frightened young author." She read her works in progress to them, including *The Story of Avis*, and respected their judgment. She viewed James as the ideal man and editor, believing that "[h]is fastidious and cultivated literary taste was sensitive to the position of women in letters. He was incapable of that literary snobbishness which undervalues a woman's work because it is a woman's."[54]

Unfortunately, Phelps's relationship with Fields's successors was not as unproblematic. As Susan Coultrap-McQuin has shown, the number of pieces she published in the *Atlantic* declined over the years. And Phelps herself was increasingly aware of the magazine's less than enthusiastic response to her work in the 1880s and after. The publisher Henry Houghton, for one, did not meet the standard of the "gentleman publisher" that Fields had set, and she seems to have felt that he didn't value women's writing as highly as Fields did. "I feel more than sorry to see the 'women' left out of your 'Men of Letters' series," she wrote to him. "Surely, as Mr. Fields said, it is too late for that." She also had differences with Howells. In 1871, his first year as editor, when he rejected one of her stories, Phelps complained to then-publisher James R. Osgood, "Mr. Fields never returned me a story—since I was a school-girl." She recognized that she differed widely "from his [Howells's] views of the province of art in fiction" because he "never does nor ever will like, an 'unpleasant' story," and she asked that Mary Livermore review *The Silent Partner* instead of Howells because he "would never feel interested in 'my style.'"[55] Shortly thereafter, Phelps insisted to Osgood that "I must go where I am most wanted, and best paid," signaling that she did not feel valued by the *Atlantic*. In 1874, she told Howells that if he wished to receive stories from her, he would have to wait in line behind four other magazines that she considered "more faithful and generous friends." Her relationship with Howells was always rocky. She bristled under his criticism of her poetry and raised objections when he wished to cut an installment of her novel *Friends: A Duet* to accommodate Henry James. "It is the most important climax in the book," she insisted. "The very fact that there is so much of Mr. James makes it more important to me that my story should have its fair artistic effect." Just as Woolson suspected, Howells was privileging James's work over that of lesser-valued women writers. In 1876, when Osgood was very slow in responding to

Phelps's letters about two books she was publishing with his firm, she wrote to him of her "sense of neglect and general injury," summing up her relationship with the *Atlantic* during this decade.[56]

In the 1880s and 1890s, Phelps became increasingly aware that her work was even less welcome at the *Atlantic* than it had been under Howells's editorship, which ended in 1881. To Aldrich she wrote, "I shall not overburden your pages with either my 'gloom' or my theology," apparently quoting his criticisms of her work. And she also knew that Horace Scudder, one of the magazine's most prominent reviewers and editorial assistants, did not like her work. In fact, she refused to send him her submissions, routing them through Houghton, who continued to desire to publish her books, undoubtedly because of her high sales. It was a shrewd business decision on her part to exploit her relationship with the publisher in order to gain further exposure in the *Atlantic.* Coultrap-McQuin suspects, for instance, that Houghton made Scudder publish her novel *A Singular Life,* about a Christian reformer, in the *Atlantic* despite the latter's dislike for it, in order "to promote book sales."[57]

In addition to much behind-the-scenes ill will, Phelps's reputation also declined very visibly over the years in the *Atlantic*'s pages. The first review in the *Atlantic* of any of her novels bestowed the highest praise she would receive from the magazine's critics. *Hedged In* (1870) was hailed as "a work of art." There is nothing but admiration in this review, which declares that "in power [the novel] exceeds anything else which the author has written." More specifically, Phelps is praised for her "hopeful look at the worst side of things." The reviewer finds no fault with the Christian theology of the novel, respects her earnestness, and insists that "there is nothing acrid in her moral judgments." In fact, she is seen as rising above the "effeminate culture which sickens at the world as it is" and demonstrating a "faith in its destiny" that is refreshing. But when the next review of her work appeared in 1875, Howells declared of *Poetic Studies,* "we blame the poet's unwilling — it seems unwilling rather than inadequate — art, because in the inferior pieces here collected we have so often the darkness without the fascination." He then goes on to associate the work's weakness with the author's gender: "the effect is oddly marred at times by the author's inability to let well alone — by a certain feminine desire to get yet one sigh or one gasp more out of expression."[58] Howells shows his distaste for her work by aligning her with feminine sentimentalism.

The *Atlantic* reviewer Harriet Preston took an even more decided stance against *The Story of Avis,* viewing it as representative of all that was deemed to be inferior or even dangerous in women's writing. Preston took issue with the novel

on the basis of "what we believe to be a wholly erroneous theory of womanhood . . . that marriage is not a woman's best and highest destiny." The review
contains an extended discussion of the merits of marriage, even declaring that
only married women have "achieved the highest order of distinction." But Preston's strongest objections to the novel are to its "frantic" and "overwrought"
emotions and its overt moralizing, especially by a "Boston woman" (and, the implication is, an unmarried one). Preston concludes, "One is sometimes tempted to
wish that she had never written prose at all, but only poetry. . . . Surely she might
then have been better than an exceedingly popular writer, not only to-day but tomorrow. Possibly she never would have swerved from her highest line if she had
not become the prey of a stringent set of 'reformatory' ideas." Phelps's attempt to
engage issues concerning the status of women lowered her in the eyes of the
Atlantic's critics, despite the earlier praise for *Hedged In*, a novel decidedly driven
by "reformatory ideas." Preton's review provoked a lively discussion in the *Atlantic* "Contributors' Club," one protracted enough to elicit the following quip in the
March 1879 Club, almost a year after the review's first appearance: "There was
getting to be an apprehension—I might say almost an anxiety—in the public
mind . . . lest there was to be no more about Avis in the Contributors' Club; this
was happily relieved by the February number." Contributors had been remarking
on various aspects of the book and the review, many defending Phelps against
attacks by Preston and other critics. "I read Avis, and gave thanks," wrote one. "Its
feverish intensity and occasionally vicious rhetoric did not escape me, but the
brave, clear intent of the book was so all-engrossing to me . . . that I was utterly
bewildered by the hue and cry of the critics." Another insisted that the unknown
reviewer was wrong about matrimony's being a precondition for women to create
great art, and that *The Story of Avis* did not deserve the "brittle statements" that
"newspaper men" echoed in the belief that they were serving "the public good."[59]
Despite her defenders, though, those in power at the *Atlantic* continued to classify
her as a "feminine," "overwrought" writer unworthy of a serious reputation. In
fact, serious treatment of her publications dwindled over the years so that when
Horace Scudder wrote about her novel *Beyond the Gates* (1883) in an article on
depictions of heaven, only a plot summary was provided.[60] It is likely that the
Atlantic's reviewers were told to tone down their criticism of an author whom the
magazine's publisher valued very much. Therefore, she remained one of their
most visible contributors, but she was on very uncertain footing with those who
had power to grant her inclusion among the literary elite.

Woolson's relationship with the *Atlantic* was more encouraging but also more limited, owing to Woolson's stronger relationship with Harper and Brothers, her main publisher. During Howells's editorship in the 1870s, the *Atlantic* had begun to gather a promising new crop of contributors, and Woolson was among them. In the early years of his tenure, Howells was most concerned with maintaining the magazine's reputation and pleasing his Brahmin mentors by continuing to publish and favorably review the Boston literary lions who had made the magazine. But he was also keenly interested in promoting realism and the new writers who were producing it. Many of these were women, and in the 1870s the percentage of stories by women increased to about 70 percent.[61] But Howells was incorrect when he surmised that "there were more women than men" among the new contributors he brought to the *Atlantic*. (His list of the best young writers he introduced to the magazine's readers — fifty-nine in all — included only nineteen women.)[62] Nevertheless, Howells supported many of the women local colorists.

Woolson found her regionalist stories appreciated by Howells, and in the fall of 1874 she wrote to him, "It has given me great pleasure to enter within the 'Atlantic' circle." In 1877, Howells brought her farther into the inner circle by including her in his new "Contributors' Club." Late that year she sent him a piece "for the 'Club'" and told him, "I am much pleased to be put into the Atlantic announcements for 1878."[63] She was developing a professional relationship with Howells that began with an acquaintanceship in St. Augustine, Florida, a favorite vacation spot.

Initially, at least, Woolson might have felt that she was included among Howells's favorites. While writers like her friend Paul Hamilton Hayne were trying to get Howells's notice, she was accomplishing that. Howells's review of her first book, the collection of stories titled *Castle Nowhere* (1875), was cautiously encouraging. He found three of the stories (those that had been published in the *Atlantic*) to be a "triumph" and a "success," although he criticized the romanticism of the title story. Thomas Sargeant Perry reviewed her next book, *Rodman the Keeper* (1880), and found many of her characters to "read like what one finds oftener in poor novels than in real life," although he believed that she could "do good work if she will keep 'closer to the record.'" But when her novel *Anne* (1882) appeared, the review was one of the most laudatory that had appeared in the *Atlantic*'s pages. The reviewer, Horace Scudder, was optimistic about her future success and compared her favorably to James and Howells. Her abilities, he wrote, hint "at a power which may possibly give her singular success." Significantly, however, he began his reflections on her work by invoking the memory of two of the *Atlantic*'s most prestigious legacies. "We shall remember when Longfellow and Emerson died and were buried," he writes, "can it be possible that we were then reading the works of men and women who now have an enduring fame, and did not recognize how surely they were in the succession of literature?" Scudder's remarkable suggestion is that he foresees such an eminent place in the succession for Woolson, a place, if not directly next to Emerson and Longfellow, then at least in the canon of America's high literature. The assumption is that their successors would be women as well as men and that Woolson was foremost among the women writers of her day and most likely to attain such an eminent position. However, Scudder goes on to cite evidence of the "immaturity of the book" and asserts that *Anne* will be remembered "chiefly as a marking stage in the author's development." Despite the author's promise, he implies, she has not yet arrived, and she must carefully heed his advice if she desires to do so.[64]

By the time this review appeared, Woolson had already published her last piece in the *Atlantic*. Although the editor, Thomas Bailey Aldrich, asked her to contribute a serial work, a sign of great respect for her, she declined, claiming previous obligations. "It gratified me much to be asked," she told him, because of her "especial regard for the magazine,"[65] but she had allied herself with her publishers, the Harpers. All of her novels after 1883 appeared first in the pages of their magazine and then in book form under their firm's name. As a highly respected firm with a first-rate magazine, the Harpers offered Woolson a certain level of prestige that could compete with that offered by the more austere *Atlantic* and could pay her a great deal more, which was a significant consideration for Woolson and most women writers of her day.

However, the *Atlantic* continued to review her work, expressing great disappointment with how she developed as an author. When Woolson's second novel, *For the Major* (1883), was published, Scudder reverted to a paternalistic stance, foregrounding her gender and its influences on her novel. Acknowledging that "[w]e took up Miss Woolson's little book with special interest, from a desire to know what effect Anne had upon her," he was disappointed in his earlier predictions for her, and he now treated Woolson with considerably less regard. He especially criticized the "artificial" "construction" of the story, concluding, "We noticed in Anne something of the same tendency . . . and we hope that it will not increase in her work." In his review of her third novel, *East Angels* (1886), Scudder was once again put off by the "excess of invention," claiming that the major characters are not "true" and that she "presses too hard" the technique of contrast. Gone are the comparisons with Howells and James. Scudder claimed that the novel is "immensely clever in its separate passages" but disappointing "as a whole." Again he closed with advice, this time that she use her "power" in a "swiftly accomplished tale" with "quickness of movement" rather than in a novel concerned with "subtlety of motive."[66] He obviously did not appreciate her attempts to rise above current popular tales into the realm of psychological realism. It seems likely that she was not meeting his expectations of a woman writer.

In the case of all four writers, but particularly Phelps and Woolson, initial successes with the *Atlantic*'s editors and critics did not lead to lasting reputations. Their associations with the magazine are indicative of its general treatment of women writers. While Lowell, Fields, and Howells each can be credited with welcoming young women writers to the magazine, they and the reviewers made it clear that female authors would not achieve the stature of male luminaries. The overall tendency of the magazine in the 1880s was to exclude women as it canonized its great male authors, a trend visible in the critical treatment of post-bellum women writers in the literary world generally.

In the Hands of the Critics

The ambitions of Alcott, Phelps, Stoddard, and Woolson are most visible in their desires to gain the attention of the nation's growing cadre of critics — most of whom were men — rather than only the reading public. As Woolson explained, she envisioned a clear hierarchy in the reading world: " 'the Mass,' " which she called "ordinary readers," existed "below the region of the critics and the few really cultivated people we have in this new country of ours." Like Stoddard, she did "not care a copper" for "common praise." Instead, she rested her hopes on receiving the approbation of the critics, who, she wrote to Howells in 1875, "seem to hold my life in their hands," suggesting the extent to which she may have identified with her creation Miss Crief. Woolson and many of her contemporaries — such as Stoddard, who believed that Lowell had "saved" her; Phelps, who claimed that Higginson's and Whittier's praise was a "life-preserver"; and Dickinson, who wrote to Higginson, "you saved my Life"[67] — felt as if the male literary elite could make or break not only their careers but also their very lives. These quotes indicate the extent to which, for this generation of serious women writers, authorial and personal identities could not be disentangled. They thought of the nation's critics as omnipotent, and they felt particularly at their mercy. However, there was little they could do to disabuse most critics of the assumption that women writers were not worthy of serious recognition, a factor contributing significantly to their personal and professional grief.

Although Alcott, Phelps, Stoddard, and Woolson did not expect to completely elude the gender bias of male reviewers, they did hope to be treated fairly and to be considered worthy contributors to America's high literature. However, they had to contend with the general critical attitude, which was dismissive of female writers, as is conveyed in an 1853 article in the *United States Review:* "Where is American genius? Where are the original, the brilliant, the noble works, in whose publication we might take a lasting and national pride . . . ? Where are the men to write them? . . . American authors, be men and heroes! . . . Do not leave [American] literature in the hands of a few industrious females."[68] When Stoddard called for an American Brontë or Sand "to offer to our enemies, the critics," she registered her disdain for the attitude expressed by this reviewer.[69] Stoddard was calling for the model of female genius to prove that women were capable of contributing to the national high literature for which such critics were clamoring. As the critic's statement reveals, though, he will not be looking to women, but exclusively to men, for evidence of "American genius." In fact, he will not take women's writings seriously at all.

Another critic for the *North American Review* explained in 1851 how the critics generally dealt with women writers: "It is the custom to praise lady authors. . . . [T]o throw a damper upon harmless vanity, by pointing out an exuberance to be restrained, or a more vigorous tone of thought to be wrought for, is hardly worth the while. And thus the enterprises of full-fledged ambition among the scribbling fair, are dealt with by good-natured critics." Stoddard was well aware of this practice, as she wrote in 1854: "No criticism assails [women writers]. Men are polite to the woman, and contemptuous to the intellect. They do not allow woman to enter their intellectual arena to do battle with them." Eighteen years later, after her own bouts with the critics, Stoddard continued her attack on men who "sneer" at the efforts of women artists. In her article on the artist Rosa Bonheur, she declared that "there is certainly much in such a story as hers to . . . rebuke the supercilious critic, who stands ready to sneer at every woman who aspires to make use of the talents with which God intended her to adorn the walks of literature or art."[70] Woolson also took on male critics who belittled women writers in an anonymous review of Alice Perry's *Esther Pennefather* in the *Atlantic*'s "Contributors' Club." Although the novel, she admitted, was "the most utterly ridiculous book of the season," she thought it showed "originality" and "promise." She continued, "I have observed that the critics who have noticed it all have politely advanced the supposition that the author was very young, and then, hiding their smiles behind their tall hats, have hastily retired." Undoubtedly, Woolson sympathized with the young author who had suffered the "laughter" of male critics and wanted to give her some reassurance, taking her seriously in a way that they would not.[71]

Unfortunately, Alcott, Phelps, Stoddard, and Woolson were themselves unable to escape such ridicule. For instance, *The Literary World*'s review of Woolson's *Jupiter Lights* concluded, "Paul Tennant is one of those curious 'women's-men' at whom the masculine critic can only smile. We should have thought Miss Woolson superior to such crudity of portraiture, and to the melodrama of the last chapter — as absurd in its way." Likewise, *The Critic* wrote about Woolson's *Anne* that when the novel concluded with "melodramatic clap-trap of the cheapest variety . . . the artistic mistake is so colossal, so incongruous, so incredible, that we are not merely disappointed; we laugh."[72] These are only the most blatant examples of how male critics put these women authors in their place. But critics also found other, more subtle ways to tell them that their faults were due to their gender. In his review of Alcott's *Moods*, James claimed, "The two most striking facts with regard to 'Moods' are the author's ignorance of human nature, and her self-confidence in spite of this ignorance. Miss Alcott doubtless knows men and women well enough to deal successfully with their every-day virtues and temptations, but not well enough to handle great dramatic passions." Her "ignorance of human nature," he implies, is due to the fact that she is single and hence could know little about men. In fact, one of his greatest critiques is reserved for the hero, Adam Warwick, who, he suggests, is not realistic but is a product of a schoolgirl's romantic imagination. "Miss Alcott has probably mused upon Warwick so long and so lovingly that she has lost all sense of his proportions," he writes, and he likens Warwick to the "impossible heroes" of "lady novelists" generally.[73] Phelps received similar criticism for *The Story of Avis* from the *New York Times*. The reviewer declared that although "Miss Phelps does understand something about women before marriage," her male characters were "unnatural" and "her notions of the married state" were "singular." The result was that her novel should not be regarded as "a literary work."[74] Women authors, these men insinuated, were limited in their ability to create works of art because they could not move beyond their circumscribed experiences. Therefore, single women were unable to truthfully depict marriage and women generally were unfit to depict men. The *Nation*'s reviewer said as much about Stoddard's *Temple House:*

> The chief figure in "Temple House" is Argus Gates, a man of the sort which female novelists, considered as intellectual beings, have been for a long time asking us to admire. Next is Sebastian Ford, a man of the sort which female novelists, considered

as creatures of sentiment and poetic passion, depict as all but irresistible. Then we have John Carfield, who addresses himself to the animal side of female novelists.

All of these men are types that "female novelists" have invented and that the reviewer finds predictable.[75] The *Nation* similarly judged Woolson's fiction as marred by its femininity: "she solved the emotional problems of life in the clear-eyed, American-maiden way — a way that is often more entertaining than convincing to the rest of the world." Phelps's short story collection *Men, Women, and Ghosts* was also criticized in a manner that was meant to point out the limitations of women writers. Although the "nervous energy" the stories displayed was the cause of her popularity, "The critic, however, will be apt to observe, that while this nervous power exceeds the ordinary feminine limit, it is still limited by feminine weakness, and can never be mistaken for continuous masculine strength," the latter of which is no doubt preferable.[76] The *Nation's* reviewer offered similar opinions about Phelps's *Hedged In*, classing her as one of "our American authoresses," most of whom display "an uncontrolled tendency to dwell upon what is morbid and painful in life." The review of *The Story of Avis* in the *New York Times* summed up the general response to her work: "There are persons to whom *The Gates Ajar* [her first and most popular novel] is a standard to which they refer books they admire intensely, and there are others who use the same volume as a measure of their contempt for trashy, overstrained 'feminine' literature. The same thing is likely to befall this latest novel by Elizabeth Stuart Phelps."[77] The reviewer implies that the first group of readers were of the popular sort, and the latter were no doubt of the masculine and critical sort. In each case, the reviewer established his (most likely) authority by stressing the femininity and hence the inferiority of Phelps's works.

Even when reviewers did not view the female gender of these authors as a liability, they often grouped them with other women writers, suggesting that they belonged to a literary class based on gender. For example, the reviewer for the *New York Times* saw Woolson as "the most promising of our women novelists." The *Literary World* considered her "one of the most vigorous woman writers of this country" and declared, "If *Anne* placed the author in the highest rank among women writers of today, *For the Major* gives further proof of her right to be there." But the *Critic* offered perhaps the most interesting opinion about Woolson's place in American letters:

> If Miss Woolson has stood easily at the head of American women novelists, it is less because she has given us the best, than because she has given us little but the best. In

Miss Phelps we have to forgive some superfluous sentiment; in Rebecca Harding Davis, an extreme degree of the uncanny element; in Mrs. Burnett, the impossible refinement of her "lower class" characters; in Harriet Prescott Spofford, a Disraelish tendency to mother-of-pearl bedsteads and diamond-studded thimbles. Miss Woolson makes no demands of this sort upon our clemency.

As this review makes clear, women writers were usually judged in the company of other American women writers. While Woolson's work warranted comparison to James's as much as, if not more than, to George Eliot's (and certainly more than to Phelps's and Davis's), such a comparison was rarely made. Even James himself, who wrote an essay on her for *Harper's Weekly*, considered her chiefly as a *female* author, viewing her as a "striking illustration" of his principle that women's private lives lend themselves particularly well to the pursuit of literature.[78] In a similar vein, Howells considered Stoddard's *Two Men* to be "one of the most original books written by an American woman." The "peculiar charm" of Alcott's *Work* was due in part to "the summer cheerfulness infused through all of its pages by the glow of a woman's bright, trusting, and loving heart." Her *Hospital Sketches* "shows, with genuine feeling, all a woman's sympathy for suffering, and all a woman's tact in relieving it," and, according to another reviewer, "no lover of woman, should delay reading" this book. About Phelps's *Story of Avis*, the *Literary World*'s reviewer wrote, "only a woman could have written it," and the *Independent*'s obituary after her death declared Phelps "at the head of our women writers."[79]

The highest praise these authors received, though, was not to be ranked highly among other American women writers but to be considered, essentially, masculine writers who could compete with male authors. Of the four, Stoddard was most often characterized as "masculine," an adjective meant to be thoroughly positive. George Parsons Lathrop wrote that her works exhibit "a woman writing with that sort of vigor which, for want of a more searching and pliable term, we call masculine." Then he explained that her writing was "masculine" because she was able to "rise out of this little individuality [dictated by convention] into the larger one of a free, observant, independent mind." This, he admitted, was unusual for a woman, but "[i]f this privilege is to be denied to women, it is clear that their function as authors must be seriously limited." The "privilege," of course, belonged to men, and whether or not it would be granted to women remained uncertain. Julian Hawthorne, who deeply admired Stoddard, addressed the individuality of her works in an equally suggestive manner:

"Most women novelists try to write like men," he wrote. "Mrs. Stoddard writes like nobody else." While Lathrop considered her originality "masculine," Hawthorne was not quite sure how to label it: "there is no aping of the masculine voice: yet the virility, austerity, and . . . taciturnity of her style still less recall the conventional feminine tone. She is, in fact, the artist pure and simple." Hawthorne thus paid Stoddard the highest of compliments, equating her ability to avoid the conventionally feminine with a gender-neutral artistry.[80] Phelps was also deemed above her sex on at least one occasion: the *Philadelphia Press* wrote of *Friends: A Duet*, "The book is marked by that strength of touch — at times almost masculine — observable in all the works of this author." Interestingly, the *Literary World* claimed Woolson to be "one of the most vigorous woman writers of this country," raising her above her sex and comparing her to other female authors at the same time.[81]

Perhaps even more noteworthy, though, were the occasional assessments ranking them highly among authors generally or in comparison to male authors who had themselves achieved the highest stature. For example, the *Literary World* wrote of Phelps's *Story of Avis*, "in intellectual power, in loftiness of tone, in pureness and yet passionateness of feeling, in depth of experiences described, in subtlety of psychical analysis, and in mere superficial finish, this is the most notable American product of its class in many years, and in our judgment easily lifts its author to a place among the masters of modern fiction." *Harper's Weekly* wrote of Alcott's *Moods*, "After Hawthorne we recall no American love-story of equal power." Julian Hawthorne thought *The Morgesons* "one of the best novels ever written by a woman, and superior to all but a very few produced before or since by any American author." And the reviewer for the *Literary World* wrote of Woolson, "Some of the finest work in America has been done by her hand."[82]

However, even as these passages suggest that Alcott, Phelps, Stoddard, and Woolson were at one time or another considered to be among the highest-ranking American authors, such voices were in the minority. When these writers weren't being judged against others of their sex, they were deemed in various ways to have fallen short of the bar set by critics — the accurate portrayal of "truth." Predictably, critics did not agree on what "truth" was nor on how successful these writers were at depicting it. Some applauded these four writers for their adherence to "reality," while others did not recognize their characters as "real." Some appreciated their willingness to tackle tough subjects — such as passion or poverty — although others criticized them for addressing such unseemly or "gloomy" topics. Ultimately, though, none of these authors achieved the level of prestige she desired. None were accepted by the critics as an American Eliot or Brontë or a female Hawthorne. Even though they were given much encouragement early in their careers, reviewers were inclined to withhold full acceptance. This was a common chord struck by the critics as they reviewed "promising" women writers. Alcott, Phelps, Stoddard, and Woolson were all acknowledged as important candidates for the coming vanguard of American literature, but the critics were careful to point out the faults that must be eliminated in order for their predictions to come true. Much like the male writer in "'Miss Grief,'" male critics routinely found flaws (usually attributed to inexperience or the author's sex) that they believed would preclude widespread respect for their work. What we see in these reviews is little consensus about what constitutes good literature, which befits this period in which literary tastes were in flux. The inability of any of the four writers to gain immortality as serious artists has as much to do with their gender as with the fact that they wrote during this transitional period. None of them was as staunchly or consistently a realist as Henry James was or as much a romanticist as Nathaniel Hawthorne was. The critics' disagreement about them, therefore, reflects the fact that they cannot be firmly placed in a literary camp, making their reputations even more tenuous.

Phelps and Alcott were judged very similarly by critics, attacked for their critical depictions of marriage in *Avis* and *Moods* and either praised or considered second-rate for the moral purpose of their works. They were even lumped together, in retrospect, by a reviewer for the *Nation*, who wrote in 1909 that Phelps's fiction "belongs to the same school" as Alcott's, "and we may fairly say, to the same period of unabashed sensibility."[83] By that time they were permanently removed from the category of high literature, which was then firmly associated with realism, and their early contributions to that movement were suppressed as they were categorized with other women writers as sentimentalists. During their day, however, the critical verdict was much more equivocal.

Alcott's foremost bid for immortality, her novel *Moods*, was both highly praised and considered "dangerous" for its ideas about marriage. Unfortunately, *Moods* came out just after *Emily Chester*, another novel dealing with unhappiness in marriage, and many reviewers discussed the two novels together, assailing the "dangerous nonsense" and "excessively unhealthy influence" they had on readers, even arguing that such novels contributed to divorce. As one reviewer wrote, "it is high time that the critical world should begin to consider [novels'] moral bearing as well as their literary execution." Alcott was dismayed by this focus on her work's moral implications and by what she felt was a serious misrepresentation of her views. She wrote to a friend, "I find myself accused of Spiritualism, Free Love, Affinities & all sorts of horrors that I know very little about & dont [*sic*] believe in."[84] She felt that she had failed to deliver her message about the importance of choosing a mate carefully. However, Alcott did manage with *Moods* to please a great many critics, who felt, as one wrote, that although here was "a lady whose brilliant abilities are rapidly winning for her a first place among the best writers of the time," she was "capable of something better than this work." Although much of Henry James's review in the *North American Review* was condescending, his final paragraph was full of praise and encouragement:

> there is no reason why Miss Alcott should not write a very good novel, provided she
> will be satisfied to describe only that which she has seen. When such a novel comes,
> as we doubt not it eventually will, we shall be among the first to welcome it. With
> the exception of two or three celebrated names, we know not, indeed, to whom, in
> this country, unless to Miss Alcott, we are to look for a novel above the average.

Similarly, the *Harper's Weekly* critic praised *Moods* for its "freshness and self-reliance," predicting "remarkable works hereafter."[85]

Published after Alcott had become known as a children's author, her other serious adult novel, *Work* (1873), received mostly negative reviews. The *Literary World*'s was the most positive, claiming that the characters were "life-like" and seeing no conflict in calling it "a very well-written work" that "will come very near doing positive good." Others, however, objected to its engagement with social issues. The *Nation* declared it "a contribution to the literature of the 'labor question' and the 'woman question,' . . . under the veil of fiction," making it ultimately "nothing as a work of art." *Appletons'* pointed out the "inartistic indication of . . . its moral," and *Harper's* objected that it "is not a novel at all, but a serious didactic essay on the subject of woman's work," "impair[ing] it as a work of art."[86]

Similar critiques were leveled at many of Phelps's novels. For instance, the *Nation*'s critics wrote about *Avis*, "Under the guise of fiction the book is really a protest against marriage." However, some of her critics did not object to her ethical realism, finding that the moral and "art" were not mutually exclusive categories in her hands. *Harper's* thought that *The Silent Partner* (1871) taught "a terribly needed lesson," while praising it for being "more effective and artistic" than her last novel. The *Literary World* wrote about the same novel that it showed "evidence of true creative genius" and that "her pictures of work-life, the home-life, and the street-life of mill-operatives, have all the realism of photographs." At the same time, "As a revelation of the wrongs and sufferings of the manufacturing population of New England, 'The Silent Partner' will command general attention, and will do much to arouse public sentiment to insist upon needed reforms."[87] However, Phelps appears to have been most successful with the critics when she leaned more toward objective realism and away from the ethical, which could, some believe, veer toward the sentimental. About *Hedged In* (1870), the *Nation*'s reviewer wrote, "the chief impression that it makes is that there must be those who love to indulge themselves in wanton grieving and who enjoy a laceration of the heart more or less real." The critics' general assessment of Phelps's work was that she overindulged in sentimentality.[88]

As their careers progressed, however, Phelps and Alcott paid less and less attention to the critics. Having found her niche as a children's writer, Alcott did not have to seek their favor anymore. After the publication of *The Gates Ajar* (1868), Phelps had vowed no longer to pay attention to the critics' opinions of her work, although she knew "in a general way . . . if some important pen has shown a comprehension of what [I] meant to do . . . or has spattered venom." Actually, though, Phelps must have paid some attention, as her autobiography clearly implies: "I sometimes think, good brother critics, that I have had my share of the attentions of poisoned weapons." But she contended that she did not heed their criticisms — "they stab at the summer air." When she learned that George Eliot also ignored her critics, she "felt reinforced by this great example." Eliot's letter to Phelps on this subject reveals how potent the critics' views could be to the woman writer struggling to be an artist. "I adopted this rule [of not reading reviews] many years ago," Eliot wrote her, "as a necessary preservative against influences that would have ended by nullifying my power of writing."[89] Only by ignoring the critics could women writers maintain power over themselves and their art. But they weren't always successful at doing this.

Despite her protestations that she didn't listen to the critics, Phelps did take their "abuse" and "misapprehension" to heart in the case of *The Story of Avis*. She called it a "woman's book, hoping for small hospitality at the hands of men," but the harsh attacks it generated for its style and theme disheartened her. The *Harper's* reviewer declared that Phelps had heeded previous criticism — "There are no careless passages in it, no marks of haste, no writing for the market, no hurry-scurry to catch the fall trade" — but ultimately felt the novel was "sometimes perhaps too finely finished, as though the language of passionate feeling had been fashioned with too great a thought of artistic perfection." Most other reviewers also criticized its style; however, they reserved their greatest venom for the novel's critique of marriage. So widespread was the disapproval that one reviewer, wishing to praise the novel, wrote, "its faults having been already so thoroughly discussed by almost all critics, it is unnecessary here to restate them."[90] Having invested more of herself, her time, and her ambition in trying to gain serious recognition with *Avis* than she had with any previous work, she did not do so again. After this experience, she seems to have closed her eyes almost completely to reviews of her work. Like Alcott, she learned to focus more of her attention on her many appreciative readers rather than on critics who could not be satisfied with her work because of its dark themes, sometimes exuberant style, and concern with social reform.

Woolson was also very sensitive to criticism about her writings, especially when she first started to publish in book form. When her friend Hayne gave her a positive "notice" of her short story "Castle Nowhere," she wrote to him, "when I had finished [the story] I said 'it is my best.' But as no one else said so, I began to doubt my own judgment; a very unsettling state of mind, don't you think? Now comes your letter, the clouds part, and I take courage again." She was upset about Howells's review of the collection *Castle Nowhere* (1875) in the *Atlantic*, especially his comments about the title story. When the review appeared, she wrote to Hayne about it, explaining that "I had been abused so for writing such deadly 'real' stories, that I did branch out, in that one, into the realm of imagination." She had tried to please her critics with a more romantic atmosphere and ideal construction in "Castle Nowhere," but Howells found it to be the "least satisfactory of the stories." While many magazine men still clung to romanticism, Howells was articulating a new critical aesthetic, leaving Woolson perhaps a bit confused about how best to please reviewers. Of this story, Howells complained, "one is harassed from beginning to end by a disagreeable fantasticality." Although the rest of the review was, as she wrote to him, "very high praise" and gave her "much delightful encouragement for the future," these criticisms stayed with her. "I am, shall I say unfortunately, excessively sensitive to praise and to blame; these critics seem to hold my life in their hands. I go sleepless, often, after reading what they say, whether for good or for ill." However, she continued, "Your friend Miss Phelps is above all that."[91] While Phelps for the most part ignored the critics' prescriptions for her work, Woolson could not. As in "'Miss Grief,'" the male critic's judgment had the power to "nullify" her, in Eliot's phrase.

But Howells's praise elsewhere in the review was also encouraging, especially where he wrote that her tendencies to be both "poetically realistic" and "poetically fanciful . . . rest upon the same solid basis — truth to human nature." In fact, most of her early reviews were encouraging. As the *Appletons'* reviewer wrote about *Castle Nowhere*, "The promise of the early work that she has done here is of more than [the] ordinary sort; her literary future looks very bright indeed." The *Literary World*, in its review of her second book, *Rodman the Keeper: Southern Sketches* (1880), called her a "genuine artist" and credited her with "virile force."[92] When *Anne* was published, most reviewers agreed, however, that it was exquisite in its description and details, but that the "sensational scenes" that closed the book were a disappointment. The *Literary World* suggested that such scenes should be left to the likes of Wilkie Collins, but the reviewer proceeded to equate this failing with her sex: "We should wish for a writer of her force and growing influence a diminished acquaintance with or interest in the trick[er]y of her own sex."[93] Critics were ultimately divided, though, on how to classify her. The *Century* believed that "she carries out the picture with the utmost particularity as to details until the scene stands before one as if in a photograph" and that "Miss Woolson adds to her observation of scenes and localities an unusual insight into the human heart," concluding that she was inheriting "the mantle of George Eliot." However, the *Literary World* declared that she had "such sympathy with the tropical currents of life." "With all Miss Woolson's realism and searching wit she was a romanticist," the reviewer maintained. And Charles Dudley Warner wrote after her death, "Her pictures are real, but they are painted with the ideality inseparable from the high-bred literary artist."[94] However, Woolson ultimately did not fare well, as all idealism in literature was viewed with increasing suspicion and she was relegated to the margins with other women writers.

Stoddard was probably the most sensitive about her critical reception as well as the most highly praised, managing to ride the waves of both romanticism in the 1860s and realism in the 1890s. When her novels first appeared in the 1860s, many reviews praised her "genius" and placed her in the company of Charlotte Brontë and Nathaniel Hawthorne, although most criticized her abrupt, enigmatic style and saw it as a sign of her inexperience as an author and a blemish that she must correct in order to achieve the "more prominent rank" the *Round Table* believed was possible in her case.[95] George Ripley of the *New York Tribune* was her most consistent and ardent admirer. He praised *The Morgesons* for its "original invention" and saw it as evidence of "a far more profound genius, as well as a higher artistic gift, than the literal narrative which consists of mere photographic copies of one's acquaintance." In this review of *Two Men* he raised her above other women writers: "In a day of exuberant demonstration, and reckless imagery, especially among popular female writers, it is a refreshment to find a woman self-possessed as the Sybil, and as impassive and reticent." Similarly, he wrote, "No weak womanly sentiment impairs the effect of the keen, merciless dissection of passion and motives which awaken an almost morbid curiosity in the reader." This was exactly the kind of response Stoddard had hoped for from male critics. She wrote to Howells that it was "the truest review yet I guess. I write things as *I* see and feel them, . . . The writer has found out my mind there is no doubt of that." Interestingly, Howells had already written his review of the novel for the *Nation*. In this review we see Howells developing his realistic theories, praising the novel for "objective processes" and comparing it favorably to *The Scarlet Letter,* a representative romance: "The author seldom vouchsafes a word of comment or explanation on anything that her people do or say; and yet, from their brief speeches and dramatic action, you have the same knowledge of motive which you acquire from the philosophization of some such subjective romance as 'The Scarlet Letter.' We think this admirable." This is very high praise, indeed, for Howells. Above all, he finds Stoddard an original author and *Two Men* "one of the most original books written by an American woman."[96]

However, reviews of *Temple House* (1867) were discouraging, particularly because she believed that she had done her best work in this novel. Reviewers continued to see unfulfilled promise. *Putnam's* reviewer recognized "the power of an artist," but the review ends, characteristically, with two jabs about the novel's "too compact structure, and too sudden conclusion," and the statement, "We are confident that she will do much better next time." But there would not be a next time. Stoddard had come to the conclusion that her novels would not meet with an appreciative audience among her contemporaries, and she wrote no more. Henry Wadsworth Longfellow wrote to her husband in 1878, "if her writings have not found that swift recognition which they merit, I hope it will not discourage her. Often the best things win their way slowly, but are pretty sure of being found out sooner or later."[97]

Stoddard's talent was "found out" when her work was republished in the late 1880s. The republication had been spurred by the rediscovery of her novels by Julian Hawthorne and Junius Browne and the support of her old friend Stedman, who was now a prominent literary critic. *Two Men* was republished first, with a laudatory preface by Stedman, in which he wrote that she had been "before her time." Her books, he continued, are "additions not merely to the bulk of reading, but to literature itself; as distinct in their kind as *Wuthering Heights*." Excitement from the press greeted the first reprinted volume, as critics were eager to see if

Stedman's claims were justified. In fact, many critics lamented that her work had not been received as it should have been when it was first published and that the author had since ceased to write novels. George Parsons Lathrop, who would write a significant appreciation of her in a *North American Review* essay, wrote to her, "Why, what has the world been about, all these years — & where have *I* been? — not to know more about this book & you? . . . Oh, why did you not just curse the world, & go on writing?" He assures her that she possesses "the most surprising, the most penetrating genius I have known in an American woman."[98]

The time had come at last, it seemed, for her novels to receive the recognition she had long believed they deserved. The trend toward realism gave her a more appreciative audience; for the stark depiction of the bleak New England of her youth and the uncompromising individuality of her characters were not so strange to readers as they once had been. Now, reviewers could look back and see how ahead of her time she had been. Undoubtedly, the proliferation of literary periodicals and the greater numbers of men (and a few women) making their living by writing reviews for them also created a larger circle of appreciative readers for her. Reviews of her republished novels appeared in the *Nation*, the *Independent*, the *Literary World*, *Lippincott's*, the *New York Times*, *Harper's*, the *Critic*, and the *Atlantic*. The tenor of the initial reviews of the first edition of her republished novels in 1888–89 was similar to the best reviews she had received in the 1860s, and they reflected the widening split between intellectual readers and the general reading public. Reviewers agreed that her genius, while somewhat raw, was of a sort that would not be recognized by the general public, only the cultivated few.[99] When the first novel to be republished appeared, Stoddard was "astonished," she wrote to Julia Dorr, "at the way in which the book has been taken by men, authors who compare me to Balzac and George Meredith!" It was precisely to these "men," authors and intellectuals, that she had all along tried to prove she was their peer. But while earlier reviews had predicted a bright future (always putting off the achievement of success until the publication of the next novel), these looked back and speculated about what might have been had she not given up writing novels. The *Nation* struck what must have been an agonizing note for Stoddard: "It is impossible not to regret that destiny silenced Mrs. Stoddard's pen many years ago, impossible not to believe that work as great as this is impressive might have crowned a persistent practice."[100] As much as she was being feted now, how much more would she have been celebrated if she had continued to write?

The triumph of her resurrected fame, however, was short-lived. As each of her novels was republished, the reviews became more negative. When the final novel to be republished, *The Morgesons*, came out, hardly anyone noticed it. In 1896, her brief glimpse of immortality was already over. "I am attempting once more to write a story," she wrote to Dorr, "but I am so snubbed, so ignored — [m]y name left out of every passing thing written that I haven't much faith in myself."[101] The absence of her name in the numerous assessments of the nation's and women's literature that were appearing during these years silenced her once and for all.

Stoddard, whose ambitions were perhaps the highest, had more difficulty redirecting her goals as an author or shutting her eyes to the critics' words. Pinning all of her feelings of worth as a writer on the prospect of recognition from literary men, Stoddard left only a small body of brilliant work behind. While personal factors also played a role, it is clear that critical neglect, especially in the absence of popular acclaim, stifled her. Had she been embraced by the public, even in the absence of unequivocal critical acclaim, as Alcott, Phelps, and Woolson were, she undoubtedly would have been less likely to give up her writing.

Although it is difficult to sum up the diverse critical response to all four writers, one thing is clear: each was judged as ultimately limited by her sex in the production of great art. None of them could escape reviewers' biases toward women as writers and their expectations for women's fiction. Although Alcott, Phelps, Stoddard, and Woolson did succeed at gaining the attention of some important critics who gave them some of the highest praise received by any women writers of their generation, such glimpses of serious recognition were not sustained or prominent enough to counter the trend toward creating an exclusive canon of male stars. While each was perceived as possessing much promise, and reviewers were on occasion willing to recognize female authors as participating in the emerging high literary culture, any provisional entrance they were granted to the upper echelons of literary achievement was rescinded by the end of the century.

CONCLUSION

The Question of Immortality

Although Alcott, Phelps, Stoddard, and Woolson had been accorded at one time
or another some of the highest praise of any women writers of their generation,
each of them was sooner or later relegated to literary obscurity. What happened
from their deaths until the national establishment of the American literary canon
in the 1920s and in the years thereafter to ensure that they would be so entirely
eclipsed? A number of factors converged, including the masculinization of literary tastes, the derogation of the "ideal" and moral aspects of literature, and the
institutionalization of American literary study in university English departments.
While all of these factors cannot be thoroughly explored here, an overview of the
early assessments of these writers' legacies and the formation of the all-male
canon of American literature gives some indications of why all four writers — as
well as their female contemporaries — were erased from the literary map. Each of
these authors, despite the tremendous differences in their works, suffered the
same fate. Even Woolson, a close friend of Henry James and widely considered to
be the best woman writer of her generation (perhaps next to Jewett), would not
be remembered. In fact, there was so little consensus on matters of literary
excellence during this period that the perceived quality of their work, running the

gamut from the highest to the lowest rank, was the least significant factor in determining the fate of their literary reputations. Instead, the growing bias of the male literary elite against women writers and the masculinization of high literature were arguably the main reasons their reputations declined so precipitously.

Early Assessments

Nearly all women writers of this generation who were at one time considered worthy of high praise experienced a decline in their reputations. Helen Hunt Jackson, according to Susan Coultrap-McQuin, was never able to solidify her considerable literary status owing to her use of multiple pseudonyms and anonymity. When she died in 1885, therefore, her popular novel *Ramona* (1884) and her report of wrongs committed against Native Americans, *A Century of Dishonor* (1881), both of which she claimed with her real name, were foremost among her legacy. As a result, any high cultural status she achieved through her association with the *Atlantic Monthly* became overshadowed by her commitment to this social reform. Similarly, Emma Lazarus was remembered after her death in 1887 as a crusader for Jewish causes, to which she devoted herself in the last five years of her life. Her sister memorialized her in the introduction to her posthumous selected poems as "too distinctly feminine to wish to be exceptional or to stand alone and apart," a view adopted by almost all subsequent biographers. Interestingly, however, she gained perhaps more lasting recognition than any other writer of her generation because lines from her sonnet "The New Colossus," inscribed on the Statue of Liberty, entered into the national consciousness: "Give me your tired, your poor, / Your huddled masses . . . "[1]

Part of the problem for many writers was their varied output, especially when it appeared in less serious venues. Both Harriet Prescott Spofford and Rebecca Harding Davis, who had been so closely aligned with the *Atlantic Monthly* in its early years, were harmed by their popularity. Alfred Bendixen explains, "During her final years, Spofford seems to have accepted her position as a popular writer of magazine fiction, whose early romantic tales had once been acclaimed." Never having completely abandoned romanticism, Spofford nonetheless became a (minor) figure among local colorists, who were the primary producers of popular stories for the magazines in the 1890s. Well into the next century, Rebecca Harding Davis continued to produce works that combined stark realism with the idealistic purpose of transforming society, but in her last years critics and readers remembered only "Life in the Iron Mills" (1861), suggesting that her career had peaked at that early date and that she had left nothing else of significance behind. Upon her death in 1910, as Sharon Harris has determined, she was less widely eulogized than her husband had been six years earlier, and, according to Tillie Olsen, "No literary journal noted her passing." In one of the few notices of her death, she was identified only as the "widow of L. Clarke Davis" and not as an author in her own right. Similarly, the *New York Times* announced, "Mother of Richard Harding Davis Dies." Her career was eclipsed by her famous author son, who, despite his lack of association with the realists, was more widely remembered among literary critics and scholars than his mother, the pioneering realist.[2]

The four writers examined in this study experienced varying degrees of recognition upon their deaths, but, like their sister authors, they were forgotten almost completely by the time the American literary canon was solidified in the twentieth century. Alcott, the first of the group to die, was also the least respected by literary critics. The obituaries marking her death in 1888 stressed her popularity as a children's author, her enormous income from her books (estimated at $100,000), and her devotion to her family, especially her infirm father. In fact, having died two days apart, they were often eulogized together, and their pathetic last days were recounted as evidence that Alcott was the dutiful daughter even in death. None of the obituaries mentioned her early work in the *Atlantic*, and most neglected to mention her serious novels for adults. Instead, they focused on the lasting impression made by *Little Women*.[3] In response to the many laudatory obituaries, Thomas Wentworth Higginson, who had once encouraged Alcott, wrote an article for *Harper's Bazar* warning the "young girls" who revered her. "Her muse was domestic, simple, and sociable," he argued; "the instinct of art she never had: it is difficult to imagine her as pondering a situation deeply, still less as concerning herself about phrase or diction." She should not be a model for young writers, he cautioned, "if they are moved by a profound passion for the art of literature itself; if they wish to reach an audience remoter than that of to-day; if they wish to do something that shall add to the lasting treasure of the great literature on which they have fed." Higginson claimed that she was nothing more than a popular author who dashed off copy with no thought for "the art of literature."[4]

In the ensuing decades, Alcott was almost always remembered as the "children's friend," as Ednah D. Cheney memorialized her, and as the daughter of her Transcendentalist father. Her work came to be associated with the sentimental literature widely viewed by male critics to have debased American literature. G. K. Chesterton wrote in the *Nation* that he believed she had anticipated realism by twenty to thirty years, yet he could not place, analyze, or even "understand" her works because they belonged exclusively to women. He took up Alcott in order to explore her enduring popularity and ended by dismissing her as outside of the purview of a male critic. Thomas Beer, in his work on the 1890s, *The Mauve Decade* (1926), claimed she represented the genteel womanhood in American letters that young male writers were battling. He discussed her in his chapter "The Titaness," which refers to the prudish woman reader who holds Alcott as the apotheosis of good and tasteful literature. In essence, he blamed Alcott for creating an effeminate, emasculated literature that had to be overcome by a new generation of male writers.[5] Given the fact that Alcott had primarily devoted herself to writing children's literature, these assessments are not too surprising. But it is important to remember that her publication of *Work* in 1872 and her republication of the revised *Moods* in 1882 were completely eclipsed by her works for children. Her legacy would be one of tremendous popular influence, particularly on children and female readers, but not one of artistic achievement.

In contrast, Woolson, despite the varied response to her works during her lifetime, was accorded great respect as an artist upon her death in 1894. As *Harper's* argued, "to the last her standard was not popular favor, but her own high conception of her office as a writer. . . . This patience in creative genius is not common." Most of the other notices joined Margaret Sangster in commenting on her industry and high standards: "Her work was performed with the utmost sincerity, never slurred over or hastened, and into it she put the best of herself — her finest thought." Woolson could have quickly produced abundant publishable copy, Henry Mills Alden wrote in *Harper's Weekly*, but "like a true artist, she sought difficulty." Many commented on her "genius" and her high rank as an author. The *Critic* quoted Edmund Clarence Stedman as declaring her "one of the leading women in American literature of the century." The *Dial* noted, "By the death of Miss Constance Fenimore Woolson . . . America lost one of the best of its fiction writers." And the *New York Times* claimed that the publication of her first novel had "placed her at once in the front rank of prose writers." The efforts of her publisher, Harper and Brothers, to keep her fame alive included a promotional page in the back of her last (posthumously published) book, *The Front Yard and Other Italian Stories* (1895), containing the following statement from the *Boston Globe*: "Constance Fenimore Woolson may easily become the novelist laureate."[6] The consensus was that Woolson was one of the foremost writers of her generation.

But this estimation of her very high rank was short-lived. The new literary histories had relatively little to say about her place in American literature. In *American Literature, A Text-Book* (1892), Julian Hawthorne and Leonard Lemmon gave her work a token four lines, placing her among the "analytic novelists [who] take their cue from James and Howells," the true "Innovators." In *Introduction to American Literature* (1897), F. V. N. Painter mentioned her briefly among sixty-one "Prominent Writers" of the "Second National Period." In *American Writers of To-Day* (1894), Henry C. Vedder ignored her, as did Fred Lewis Pattee in his *History of American Literature* (1896). But Pattee remembered her in his *History of American Literature since 1870* (1917): "During the eighties Miss Woolson was regarded as the most promising of the younger writers," with *Castle Nowhere* "ranking as a pioneer book in a new field [regionalism]." And he quoted Stedman as saying, " 'No woman of rarer personal qualities, or with more decided gifts as a novelist, figured in her own generation of American writers.' But," Pattee concluded, "time has not sustained this contemporary verdict. . . . She must take her place as one of the pioneers of the period who discovered a field and prepared an audience for writers who were to follow." He repeated this verdict in his *Development of the American Short Story* (1923), again calling her a "pioneer" who did not live up to expectations. Pattee set the tone for his successors, such as Vernon Louis Parrington, who also called her a "pioneer," and John Dwight Kern, who published an entire study of her work titled *Constance Fenimore Woolson: Literary Pioneer* (1934).[7] Within the four decades after her death, Woolson had gone from "novelist laureate" to an author who had not fully realized her promise.

Stoddard, who had been so highly regarded by influential critics like Julian Hawthorne in the 1880s and 1890s, lived to see her reputation sink once again into obscurity. Upon her death in 1902, she was the least recognized of the four, and, like Davis and Alcott, she was overshadowed by a male relative, her husband. The only lengthy obituary she received was in the *New York Times*. It had little to say about her writings, although Stedman was quoted as saying that her novels found "many readers who valued them above most other American novels." Three months after her death, the *Bookman* published a tribute to her work by Mary Moss, which reads more like an apology. While ostensibly making a claim for the lasting recognition of Stoddard's novels, Moss repeatedly points out her faults. "[S]he had genius of a high order, but totally undisciplined, with scant capacity for taking pains." Besides these two pieces, Stoddard appears to have passed almost completely unnoticed. Even the *Critic*, which had published lengthy tributes to her husband, did not mark her death. Instead, it only mentioned her death two months later in a short passage that focused on Richard Henry Stoddard's newly solitary life.[8]

Stoddard also received the least attention from early literary scholars. Pattee recalled her in *A History of American Literature*, in his section on her husband, but he had forgotten her or set her aside by the time he wrote *A History of American Literature since 1870* and *The Development of the American Short Story*. In *American Literature*, however, Julian Hawthorne once again championed her. In a two-and-a-half-page entry on her, he and Lemmon declared, "Few men have written stories more original and powerful than [hers]." Vedder, writing in 1894, shortly after her novels had been republished, discussed her briefly in the chapter on her husband, commenting, "It is really one of the curiosities of literature that her books have not known a wider recognition." And he predicted that "tardy fame is about to overtake Mrs. Stoddard." But of the later scholars, only Van Wyck Brooks acknowledged her work. In his book *New England: Indian Summer, 1865–1915* (1940), he mentioned her, along with Stowe and Cooke, as a precursor to Howells, James, Jewett, and Freeman.[9] While the rekindling of her literary fame had coincided with the first significant literary histories, she would, like Woolson, be either forgotten or considered an incomplete artist whose promise had been unfulfilled.

Phelps's prolific literary output, long life, and continued popularity ensured that she would not be as easily dismissed or forgotten. The early assessments of her work, while she was still alive, indicate that many literary historians considered her an artist of high rank. Vedder wrote that the success of *The Gates Ajar* was "of the first magnitude," although *Avis* was the "favorite" of most of her readers. Although he deemed her "didactic," he felt that she had not sacrificed "artistic purpose and method." He concluded his lengthy discussion of her with the observation: "Of all our American women of letters, Miss Phelps impresses one as the most intense, the most high-purposed, the most conscientious in her art." Painter listed Phelps among five female writers "who have achieved eminence" and have "exploded" the "old theory of the intellectual inferiority of woman." In 1896, Pattee concluded that "No one of the group [of New England women writers] has written stronger or more finished work than Elizabeth Stuart Phelps." The one dissenting opinion was that of Hawthorne and Lemmon, who wrote a very negative appraisal of her work, although they featured her prominently in their textbook, even including her portrait. "She is vividly emotional, — at times almost hysterical," they wrote. In the end, the "merits and beauties [of her work] cannot, like their faults, be analyzed."[10]

When Phelps died in 1911, the verdict was more mixed. Only the religious periodical the *Independent* ranked her "at the head of our women writers." The *New York Times* declared her to be "the well-known authoress of several spiritual romances," hardly a claim to lasting fame. And the *Dial* argued that her books "always maintained the same high ethical and religious level, impressing their lessons indeed with some straining of incident, some undue shrillness in the note struck," although it also found "her work . . . not unworthy of comparison with the best of the good old New England school to which she properly belonged." As these obituaries suggest, Phelps's brand of literature by then had fallen out of style. She was deemed old-fashioned. The *Independent* even believed her to have "led the elder generation of women authors who were contemporary with Mrs. Stowe." (Stowe was born in 1811, thirty-three years before Phelps.) As Susan Coultrap-McQuin notes, Phelps's obituaries stressed the ethical aspect of her fiction, and, "[w]hile laudatory, these appraisals were actually the last hurrah for a fading literary reputation in a culture that no longer emphasized the ethical imperative in literature."[11]

When Phelps was mentioned in scholarly studies after her death, commentators followed Hawthorne's and Lemmon's lead in viewing her as an overly emotional female writer. Many still considered her prominent among women writers, but she represented, like Alcott, all that needed to be discredited in order to solidify America's literary reputation. As Parrington wrote in *Main Currents in American Thought* (1927), her novel *The Silent Partner* (1871) was "sticky with sentiment" and "belongs to the emotional fifties" rather than to the "Beginnings of Critical Realism" he was chronicling. In *The Great Tradition: An Interpretation of American Literature* (1933), Granville Hicks called Phelps "that arch romanticist and sentimentalist," ignoring her contributions to the realist movement. Brooks found her work "too consciously righteous" in its "missionary spirit," and he launched from a discussion of her work into lamentations about "the feminization of literature." Pattee changed his tune about her in 1917, criticizing her preachiness: "she has pleaded rather than created," and "[t]he artist within her was dominated ever by the preacher; the novelist by the Puritan." In 1923, he saw her as a "pioneer in New England *genre* fiction," although he focused on "the emotional" in her stories. He also declared, "She was a realist because of the limitations of her imagination"; she was "not intentionally . . . an innovator."[12] Whether Phelps was classified as a romanticist, a sentimentalist, or a realist, her work was identified as lacking in aesthetic accomplishment because of its "feminine" qualities, making it emotional, didactic, or lacking in imagination. All of these labels were increasingly used to condemn women's writings as not only of lesser value but also completely outside the realm of "art."

As the early assessments of Alcott, Phelps, Stoddard, Woolson, and other women writers of their generation make clear, there was little concrete consensus on where these authors fit and why they did not belong on the map of American literature these critics were drawing. Alcott and Phelps were deemed to be either part of an outmoded school of literature or simply not literary artists. Stoddard seemed to disappear for similar reasons. Although not associated as much with a feminized literary culture, she was, however, part of an earlier literary age, despite her originality. She simply didn't belong in any convenient grouping. And Woolson was dismissed as not belonging to the later literary movement of regionalism. Woolson's relatively early death and Stoddard's early literary retirement also left critics, many of whom saw in their works "genius," with the impression that they had not fully realized their potential or had left their careers unfinished. In addition, there was little consensus on the quality or significance of these authors' works, and in some cases, earlier high appraisals were forgotten, weakening any claim that objective aesthetic standards determined the fate of their literary reputations. Much more contingent factors were at work.

Some important works of early American literary history did not mention them at all,[13] and when they were mentioned, it was usually in connection with other women writers, who were, as a class, considered minor. They were relegated, because of their gender, to the margins of American literature. The distinct cleavage between major male authors and minor female authors became solidified in the decades when the question of these writers' literary immortality was decided. Therefore, their erasure from the literary map cannot be explained merely by the fact that literary tastes were changing. A sea change was under way that would erase all but a few male authors.

The Formation of the American Literary Canon

As the careers of Alcott, Phelps, Stoddard, and Woolson came to a close, the project of defining the American pantheon gained urgency. The old masters (Emerson, Longfellow, Whittier, and others) were passing away, and the question of who would take up their mantle was unresolved. Many lamented that while several authors showed promise, none rose above the rest. Whereas midcentury discussions about American literature had focused on its future and the coming master "genius," at the end of the century attention was focused on

America's literary past and defining the American pantheon. Like earlier discussions of "genius," there were competing visions of what shape this group should take.

Authors of some of the early anthologies and literary histories, especially, presented an inclusive view of America's literary past. For example, from 1883 to 1890 Stedman and Ellen Mackay Hutchinson edited an eleven-volume anthology titled *A Library of American Literature from the Earliest Settlement to the Present Time*. This exhaustive collection contained selections from more than fifteen hundred authors, many of them unknown today and many of them women. Alcott, Phelps, Stoddard, and Woolson were all well represented with prose selections and poems, and Stoddard and Woolson were both honored with prominent portraits. In the final volume the editors looked back on their series and concluded, "we have respected our title, which is neither a 'Thesaurus' nor a 'Valhalla,' but 'A Library' of American literature, and thus denotes a compilation varied in subject, treatment, and merit, and above all — inclusive. . . . It is not confined to masterpieces." Had they chosen to compile an "exclusive miscellany," they surmised, "less than fifty authors" would have been represented.[14] Some of the early literary histories published by the new scholars of American literature also made room for a wide variety of authors, usually considered minor, in addition to the major male authors. Examples include the four-volume *Cambridge History of American Literature* (1913–21), Charles F. Richardson's influential *American Literature, 1607–1885* (1886–88), F. V. N. Painter's *Introduction to American Literature* (1897), Walter Bronson's *Short History of American Literature* (1908), and, much later, Granville Hicks's *Great Tradition* (1933).[15]

But the tendency in many textbooks, anthologies, and scholarly studies was toward a radically reduced representation of authors. The desire to delineate a "Valhalla" won out over the perceived need to provide a "Library." As the *Atlantic*'s review of Stedman's and Hutchinson's *Library* opined, "The reputation of a nation for letters must depend upon its eminent authors, and arises rather from quality than quantity." A few "eminent authors" rather than a multitude of voices must be selected in order to establish an American literary tradition.[16] As a result, the authorities — increasingly university-affiliated scholars — trimmed down the list of significant American authors considerably, resulting in a selective group from which women writers and writers of color were excluded. For example, in *The Chief American Prose Authors* (1916), Norman Foerster represented all of American literature by nine (white male) authors. Richard Burton's *Literary Leaders of America* also represents this tendency. Between "The Earlier Period" and "The Present Day" are individual chapters on twelve authors, all white males. Edwin W. Bowen's *Makers of American Literature: A Class-Book on American Literature* (1908) covers fourteen white male authors. And Horace E. Scudder's *American Prose* (1885) presents Hawthorne, Irving, Longfellow, Whittier, Holmes, Lowell, Thoreau, and Emerson as the sole representatives of American prose "literature."[17]

This trend toward exclusivity in large part reflected the desires of male scholars, authors, and critics to create a more masculine national literature. As Charlene Avallone has forcefully explicated, the discourse of an "American Renaissance," which emerged in the 1880s, sought to legitimize an American literary tradition by linking it to classical conceptions of art and the Anglo-Saxon race, excluding African Americans, immigrants, and women. In addition, from the 1890s to the 1920s, the literary establishment that had given birth to America's high literature and that had partially and provisionally included Phelps, Stoddard, and Woolson (and, much earlier, Alcott) lost much of its clout. As Nancy Glazener explains, "the *Atlantic* group" of magazines was under fire for its promotion of "genteel" realism and middle-class culture. As William Dean Howells, Thomas Bailey Aldrich, Richard Henry Stoddard, and others were cast by George Santayana, Van Wyck Brooks, Frank Norris, and H. H. Boyeson as members of an effeminate, bourgeois literary elite that had to be usurped, it is no wonder that Alcott and Phelps were dismissed out of hand for their sentimental tendencies, and that Stoddard and Woolson became tainted by their association with the genteel literary establishment. In the battles over literary turf at the turn of the century, critics, in Glazener's words, resorted to "feminization as a way of discrediting an ideological opponent," leading to "women's being blamed for the establishment's taboos."[18]

An illuminating example of how the prejudices of the literary establishment affected the institutionalization of a white male literary canon can be found in the pages of the *Critic*. On April 12, 1884, the magazine announced the results of a readers' poll under the title "Our 'Forty Immortals.'" Readers had been asked to elect authors to "membership in a possible American Academy, formed on the same general principle as the famous French literary institution." At the moment, it was assumed, no authoritative institution existed that could establish the American pantheon for which critics, authors, and editors had been longing. The proposed academy could be such an institution. The results of the ostensibly democratic election read like a who's who of the literary elite. Holmes, Lowell, and Whittier were the top three choices. Howells ranked fifth, James thirteenth, and Samuel Clemens fourteenth. (Only living authors were considered, hence the exclusion of Hawthorne, Emerson, and Longfellow.) The editors also listed the names of every individual who received at least one vote. Of these "at least three hundred candidates," not one was a woman, the editors having stipulated that to be eligible, authors must be "of the sterner sex." But this did not stop some readers from sending in the names of women. The most frequently mentioned were listed separately. Stowe, of course, led the list. Phelps and Woolson were also mentioned, as were Jackson and Spofford.[19] Notwithstanding the devotion of readers who wrote in these "ineligible" names, in the eyes of the *Critic*, women could not be considered "immortal." The very idea of an academy of the greatest authors (like the notion of the "artist" or "genius" on an individual scale) was irrevocably male. Therefore, when readers requested that a parallel poll of the " 'Forty Immortals' of the gentler sex" be conducted, the *Critic*'s editors did not take the idea seriously. Two weeks later, the following explanation appeared: "this would never do. The embarrassment of riches is too great. To hold all the American women worthy of membership in such an institution, the Academy would have to be composed of four hundred, rather than of forty, ladies." The implication was that ranking women writers was futile. Virtually any woman who wrote books or articles would have to be included because none was better or more worthy of lasting recognition than another. Such a view is corroborated in a piece on "American Women of Letters" published the previous year in the *Literary World*. The anonymous author, claiming the authority of the literary establishment, declared that no American women were worthy of the designation "women of letters." "American men of letters we certainly have — or have had, men worthy to stand by the side of any but the very chief of the men of letters across the sea; but where in America can we find a George Eliot or a Mrs. Browning?" Stoddard's complaint, written in 1855, remained, according to this critic. No American woman exhibited enough "masculinity in her composition" to join "our Pantheon."[20]

When the National Institute of Arts and Letters was formed in 1898, and the American Academy of Arts and Letters followed six years later, these institutions carried out the formerly hypothetical process of selecting "Forty Immortals" and put into practice the exclusive cultural hierarchy of the *Critic*'s imaginary academy. As Thomas Bender writes, many of the men who belonged to these organizations "were united by a commitment to Anglo-Saxonism in literature and life; they were deeply worried about democracy, immigration, and modernism." Their concern over New Women and the suffrage movement certainly also played a significant role. And when the two organizations held a joint convention in 1911, a photo of their chief members appeared in the *Book News Monthly* under the heading "Group of Immortals."[21] Once again, immortality was reserved exclusively for white males.

The *Atlantic*'s publishers and editors also played a large role in these conservative canonizing efforts at the end of the century. Even though the literary establishment led by the magazine was losing cultural authority in favor of the universities, they still had a tremendous impact on canon formation, and while they had once included women in their project of creating a national high literature, those same women were now out of the picture. During the 1880s and 1890s, the *Atlantic*, which helped establish Hawthorne, Emerson, Longfellow, Whittier, Holmes, and Lowell as the representatives of America's unique literary legacy, returned to its roots in Brahmin culture. The ghosts of the *Atlantic*'s illustrious past loomed large in its pages, as is evidenced by the numerous poems and essays in the 1880s paying tribute to its founding fathers. Meanwhile, Horace Scudder, the magazine's most prolific reviewer and its editor during the 1890s, published a number of anthologies and reviews of the Old Guard's works and lobbied for their inclusion in school curricula.[22] From 1881 to 1896, Houghton, Mifflin, the publisher of the *Atlantic*, produced the *American Men of Letters* series, which featured only one woman, Margaret Fuller, and no people of color. This series, as Scott E. Casper writes, "established the ground on which future scholars built." And the growing textbook market for secondary schools, led by Houghton, Mifflin, also reflected the conservative tendencies of canon formation in focusing on the elite authors promoted by the *Atlantic*.[23]

Women writers' exclusion from the canon that the *Atlantic* helped to create reflected much more than shifting literary tastes. It also was the result of the male establishment's conservative reaction against the pluralist culture of which women were a prominent part. The biases against female authors and the "feminine" in literature were reinforced as the literary elite feared that a diverse culture was set to replace the one in which privileged Anglo-Saxon males had a monopoly on cultural power. The growing consensus that American literature should be masculine and therefore grounded in manly realism and naturalism was part of the reaction of male elites against the new factions whose voices were clamoring for recognition. As African American males gained the ballot, Irish immigrants took over the political machines of northern cities, workers staged strikes, and women demanded with increasing intensity the right to vote, the Old Guard and the younger men who saw themselves as their inheritors felt that their authority as the creators and monitors of America's culture was threatened. Fearing these cultural and political changes, male critics and scholars decried what they per- ceived as the feminine domination of American letters and attacked ambitious women writers, establishing themselves as "cultural custodians," as authori- ties who knew better than the (feminine) multitudes what should constitute the American literary pantheon. The hegemony these men had enjoyed was threat- ened on many fronts, but they were determined to maintain their hold on Ameri- can letters and high culture. Meanwhile, many women and African Americans focused their attention on gaining social and political rights, which they deemed of the greatest importance.

Echoing the conservative desire at the turn of the century for social stability in the face of upheaval, American literary discourse tended toward the nostalgic and homogeneous. Canonization itself was essentially an attempt of the "genteel" forces in American letters to create an American literary tradition that was largely uniform and stable rather than diffuse and disorganized. The desire for a select canon of American literature was by its very nature exclusionary rather than anthological and effectively suppressed the impulses toward a democratic na- tional literature, which had competed with elitist tendencies throughout the century. By the 1880s and 1890s, a sharp division between high and low literature had displaced the pluralistic model that would potentially include women writers in a tier just below the lords of American literature. Whereas the names of Alcott, Phelps, Stoddard, and Woolson previously had been uttered in the same breath as Hawthorne, Emerson, James, Brontë, and Eliot, such comparisons between male and female writers or between American and British were no longer possible.

Making a Place in the Canon

The reconfiguration in the late-twentieth and the early-twenty-first centuries of the white, all-male canon to include women and people of color has meant, to some extent, that the works of Alcott, Phelps, Stoddard, and Woolson have been revalued as important contributions to America's literary heritage. But the posi- tions of these writers are not secure for some of the same reasons that their works were not canonized in the nineteenth century. Alcott, Phelps, Stoddard, and Woolson were deemed to be "pioneers" who participated in a turn toward real- ism and local color without actually being influential members of those move- ments. Today they still don't seem to belong to a single identifiable period;

rather, they are viewed as products of a transitional period in American literary history and as authors who wrote a great variety of works, making it difficult to fit them into current literary categories. These four writers don't belong to the so-called women's categories of domestic literature or local color, nor to the so-called men's movements of romanticism and realism; rather, they straddled male and female literary realms, breaking down the classification of women's writing as low- or middlebrow literature and the idea that high literature was reserved exclusively for men. As a result, they posed a serious threat to the male literary elite, which was trying to establish America's literary reputation on the world stage and which would do so, in part, by erasing these writers from the literary map altogether. When their works have been considered, they have seemed to exist in a barren middle ground between the "feminine fifties" and the local color 1890s. As Mary Moss wrote of Stoddard in 1902, "her books form no link in the chain of literature, since she exerted no influence."[24] This image has persisted about all four writers and is essentially accurate. They were quickly neglected not only by scholars and critics but also by subsequent writers. The same is true of Davis, Spofford, Lazarus, and Jackson. Charlotte Forten Grimké and Sherwood Bonner, despite their early ambitions, did not live long enough or publish enough to have an impact on the critics of their day, so were doomed more completely to obscurity.

Another force that helped to erase this link of the postbellum generation of women writers in the chain of American literature was subsequent female authors themselves. Edith Wharton and Willa Cather, who have loomed large in the discussions of women writers adopting identities as serious artists, tried to establish themselves by participating in an increasingly masculine literary world. Therefore, they did not recognize Alcott, Phelps, Stoddard, Woolson, or any of the others as their literary ancestors. Cather's relation to Jewett, however, helped to secure the latter's reputation. If, as Sharon Dean has suggested, Wharton was influenced by Woolson,[25] this connection remained hidden during Wharton's lifetime, and so her recognition did not extend to her literary foremother. In fact, Wharton ignored the earlier generation altogether. Donna M. Campbell reflects Wharton's view of her predecessors when she writes, "Identifying local colorists Jewett and Freeman rather than the previous generation of sentimentalists as her 'predecessors,' Wharton defines herself as a rebel against the tradition of women's local color fiction rather than as a practitioner of it." By dismissing the earlier sentimentalists and distinguishing herself from the later local colorists, she helped to obscure the innovations of the intervening generation of women writers. To a significant extent, Wharton's and Cather's erasure of postbellum women writers has led scholars to assume that women's literature before the 1890s was only sentimental or domestic, as Deborah Lindsay Williams does when she writes of Wharton and Cather: "Claiming the role of artist for themselves marks a significant departure from the tradition of nineteenth-century female authorship," represented in Williams's study by the antebellum writers Stowe, Fanny Fern, and E. D. E. N. Southworth. Similarly, Amy Kaplan declares, "By pitting professional authorship against domesticity, Wharton defines herself against an earlier generation of American women novelists, known as the sentimental or domestic novelists."[26] If we let Wharton and Cather dictate our understanding of women's literary tradition, the postbellum generation disappears.

It also seems appropriate to return to the question of Jewett's importance. As I mentioned at the outset and have tried to convey throughout, she can be viewed as participating in many of the developments I chart here. She certainly devoted herself to her art and received recognition from the literary elite. She wrestled with her early ambitions and found a way to modify them in order to gain access to the high culture periodicals. And she, in essence, achieved what Alcott, Phelps, Stoddard, and Woolson could not—immortality as an artist. However, it is fair to say that the fact that she did not challenge the male literary elite helped to facilitate her lasting reputation. She represented for them a nonthreatening woman writer who knew her place, so to speak. She gained their respect by not asking for inclusion in their pantheon. Her work did not exhibit the kind of ambitions visible in some of Alcott's, Phelps's, Stoddard's, and Woolson's works. It is important to note that many recent scholars have argued against the "minor" or "small" status of Jewett's fiction, seeing much larger implications for nation building and feminizing American culture in her work, particularly *The Country of the Pointed Firs.*[27] However, my concern here is with how Jewett has been viewed since the late nineteenth century and on what terms she had been granted a place in the canon.

I do not wish to discredit Jewett's contribution to American literature or suggest that her work is of less value that that of Alcott, Phelps, Stoddard, or Woolson. On the contrary, if Jewett is worthy of serious attention, as she certainly is, then other women writers of her generation are equally deserving of the prestige that has been primarily or even solely granted to Jewett. My desire is that Jewett will no longer be seen as the single figure representing postbellum women writers, in part because she does not represent the full scope of their growing ambitions and participation in America's emerging high literary culture. By continuing to focus on Jewett and the local color writers of the 1890s, scholars perpetuate the notion of a separate sphere for women writers in the second half of the nineteenth century. When we expand our horizon to include the emerging artists of the 1860s–80s, divisions between a male and a female American literature begin to dissolve.

In addition, the writings of Alcott, Phelps, Stoddard, and Woolson challenge the dominant image of the American woman literary artist as essentially "private," "hidden," and "reticent," an image encapsulated by Emily Dickinson.[28] Often taken as the most accomplished woman writer of the nineteenth century, Dickinson has come to represent the impossibility of any female author openly subverting taboos against women's devotion to art. While the careers of Alcott, Phelps, Stoddard, Woolson, and many of their female contemporaries exhibit strategies to deflect criticism of their ambitions, they certainly do not display the degree of reticence that Dickinson did. Again, it is important that we begin to reconfigure our understanding of American women writers and literary traditions in order to move beyond the kind of stereotype created by viewing Dickinson as *the* model of the nineteenth-century American female literary artist.

The careers of Alcott, Phelps, Stoddard, and Woolson make clear that our understanding of American women's literary history as advancing from sentimentalism to domestic literature to local color to modernism obscures the value of many women writers who do not fit neatly into any of those categories. We create the wrong impression when we teach students the Fuller-Stowe-Dickinson-Jewett-Chopin line of women writers' development and hold up a few shining examples of women's authorship without illuminating the diversity of women's voices and ambitions that flourished in the nineteenth century, particularly in the postbellum period. Such a paradigm reifies what Avallone describes as late-nineteenth-century scholars' attempts to contain female authors as "a series of exceptional individuals, not affiliated in literary traditions with one another or with men but, rather, assigned successively to a subordinate women's 'position.' "[29] Additionally, by constructing a pattern of women's writing that advances from sentimentalism to domestic fiction to local color, scholars have created a parallel to the romanticism-realism-naturalism model that has governed our understanding of mainstream (men's) American literary history. Few writers fit neatly into such narrow classifications, and by perpetuating them in scholarship and in the classroom as the dominant model of the nation's literary past, we also perpetuate the narrow view of late-nineteenth- and early-twentieth-century canonizers who sought to elevate a few writers above all others.

The conventional model of separate literary traditions for men and women also propagates the theory popular in the nineteenth century among advocates of women's "special genius" that women's writings are essentially different from men's. Our understanding of this period's construction of a national literature should be much more complex and multifaceted than it has been, and we should resist resurrecting old hierarchies. Of course, even as Alcott, Phelps, Stoddard, and Woolson sought entrance to high literary culture, they also understood themselves as different from male writers. But their writings and careers show us that difference does not necessarily mean entirely separate. Julia Ward Howe's view of a separate literary firmament for George Sand, or Phelps's depiction of the hierarchy of male and female writers at Holmes's breakfast, suggest how this generation of writers envisioned literary immortality for women writers and a place in the high literary culture, albeit distinct from the highest level, inhabited by the major male writers. This two-tiered view of the literary pantheon is much more inclusive than the all-male canon that prevailed, and therefore should be recognized as a competing model of a national literature. However, such a distinction should not be replicated today as we restructure the canon. For inherent in it is the assumption that women's writings are essentially different and inferior. It is important to recognize the potency of this belief when studying the literature of this period, but we must find alternative paradigms to govern our reconstruction of the American literary map.

As we do so, we should pay much more attention to Alcott, Phelps, Stoddard, Woolson, and their contemporaries and no longer view them as isolated figures, disconnected from each other and from male writers. An important next step is to more fully consider how women writers of this generation participated in and challenged the major literary movements of the nineteenth century, particularly romanticism and realism, both of which scholars today still construct as composed almost exclusively of male authors. Many postbellum women writers produced texts displaying their serious engagement with the hotly contested issues that arose from their period's shifting literary aesthetics and solidifying artistic standards. In my next project, an extension of this one, I will consider how Alcott, Phelps, Stoddard, Woolson, and other postbellum women writers formulated their theories of literary art and put them into practice. I will argue that by adopting the aim of the artist as "truth-teller," they were engaged in the most central literary issues of their day, confronting the obstacles to women writers within romanticism and realism and making serious efforts to find room for women in America's emerging high literary culture.

Chronology

This chronology is not exhaustive but highlights events discussed in this book on a timeline that allows for a comparison of the four authors' biographies.

1823   Elizabeth Barstow [Stoddard] is born on May 6 in Mattapoisett, MA.

1832   Louisa May Alcott is born on November 29 in Germantown, PA.

1840   Abby May Alcott is born on July 26 in Concord, MA. (She will later go by May.)

        Constance Fenimore Woolson is born on March 5, in Claremont, NH.

1843   The Alcotts undertake their Fruitlands experiment in June, and it will last until January 1844.

1844   Mary Gray Phelps [Elizabeth Stuart Phelps] is born on August 31.

1849   Stoddard's mother, Betsy Barstow, dies.

1851   Alcott's first publication, the poem "Sunlight," by "Flora Fairfield," appears in *Peterson's Magazine*.

        Stoddard begins her friendship with Margaret Sweat, which will last until 1854. Stoddard attends literary gatherings in New York City and meets Richard Henry Stoddard and his circle of poet friends.

1852   Phelps's mother dies, after which the daughter adopts her mother's name, Elizabeth Stuart Phelps.

        Stoddard's first publication, the sketch "Phases," appears in the *Literary World* in October. Her father goes bankrupt in the same month, breaking up her family in Mattapoisett. She marries Richard Henry Stoddard in December.

1853   Phelps's mother's story, "The Husband of a Blue," is published posthumously.

1854   Alcott's first book, *Flower Fables*, is published in December.

        Stoddard begins to publish her column in the *Daily Alta California* in October; the column will run until February 1858.

1855   Stoddard gives birth to a son, Wilson (Willy).

1857   Elizabeth Gaskell's biography *The Life of Charlotte Brontë* is published.
        Stoddard and Alcott are inspired by the book and write about it, Stoddard
        in her *Daily Alta* column and Alcott in her journal.

        The *Atlantic Monthly* is founded.

1860   Alcott's first publication in the *Atlantic*, the story "Love and Self-Love,"
        appears in March. A second story, "A Modern Cinderella," is published in
        the *Atlantic* in October. Her antislavery story "M.L." is rejected. Alcott
        writes the first draft of *Moods* in four weeks in August.

        Phelps reads *Aurora Leigh* and decides to commit herself to authorship.

        Stoddard's first short story, "My Own Story," is published in the *Atlantic*
        in May.

1861   Alcott revises *Moods*.

        Stoddard's son Willy dies.

1862   In January, James T. Fields, publisher of the *Atlantic*, tells Alcott to give
        up writing and gives her money to run a kindergarten, which she does
        from January to April while living with the Fieldses in Boston. In
        December, Alcott begins her secret life as a writer of sensation stories,
        winning a hundred-dollar prize from *Frank Leslie's Illustrated Newspaper*.
        She also begins her stint as a Civil War nurse in Washington, D.C., which
        will end in January 1863.

        Stoddard's first novel, *The Morgesons*, is published.

1863   Alcott's *Hospital Sketches* are published in the *Boston Commonwealth* in May
        and June and then in book form. She has three works published in the
        Atlantic: the story "Debby's Début" in August (almost three years after it
        was accepted), the poem "Thoreau's Flute" in September, and the story
        "The Brothers" (later retitled "My Contraband") in November. In
        December, Alcott publishes a collection of her Civil War stories, *On
        Picket Duty, and Other Tales*.

        Stoddard's second son, Lorimer (Lorry), is born.

1864   Alcott's novel *Moods* is published in December. Fields rejects her story
        "An Hour" for the *Atlantic*, and the assistant editor accepts "Nelly's
        Hospital" for *Our Young Folks*. Her relationship with the publishing firm
        Ticknor and Fields and their magazines terminates.

1865   Alcott travels to Europe in July and returns in July 1866.

        Stoddard's second novel, *Two Men*, is published.

1866   Stoddard keeps her writer's journal during the summer in Mattapoisett.

1867   Stoddard publishes her final novel, *Temple House*.

1868   Alcott's sensation *Little Women* is published, part 1 in October, and part 2
        in April 1869.

Alcott publishes "Psyche's Art" in book form.

Phelps's first novel, *The Gates Ajar*, is published to much popular acclaim. Her first story in the *Atlantic*, "The Tenth of January," appears and gains her the recognition of the literary elite.

1869   Woolson's father, Charles Jarvis Woolson, Sr., dies.

1870   In April, Alcott travels to Europe with her sister May and May's friend Alice Bartlett; she will return in June 1871.

Phelps publishes *Hedged In*.

Stoddard publishes her only story about a woman writer, "Collected by a Valetudinarian," in *Harper's*.

Woolson's first publications appear in July, "The Happy Valley" in *Harper's* and "Fairy Island" in *Putnam's*.

1871   Phelps publishes *The Silent Partner*. She also publishes her essays "Unhappy Girls" and "The True Woman" in the *Independent*.

Stoddard publishes "A Literary Whim" in *Appletons' Journal*. Over the next two years, with her husband as editor, she publishes many pieces (some under pseudonyms) in the *Aldine Press*.

1872   Alcott publishes *Aunt Jo's Scrap-Bag: Shawl Straps*. In December, serialization of her novel *Work* begins.

Woolson's first publication in the *Atlantic*, the poem "Ideal. (The Artist Speaks.)," appears in October.

1873   Woolson begins her extensive travels through the South with her mother, continuing through 1879. Her first book, *The Old Stone House*, a book for children, is published under the pseudonym "Anne March."

1874   Stoddard publishes her children's book, *Lolly Dink's Doings*.

1875   Woolson's first collection, *Castle Nowhere: Lake Country Sketches*, is published.

1876   May Alcott returns to Europe, where she will live until her death.

Phelps gives her lectures on George Eliot at Boston University and builds her house, which she called her "old maid's paradise," in Gloucester.

Woolson publishes her poem "To George Eliot" in the *New Century for Woman*.

1877   Alcott publishes *A Modern Mephistopheles* in Roberts Brothers' No Name series. Her mother, Abigail Alcott, dies in November.

Phelps publishes *The Story of Avis*.

1878   May Alcott marries Ernest Nieriker in March. Alcott begins to write *Diana and Persis*.

1879   May Alcott gives birth to a daughter, Lulu, and dies seven weeks later, December 29, in Paris.

Alcott stops writing *Diana and Persis*.

Phelps publishes *An Old Maid's Paradise* about her residence in Gloucester.

In January and February, Woolson publishes two reviews of James's *Europeans* in the *Atlantic*'s "Contributors' Club." Her mother, Hannah Cooper Pomeroy Woolson, dies on February 13. In November, Woolson travels to Europe. She will not return to the United States.

1880   Lulu Nieriker arrives from Europe to be cared for by Alcott.

Phelps publishes "A Plea for Immortality" in the *Atlantic*.

Woolson meets Henry James in late April in Florence. In May, her story "'Miss Grief'" is published in *Lippincott's*. In December, her first novel, *Anne*, begins serialization in *Harper's*. It will be published in book form in 1882.

1882   Phelps publishes *Dr. Zay*.

Woolson publishes her story "The Street of the Hyacinth" in *Century* magazine in May and June.

Alcott publishes a revised *Moods* to little critical notice.

1883   Woolson publishes her second novel, *For the Major*.

1886   Alcott publishes *Jo's Boys*, the final book in the *Little Women* trilogy.

Phelps's close friend, Dr. Mary Briggs Harris, with whom she sometimes lived, dies.

Woolson lives in Aurora Leigh's villa at Bellosguardo in Florence with artist friends and publishes her novel *East Angels*.

1887   Woolson publishes "At the Château of Corinne" in *Harper's* in October.

1888   Bronson Alcott dies on March 4; Louisa May Alcott dies on March 6.

Phelps marries Herbert Dickinson Ward.

With the help of Edmund Clarence Stedman, Stoddard's novels *Two Men* and *Temple House* are republished, the former with a laudatory introduction by Stedman.

1889   Ednah D. Cheney publishes *Louisa May Alcott: Her Life, Letters, and Journals*.

Stoddard's novel *The Morgesons* is republished.

1893   Phelps publishes the story "The Rejected Manuscript" in *Harper's*.

1894   Shortly after finishing her final novel, *Horace Chase*, and suffering from influenza, Woolson commits suicide in Venice on January 24.

1895   Stoddard's selected *Poems*, spanning her entire career, are published by Houghton, Mifflin.

Phelps publishes her autobiography, *Chapters from a Life*.

1897   The Authors' Club honors Richard Henry Stoddard with a public dinner to commemorate his career, and Elizabeth Stoddard, although she must sit in the balcony with the other women, is also honored.

1901   All three of Stoddard's novels are again republished. *The Morgesons* contains a new preface by the author, including recollections of how she developed as a writer and an excerpt from a letter by Hawthorne.

1902   Stoddard dies on August 1.

Phelps publishes the novel *Confessions of a Wife*.

1911   Phelps dies on January 28.

Notes

ABBREVIATIONS

Manuscript Collections

BPL	Boston Public Library, Department of Rare Books and Manuscripts, Boston, MA
MH	Houghton Library, Harvard University, Cambridge, MA
NYCol-SC	Stedman Collection, Columbia University, Rare Book and Manuscript Library, Butler Library, New York, NY
PSt-Sh	Shelley Collection, Rare Books, University Libraries, Pennsylvania State University, University Park, PA
UVA	Clifton Waller Barrett Library, Albert and Shirley Small Special Collections Library, University of Virginia, Charlottesville, VA
VTMC	Abernethy Library, Special Collections, Middlebury College, Middlebury, VT
WRHS	Mather Family Papers, 1834–1967, Western Reserve Historical Society, Cleveland, OH

Persons

CFW	Constance Fenimore Woolson
EBS	Elizabeth Barstow Stoddard
ECS	Edmund Clarence Stedman
ESP	Elizabeth Stuart Phelps
LMA	Louisa May Alcott
RHS	Richard Henry Stoddard

Introduction

1. Kate G. Wells, "The Transitional American Woman," *Atlantic Monthly* 46 (Dec. 1880): 817–823; quotes on 817–818, 821, 819. See Kristen Swinth, *Painting Professionals: Women Artists and the Development of Modern American Art, 1870–1930* (Chapel Hill: University of North Carolina Press, 2001), for an examination of the dawning ambition of many women visual artists during this period.

2. Catharine Maria Sedgwick, *Life and Letters*, ed. Mary E. Dewey (1871); quoted in Judith Fetterley, ed., *Provisions: A Reader from Nineteenth-Century American Women*

(Bloomington: Indiana University Press, 1985), 44. Sedgwick to William Minot, Oct. 5, 1851; quoted in Mary Kelley, introduction to *The Power of Her Sympathy: The Autobiography and Journal of Catharine Maria Sedgwick* (Boston: Massachusetts Historical Society, 1993), 3.

3. CFW to Katherine Mather, 1880, WRHS. ESP, *Chapters from a Life* (Boston: Houghton, Mifflin, 1895), 253. LMA, Feb. 1861, *The Journals of Louisa May Alcott*, ed. Joel Myerson, Daniel Shealy, and associate ed. Madeleine B. Stern (Boston: Little, Brown, 1989), 103. EBS to Whitelaw Reid, n.d. (Monday evening), Reid Family Papers, Library of Congress, Manuscript Division, Washington, D.C.

4. Nina Baym, *Woman's Fiction: A Guide to Novels by and about Women in America, 1820–1870*, 2d ed. (Urbana: University of Illinois Press, 1993), 32. Fetterley, introduction to *Provisions*, 7, 6.

5. Baym, *Woman's Fiction*, 32. Elaine Showalter, *Sister's Choice: Tradition and Change in American Women's Writing* (New York: Oxford University Press, 1994), 67. Joanne Dobson, "The American Renaissance Reenvisioned," in *The (Other) American Traditions: Nineteenth-Century Women Writers*, ed. Joyce W. Warren (New Brunswick, NJ: Rutgers University Press, 1993), 177.

6. CFW to ECS, July 23, [1876], NYCol-SC. LMA to Mrs. A. D. Moshier, April 6, [1878], in *The Selected Letters of Louisa May Alcott*, ed. Joel Myerson, Daniel Shealy, and associate ed. Madeleine B. Stern (Athens: University of Georgia Press, 1995), 228.

7. Elizabeth Ammons, *Conflicting Stories: American Women Writers at the Turn into the Twentieth Century* (New York: Oxford University Press, 1991), 4–5.

8. Ammons's study, *Conflicting Stories*, explores a generation of women writers at the turn of the century that was more culturally, regionally, and racially diverse.

9. The critical studies that most influenced me include Sarah Elbert, *A Hunger for Home: Louisa May Alcott's Place in American Culture* (New Brunswick, NJ: Rutgers University Press, 1987); Richard H. Brodhead, *Cultures of Letters: Scenes of Reading and Writing in Nineteenth-Century America* (Chicago: University of Chicago Press, 1993), chap. 3; Carol Farley Kessler, *Elizabeth Stuart Phelps* (Boston: Twayne, 1982), and "A Literary Legacy: Elizabeth Stuart Phelps, Mother and Daughter," *Frontiers* 5 (fall 1980): 28–33; Susan Coultrap-McQuin, "Elizabeth Stuart Phelps" (Ph.D. diss., University of Iowa, 1979), and *Doing Literary Business: American Women Writers in the Nineteenth Century* (Chapel Hill: University of North Carolina Press, 1990), chap. 7; Sandra Zagarell, "Legacy Profile: Elizabeth Drew Barstow Stoddard (1823–1902)," *Legacy* 8 (spring 1991): 39–49; Lawrence Buell and Sandra Zagarell, "Biographical and Critical Introduction," *The Morgesons and Other Writings, Published and Unpublished*, by Elizabeth Stoddard (Philadelphia: University of Pennsylvania Press, 1984); Sharon Dean, *Constance Fenimore Woolson: Homeward Bound* (Knoxville: University of Tennessee Press, 1995); Cheryl Torsney, *Constance Fenimore Woolson: The Grief of Artistry* (Athens: University of Georgia Press, 1989); and Joan Myers Weimer, introduction to *Women Artists, Women Exiles: "Miss Grief" and Other Stories*, by Constance Fenimore Woolson (New Brunswick, NJ: Rutgers University Press, 1988), ix–xliii.

10. Reprints of their works include LMA, *Moods*, ed. Sarah Elbert (New Brunswick, NJ: Rutgers University Press, 1991); LMA, *Alternative Alcott*, ed. Elaine Showalter (New Brunswick, NJ: Rutgers University Press, 1988); ESP, *The Story of Avis*, ed. Carol Farley Kessler (New Brunswick, NJ: Rutgers University Press, 1985); EBS, *The Morgesons and*

Other Writings; EBS, *The Morgesons,* ed. Lawrence Buell and Sandra Zagarell (New York: Penguin, 1997); and CFW, *Women Artists, Women Exiles.*

11. Brodhead, *Cultures of Letters,* 173, 175.

12. Jane Tompkins, *Sensational Designs: The Cultural Work of American Fiction, 1790–1860* (New York: Oxford University Press, 1985). Nina Baym, *American Women Writers and the Work of History, 1790–1860* (New Brunswick, NJ: Rutgers University Press, 1995), 1. Monika M. Elbert, introduction to *Separate Spheres No More: Gender Convergence in American Literature, 1830–1930* (Tuscaloosa: University of Alabama Press, 2000), 2. The literary separate spheres model was influenced by that developed by historians in the 1970s and 1980s. Both the literary and historical models are undergoing significant revision. Elbert provides an extensive overview of the debate in her introduction to *Separate Spheres No More.* For some of the most important work revising or challenging the separate spheres model, see Gillian Brown, *Domestic Individualism: Imagining Self in Nineteenth-Century America* (Berkeley: University of California Press, 1990); Barbara Bardes and Suzanne Gossett, *Declarations of Independence: Women and Political Power in Nineteenth-Century American Fiction* (New Brunswick, NJ: Rutgers University Press, 1990); Michael Newbury, *Figuring Authorship in Antebellum America* (Stanford, CA: Stanford University Press, 1997); Lora Romero, *Home Fronts: Domesticity and Its Critics in the Antebellum United States* (Durham, NC: Duke University Press, 1997); Cathy Davidson, ed., "No More Separate Spheres," special issue of *American Literature* 70, no. 3 (1998); Karen Kilcup, ed., *Nineteenth-Century American Women Writers: A Critical Reader* (Malden, MA: Blackwell, 1998); Karen Kilcup, ed., *Soft Canons: American Women Writers and Masculine Tradition* (Iowa City: University of Iowa Press, 2000); and Elbert, *Separate Spheres No More.*

13. Romero, *Home Fronts,* 5, and chap. 5. Newbury, *Figuring Authorship,* 32.

14. Elbert, *Separate Spheres No More,* 1. I support Elbert in her argument that Cathy Davidson's "No More Separate Spheres" issue of *American Literature* tends to present another binary by dividing critics into two camps—those who still believe in separate spheres and those who don't. "[I]t is more productive to analyze the overlap of private and public, of female and male, than to create an artificial either-or situation," Elbert writes (21).

15. For discussions of this issue, see Susan K. Harris, " 'But is it any *good?':* Evaluating Nineteenth-Century American Women's Fiction," in Warren, *The (Other) American Traditions,* 263–279; and Jane Tompkins, " 'But Is It Any Good?': The Institutionalization of Literary Value," in *Sensational Designs,* 186–201.

16. Buell and Zagarell, "Biographical and Critical Introduction," *The Morgesons,* xi.

17. Baym, *Woman's Fiction,* 14.

CHAPTER ONE: Solving the "Old Riddle of the Sphinx"

1. CFW, *Anne* (1882; reprint, New York: Harper & Bros., 1910), 91, 380. The novel began serialization in *Harper's* in December 1880.

2. LMA, *Moods,* ed. Sarah Elbert (1864; reprint New Brunswick, NJ: Rutgers University Press, 1991), 84. EBS, "The Prescription," *Harper's* 28 (May 1864): 797.

3. Thomas Wentworth Higginson, "Literature as an Art," *Atlantic Monthly* 20 (Dec. 1867): 746–747. His review of Harriet Prescott's *Azarian, Atlantic Monthly* 14 (Oct. 1864), expresses doubt about the ability of women to become serious authors.

4. EBS, *Daily Alta California*, Oct. 22, 1854, in *The Morgesons and Other Writings, Published and Unpublished*, ed. Lawrence Buell and Sandra Zagarell (Philadelphia: University of Pennsylvania Press, 1984), 314.

5. "Female Authors," *North American Review* 72 (Jan. 1851): 163–164. Margaret Fuller, *Woman in the Nineteenth Century*; reprinted in *The Portable Margaret Fuller*, ed. Mary Kelley (New York: Penguin, 1994), 288.

6. Martha Woodmansee, *The Author, Art, and the Market: Rereading the History of Aesthetics* (New York: Columbia University Press, 1994), 37.

7. Thomas Carlyle, *On Heroes, Hero-Worship, and the Heroic in History* (1841; reprint, Boston: Ginn, 1901), 179–180.

8. *North American Review* quoted in Russel B. Nye, *The Cultural Life of the New Nation, 1776–1830* (New York: Harper & Row, 1960), 241.

9. Review of *The House of Seven Gables* and *The Blithedale Romance*, by Nathaniel Hawthorne, *North American Review* 76 (Jan. 1853): 228. James Russell Lowell, review of *Sir Rohan's Ghost*, by Harriet Prescott (Spofford), *Atlantic Monthly* 5 (Feb. 1860): 253. Nathaniel Hawthorne, "A Select Party," *United States Magazine and Democratic Review* (July 1844): 36.

10. *Harper's* quoted in Nina Baym, *Novels, Readers, and Reviewers: Responses to Fiction in Antebellum America* (Ithaca, NY: Cornell University Press, 1984), 247.

11. Herman Melville, "Hawthorne and His Mosses," *New York Literary World* (Aug. 17 and 24, 1850); reprinted in Gordon Hutner, ed., *American Literature, American Culture* (New York: Oxford University Press, 1999), 101. Hawthorne quoted in Caroline Ticknor, *Hawthorne and His Publisher* (Boston: Houghton, Mifflin, 1913), 141–142.

12. Michael Gilmore, *American Romanticism and the Marketplace* (Chicago: University of Chicago Press, 1985), 81–82.

13. Ralph Waldo Emerson, "The American Scholar" (1837), in *The Collected Works of Ralph Waldo Emerson*, ed. Alfred R. Ferguson, Joseph Slater, Douglas Emory Wilson, et al., 5 vols. (Cambridge: Harvard University Press, 1971), 1:56–57. Melville, "Hawthorne and His Mosses," 97.

14. Stephen Mintz, *A Prison of Expectations: The Family in Victorian Culture* (New York: New York University Press, 1983), 31.

15. This is Christine Battersby's argument in *Gender and Genius: Towards a Feminist Aesthetics* (Bloomington: Indiana University Press, 1989). Battersby focuses solely on European and British ideals of gender and genius.

16. Margaret Fuller, review of *Essays: Second Series*, by Ralph Waldo Emerson, *New York Daily Tribune*; reprinted in *The Portable Margaret Fuller*, 365. Rebecca Harding Davis, "Boston in the Sixties" (1904); reprinted in *A Rebecca Harding Davis Reader*, ed. Jean Pfaelzer (Pittsburgh: University of Pittsburgh Press, 1995), 450. Katherine McDowell [Sherwood Bonner], "Ralph Waldo Emerson Interviewed by a Fair Southron" (1874); reprinted in *A Sherwood Bonner Sampler, 1869–1884*, ed. Anne Razey Gowdy (Knoxville: University of Tennessee Press, 2000), 17.

17. Ralph Waldo Emerson, "Genius," (1839), in *The Early Lectures of Ralph Waldo Emerson*, ed. Robert Spiller, Stephen E. Whicher, and Wallace E. Williams, 3 vols. (Cambridge: Harvard University Press, Belknap Press, 1959–72), 3:81. My interpretation of Emerson's notion of "genius" is, admittedly, simplified. I have chosen not to elaborate on Emerson's concern with the incommunicability of language because I wish to focus on

those parts of his philosophy of the artist/genius that were more available for popularization and that inspired the majority of American writers.

18. Emerson, "Self-Reliance" (1841), *Collected Works*, 2:29. Henry David Thoreau, *Walden* (1854; reprint, Princeton, NJ: Princeton University Press, 1971), 8. Quote from Emerson's diary, July 15, 1839, in *The Journals and Miscellaneous Notebooks of Ralph Waldo Emerson*, ed. William H. Gilman, Ralph H. Orth, et al., 16 vols. (Cambridge: Harvard University Press, 1960–82), 4:306. Emerson's letters to Emma Lazarus in Ralph L. Rusk, ed., *Letters to Emma Lazarus in the Columbia University Library* (New York: Columbia University Library, 1939).

19. Joel Myerson notes the differing interpretations of Emerson's lecture in his headnote to the lecture in *Transcendentalism: A Reader* (New York: Oxford University Press, 2000), 615. Quote from a female audience member is in Armida Gilbert, " 'Pierced by the Thorns of Reform': Emerson on Womanhood," in *The Emerson Dilemma: Essays on Emerson and Social Reform*, ed. T. Gregory Garvey (Athens: University of Georgia Press, 2001), 107. Jeffrey Steele, "The Limits of Political Sympathy: Emerson, Margaret Fuller, and Woman's Rights," in Garvey, *Emerson Dilemma*, 115, 132. I am grateful for the comments of Jay Grossman at the "New Frontiers in Early American Literature" conference at the University of Virginia (2002), which helped me to clarify my position on Emerson's influence.

20. Fuller, *Woman*, 329, 330.

21. Fuller, *Woman*, 327, 294.

22. ESP, "The True Woman," *Independent* 23 (Oct. 12, 1871): 1; reprinted in ESP, *The Story of Avis*, ed. Carol Farley Kessler (1877; reprint, New Brunswick, NJ: Rutgers University Press, 1985), 269, 271, 272.

23. Alcott quoted in LaSalle (Corbell) Pickett, *Across My Path: Memories of People I Have Known* (1916; reprint, Freeport, NY: Books for Libraries, 1970), 108. CFW to Samuel Mather, Jan. 22, [1887?], WRHS. Charlotte Forten Grimké, *The Journals of Charlotte Forten Grimké*, ed. Brenda Stevenson (New York: Oxford University Press, 1988), 279. Emily Dickinson, *The Letters of Emily Dickinson*, ed. Thomas H. Johnson (Cambridge: Harvard University Press, 1965), 913.

24. Jewett quoted in Elizabeth Silverthorne, *Sarah Orne Jewett: A Writer's Life* (Woodstock, NY: Overlook Press, 1993), 72. Bonner quoted in Hubert H. McAlexander, *The Prodigal Daughter: A Biography of Sherwood Bonner* (Baton Rouge: Louisiana State University Press, 1981; reprint, with a new introduction, Knoxville: University of Tennessee Press, 1999), 60. Lazarus in Bette Roth Young, *Emma Lazarus in Her World: Life and Letters* (Philadelphia: Jewish Publication Society, 1995), 72, 122.

25. LMA to Bronson Alcott, Oct. 13, [1877], in *The Selected Letters of Louisa May Alcott*, ed. Joel Myerson, Daniel Shealy, and associate ed. Madeleine B. Stern (Athens: University of Georgia Press, 1995), 321. LMA, "Reminiscences of Ralph Waldo Emerson," *Youth's Companion* (May 25, 1882): 213. LMA to Maggie Lukens, Feb. 14, [1884], in *Selected Letters*, 280; see also editors' note on 287. LMA, Scrapbook, 1855, bMS Am 1817.2 (24), MH. She also recorded in her journal having attended one of Emerson's classes on "Genius," indicating that she was invited by Emerson, "a great honor, as all the learned ladies go." LMA, Dec. 1860, in *The Journals of Louisa May Alcott*, ed. Joel Myerson, Daniel Shealy, and associate ed. Madeleine B. Stern (Athens: University of Georgia Press, 1997), 101.

26. LMA, *Moods*, 1. Epigraph to *Two Men* quoted in James Matlack, "The Literary Career of Elizabeth Barstow Stoddard" (Ph.D. diss., Yale University, 1967), 341. EBS to Margaret Sweat, Apr. 14, [1852], PSt-Sh. EBS, Journal, in *The Morgesons*, 354. Emerson, "Self-Reliance," 47.

27. CFW to ECS, Sept. 16, [1877], NYCol-SC. Strikethrough in original. CFW to ECS, Apr. 30, [1883], NYCol-SC.

28. Fuller, *Woman*, 280, 294.

29. Lawrence Buell, *New England Literary Culture from Revolution through Renaissance* (Cambridge: Cambridge University Press, 1986), 377. RHS to R. S. Mackenzie, n.d.; quoted in Matlack, "Literary Career," 337–338.

30. EBS to Rufus Griswold, quoted in Matlack, "Literary Career," 122. EBS, *Daily Alta California*, Nov. 18, 1855, quoted in Matlack, 156. CFW, "To George Eliot," *New Century for Women*, no. 2 (May 20, 1876): 1.

31. Dickinson, *Letters*, 376.

32. Theophilus Parsons, "Life and Writings of Madame de Staël," *North American Review* 11 (July 1820): 139. "Madame de Staël," *Appletons' Journal*, n.s., 10 (May 1881): 439.

33. LMA, 1852, *Journals*, 67. EBS, *The Morgesons*, 106. CFW, "At the Château of Corinne" (1887), in *Women Artists, Women Exiles: "Miss Grief" and Other Stories*, ed. Joan Myers Weimer (New Brunswick, NJ: Rutgers University Press, 1988), 229. Ellen Moers, *Literary Women* (Garden City, NY: Doubleday, 1976), 174.

34. See Baym, *Novels*, 259–260.

35. Julia Ward Howe, "George Sand," *Atlantic Monthly* 8 (Nov. 1861): 514, 533. Justin McCarthy. "George Sand," *Galaxy* 9 (May 1870): 663, 661.

36. EBS, *Daily Alta California*, June 19, 1855, in *The Morgesons*, 318. LMA, "Odds and Ends," bMS Am 1817 (24), MH. CFW to ECS, Sept. 28, [1874?], NYCol-SC. Lazarus in Young, *Emma Lazarus*, 183, 192.

37. "Novels of the Season," *North American Review* 67 (Oct. 1848): 355–357.

38. Margaret J. Sweat, "Charlotte Brontë and the Brontë Novels," *North American Review* 85 (Oct. 1857): 315, 316.

39. EBS, *Daily Alta California*, June 2, 1857, quoted in Matlack, "Literary Career," 168. (Matlack incorrectly cites the year as 1855, but the biography was published in 1857.) LMA, June 1857, *Journals*, 85.

40. C. C. Everett, "Elizabeth Barrett Browning," *North American Review* 85 (Oct. 1857): 415, 418. Edward Eggleston, "George Eliot and the Novel," in *Essays from "The Critic"* (Boston: James R. Osgood, 1882), 49–53.

41. "Mrs. Browning's New Poem," *Putnam's* 9 (Jan. 1857): 32. Kate Field, "Elizabeth Barrett Browning," *Atlantic Monthly* 8 (Sept. 1861): 375.

42. EBS, *Daily Alta California*, Jan. 11, 1857, quoted in Sybil B. Weir, "Our Lady Correspondent: The Achievement of Elizabeth Drew Stoddard," *San José Studies* 10 (spring 1984): 87–88. ESP, *Chapters from a Life* (Boston: Houghton, Mifflin, 1895), 64, 65–66. Grimké, *Journals*, 201.

43. "George Eliot," *Spectator*; reprinted in *Appletons' Journal*, n.s., 10 (Mar. 1881): 258.

44. Dickinson, *Letters*, 700. CFW, "To George Eliot," 1. Lazarus in Young, *Emma Lazarus*, 121.

45. ESP, "George Eliot," *Harper's Weekly* 29 (Feb. 14, 1885): 103. See also ESP, "Last Words from George Eliot," *Harper's* 64 (Mar. 1882): 568–571; and ESP, "George Eliot's

Short Stories," *Independent* 37 (Apr. 30, 1885): 1–2. ESP describes her lectures on Eliot in a letter to Eliot, Dec. 1, 1876, George Eliot and George Henry Lewes Collection, Beinecke Rare Book and Manuscript Library, Yale University, New Haven, CT.

46. Julia Ward Howe, "George Sand," *Atlantic Monthly* 8 (Nov. 1861): 534.

47. Fuller quoted in R. W. Emerson, W. H. Channing, and J. F. Clarke, *Memoirs of Margaret Fuller Ossoli*, vol. 1 (New York: Tribune Association, 1869), 297. Helen Gray Cone, "Woman in American Literature," *Century Magazine* 40 (Oct. 1890): 924. This view of Fuller as a superior conversationalist but an incomplete artist was also promoted by Emerson, Channing, and Clarke in the *Memoirs*.

48. Molly Vaux, " 'But Maria, did you *really* write this?': Preface as Cover Story in Lydia Maria Child's *Hobomok*," *Legacy* 17, no. 2 (2000): 131. Carolyn Karcher, *The First Woman in the Republic: A Cultural Biography of Lydia Maria Child* (Durham, NC: Duke University Press, 1994), 102. Lydia Maria Child refers to Sand as her "twin sister" in a letter to Lucy and Mary Osgood, June 12, 1858, in *Lydia Maria Child: Selected Letters, 1817–1880*, ed. Milton Meltzer and Patricia G. Holland (Amherst: University of Massachusetts Press, 1982), 315.

49. Susan Phinney Conrad, *Perish the Thought: Intellectual Women in Romantic America, 1830–1860* (New York: Oxford University Press, 1976), 220.

50. Cone, "Woman in American Literature," 926.

51. Hale quoted in Patricia Okker, *Our Sister Editors: Sarah J. Hale and the Tradition of Nineteenth-Century American Women Editors* (Athens: University of Georgia Press, 1995), 38. Nina Baym, "From Enlightenment to Victorian: Toward a Narrative of American Women Writers Writing History," in *Feminism and American Literary History: Essays* (New Brunswick, NJ: Rutgers University Press, 1992), 107.

52. The term is Mary Kelley's, in *Private Woman, Public Stage: Literary Domesticity in Nineteenth-Century America* (New York: Oxford University Press, 1984), 181–184.

53. Ellen Olney Kirk, "Women Fiction Writers of America," *The National Exposition Souvenir: What America Owes to Women* (Buffalo, NY: Charles Wells Moulton, 1893), 199. Cone, "Woman in American Literature," 926. Elsewhere, I have stressed women writers' exclusion from the magazine. See " 'What! Has she got into the "*Atlantic*"?': Women Writers, the *Atlantic Monthly*, and the Formation of the American Canon," *American Studies* 39 (fall 1998): 5–36. But here I wish to show the ways in which it also offered, particularly in its early years, a unique opportunity for women writers.

54. Thomas Wentworth Higginson, *Letters and Journals of Thomas Wentworth Higginson, 1846–1906*, ed. Mary Thacher Higginson (1921; reprint, New York: Da Capo Press, 1969), 103, 107.

55. LMA mentioned Spofford's stories in a letter to Alfred Whitman, May 11, [1862], *Selected Letters*, 77. Davis described meeting LMA in "Boston in the Sixties," 447–448. LMA, May 1862, *Journals*, 109. ESP, "Stories That Stay," *Century* 81 (Nov. 1910): 119–120.

56. ESP, "Unhappy Girls," *Independent* 23 (July 27, 1871): 1.

57. See Linda W. Rosenzweig, " 'The Anchor of My Life': Middle-Class American Mothers and College-Educated Daughters, 1880–1920," *Journal of Social History* 25 (fall 1991): 5–25.

58. Joyce Vantassel-Baska, "The Talent Development Process in Women Writers: A Study of Charlotte Brontë and Virginia Woolf," in *Remarkable Women: Perspectives on Female Talent Development*, ed. Karen D. Arnold, Kathleen Diane Noble, and Rena Faye

Subotnik (Creskill, NJ: Hampton Press, 1996), 298; and R. Ochse, *Before the Gates of Excellence: The Determinants of Creative Genius* (Cambridge: Cambridge University Press, 1990), have stimulated my thinking in devising this list.

59. Ochse, *Before the Gates*, 149.

60. Jewett quoted in Blanchard, *Sarah Orne Jewett*, 31. LMA, "Sketch of Childhood," in *Life, Letters, and Journals*, ed. Ednah Cheney (1889; reprint, New York: Gramercy Books, 1995), 15. ESP, *Chapters*, 20.

61. EBS to ECS, Apr. 24, n.y., NYCol-SC. Hawthorne quoted in Joyce W. Warren, introduction to Fanny Fern, *Ruth Hall and Other Writings* (New Brunswick, NJ: Rutgers University Press, 1986), xxxv. LMA, *Journals*, 55–56. Child, *Selected Letters*, 534.

62. ESP, *Chapters*, 103–104. The incident with the thimble is recorded in Elizabeth T. Spring, "Elizabeth Stuart Phelps," in *Our Famous Women: An Authorized Record of the Lives and Deeds of Distinguished American Women of Our Times* (Hartford, CT: A. D. Worthington, 1888), 566. Phelps developed an interest in art before literature. ESP, *Chapters*, 19. Dickinson, *Letters*, 82. ESP, *Chapters*, 82.

63. LMA, June 1860, *Journals*, 99. EBS, "Literary Folk as They Came and Went with Ourselves," *Saturday Evening Post* 172 (June 30, 1900): 1223. ESP, *Chapters*, 22, 79. LMA to Bronson Alcott, Nov. 29, 1856, in *Selected Letters*, 26.

64. Statistics cited by Sharon L. Dean in *Constance Fenimore Woolson: Homeward Bound* (Knoxville: University of Tennessee Press, 1995), 102. Susan Coultrap-McQuin, "Elizabeth Stuart Phelps: The Cultural Context of a Nineteenth-Century Professional Writer," (Ph.D. diss., University of Iowa, 1979), 6–7. ESP, *Chapters*, 77. Cheryl B. Torsney, *Constance Fenimore Woolson: The Grief of Artistry* (Athens: University of Georgia Press, 1989), 164. Dean, *Woolson*, 104. Woolson's letter to Samuel Mather, Jan. 1891, about Spaulding, quoted in Dean, *Woolson*, 104.

65. LMA, "Happy Women" (1868), in *Alternative Alcott*, ed. Elaine Showalter (New Brunswick, NJ: Rutgers University Press, 1988), 203, 206.

66. Kelley, *Private Woman*, 37.

67. One of Woolson's first publications, "The Haunted Lake," about her great-uncle, appeared under the name of "Constance Fenimore" in *Harper's* 44 (Dec. 1871): 20–30. On Woolson's intention to use "Constance Fenimore" as her nom de plume, see her letter to Mary L. Booth, Feb. 2, 1871, Princeton University Library, Princeton, NJ. She capitalized on her Cooper connection throughout her life: "I am still sailing on my middle name — as I have done ever since I came abroad," she wrote to Samuel Mather, Jan. 10, [1882?], WRHS. Her mother's autobiographical writings appear in Clare Benedict, ed., *Voices out of the Past*, vol. 1 of *Five Generations* (London: Ellis, 1929), 119–221.

68. CFW to ECS, Sept. 28, 1874, in Laura Stedman and George M. Gould, *Life and Letters of Edmund Clarence Stedman*, vol. 1 (New York: Moffat, Yard, 1910), 522. In this letter she writes of her reading the *Atlantic* "ten years ago." Clara Benedict to Miss Mary Harris, n.d., in Benedict, *Voices out of the Past*, 292. CFW to Mrs. Lawson Carter, 1883, in Benedict, 254. Joan Myers Weimer, in her introduction to *Women Artists, Women Exiles*, xi–xii, discusses her mother's literary legacy to her and refers specifically to Woolson's desire to publish her mother's writings and Woolson's comments that her mother's literary abilities in some ways exceeded her own.

69. CFW to ECS, July 8, [1877], Oct. 1, [1876], NYCol-SC.

70. CFW to Paul Hamilton Hayne, May 1, 1875, in Jay B. Hubbell, ed., "Some New Letters of Constance Fenimore Woolson," *New England Quarterly* 14 (Dec. 1941): 717.

CFW to Mrs. Washburn, n.d., in Clare Benedict, ed., *Constance Fenimore Woolson*, vol. 2 of *Five Generations* (London: Ellis, 1932), 20. CFW to Paul Hamilton Hayne, Feb. 16, [1880], in Hubbell, "Some New Letters," 734. CFW to Samuel Mather, Feb. 27, [1887?], WRHS.

71. ESP, *Chapters*, 12.

72. Austin Phelps, "Memorial," in *The Last Leaf from Sunny Side*, by H. Trusta [Elizabeth Stuart Phelps] (Boston: Phillips, Sampson, 1853), 36, 37–38, 104.

73. Austin Phelps, "Memorial," 65. ESP, *Chapters*, 12, 13.

74. ESP, *Chapters*, 15.

75. ESP, *Chapters*, 82, 101–103, 115.

76. LMA, *Journals*, 110. Bronson Alcott explicated his ideas on genius in the introduction to his *Conversations with Children on the Gospels*, vol. 1 (Boston: James Munroe, 1836); quotes on xxvii, xviii.

77. Account of Bronson's gift on her fourteenth birthday in Cynthia H. Barton, *Transcendental Wife: The Life of Abigail May Alcott* (Lanham, MD: University Press of America, 1996), 128. Quote about gaining fame in Madelon Bedell, *The Alcotts: Biography of a Family* (New York: Clarkson N. Potter, 1980), 245. Bronson Alcott to LMA, *The Letters of A. Bronson Alcott*, ed. Richard L. Herrstadt (Ames: Iowa State University Press, 1969), 377, 379.

78. Barton, *Transcendental Wife*, 46. Barton describes the busts arrayed in Bronson's Temple School as those of Milton, Shakespeare, Plato, and others, 40; those in his study likely were similar.

79. In *Alcott Memoirs* (Boston: Richard G. Badger, 1915), Frederick L. H. Willis, who was a kind of "son" in the family for about ten years, describes at length Bronson Alcott's "impracticability" and the burden it placed on his wife. LMA, "Transcendental Wild Oats" (1873), in *Alternative Alcott*, 375. Emerson's journal, 1842, in *Journals and Miscellaneous Notebooks*, 8:213. Bronson often felt that he could only realize his full spiritual potential in the absence of his wife and daughters.

80. LMA quoted in Willis, *Alcott Memoirs*, 41. Abigail Alcott quoted in Barton, *Transcendental Wife*, 92.

81. Abigail Alcott quoted in Barton, *Transcendental Wife*, 156. LMA, *Journals*, 59.

82. Charles Strickland, *Victorian Domesticity: Families in the Life and Art of Louisa May Alcott* (University: University of Alabama Press, 1985), 43. Bedell, *The Alcotts*, 239.

83. LMA, "To Mother," in Cheney, *Life*, 11.

84. Cheney, *Life*, 8. Abigail Alcott's poem and "Lift up your soul" quoted in Bedell, *The Alcotts*, 239. Abigail Alcott, diary, June 14, 1863, and Oct. 18, 1864, bMS Am 1130.14 (2), MH. Dedication of *Moods* in LMA, Oct. 1864, *Journals*, 133. Letter to her mother about *Flower Fables* in Cheney, *Life*, 52.

85. Cheney, *Life*, 10.

86. LMA, Mar. 1846, *Journals*, 59. Dickinson quoted in Cheryl Walker, *The Nightingale's Burden: Women Poets and American Culture before 1900* (Bloomington: Indiana University Press, 1982), 103.

87. LMA to the *Springfield Republican*, May 4, 1869, in *Selected Letters*, 127. LMA to Louisa Caroline Greenwood Bond, Sept. 17, 1860, in *Selected Letters*, 60–61.

88. LMA, Nov. 1862, *Journals*, 110. LMA to Abigail Alcott, Dec. 25, 1854, in *Selected Letters*, 11. LMA to Hannah Stevenson, *Massachusetts Historical Society Miscellany*, no. 65 (fall 1996): 4.

89. EBS, 1901 Preface, *The Morgesons*, 259.

90. RHS, *Recollections, Personal and Literary* (New York: A. S. Barnes, 1903), 108. EBS to Lillian Whiting, June 20, n.y., BPL.

91. EBS, *Daily Alta California*, Jan. 29, 1855, reprinted in *The Morgesons*, 315. For Stoddard's fiction in which the sea plays such a role, see "The Prescription," *Harper's* 28 (May 1864): 794–800; and *The Morgesons*.

92. RHS, *Recollections*, 110. EBS to ECS, Feb. 3, n.y., NYCol-SC. EBS to Lillian Whiting, June 20, n.y., BPL. See also EBS to ECS, Apr. 24, n.y., NYCol-SC.

93. Matlack, "Literary Career," 40–41. EBS to Margaret Sweat, July 20, 1852, PSt-Sh.

94. EBS to Margaret Sweat, n.d., PSt-Sh. (I believe this is Stoddard's first letter to Sweat, probably written in the fall of 1851, as it begins with "I remember you well.") EBS to Margaret Sweat, July 11, [1852], May 4, [1852], PSt-Sh.

95. EBS to Margaret Sweat, Oct. 22, [1852], Dec. 23, [1852], Feb. 10, [1853], PSt-Sh.

96. Sandra Zagarell, in "Legacy Profile: Elizabeth Drew Barstow Stoddard," *Legacy* 8, no. 1 (1991): 39–49, discusses Stoddard's marriage and "crisis of identity." EBS, "Tuberoses," *Harper's* 26 (Jan. 1863): 191–197. EBS to Margaret Sweat, May 4, [1853], Apr. 14, [1853], May 12, [1853], Sept. 14, [1853], PSt-Sh. I have based the assumption that she did not publish anything for the first two years of her marriage on the bibliography assembled by Matlack, which he admits is incomplete. She may have published something anonymously or pseudonymously that he was unable to trace.

97. RHS, *Recollections*, 114. EBS to Margaret Sweat, Aug. 31, [1854], Aug. 24, [1853 or 1854], PSt-Sh.

98. EBS, 1901 Preface, *The Morgesons*, 259.

99. RHS, *Recollections*, 50. EBS, *Daily Alta California*, Jan. 20, 1856; quoted in *The Morgesons*, 323.

100. EBS, "The Poet's Secret," *Harper's* 20 (Jan. 1860): 194.

101. EBS to ECS, Nov. 3, n.y., NYCol-SC. EBS to Margaret Sweat, Mar. 20, [1854], PSt-Sh. EBS to William Dean Howells, Nov. 24, n.y., bMS AM 1784 (460), MH.

102. EBS to ECS, Oct. 25, n.y., NYCol-SC. The sexist nature of RHS's literary circle and other factors that contributed to EBS's increasing self-doubt will be explored more fully in Chapter 4.

CHAPTER TWO: "Prov[ing] Avis in the Wrong"

1. ESP, "What Shall They Do?" *Harper's* 35 (Sept. 1867): 519. LMA, "Happy Women" (1868), in *Alternative Alcott*, ed. Elaine Showalter (New Brunswick, NJ: Rutgers University Press, 1988), 205.

2. Lazarus in Bette Roth Young, *Emma Lazarus in Her World: Life and Letters* (Philadelphia: Jewish Publication Society, 1995), 92.

3. LMA to Mrs. A. D. Moshier, Apr. 6, [1878], in *The Selected Letters of Louisa May Alcott*, ed. Joel Myerson, Daniel Shealy, and associate ed. Madeleine B. Stern (Athens: University of Georgia Press, 1995), 228.

4. Marriage and divorce rates in Catherine Clinton and Christine Lunardini, *The Columbia Guide to American Women in the Nineteenth Century* (New York: Columbia University Press, 2000), 96, 129. Elizabeth Cady Stanton, "Declaration of Sentiments" (1848), in *The Heath Anthology of American Literature*, ed. Paul Lauter, 4th ed. (Boston: Houghton Mifflin, 2002), 2043.

5. See Clinton and Lunardini, *Columbia Guide*, 102–107. Sarah Grimké, "Marriage"

(unpublished essay), in Gerda Lerner, ed., *The Female Experience: An American Documentary* (Indianapolis: Bobbs-Merrill, 1977), 91, 92, 94.

6. Catherine Beecher cited in Glenna Matthews, *"Just a Housewife": The Rise and Fall of Domesticity in America* (New York: Oxford University Press, 1987), 31. For first-person accounts of women's daily tasks, see Abby Diaz, "A Domestic Problem" (1875), quoted in Matthews, 98–99; "Cleo Dora," letter to the editor, *Anti-Slavery Bugle* (1846), in Lerner, *Female Experience,* 119–120; and Lydia Maria Child, diary (1864), in Lerner, 124–146. ESP, "What Shall They Do?" 519.

7. Alexis de Tocqueville, *Democracy in America* (1840; reprint, New York: Mentor, 1984), 235.

8. Joanne Dobson, " 'The Invisible Lady': Emily Dickinson and Conventions of the Female Self," *Legacy* 3, no. 1 (spring 1986): 41–55.

9. Tocqueville, *Democracy in America,* 236.

10. Grimké, "Marriage," 94.

11. Stephen Mintz, *A Prison of Expectations: The Family in Victorian Culture* (New York: New York University Press, 1983), 123.

12. LMA to Thomas Niles, July 20, 1880, in *Selected Letters,* 249.

13. Lee Virginia Chambers-Schiller, *Liberty, A Better Husband: Single Women in America, The Generations of 1780–1840* (New Haven, CT: Yale University Press, 1984), 134; see also all of chap. 7. While Chambers-Schiller discusses primarily sibling relationships, her remarks can be applied to relationships between women who were not sisters. ESP's "Since I Died" and CFW's " 'Miss Grief' " and "Felipa" are included in the anthology *Two Friends and Other Nineteenth-Century Lesbian Stories by American Women,* ed. Susan Koppelman (New York: Meridian, 1994). For discussions of lesbian themes in their fiction, see Josephine Donovan, *New England Local Color Literature: A Women's Tradition* (New York: Ungar, 1983), 90; Koppelman's introduction to *Two Friends;* and Kris Comment, "The Lesbian 'Impossibilities' of Miss Grief's 'Armor,' " in *Constance Fenimore Woolson's Nineteenth Century: Essays,* ed. Victoria Brehm (Detroit: Wayne State University Press, 2001), 207–223.

14. LMA quoted in Louise Chandler Moulton, "Louisa May Alcott," in *Our Famous Women: An Authorized Record of the Lives and Deeds of Distinguished American Women of Our Times* (Hartford, CT: A. D. Worthington, 1884), 49. For a recent survey of the critical views on Dickinson's relationship with Susan, and a strong argument in favor of viewing it as lesbian, see Kristin M. Comment, "Dickinson's Bawdy: Shakespeare and Sexual Symbolism in Emily Dickinson's Writing to Susan Dickinson," *Legacy* 18, no. 2 (2001): 167–181.

15. On ESP's relationship with Annie Fields, see Susan Coultrap-McQuin, "Elizabeth Stuart Phelps: The Cultural Context of a Nineteenth-Century Professional Writer," (Ph.D. diss., University of Iowa, 1979), 148; and ESP's correspondence with Annie Fields at the Huntington Library, Department of Manuscripts, San Marino, CA. On ESP's friendship with Mary Briggs Harris, see Carol Farley Kessler, *Elizabeth Stuart Phelps* (Boston: Twayne, 1982), 64, 73. CFW, "Contributors' Club," *Atlantic Monthly* 42 (Oct. 1878): 503. CFW's friendship with Arabella Carter is documented in letters; see Clare Benedict, ed., *Constance Fenimore Woolson,* vol. 2 of *Five Generations* (London: Ellis, 1932), 17–19. For Stoddard's relationship with Sweat, see her letters to Sweat in PSt-Sh.

16. CFW to Arabella Carter (later Mrs. Washburn), n.d., in Benedict, *Constance Fenimore Woolson,* 18, 19.

17. CFW to Flora Payne, n.d., in Benedict, *Constance Fenimore Woolson*, 16–17. Evidence in the letter indicates that she is in her teens or twenties. CFW to Samuel Mather, Feb. 8, 1892, WRHS.

18. CFW, notebooks, n.d., in Benedict, 111–112. CFW to Miss Emily Vernon Clark, n.d., in Benedict, 27–29.

19. CFW to Samuel Mather, Jan. 21, 1891; quoted in Rayburn Moore, *Constance F. Woolson* (New Haven, CT: Twayne, 1963), 154. To Samuel Mather she wrote, "the only importance I have is that of an aunt," Feb. 8, 1892, WRHS. CFW, notebooks, n.d., in Benedict, *Constance Fenimore Woolson*, 124.

20. See for example, "Miss Elisabetha," *Appletons' Journal* 13 (Mar. 13, 1875): 327–334; "In Sloane Street," *Harper's Bazar* 25 (June 11, 1892): 473–478; "Ballast Island," *Appletons' Journal* 9 (June 28, 1873): 833–839; and "'Miss Grief'" (1880), in *Women Artists, Women Exiles: "Miss Grief" and Other Stories*, ed. Joan Myers Weimer (New Brunswick, NJ: Rutgers University Press, 1988), 248–269.

21. Sharon L. Dean, *Constance Fenimore Woolson: Homeward Bound* (Knoxville: University of Tennessee Press, 1995), 109, and all of chap. 6.

22. LMA to Annie Maria Lawrence, Feb. 3, 1865, in *Selected Letters*, 107. Ednah D. Cheney discusses LMA's marriage offer in *Life, Letters, and Journals* (1889; reprint, New York: Gramercy Books, 1995), 64.

23. LMA to Elizabeth Powell, Mar. 20, [1869], in *Selected Letters*, 125. LMA to Samuel Joseph May, Jan. 22, [1869], in *Selected Letters*, 121–122.

24. LMA, "Happy Women," 203, 205.

25. ESP, "What Shall They Do?" 522. ESP, *The Silent Partner* (1871; reprint, New York: Feminist Press, 1983), 260, 291, 302.

26. ESP, "The True Woman," *Independent* 23 (Oct. 12, 1871): 1; reprinted in ESP, *The Story of Avis*, ed. Carol Farley Kessler (1877; reprint, New Brunswick, NJ: Rutgers University Press, 1985), 272.

27. ESP to John Greenleaf Whittier, May 14, 1882, Barrett-Ward Collection, UVA. ESP, *Dr. Zay* (1882; reprint, New York: Feminist Press, 1987). For another woman writer's negative response to the happy ending of this novel, see Lucy Larcom to ESP, Oct. 20, 1882, Benjamin Allen Miller Collection, Schlesinger Library, Radcliffe College, Cambridge, MA.

28. ESP to Annie Fields, Nov. 18, 1881, Huntington Library, Department of Manuscripts, San Marino, CA. ESP, "George Eliot," *Harper's Weekly* 29 (Feb. 14, 1885): 103.

29. Kessler, *Elizabeth Stuart Phelps*, 78–79. Kessler points to an article in which Phelps had written approvingly of the marriages of de Staël, Brontë, Fuller, and Eliot to younger men ("The Empty Column," *Independent* 36 [Sept. 4, 1884]). ESP, *Chapters from a Life* (Boston: Houghton, Mifflin, 1895), 243.

30. ESP to Harriet Prescott Spofford, Feb. 2, 1908, Miscellaneous Manuscripts "W," American Antiquarian Society, Worcester, MA.

31. See EBS, "My Own Story," *Atlantic Monthly* 5 (May 1860): 526–547; EBS, "The Prescription," *Harper's* 28 (May 1864): 794–800; and EBS, "Tuberoses," *Harper's* 26 (Jan. 1863): 191–197.

32. LMA, 1873, Mar. 1877, *The Journals of Louisa May Alcott*, ed. Joel Myerson, Daniel Shealy, and associate ed. Madeleine B. Stern (Athens: University of Georgia Press, 1997), 189, 204. ESP to George Eliot, Dec. 1, 1876, George Eliot and George Henry Lewes Collection, Beinecke Rare Book and Manuscript Library, Yale University, New Haven, CT.

33. EBS, *Daily Alta California*, [Oct. 8, 1854], in *The Morgesons and Other Writings, Published and Unpublished*, ed. Lawrence Buell and Sandra Zagarell (Philadelphia: University of Pennsylvania Press, 1984), 313–314. EBS to ECS, Aug. 25, [1861], NYCol-SC. EBS to RHS, n.d. [James Matlack, in "The Literary Career of Elizabeth Barstow Stoddard" (Ph.D. diss., Yale University, 1967), dates the letter as late Nov. or early Dec. 1861], Hitchcock Collection, Columbia University, Rare Book and Manuscript Library, Butler Library, New York, NY.

34. EBS, "Nameless Pain," in *Poems* (Boston: Houghton, Mifflin, 1895), 43. EBS to ECS, Jan. 24, 1862, NYCol-SC.

35. Matlack, "Literary Career," 564.

36. EBS, Journal, Apr. 22, 23, 25, 26, and May 8, 1866, in *The Morgesons*, 348, 349, 350–351.

37. EBS, Journal, May 18, 29, June 1, 17, 25, July 6, Sept. 5, Oct. 7, 1866, in *The Morgesons*, 352, 353, 354, 355, 357, 358.

38. See Matlack's discussion of *Lolly Dink's Doings*, in "Literary Career," 505–506.

39. Linda Huf, *A Portrait of the Artist as a Young Woman: The Writer as Heroine in American Literature* (New York: Ungar, 1983), 32. Fanny Fern, *Ruth Hall and Other Writings*, ed. Joyce W. Warren (New Brunswick, NJ: Rutgers University Press, 1986), 174 (italics in original), 182. Augusta Jane Evans, *St. Elmo* (Tuscaloosa: University of Alabama Press, 1992), 274, 275, 276, 365.

40. Madame de Staël, *Corinne, or Italy*, trans. Avriel H. Goldberger (New Brunswick, NJ: Rutgers University Press, 1987), 46. Subsequent references will be made in the text.

41. Elizabeth Barrett Browning, *Aurora Leigh* (1856), in *The Poetical Works of Elizabeth Barrett Browning*, Cambridge ed., ed. Ruth M. Adams (Boston: Houghton Mifflin, 1974), 1.304–305. Subsequent references will be made in the text.

42. EBS, "Collected by a Valetudinarian," in *The Morgesons*, 285, 289. Subsequent references will be made in the text.

43. "Explanatory Notes," in the back of *Corinne*, 431. Madelyn Gutwrith points out, in "*Corinne* and *Consuelo* as Fantasies of Immanence," *George Sand Studies* 8, nos. 1–2 (1986–1987): 21–27, that the woman artist's rival in Sand's *Consuelo* is named Corilla, a name that Gutwrith claims is "the original (that is, the Pindaric) name of Staël's protagonist" (22).

44. For discussions of bird imagery in *Jane Eyre* and other women's works, see Ellen Moers, *Literary Women* (Garden City, NY: Doubleday, 1976), 245–251; and Cheryl Walker, *The Nightingale's Burden: Women Poets and American Culture before 1900* (Bloomington: Indiana University Press, 1982).

45. Matlack, in "Literary Career," sees the story as a "compensatory fable" (479). Ellen Weinauer, "Alternative Economies: Authorship and Ownership in Elizabeth Stoddard's 'Collected by a Valetudinarian,'" *Studies in American Fiction* 25, no. 2 (1997): 167–182, calls it "a consoling fiction" (178). Lisa Radinovsky, in "Negotiating Models of Authorship: Elizabeth Stoddard's Conflicts and Her Story of Complaint," in Brehm, *Constance Fenimore Woolson's Nineteenth Century*, reads it as "a combination of wish fulfillment or escapist fantasy and carefully veiled complaint" (45).

46. George Eliot, "Armgart," *Atlantic Monthly* 28 (July 1871): 94–105. This poem was later published in Eliot's collection *The Legend of Jubal* (1874). Quotes on 96, 98, 99, 100.

47. Eliot, "Armgart," 100, 102, 104, 105.

48. H. Trusta [Elizabeth Stuart Phelps], "The Husband of a Blue," in *The Tell-Tale; or,*

Home Secrets Told by Old Travellers (Boston: Phillips, Samson, 1853), 99. Subsequent references will be made in the text.

49. I am grateful to Catherine Loomis for alerting me to the significance of Mrs. Graves's name.

50. H. Trusta [Elizabeth Stuart Phelps], *The Angel over the Right Shoulder* (Andover: Warren F. Draper, 1852, 1868); excerpt reprinted in Judith Fetterley, ed., *Provisions: A Reader from Nineteenth-Century American Women* (Bloomington: Indiana University Press, 1985), 209–215; quote on 215.

51. ESP, *Avis*, 23. Subsequent references will be made in the text.

52. In her notes to the novel, Kessler discusses the symbol of the Sphinx, which in its oldest forms had a female face and bird's wings; ESP, *Avis*, 258 n. 9.

53. Karen Tracey, *Plots and Proposals: American Women's Fiction, 1850–1890* (Urbana: University of Illinois Press, 2000), 159.

54. Jack H. Wilson, "Competing Narratives in Elizabeth Stuart Phelps's *The Story of Avis*," *American Literary Realism, 1870–1910* 26, no. 1 (1993): 73.

55. Carol Farley Kessler, "A Literary Legacy: Elizabeth Stuart Phelps, Mother and Daughter," *Frontiers* 5 (fall 1980): 31.

56. Bayard Taylor, a friend of the Stoddards, wrote to his wife that "She [EBS] told me that if Wilson [her brother] got a certain appointment, she would go with him to Europe; *Wilson* thought it necessary for her development!" Quoted in Matlack, "Literary Career," 409.

57. ESP to Annie Fields, June 19, 1882, Huntington Library, Department of Manuscripts, San Marino, CA.

58. James Buzard, "A Continent of Pictures: Reflections on the 'Europe' of Nineteenth-Century Tourists," *PMLA* 108 (Jan. 1993): 32.

59. Leonardo Buonomo, *Backward Glances: Exploring Italy, Reinterpreting America (1831–1866)* (Madison, NJ: Fairleigh Dickinson University Press, 1996), 30. Harriet Hosmer to Miss C., Apr. 22, 1853, in *Harriet Hosmer: Letters and Memories*, ed. Cornelia Carr (London: John Lane the Bodley Head, 1913), 27. Lydia Maria Child, "Miss Harriet Hosmer," *Living Age* 56 (Mar. 13, 1858): 697. Nathaniel Hawthorne, *The Marble Faun, or The Romance of Monte Beni* (1860; reprint, New York: Signet, 1961), 47.

60. Mary Suzanne Schriber, *Writing Home: American Women Abroad, 1830–1920* (Charlottesville: University Press of Virginia, 1997), 2.

61. Leo Hamalian, in introduction to *Ladies on the Loose: Women Travellers of the Eighteenth and Nineteenth Centuries* (New York: Dodd, Mead, 1981), x.

62. LMA, July and Aug. 1865, *Journals*, 14.

63. For evidence that Louisa and May shared the family responsibilities, see LMA to Lukens Sisters, Dec. 18., n.y., BPL, where Alcott writes that she "cannot leave home to go any where till May comes in April to mount guard & let[s] me have a vacation." LMA to Anna Alcott Pratt [after Dec. 17, 1860], in *Selected Letters*, 62. Caroline Ticknor, *May Alcott: A Memoir* (Boston: Little, Brown, 1928), 3.

64. Quoted in Ticknor, *May Alcott*, 74, 83.

65. LMA, *Aunt Jo's Scrap-Bag. Shawl-Straps* (Boston: Roberts Bros., 1872), vi, 1.

66. LMA, *Shawl-Straps*, 79, 50, 138–139, 119, 187.

67. LMA, *Shawl-Straps*, 224, 225.

68. Quoted in Ticknor, *May Alcott*, 144–145.

69. Quoted in Ticknor, *May Alcott*, 108–109.

70. May Alcott, *An Artist's Holiday*, chap. 3, "An English Outing/How We Saw the Shah," chap. 8, "Playing Vagabond," and "London Larks," bMS Am 1817 (54), MH. May did publish, under the name Abigail May Alcott Nieriker, *Studying Art Abroad and How to Do It Cheaply* (Boston: Roberts Bros., 1879). It is primarily a how-to guide.

71. May quoted in Ticknor, *May Alcott*, 171.

72. Quoted in Ticknor, *May Alcott*, 263–264. May Nieriker to Alcott family, dated "Mendon/78," "Letters home, 1878–1879," bMS Am 1130.14 (17), MH.

73. LMA, Apr. and May 1878, *Journals*, 209, 210. In "Notes and Memoranda" for 1878 in her *Journals*, Alcott recorded, "Spent a month in Boston writing about May's artist life" (211).

74. Natania Rosenfeld, "Artists and Daughters in Louisa May Alcott's *Diana and Persis*," *New England Quarterly* 64 (Mar. 1991): 17.

75. LMA, *Diana and Persis* (1879), in *Alternative Alcott*, 392. Subsequent page references will be made in the text. Showalter, in her introduction to *Alternative Alcott*, explores the connections between Diana and Harriet Hosmer (xli).

76. Rosenfeld, "Artists and Daughters," 13.

77. Puck was also the name of a famous sculpture by Harriet Hosmer.

78. Strickland, *Victorian Domesticity*, 117.

79. The open ending has received different interpretations. See Strickland, *Victorian Domesticity*, 81; Sarah Elbert, *A Hunger for Home: Louisa May Alcott's Place in American Culture* (New Brunswick, NJ: Rutgers University Press, 1987), 254; and Showalter, introduction to *Alternative Alcott*, xlii.

80. LMA to Mrs. [Clementia] Taylor, Nov. 2, [1880], uncat MS Vault 764, Betsy Beinecke Shirley Collection of American Children's Literature, Beinecke Rare Book and Manuscript Library, Yale University, New Haven, CT.

81. LMA to Mary Mapes Dodge, May 29 [1880], in *Selected Letters*, 248. LMA to Mary Preston Stearns, Feb. 21, 1881, in *Selected Letters*, 254.

82. Quoted in Ticknor, *May Alcott*, 140–141.

83. Lucy H. Hooper, "American Women Abroad," *Galaxy* 21 (June 1876): 820. Albert Rhodes, "Shall the American Girl Be Chaperoned?" *Galaxy* 24 (Oct. 1877): 457.

84. [John Hay], Contributors' Club, *Atlantic Monthly* 43 (Mar. 1879): 399–400. CFW to John Hay, Mar. 14, 1879; quoted in Sara Foose Parrott, "Expatriates and Professionals: The Careers in Italy of Nineteenth-Century American Women Writers and Artists" (Ph.D. diss., George Washington University, 1988), 149.

85. Hooper, "American Women Abroad," 819, 820.

86. CFW to ECS, July 23, [1876], NYCol-SC.

87. CFW, "A Florentine Experiment," *Atlantic Monthly* 46 (Oct. 1880): 502–530; "The Roman May, and a Walk," *Christian Union* 24 (July 26, 1881): 76–77; and "In Venice," *Atlantic Monthly* 49 (Apr. 1882): 488–505.

88. CFW to Henry James, May 7, [1873], in Leon Edel, ed., *The Letters of Henry James* (Cambridge: Harvard University Press, 1974–80), 3:555.

89. CFW to Mary Mapes Dodge, Sept. 13, n.y., Manuscripts Division, Department of Rare Books and Special Collections, Princeton University Library, Princeton, NJ. CFW to Katherine Loring, Oct. 9, 1887, Beverly Historical Society, Beverly, MA. CFW to John Hay, July 30, [1886], in Alice Hall Petry, " 'Always Your Attached Friend': The Un-

published Letters of Constance Fenimore Woolson to John and Clara Hay," *Books at Brown* 29–30 (1982–83): 87. CFW to Katherine Loring, Oct. 9, 1887, Beverly Historical Society, Beverly, MA.

90. CFW to Mrs. Croswell, Apr. or May 1880, in Benedict, *Constance Fenimore Woolson*, 184. CFW to Katherine Mather, Jan. 16, 1881, WRHS. CFW to Henry James, May 7, [1883], in Edel, *Henry James Letters*, 550.

91. CFW to ECS, Apr. 30, [1883], NYCol-SC. CFW, "In Sloane Street," *Harper's Bazar* 25 (June 11, 1892): 473–478. CFW, "A Florentine Experiment."

92. CFW, " 'Miss Grief,' " in *Women Artists*, 248–269. CFW, "The Street of the Hyacinth," in *Women Artists*, 209.

93. Cheryl B. Torsney, *Constance Fenimore Woolson: The Grief of Artistry* (Athens: University of Georgia Press, 1989), 106–107. CFW, "At the Château of Corinne," in *Women Artists*, 222. Subsequent references will be made in the text.

94. Torsney, *Constance Fenimore Woolson*, 107. Joan Weimer translates the lyrics as "Time passes, times passes, my lady." See "Explanatory Notes," *Women Artists*, 289 n. 8.

CHAPTER THREE: "The Crown and the Thorn of Gifted Life"

1. Rebecca Harding Davis, "Boston in the Sixties" (1904); reprinted in *A Rebecca Harding Davis Reader: "Life in the Iron-Mills," Selected Fiction, and Essays*, ed. Jean Pfaelzer (Pittsburgh: University of Pittsburgh Press, 1995), 447.

2. ESP, "A Plea for Immortality," *Atlantic Monthly* 45 (Feb. 1880): 278, 279.

3. ESP, "Plea," 279.

4. Nina Baym, *Novels, Readers, and Reviewers: Responses to Fiction in Antebellum America* (Ithaca, NY: Cornell University Press, 1984), 257.

5. Duff and Lombroso quoted in Christine Battersby, *Gender and Genius: Towards a Feminist Aesthetics* (Bloomington: Indiana University Press, 1989), 4, 79. Kant is paraphrased and quoted in Battersby, 77. ESP, *The Story of Avis*, ed. Carol Farley Kessler (1877; reprint, New Brunswick, NJ: Rutgers University Press, 1985), 33.

6. Deborah Barker, *Aesthetics and Gender in American Literature: Portraits of the Woman Artist* (Lewisburg, PA: Bucknell University Press, 2000), 38. Madame de Staël, *Corinne, or Italy*, trans. Avriel H. Goldberger (New Brunswick, NJ: Rutgers University Press, 1987), 46. Justin McCarthy, "George Sand," *Galaxy* 9 (May 1870): 663.

7. Battersby, *Gender and Genius*, 90. In America, such beliefs were popularized by Dr. Edward H. Clarke, in his *Sex in Education; or, A Fair Chance for the Girls* (1873); see George Cotkin, *Reluctant Modernism: American Thought and Culture, 1880–1890* (New York: Twayne, 1992), 77–79.

8. C. C. Everett, "Elizabeth Barrett Browning," *North American Review* 85 (Oct. 1857): 416–417. Elizabeth Barrett Browning, *Aurora Leigh* (1856), in *The Poetical Works of Elizabeth Barrett Browning*, Cambridge ed., ed. Ruth M. Adams (Boston: Houghton Mifflin, 1974), 2:183–189; 8.605–610.

9. Quote from *North British Review* in Elizabeth K. Helsinger, Robin Lauterbach Sheets, and William Veeder, *The Woman Question: Society and Literature in Britain and America, 1837–1883*, vol. 3, *Literary Issues* (Chicago: University of Chicago Press, 1983), 53. CFW, "At the Château of Corinne," in *Women Artists, Women Exiles: "Miss Grief" and Other Stories by Constance Fenimore Woolson*, ed. Joan Myers Weimer (New Brunswick, NJ: Rutgers University Press, 1988), 233.

10. Barker, *Aesthetics and Gender,* 17. De Staël, *Corinne,* 322. ESP, *Avis,* 59.

11. Susan Wolfson, "Gendering the Soul," in *Romantic Women Writers: Voices and Countervoices,* ed. Paula R. Feldman and Theresa M. Kelley (Hanover, NH: University Press of New England, 1995), 34. On Enlightenment theories of gender, see Nina Baym, "From Enlightenment to Victorian: Toward a Narrative of American Writers Writing History," in *Feminism and American Literary History: Essays* (New Brunswick, NJ: Rutgers University Press, 1992), 105–120.

12. Baym, "From Enlightenment to Victorian," 117. Quotes from Hale in Baym, 119, and Patricia Okker, *Our Sister Editors: Sarah J. Hale and the Tradition of Nineteenth-Century American Women Editors* (Athens: University of Georgia Press, 1995), 105.

13. Sarah E. Henshaw, "Are We Inferior?" *Galaxy* 7 (Jan. 1869): 127, 129.

14. Charlotte Forten Grimké, *The Journals of Charlotte Forten Grimké,* ed. Brenda Stevenson (New York: Oxford University Press, 1988), 261.

15. S. E. Wallace, "Another Weak-Minded Woman. A Confession," *Harper's* 35 (Nov. 1867): 793–796.

16. Grimké, *Journals,* 190. Jewett quoted in Paula Blanchard, *Sarah Orne Jewett: Her World and Her Work* (Reading, MA: Addison-Wesley, 1994), 77. Blanchard argues that the Harvard professor Theophilus Parsons, a mentor to Jewett, "absolved her from her guilt" by encouraging her, in his words, to " 'be the instrument of God' " (77).

17. Rebecca Harding Davis, "Women in Literature" (1891); reprinted in *A Rebecca Harding Davis Reader,* 402, 404.

18. Theophilus Parsons, "Life and Writings of Madame de Staël," *North American Review* 11 (July 1820): 139–140. Everett, "Elizabeth Barrett Browning," 419. McCarthy, "George Sand," 668. "The Genius of George Eliot," *Southern Review* 13 (July 1873): 206.

19. See Lannom Smith, "Howells and the Battle of Words over 'Genius,' " *American Literary Realism, 1870–1910* 13 (spring 1980): 101–107.

20. See Flavia Alaya, "Victorian Science and the 'Genius' of Woman," *Journal of the History of Ideas* 38 (1977): 261–280.

21. EBS to Lillian Whiting, June 25, n.y., BPL. EBS, Journal, Apr. 22, 1866, in *The Morgesons and Other Writings, Published and Unpublished,* ed. Lawrence Buell and Sandra Zagarell (Philadelphia: University of Pennsylvania Press, 1984), 348. EBS, *Daily Alta California,* May 19, 1855, in *The Morgesons,* 317.

22. EBS, "The Chimneys," *Harper's* (Nov. 1865); reprinted in *Legacy* 7 (fall 1990): 32. EBS, "A Literary Whim," *Appletons' Journal* 6 (Oct. 4, 1871): 441.

23. EBS to Lillian Whiting, Sept. 15, n.y., Oct. 6, n.y., BPL. EBS to ECS, Aug. 28, 1891, NYCol-SC.

24. EBS to Margaret Sweat, July 11, [1852], PSt-Sh.

25. EBS to ECS, n.d., NYCol-SC.

26. EBS, *Daily Alta California,* Oct. 22, 1854, in *The Morgesons,* 314. EBS, *Daily Alta California,* Nov. 18, 1855, quoted in James Matlack, "The Literary Career of Elizabeth Barstow Stoddard" (Ph.D. diss., Yale University, 1967), 156.

27. Although Matlack does not include this publication in his bibliography of Stoddard's works in "Literary Career," I cautiously attribute the anonymous article, "Woman and Art," *Aldine Press* 3 (Jan. 1870): 3–4, to Stoddard based on the letter she wrote to Whitelaw Reid, n.d. (Monday evening), Reid Family Papers, Library of Congress, Manuscript Division, Washington, D.C., in which she discusses an article on the subject that her husband has counseled her to publish anonymously. It is highly possible that after Reid,

editor of the *New York Tribune*, rejected the article, she published it instead in the *Aldine*, where she later published many articles and stories, many of them under pseudonyms, in 1872–1873, while her husband was the editor.

28. Elizabeth Leonard [EBS], "Woman in Art. — Rosa Bonheur," *Aldine* 5 (July 1872): 145.

29. EBS, *Daily Alta California*, Dec. 3, 1855, and Aug. 3, 1856, in *The Morgesons*, 322, 325–326.

30. EBS, "Me and My Son," *Harper's* 41 (July 1870): 213. Subsequent references will be made in the text.

31. EBS, "Collected by a Valetudinarian," in *The Morgesons*, 296. Subsequent references will be made in the text.

32. Everett, "Aurora Leigh," 416. Ralph Waldo Emerson, *Nature* (1836), in *The Collected Works of Ralph Waldo Emerson*, ed. Alfred R. Ferguson, Joseph Slater, Douglas Emory Wilson, et al., 5 vols. (Cambridge: Harvard University Press, 1971–), 1:9, 10.

33. EBS, *Daily Alta California*, June 2, 1855, in *The Morgesons*, 317.

34. CFW, "Miss Elisabetha," in *Women Artists, Women Exiles*. CFW, *East Angels* (New York: Harper & Bros., 1886), 100.

35. CFW to ECS, July 23, [1876], NYCol-SC. Sharon L. Dean, *Constance Fenimore Woolson: Homeward Bound* (Knoxville: University of Tennessee Press, 1995), 174. CFW to Katherine Loring, Sept. 19, [1890?], Beverly Historical Society, Beverly, MA. CFW's marginalia quoted in Clare Benedict, ed., *Constance Fenimore Woolson*, vol. 2 of *Five Generations* (London: Ellis, 1932), 93.

36. CFW to Mrs. Washburn, n.d., in Benedict, *Constance Fenimore Woolson*, 20.

37. On her fear of entering the public sphere as a writer, see CFW to Mrs. Washburn, n.d., in Benedict, *Constance Fenimore Woolson*, 20. CFW to Henry James, Feb. 12, [1882], in *The Letters of Henry James*, ed. Leon Edel (Cambridge: Harvard University Press, 1974–80), 3:532.

38. Bette Roth Young, *Emma Lazarus in Her World: Life and Letters* (Philadelphia: Jewish Publication Society, 1995), 28. Emma Lazarus, "Echoes," in Young, 28. Paula Bennett, "'The Descent of the Angel': Interrogating Domestic Ideology in American Women's Poetry, 1858–1890," *American Literary History* 7 (1997): 596.

39. CFW, Notebooks, in Benedict, *Constance Fenimore Woolson*, 107–108. This story was never completed.

40. CFW, Notebooks, in Benedict, *Constance Fenimore Woolson*, 96, 99.

41. CFW to Mrs. Washburn, n.d. (two different letters), in Benedict, *Constance Fenimore Woolson*, 21–22, 20.

42. CFW to Paul Hamilton Hayne, "All Saints Day," [1875], Jan. 16, 1876, in Jay B. Hubbell, ed., "Some New Letters of Constance Fenimore Woolson," *New England Quarterly* 14 (Dec. 1941): 725, 729.

43. For examples as well as surveys of other such criticism, see Patricia E. Johnson, "The Gendered Politics of the Gaze: Henry James and George Eliot," *Mosaic* 30, no. 1 (1997): 39–54; and Eva Gold and Thomas H. Fick, "A 'masterpiece' of 'the educated eye': Convention, Gaze, and Gender in Spofford's 'Her Story,'" *Studies in Short Fiction* 30 (1993): 511–523.

44. ESP, *Avis*, 38, 39, 54.

45. CFW, "The Street of the Hyacinth" (1882), in *Women Artists, Women Exiles*, 183. Subsequent references will be made in the text.

46. In "The Gendered Politics of the Gaze," Johnson examines *Middlemarch* and James's *Portrait of a Lady*, which also may have influenced Woolson in writing "Street," although I wish to highlight the influence of "Daisy Miller."

47. Most of these similarities are pointed out by Cheryl B. Torsney, in *Constance Fenimore Woolson: The Grief of Artistry* (Athens: University of Georgia Press, 1989), 108–109, although she does not analyze the similarities in perspective.

48. Barker, *Aesthetics and Gender*, 37.

49. Torsney, *Constance Fenimore Woolson: The Grief of Artistry*, 115.

50. George Eliot, *Middlemarch* (1872; reprint, New York: Penguin, 1994), 220, 206. Johnson, "Gendered Politics," 46, 48.

51. Johnson, "Gendered Politics," 53.

52. Torsney, *Constance Fenimore Woolson: The Grief of Artistry*, 124.

53. ESP, *Chapters from a Life* (Boston: Houghton, Mifflin, 1895), 82, 103.

54. ESP, *Chapters*, 94–95, 76–77, 66, 110. ESP to John Greenleaf Whittier, Feb. 27, 1879, bMS Am 1844 (325), MH.

55. Veronica Bassil, "The Artist at Home: The Domestication of Louisa May Alcott," *Studies in American Fiction* 15 (autumn 1987): 187. Richard H. Brodhead, *Cultures of Letters: Scenes of Reading and Writing in Nineteenth-Century America* (Chicago: University of Chicago Press, 1993), 88–89.

56. LMA, Feb. 1861, Feb. 1862, *The Journals of Louisa May Alcott*, ed. Joel Myerson, Daniel Shealy, and associate ed. Madeleine B. Stern (Athens: University of Georgia Press, 1997), 103–104, 108. LMA, *Little Women* (1868; reprint, New York: Signet, 1983), 246. Susan Naomi Bernstein, "Writing and *Little Women*: Alcott's Rhetoric of Subversion," *ATQ*, n.s., 7 (Mar. 1993): 35.

57. LMA, Nov. 1858, *Journals*, 92.

58. Abigail Alcott, diary, Dec. 25, 1854, bMS Am 1130.14 (2), MH. The published version of the letter can be found in LMA, *Life, Letters, and Journals*, ed. Ednah D. Cheyney (1889; reprint, New York: Gramercy Books, 1995), 51–52. Both versions of the letter are also included in *The Selected Letters of Louisa May Alcott*, ed. Joel Myerson, Daniel Shealy, and associate ed. Madeleine B. Stern (Athens: University of Georgia Press, 1995), where the editors also attribute the revision of Abigail's diary to Louisa (11–12).

59. LMA, Aug. 1860, *Journals*, 99. LMA to Louisa Caroline Greenwood Bond, Sept. 17, [1860], in *Selected Letters*, 61. LMA to James Redpath, [Feb. ? 1864?], in *Selected Letters*, 103.

60. Jewett quoted in Blanchard, *Sarah Orne Jewett*, 66.

61. LMA, "A Modern Cinderella," *Atlantic Monthly* 6 (Oct. 1860): 427, 440.

62. Howard M. Ticknor to LMA, Mar. 13, 1860, bMS Am 800.2 (3), MH. Charles Nordhoff, "Elkanah Brewster's Temptation," *Atlantic Monthly* 4 (Dec. 1859): 710–721; quote on 721.

63. LMA, Sept. 1860, *Journals*, 100.

64. LMA to Maggie Lukens, Feb. 5, [1884], in *Selected Letters*, 277. LMA, "The Freak of a Genius" (1866), in *Freaks of Genius: Unknown Thrillers of Louisa May Alcott*, ed. Daniel Shealy (New York: Greenwood Press, 1994), 122. LMA, Feb. 1864, *Journals*, 128.

65. LMA, "Psyche's Art" (1868), in *Alternative Alcott*, ed. Elaine Showalter (New Brunswick, NJ: Rutgers University Press, 1988), 207. Subsequent references will be made in the text.

66. LMA, "Diana and Persis" (1879), in *Alternative Alcott*, 391.

67. CFW to ECS, July 23, [1876], NYCol-SC. Fanny Fern, *Ruth Hall and Other Writings*, ed. Joyce W. Warren (New Brunswick, NJ: Rutgers University Press, 1986), 175. Torsney, *Constance Fenimore Woolson: The Grief of Artistry.*

68. Cheryl Walker, *The Nightingale's Burden: Women Poets and American Culture before 1900* (Bloomington: Indiana University Press, 1982), 88.

69. ESP, "The Rejected Manuscript," *Harper's* 86 (Jan. 1893): 286. Subsequent references will be made in the text.

70. LMA to James Redpath, [Feb.? 1864?], in *Selected Letters*, 103. LMA, *An Old-Fashioned Girl* (1870), in *Alternative Alcott*, 234. Davis depicts such downtrodden artists as Hugh in "Life in the Iron Mills," the neuralgic journalist Jenny Derby in "Earthen Pitchers," and the impoverished female writer in "Marcia."

71. Gustavus Stadler, "Louisa May Alcott's Queer Geniuses," *American Literature* 71 (Dec. 1999): 662. Although Stadler's focus is on "currents of queerness" as they are revealed in Alcott's story "The Freak of a Genius," the gender bending he identifies corresponds in some ways to the argument I am making here.

72. Elaine Showalter, *The Female Malady: Women, Madness, and English Culture, 1830–1980* (New York: Pantheon, 1985), 121, 123.

73. Jean Strouse, *Alice James: A Biography* (Boston: Houghton Mifflin, 1980), 291.

74. CFW to Samuel Mather, Feb. 8, 1892, WRHS.

75. CFW to John Hay, Jan. 27, 1884, in Alice Hall Petry, "'Always Your Attached Friend': The Unpublished Letters of Constance Fenimore Woolson to John and Clara Hay," *Books at Brown* 29–30 (1982–83): 64. Charlotte Forten Grimké's depression also stemmed from the racism she encountered as well as her estrangement from her father, but her difficulty in finding a voice as a writer certainly played a significant role as well.

76. ESP, *Chapters*, 233. CFW to Mrs. Lawson Carter, 1883, in Clare Benedict, ed., *Voices out of the Past*, vol. 1 of *Five Generations* (London: Ellis, 1929), 254. CFW to Kate Mather, July 2, 1893, WRHS.

77. LMA to Maria S. Porter, [after Oct. 24, 1882], in *Selected Letters*, 261. LMA, Jan. 1867, *Journals*, 157. ESP to Harriet Lothrop, July 23, 1890, BPL. Alcott refers to a "breakdown" after writing *Jo's Boys* in a letter to Thomas Niles, July 13, 1885, in *Selected Letters*, 290. Phelps broke down most severely after she wrote *The Story of Avis*; see *Chapters*, 229–242. Dean discusses Woolson's depressions after writing her novels, in *Constance Fenimore Woolson: Homeward Bound*, 8.

78. CFW to Mrs. Washburn, n.d., in Benedict, *Constance Fenimore Woolson*, 20. ESP, *Chapters*, 86–87, 267, 266.

79. CFW to John Hay, Dec. 26, 1885, in Petry, "'Always Your Attached Friend,'" 83. ESP, *Chapters*, 12. LMA to Roberts Brothers, Dec. 28, 1869, in *Selected Letters*, 129.

80. CFW to Emily Vernon Clark, n.d., in Benedict, *Constance Fenimore Woolson*, 28. EBS, *Daily Alta California*, June 2, 1857, quoted in Matlack, "Literary Career," 168. EBS, "Collected," 290. CFW to Linda Guilford, n.d., in Benedict, *Constance Fenimore Woolson*, 43.

81. CFW, "A Florentine Experiment," *Atlantic Monthly* 46 (Oct. 1880): 520. EBS to Lillian Whiting, Oct. 4 or 7, n.y., BPL. ESP, *Chapters*, 237, 233, 234.

82. CFW to John Hay, Jan. 27, 1884, in Petry, "'Always Your Attached Friend,'" 65. ESP to Henry Wadsworth Longfellow, Apr. 10, 1877, bMS Am 1340.2 (5815), MH.

83. CFW to Paul Hamilton Hayne, Jan. 16, 1876, in Hubbell, "Some New Letters," 728–729.

CHAPTER FOUR: "*Recognition* is the Thing."

1. EBS, "A Literary Whim," *Appletons' Journal* 6 (Oct. 14, 1871): 440–441. EBS to Lillian Whiting, June 20, n.y., BPL.

2. Nina Baym, *Woman's Fiction: A Guide to Novels by and about Women in America, 1820–1870*, 2d ed. (Urbana: University of Illinois Press, 1993), xvii.

3. Richard Stoddard quoted in James Matlack, "The Literary Career of Elizabeth Barstow Stoddard" (Ph.D. diss., Yale University, 1967), 219.

4. Nancy Glazener, *Reading for Realism: The History of a U.S. Literary Institution, 1850–1910* (Durham, NC: Duke University Press, 1997), 20.

5. Jackson quoted in Alfred Habegger, *My Wars Are Laid Away in Books: The Life of Emily Dickinson* (New York: Random House, 2001), 555–556. Jewett quoted in Paula Blanchard, *Sarah Orne Jewett: Her World and Her Work* (Reading, MA: Addison-Wesley, 1994), 112.

6. LMA to Mary E. Channing Higginson, Oct. 18, [1868], in *The Selected Letters of Louisa May Alcott*, ed. Joel Myerson, Daniel Shealy, and associate ed. Madeleine B. Stern (Athens: University of Georgia Press, 1995), 118. Dickinson to T. W. Higginson, June 7, 1862, in Emily Dickinson, *The Letters of Emily Dickinson*, ed. Thomas H. Johnson (Cambridge: Harvard University Press, 1965), 409.

7. Henry Wadsworth Longfellow to ESP, Apr. 6, 1876, BPL. Oliver Wendell Holmes to ESP, Oct. 29, 1879, in John T. Morse, *Life and Letters of Oliver Wendell Holmes* (Boston: Houghton, Mifflin, 1896), 260–261. ESP to Longfellow, May 17, n.y., bMS Am 1340.2 (5815), MH.

8. ESP to John Greenleaf Whittier, Dec. 7, 1879, UVA. ESP to Whittier, Dec. 22, 1879, Mar. 13, 1868, Apr. 5, 1878, bMS Am 1844 (325), MH.

9. ESP, *Chapters from a Life* (Boston: Houghton, Mifflin, 1895), 153, 166. Susan Coultrap-McQuin, "Elizabeth Stuart Phelps" (Ph.D. diss., University of Iowa, 1979), 136.

10. For her critique of Howells, see ESP, *Chapters*, 260–264. ESP, "The Man without a Country," *Independent* 32 (May 6, 1880): 1–2.

11. Leon Edel, *The Life of Henry James*, 5 vols. (Philadelphia: Lippincott, 1953–72), 2:411–412, 417.

12. In 1875 Woolson remarked to her friend Paul Hamilton Hayne that James was among her favorite authors; quoted in Jay B. Hubbell, ed., "Some New Letters of Constance Fenimore Woolson," *New England Quarterly* 14 (Dec. 1941): 724. CFW, "The Contributors' Club," *Atlantic Monthly* 43 (Jan. 1879): 106–108; (Feb. 1879): 259.

13. CFW, "'Miss Grief'" (1880), in *Women Artists, Women Exiles: "Miss Grief" and Other Stories by Constance Fenimore Woolson*, ed. Joan Myers Weimer (New Brunswick, NJ: Rutgers University Press, 1988), 248, 250. Subsequent references will be made in the text. In *The Life of Henry James*, Edel points out two of the similarities noted here, and he argues that the story "reflects a close reading of Henry's work" (2:416).

14. CFW to Paul Hamilton Hayne, Feb. 13, [1876], in Hubbell, "Some New Letters," 730. CFW to Henry James, Feb. 12, 1882, in *The Letters of Henry James*, ed. Leon Edel (Cambridge: Harvard University Press, 1974–80), 3:529.

15. Edel, *Life of Henry James*, 2:417. Alfred Habegger, *Henry James and the "Woman Business"* (Cambridge: Cambridge University Press, 1989), 25, 4. CFW to Henry James, Feb. 12, 1882, in Edel, *Letters of Henry James*, 3:535.

16. Edel, *Life of Henry James*, 2:309.

17. CFW to Henry James, May 7, 1883, in Edel, *The Letters of Henry James*, 3:550–551.

18. Priscilla L. Walton, *Disruption of the Feminine in Henry James* (Toronto: University of Toronto Press, 1992), 38. Henry James, *Roderick Hudson*, in *Henry James, Novels 1871–1880*, ed. William T. Stafford (New York: Library of America, 1983), 293, 301–302, 270. (This edition reproduces the original American publication in 1875.)

19. See Walton, *Disruption*, 41.

20. Woolson to James, Feb. 12, [1882], in Edel, *Letters of Henry James*, 3:528.

21. CFW to John Hay, January 27, 1884, in Alice Hall Petry, " 'Always Your Attached Friend': The Unpublished Letters of Constance Fenimore Woolson to John and Clara Hay," *Books at Brown* 29–30 (1982–1983): 65. CFW to Henry James, August 30, 1882, in Edel, *Letters of Henry James*, 3:542.

22. Henry James, "Miss Woolson," in *Women Artists, Women Exiles*, 271, first published as "Miss Constance Fenimore Woolson," in *Harper's Weekly* (Feb. 12, 1887): 114–115.

23. EBS to Elizabeth Akers Allen, [1873–74], in *The Morgesons and Other Writings, Published and Unpublished*, ed. Lawrence Buell and Sandra Zagarell (Philadelphia: University of Pennsylvania Press, 1984), 341. Dedication to *The Morgesons* quoted in Matlack, "Literary Career," 223. EBS to ECS, Nov. 3, n.y., NYCol-SC.

24. EBS, *Daily Alta California*, Nov. 18, 1855; quoted in Matlack, "Literary Career," 156. (While she spoke here to the "courageous woman" author, she clearly did so from personal experience.) Bayard Taylor to EBS, Nov. 21, 1862, Rare and Manuscript Collections, Carl A. Kroch Library, Cornell University Library, Ithaca, NY. For the names they called her, see Matlack, 448, 466.

25. Bayard Taylor to EBS, Feb. 27, 1863, Rare and Manuscript Collections, Carl A. Kroch Library, Cornell University Library, Ithaca, NY. EBS to ECS, May 1, 1865, NYCol-SC. EBS to Julia Dorr, July 31, 1881, VTMC.

26. Nathaniel Hawthorne to EBS, Jan. 26, 1863, Berg Collection of English and American Literature, New York Public Library, New York, NY, Astor, Lenox, and Tilden Foundations. See 1901 preface in *The Morgesons*, 262. EBS to Lillian Whiting, June 20, n.y., BPL.

27. EBS to Julia Dorr, Oct. 5, [1888], VTMC. ECS believed that EBS was dissatisfied with his review of *The Morgesons*, according to a letter to Thomas Bailey Aldrich, quoted in Matlack, "Literary Career," 221. EBS to ECS, Nov. 25, n.y., NYCol-SC. ECS's diary quoted in Matlack, 192. ECS to James Russell Lowell, quoted in Matlack, 440. EBS to ECS, [Oct. or Nov. 1887], NYCol-SC. EBS to Julia Dorr, Oct. 5, [1888], VTMC.

28. Stedman's 1901 introduction to Stoddard's novels is included in his *Genius and Other Essays* (New York: Moffat, Yard, 1911). ECS, ed., *An American Anthology, 1787–1900* (Boston: Houghton, Mifflin, 1900).

29. Ellery Sedgwick, *The "Atlantic Monthly," 1857–1909: Yankee Humanism at High Tide and Ebb* (Amherst: University of Massachusetts Press, 1994), 40–41.

30. ESP, *Chapters*, 78, 79. LMA, Nov. 1858, *The Journals of Louisa May Alcott*, ed. Joel Myerson, Daniel Shealy, and associate ed. Madeleine B. Stern (Athens: University of Georgia Press, 1997), 92. EBS to William Dean Howells, Nov. 24, n.y., bMS Am 1784 (460), MH. CFW to Thomas Bailey Aldrich, June 30, [188?], bMS Am 1429 (4842), MH. Davis quoted in Sharon Harris, *Rebecca Harding Davis and American Realism* (Philadelphia: University of Pennsylvania Press, 1991), 99. Jackson quoted in Elizabeth A. Petrino, *Emily*

Dickinson and Her Contemporaries: Women's Verse in America, 1820–1885 (Hanover, NH: University Press of New England, 1998), 179. Final quote in the paragraph is from a speech by Mr. Howard at the *Atlantic*-Whittier Dinner, quoted in the *Boston Daily Advertiser,* Dec. 18, 1877, 1.

31. Joan Hedrick, *Harriet Beecher Stowe, A Life* (New York: Oxford University Press, 1994), 289, 290. Thomas Wentworth Higginson, *Letters and Journals of Thomas Wentworth Higginson, 1846–1906,* ed. Mary Thacher Higginson (1921; reprint, New York: Da Capo Press, 1969), 106, 108.

32. "Whittier's Birthday," *Boston Daily Advertiser,* Dec. 18, 1877, 1. "The Atlantic-Whittier Dinner—A Woman's Thoughts Thereon," *Boston Daily Advertiser,* Dec. 20, 1877, 1. Richard S. Lowry, *"Littery Man": Mark Twain and Modern Authorship* (New York: Oxford University Press, 1996), 30–40, describes and analyzes the event, where Twain gave his infamous speech, as well as the protest published in the *Daily Advertiser.* "The Absence of Women at the Whittier Dinner," *New York Evening Post,* reprinted in the *Boston Daily Advertiser,* Dec. 28, 1877, 2.

33. Arthur Gilman, "Atlantic Dinners and Diners," *Atlantic Monthly* 100 (Nov. 1907): 654, 657.

34. Hedrick, *Harriet Beecher Stowe,* 314–315.

35. See Sedgwick, *The "Atlantic Monthly,"* 48, 55; Matlack, "Literary Career," 184; and Alcott, Nov. 1859, *Journals,* 95.

36. Sedgwick, *The "Atlantic Monthly,"* 56. On the pressure Lowell felt to " 'popularize' " the magazine, see Sedgwick, 50, and Martin Duberman, *James Russell Lowell* (Boston: Houghton, Mifflin, 1966), 173–174.

37. EBS to James Russell Lowell, Jan. 12, [1860], Jan. 27, [1860], Apr. 23, [1860], bMS Am 765 (727) MH

38. EBS to Lowell, May 5, 1860, bMS Am 765 (727), MH.

39. EBS quoted in James Matlack, "Hawthorne and Elizabeth Barstow Stoddard," *New England Quarterly* 50 (1977): 299. "Recent American Fiction," *Atlantic Monthly* 64 (July 1889): 127–128. About her unhappiness with the review, see EBS to Lillian Whiting, June 27, [1889], BPL. "Some Recent Novels," *Atlantic Monthly* 88 (Dec. 1901): 848. EBS to Bliss Perry, Nov. 25, 1901; quoted in Matlack, "Literary Career," 273.

40. LMA, Nov. 1859, *Journals,* 95. Abigail Alcott, diary, Jan. 19, 1860, bMS AM 1130.14 (2), MH.

41. Howard M. Ticknor to LMA, Mar. 13, 1860, bMS Am 800.23, MH. LMA, *Journals,* Feb. 1860, 98. On the *Atlantic*'s antislavery stance, see Sedgwick, *The "Atlantic Monthly,"* 62–64.

42. LMA to Alfred Whitman, Aug. 4, [1861], Aug. 6, [1862], *Selected Letters,* 67, 72. Howard Ticknor to LMA, Dec. 7, 1861, Dec. 10, 1861, UVA.

43. For example, vol. 10 (July–Dec. 1862) features eleven fiction pieces, eight by women and three by men. Vol. 15 (Jan.–June 1865) features ten fiction pieces, four by women and six by men. Vol. 19 (Jan.–June 1867) features thirteen fiction pieces, four by women and nine by men. Richard Brodhead, *The School of Hawthorne* (New York: Oxford University Press, 1986), 87. Kenneth S. Lynn, *William Dean Howells, An American Life* (New York: Harcourt Brace Jovanovich, 1970), 140.

44. Sedgwick, *The "Atlantic Monthly,"* 74–75, 89, 97–98.

45. EBS to ECS, May 5, 1860, in *The Morgesons,* 336. On Fields's rejection of Davis, see Harris, *Rebecca Harding Davis,* 138–139.

46. LMA, May 1862, *Journals*, 109. LMA returned the forty dollars in 1871, after she had become rich with her children's books. See LMA to James T. Fields, July 3, 1871, *Selected Letters*, 160.

47. LMA describes her stay with James and Annie Fields in a letter to Alfred Whitman, Apr. 6, [1862], *Selected Letters*, 73. LMA to Annie Fields, June 24, [1863], *Selected Letters*, 84. LMA, May 1863, *Journals*, 119.

48. LMA, Aug. 1863, *Journals*, 120. LMA to James Redpath, [early Sept. 1863], *Selected Letters*, 91.

49. LMA to Thomas Wentworth Higginson, Nov. 12, [1863], *Selected Letters*, 96–97. Bronson Alcott, *The Journals of Bronson Alcott*, ed. Odell Shepard (Boston: Little, Brown, 1938), 361.

50. LMA, Oct. 1863, Nov. 1863, July 1864, Nov. 1864, *Journals*, 120–121, 131, 133.

51. LMA, Nov. 1864, *Journals*, 133. Howard M. Ticknor to LMA, June 21, 1865, July 13, 1865, Sept. 7, 1866, UVA. LMA to Lucy Larcom, [Jan.? or Feb.? 1869], *Selected Letters*, 119.

52. Review of *An Old-Fashioned Girl*, by LMA, *Atlantic Monthly* 25 (June 1870): 753. "Contributors' Club," *Atlantic Monthly* 42 (Oct. 1878): 507. G. P. Lathrop, "Recent Literature," *Atlantic Monthly* 40 (July 1877): 109.

53. "Two New England Women," *Atlantic Monthly* 65 (Mar. 1890): 420–421.

54. ESP, *Chapters*, 92, 93, 149, 143, 147.

55. Coultrap-McQuin, "Elizabeth Stuart Phelps," 182. ESP to Henry Houghton, May 20, 1882; quoted in Coultrap-McQuin, 206. ESP to James R. Osgood, June 29, 1871, June 5, 1871, May 13, 1871, bMS Am 2100 (12), MH.

56. ESP to James R. Osgood, Nov. 13, 1872, bMS Am 2100 (12), MH. ESP to William Dean Howells, Aug. 11, 1874, Feb. 9, 1881, bMS Am 1784 (515), MH. ESP to James R. Osgood, Apr. 17, 1876, bMS Am 2100 (12), MH.

57. ESP to Thomas Bailey Aldrich, Mar. 14, 1881, bMS Am 1429 (4490), MH. Coultrap-McQuin, "Elizabeth Stuart Phelps," 183.

58. Review of *Hedged In*, *Atlantic Monthly* 25 (June 1870): 756–757. William Dean Howells, Review of *Poetic Studies*, *Atlantic Monthly* 36 (July 1875): 108–109.

59. Harriet Preston, "The Story of Avis, and Other Novels," *Atlantic Monthly* 41 (Apr. 1878): 487, 489. "Contributors' Club," *Atlantic Monthly* 43 (Mar. 1879): 397. "Contributors' Club," *Atlantic Monthly* 43 (Feb. 1879): 258. "Contributors' Club," *Atlantic Monthly* 41 (May 1878): 667.

60. Horace Scudder, "The Annexation of Heaven," *Atlantic Monthly* 53 (Jan. 1884): 138–139.

61. For example, vol. 35 (Jan.–June 1875) features thirteen pieces of fiction, eight by women and five by men, and vol. 44 (July–Dec. 1879) features ten fiction pieces, seven by women and three by men.

62. Howells, "Recollections," 193, 187.

63. CFW to William Dean Howells, Oct. 27, [1874], Nov. 5, [1877], bMS AM 1784 (558), MH.

64. William Dean Howells, "Recent Literature," *Atlantic Monthly* 35 (June 1875): 736–737. Thomas Sargeant Perry, "Some Recent Novels," *Atlantic Monthly* 46 (July 1880): 125. Horace Scudder, "Recent American Fiction," *Atlantic Monthly* 50 (July 1882): 111–113.

65. CFW to Thomas Bailey Aldrich, June 30, [188?], bMS Am 1429 (4842), MH.

66. Horace Scudder, "American Fiction by Women," *Atlantic Monthly* 52 (July 1883): 119–120. Horace Scudder, "Recent Novels by Women," *Atlantic Monthly* 59 (Feb. 1887): 267. Scudder's review of her next novel, *Jupiter Lights*, was even more negative; "Recent American Fiction," *Atlantic Monthly* 65 (Jan. 1890): 126–128.

67. CFW to Paul Hamilton Hayne, Jan. 16, 1876, in Hubbell, "Some New Letters," 728. EBS to Lillian Whiting, June 20, n.y., BPL. CFW to William Dean Howells, June 28, [1875], bMS Am 1784 (558), MH. Dickinson to T. W. Higginson, June 1869, in *Letters of Emily Dickinson*, 460.

68. *United States Review* quoted in Joyce W. Warren, "Introduction: Canons and Canon Fodder," *The (Other) American Traditions: Nineteenth-Century Women Writers*, ed. Joyce W. Warren (New Brunswick, NJ: Rutgers University Press, 1993), 1.

69. EBS, *Daily Alta California*, Oct. 22, 1854, in *The Morgesons*, 314.

70. "Female Authors," *North American Review* 72 (Jan. 1851): 160. This is the same piece quoted in Chap. 1, lamenting "the entrance of the Amazonian mania into literature" (163). EBS, *Daily Alta California*, Oct. 22, 1854, in *The Morgesons*, 314. EBS, "Woman in Art. — Rosa Bonheur," *Aldine* 5 (July 1872): 145.

71. CFW, "Contributor's Club," *Atlantic Monthly* 42 (Oct. 1878): 502–503.

72. Review of *Jupiter Lights*, *Literary World* 21 (Feb. 1890): 41. "Miss Woolson's 'Anne,'" *Critic* 2 (July 15, 1882): 187.

73. Henry James, review of *Moods*, *North American Review* 101 (July 1865): 276, 281; reprinted in Louisa May Alcott, *Moods*, ed. Sarah Elbert (New Brunswick, NJ: Rutgers University Press, 1991), 223, 220.

74. Review of *The Story of Avis*, *New York Times*, Oct. 15, 1877, 2.

75. Review of *Temple House*, *Nation* 6 (Jan. 23, 1868): 74.

76. Review of *Horace Chase*, *Nation* 58 (Mar. 29, 1894): 233. Review of *Men, Women, and Ghosts*, *Overland Monthly* 3 (Sept. 1869): 292.

77. Review of *Hedged In*, *Nation* 10 (Apr. 14, 1870): 245. Review of *The Story of Avis*, *New York Times*, Oct. 15, 1877, 2.

78. Review of *For the Major*, *New York Times*, June 16, 1883, 3; reprinted in Cheryl B. Torsney, ed., *Critical Essays on Constance Fenimore Woolson* (New York: G. K. Hall, 1992), 35. Review of *For the Major*, *Literary World* (Aug. 11, 1883): 261; excerpted in *Critical Essays on Constance Fenimore Woolson*, 40. "Miss Woolson's 'Anne,'" *Critic* 2 (July 15, 1882): 187. Henry James, "Miss Woolson," reprinted in *Women Artists, Women Exiles*, 271.

79. William Dean Howells, review of *Two Men*, *Nation* 1 (1865): 537. "Editor's Literary Record," *Harper's* 47 (Sept. 1873): 619. Reviews of *Hospital Sketches* from the *New England Farmer* and the *Boston Cultivator*, quoted in advertisement, unidentified newspaper clipping no. 290, UVA. "Miss Phelps's New Novel," *Literary World* 8 (Nov. 1877): 98. "Elizabeth Stuart Phelps Ward," *Independent* 70 (Feb. 2, 1911): 269.

80. George Parsons Lathrop, "Audacity in Women Novelists," *North American Review* 150 (May 1890): 612. Julian Hawthorne, "Novelistic Habits and 'The Morgesons,'" (*Lippincott's* 44 (Dec. 1889): 869.

81. Review of *Friends: A Duet*, *Philadelphia Press*, excerpted in ESP, *An Old Maid's Paradise* (Boston: Houghton, Mifflin, 1886), endpages. "Southern Sketches," *Literary World* 11 (July 3, 1880): 223.

82. "Miss Phelps's New Novel," *Literary World* 8 (Nov. 1877): 98. Review of *Moods*, *Harper's Weekly* 9 (Jan. 21, 1865): 35. Julian Hawthorne, "Novelistic Habits and 'The Morgesons,'" 869. "Anne," *Literary World*, 12 (July 15, 1882): 227.

83. Review of *The Oath of Allegiance, Nation* 89 (Nov. 18, 1909): 487.

84. "Novel Views of Marriage," unidentified newspaper clipping no. 291, UVA. LMA to Moncure Daniel Conway, Feb. 18, 1865, in *Selected Letters*, 108.

85. "New Publications," unidentified newspaper clipping no. 291, UVA. Henry James, Jr., review of *Moods, North American Review* 101 (July 1865): 276–281; reprinted in *Critical Essays on Louisa May Alcott*, ed. Madeleine B. Stern (Boston: G. K. Hall, 1984), 71, 73. Review of *Moods, Harper's Weekly* 9 (Jan. 21, 1865): 35.

86. "Work," *Literary World* 4 (July 1873): 18–19. Review of *Work, Nation* 17 (July 31, 1873): 73. Review of *Work, Appletons' Journal* 10 (July 5, 1873): 30. "Editor's Literary Record," *Harper's* 47 (Sept. 1873): 618.

87. Review of *The Story of Avis, Nation* 26 (Mar. 21, 1878): 202. "Editor's Literary Record," *Harper's* 43 (June 1871): 300–301. Review of *The Silent Partner, Literary World* 1 (Apr. 1, 1871): 166–167.

88. Review of *Hedged In, Nation* 10 (Apr. 14, 1870): 245.

89. ESP, *Chapters*, 120, 121. George Eliot to ESP, Dec. 16, 1876, George Eliot and George Henry Lewes Collection, Beinecke Rare Book and Manuscript Library, Yale University, New Haven, CT.

90. ESP, *Chapters*, 157. Review of *The Story of Avis, Harper's* 56 (Jan. 1878): 310. "Gail Hamilton's Criticism," *Woman's Journal* 29 (Mar. 30, 1878): 99; reprinted in *The Story of Avis*, ed. Carol Farley Kessler (New Brunswick, NJ: Rutgers University Press, 1985), 275. For other reviews, see "Miss Phelps's New Novel," *Literary World* 8 (Nov. 1877): 97–98; review of *The Story of Avis, Nation* 26 (Mar. 21, 1878): 202; and review of *The Story of Avis, New York Times*, Oct. 15, 1877, 2. "New Books," *Philadelphia Inquirer*, Oct. 31, 1877; reprinted in *The Story of Avis*, 273.

91. CFW to Paul Hamilton Hayne, "May Day," 1875, and June 15, 1875, in Hubbell, "Some New Letters," 717, 720. William Dean Howells, "Recent Literature," *Atlantic Monthly* 35 (June 1875): 736. CFW to William Dean Howells, June 28, n.y., bMS Am 1784 (558), MH.

92. William Dean Howells, "Recent Literature," *Atlantic Monthly* 35 (June 1875): 736. Review of *Castle Nowhere, Appletons' Journal* 13 (Apr. 3, 1875): 438–439. "Southern Sketches," *Literary World* 11 (July 3, 1880): 223.

93. "Miss Woolson's 'Anne,'" *Critic* 2 (July 15, 1882): 188. "Anne," *Literary World* 12 (July 15, 1882): 227. See also "Recent Novels," *Nation* 31 (Aug. 31, 1882): 182; review of *Anne, Century* 24 (Aug. 1882): 635–636; and "Four American Novels," *Lippincott's* 30 (Aug. 1882): 215.

94. Review of *Anne, Century*, 635–636. Review of *Horace Chase, Literary World* 24 (Mar. 1894): 85. Charles Dudley Warner, "Editor's Study," *Harper's* 88 (May 1894): 967.

95. Quoted in Matlack, "Literary Career," 442.

96. George Ripley, review of *Two Men, New York Tribune*, Nov. 16, 1856, 6: quoted in Matlack, "Literary Career," 370–372. EBS to William Dean Howells's, n.d., bMS Am 1784 (460), MH. (A clipping of a notice with an excerpt from Howells's *Nation* review is pasted at the head of the letter.) William Dean Howells, review of *Two Men, Nation* 1 (1865): 537–538.

97. Review of *Temple House, Putnam's* 11 (Feb. 1868): 255. See also review of *Temple House, Nation* 6 (Jan. 23, 1868): 74–75; and review of *Temple House, Round Table*, Jan. 18, 1868. *The Letters of Henry Wadsworth Longfellow*, ed. Andrew Hillen, vol. 6 (Cambridge: Harvard University Press, Belknap Press, 1982), 327.

98. See Matlack, "Literary Career," 532–534, on the interest from Julian Hawthorne, Browne, and Stedman. ECS, "A Critical Estimate of Mrs. Stoddard's Novels"; reprinted as "Mrs. Stoddard's Novels," in *Genius and Other Essays* (Port Washington, NY: Kennikat Press, 1966), 154, 156. George Lathrop to EBS, Aug. 8, 1888, Papers of Richard H. Stoddard and Elizabeth B. Stoddard, Manuscripts and Archives Division, New York Public Library, Astor, Lenox, and Tilden Foundations, New York, NY.

99. See "Mrs. Stoddard's 'Two Men,'" *Literary World* 19 (July 21, 1888): 227; "A Romance of New Bedford," *New York Times*, July 15, 1888, 12; Julian Hawthorne, "Novelistic Habits and 'The Morgesons,'" *Lippincott's* 44 (Dec. 1889): 869; "Recent Fiction," *Independent* 40 (Aug. 23, 1888): 16–17; "Recent Fiction," *Critic* 9 (June 23, 1888): 305; and review of *Two Men*, *Nation* 47 (Aug. 9, 1888): 118.

100. EBS to Julia Dorr, Oct. 5, [1888], VTMC. Review of *Two Men*, *Nation* 47 (Aug. 9, 1888): 118.

101. EBS to Julia Dorr, July 29, [1896], VTMC.

Conclusion. The Question of Immortality

1. Susan Coultrap-McQuin, *Doing Literary Business: American Women Writers in the Nineteenth Century* (Chapel Hill: University of North Carolina Press, 1990), 159. [Josephine Lazarus], "Emma Lazarus," *Century* 36 (Oct. 1888): 877; quoted in Bette Roth Young, *Emma Lazarus in Her World: Life and Letters* (Philadelphia: Jewish Publication Society, 1995), 13.

2. Alfred Bendixen, introduction to *"The Amber Gods" and Other Stories* (New Brunswick, NJ: Rutgers University Press, 1989), xxi. Sharon Harris, *Rebecca Harding Davis and American Realism* (Philadelphia: University of Pennsylvania Press, 1991), 292, 307. Notice of Davis's death identifying her as the "widow of L. Clarke Davis" in Harris, 307. Tillie Olsen, "Biographical and Critical Introduction," *Life in the Iron Mills and Other Stories* (New York: Feminist Press, 1985), 152. *New York Times* obituary of Davis quoted in Olsen, 153.

3. See "Louisa May Alcott," *New York Times*, Mar. 7, 1888, 4; "The Alcotts," *Critic* 12 (Mar. 10, 1888): 119; "Louisa May Alcott," *Harper's Bazar* 21 (Mar. 3, 1888): 207; "Bronson Alcott and His Daughter," *Harper's Weekly* 32 (Mar. 17, 1888): 187; "Louisa May Alcott," *Ladies' Home Journal* 5 (May 1888): 3; and "The Alcotts," *Literary World* 19 (Mar. 17, 1888): 88.

4. Thomas Wentworth Higginson, "Women and Men. Louisa May Alcott," *Harper's Bazar* 21 (Apr. 7, 1888): 218.

5. Ednah D. Cheney, *Louisa May Alcott, the Children's Friend* (Boston: L. Prang, 1888). G. K. Chesterton, "Louisa Alcott," *Nation* (1907); reprinted in *Critical Essays on Louisa May Alcott*, ed. Madeleine B. Stern (Boston: G. K. Hall, 1984), 213, 214. Thomas Beer, *The Mauve Decade* (New York: Knopf, 1926), 61.

6. Charles Dudley Warner, "Editor's Study," *Harper's* 88 (May 1894): 966. Margaret Sangster, "Constance Fenimore Woolson," *Harper's Bazar* 27 (Feb. 3, 1894): 94. Henry Mills Alden, "Constance Fenimore Woolson," *Harper's Weekly* 38 (Feb. 3, 1894): 113. "Constance Fenimore Woolson," *Critic* 24 (Feb. 3, 1894): 14. "Constance Fenimore Woolson," *Dial* 16 (Feb. 1, 1894): 92. "Death of Constance F. Woolson," *New York Times*, Jan. 25, 1894, 2. CFW, *The Front Yard and Other Italian Stories* (New York: Harper & Bros., 1895).

7. Julian Hawthorne and Leonard Lemmon, *American Literature, a Text-Book* (Boston: Heath, 1892), 284. F. V. N. Painter, in "Prominent Writers," *Introduction to American Literature* (Boston: Sibley & Ducker, 1897), 253–258. Fred Lewis Pattee, *A History of American Literature since 1870* (New York: Century, 1917), 317, 318. Fred Lewis Pattee, *The Development of the American Short Story, an Historical Survey* (New York: Harper & Bros., 1923), 253, 254. Vernon Louis Parrington, *Main Currents in American Thought*, vol. 3, *1860–1920, The Beginnings of Critical Realism in America* (New York: Harcourt, Brace, 1927, 1930), 398. John Dwight Kern, *Constance Fenimore Woolson: Literary Pioneer* (Philadelphia: University of Pennsylvania Press, 1934).

8. "Death of Mrs. Stoddard," *New York Times*, Aug. 2, 1902, 9. Mary Moss, "The Novels of Elizabeth Stoddard," *Bookman* 16 (Nov. 1902): 262. "The Lounger," *Critic* 41 (Oct. 1902): 299. The *Critic* had published the following tributes to Richard Henry Stoddard: "Mr. Stoddard's Seventieth Birthday," 27 (July 6, 1895): 11–13; and "Honoring Mr. Stoddard," 30 (Apr. 3, 1897): 225–231. For two brief notices of Elizabeth Stoddard's death, see *New York Herald Tribune*, Aug. 2, 1902, 7; and "Chronicle and Comment," *Bookman* 16 (Aug. 1902): 5–6.

9. Fred Lewis Pattee, *A History of American Literature, with a View to the Fundamental Principles Underlying Its Development* (New York: Silver, Burdett, 1896), 362. Hawthorne and Lemmon, *American Literature*, 209. Henry C. Vedder, *American Writers of To-Day* (New York: Silver, Burdett, 1894), 279. Van Wyck Brooks, *New England: Indian Summer, 1865–1915* (New York: Dutton, 1940), 238.

10. Vedder, *American Writers*, 193, 194, 200. Painter, *Introduction*, 267–268. Pattee, *History* (1896), 415. Hawthorne and Lemmon, *American Literature*, 287.

11. "Elizabeth Stuart Phelps Ward," *Independent* 70 (Feb. 2, 1911): 269. "Mrs. E. S. P. Ward Dies in 67th Year," *New York Times*, Jan. 29, 1911, 11. Obituary for Elizabeth Stuart Phelps, *Dial* 57 (Feb. 16, 1911): 116. Coultrap-McQuin, *Doing Literary Business*, 184.

12. Parrington, *Main Currents*, 61. Granville Hicks, *The Great Tradition: An Interpretation of American Literature* (New York: Macmillan, 1933), 83. Brooks, *New England*, 82, 101. Pattee, *History* (1917), 224. Pattee, *Development*, 178, 180, 181.

13. See M. A. DeWolfe Howe, *American Bookmen: Sketches, Chiefly Biographical, or Certain Writers of the Nineteenth Century* (1898; reprint, Freeport, NY: Books for Libraries, 1972); Henry A. Beers, *Initial Studies in American Letters* (New York: Chatauqua Press, 1891); Richard Burton, *Literary Leaders of America: A Class-Book on American Literature* (New York: Scribner, 1904); and Edwin Greenlaw, *Literature and Life* (Chicago: Scott, Foresman, 1922).

14. ECS and Ellen Mackay Hutchinson, eds., *A Library of American Literature from the Earliest Settlement to the Present Time*, 11 vols. (New York: Charles L. Webster, 1883–90). Quotes from editors' preface, 11:vi, vii. Alcott and Stoddard are featured in vol. 8, Phelps and Woolson in vol. 10.

15. William Peterfield Trent et al., eds., *The Cambridge History of American Literature*, 4 vols. (New York: Putnam, 1913–21); Charles F. Richardson, *American Literature 1607–1885* (1886–88; reprint, New York: Putnam, 1893); Painter, *Introduction*; Walter Bronson, *A Short History of American Literature* (Boston: Heath, 1908); Hicks, *Great Tradition*.

16. Review of "Stedman's Library of American Literature," *Atlantic Monthly* 66 (Nov. 1890): 707.

17. Paul Lauter, "Race and Gender in the Shaping of the American Literary Canon: A Case Study from the Twenties," in *Canons and Contexts* (New York: Oxford University

Press, 1991), 24, discusses Foerster's book. Burton, *Literary Leaders*. Edwin W. Bowen, *Makers of American Literature: A Class-Book on American Literature* (New York: Neale, 1908). Horace E. Scudder, *American Prose* (Boston: Houghton, Mifflin, 1885).

18. Charlene Avallone, "What American Renaissance? The Gendered Genealogy of a Critical Discourse," *PMLA* 112 (1997): 1102–1120. Nancy Glazener, *Reading for Realism: The History of a U.S. Literary Institution, 1850–1910* (Durham, NC: Duke University Press, 1997), 229–255; quote on 235.

19. "Our 'Forty Immortals,'" *Critic* 4 (Apr. 12, 1884): 169–170. Nonwhite males were also excluded. Frederick Douglass and Sitting Bull were nominated by readers but excluded by the editors for unclear reasons. Their "only claim to eligibility consisted in the fact that they were born, and have always lived, on American soil" (170). For a reader's protest, see William F. Peck, letter to the editor, *Critic* 4 (May 3, 1884): 210.

20. "Notes," *Critic* 4 (Apr. 26, 1884): 202. "American Women of Letters," *Literary World* 14 (Apr. 21, 1883): 126.

21. Thomas Bender, *New York Intellect: A History of Intellectual Life in New York City, from 1750 to the Beginnings of Our Own Time* (New York: Knopf, 1987), 219–220. Photo of "Group of Immortals," *Book News Monthly* 29 (Mar. 1911): 443.

22. Glazener, *Reading for Realism*, 229–255. For Horace E. Scudder's efforts at canonizing the Boston Brahmins, see Ellery Sedgwick, *The "Atlantic Monthly," 1857–1909: Yankee Humanism at High Tide and Ebb* (Amherst: University of Massachusetts Press, 1994), 213; and Nina Baym, "Early Histories of American Literature: A Chapter in the Institution of New England" in *The American Literary History Reader*, ed. Gordon Hutner (New York: Oxford University Press, 1995), 83–84. Scudder's works that helped canonize these writers include *American Poems* (Boston: Houghton, Mifflin, 1879); *American Prose* (Boston: Houghton, Mifflin, 1885); *Men and Letters: Essays in Characterization and Criticism* (Boston: Houghton, Mifflin, 1887); and *Literature in School* (Boston: Houghton, Mifflin, 1888).

23. Scott E. Casper, "Defining the National Pantheon: The Making of Houghton Mifflin's Biographical Series, 1880–1900," in *Reading Books: Essays on the Material Text and Literature in America*, ed. Michele Moylan and Lane Stiles (Amherst: University of Massachusetts Press, 1996), 214. Lane Stiles, "Packaging Literature for High Schools: From the Riverside Literature Series to *Literature and Life*," in *Reading Books*, 248–275.

24. Moss, "Novels," 263.

25. Sharon Dean, *Constance Fenimore Woolson: Homeward Bound* (Knoxville: University of Tennessee Press, 1995), 200; and "Edith Wharton's Early Artist Stories and Constance Fenimore Woolson," in *Constance Fenimore Woolson's Nineteenth Century: Essays*, ed. Victoria Brehm (Detroit: Wayne State University Press, 2001), 225–239.

26. Donna M. Campbell, *Resisting Regionalism: Gender and Naturalism in American Fiction, 1885–1915* (Athens: Ohio University Press, 1997), 150. Deborah Lindsay Williams, *Not in Sisterhood: Edith Wharton, Willa Cather, Zona Gale, and the Politics of Female Authorship* (New York: Palgrave, 2001), 3, 2. Amy Kaplan, *The Social Construction of American Realism* (Chicago: University of Chicago Press, 1988), 70.

27. For a thorough overview of such criticism and the issues it raises, see June Howard, "Unraveling Regions, Unsettling Periods: Sarah Orne Jewett and American Literary History," *American Literature* 68 (June 1996): 365–384.

28. Vivian R. Pollak, in *Dickinson: The Anxiety of Gender* (Ithaca, NY: Cornell University Press, 1984), writes of "The Female Artist as a Private Poet" in chap. 8. Judith

Farr's *Passion of Emily Dickinson* (Cambridge: Harvard University Press, 1992) begins with a chapter titled "The Hidden Face." Joanne Dobson's influential study of Dickinson as representative is titled *Dickinson and the Strategies of Reticence: The Woman Writer in Nineteenth-Century America* (Bloomington: Indiana University Press, 1989).

    29. Avallone, "What American Renaissance?" 1107.

Bibliographic Essay

When I first began my research for this book in 1994, the project of recovering nineteenth-century American women writers was well under way. Studies such as Nina Baym, *Woman's Fiction: A Guide to Novels by and about Women in America, 1820–1870* (Ithaca, NY: Cornell University Press, 1978; 2d ed., Urbana: University of Illinois Press, 1993); Mary Kelley, *Private Woman, Public Stage: Literary Domesticity in Nineteenth-Century America* (New York: Oxford University Press, 1984); Susan K. Harris, *Nineteenth-Century American Women's Novels: Interpretive Strategies* (Cambridge: Cambridge University Press, 1990); Josephine Donovan, *New England Local Color Literature: A Women's Tradition* (New York: Ungar, 1983); and Elizabeth Ammons, *Conflicting Stories: American Women Writers at the Turn into the Twentieth Century* (New York: Oxford University Press, 1991) were the standards in the field, having established the study of nineteenth-century American women writers as a serious endeavor. Each of these works examined a variety of writers and works and theorized women's participation in American literature in significant and groundbreaking ways. However, Baym, Kelley, and Harris focused on the antebellum generation, and Donovan and Ammons looked at the late nineteenth century. There was no such work for the Civil War and postbellum era. While each of these studies certainly informs an examination of the intermediary period, the scholar interested in exploring the women writers who began their careers in the 1860s and 1870s has had to turn to single-author studies.

The majority of books published on Louisa May Alcott are biographies written for a general audience. The best of these is Madeleine Stern, *Louisa May Alcott: A Biography* (1950; reprint, New York: Random House, 1996). The most comprehensive scholarly biographical and critical study of Alcott is Sarah Elbert, *A Hunger for Home: Louisa May Alcott's Place in American Culture* (New Brunswick, NJ: Rutgers University Press, 1987). Elaine Showalter's introduction to *Alternative Alcott* (New Brunswick, NJ: Rutgers University Press, 1988), also provides an authoritative overview of her life and work. Richard H. Brodhead, *Cultures of Letters: Scenes of Reading and Writing in Nineteenth-Century America* (Chicago: University of Chicago Press, 1993), chap. 3, offers a compelling examination of how Alcott developed as an author. Those interested in Alcott's biography should not neglect *The Journals of Louisa May Alcott*, ed. Joel Myerson, Daniel Shealy, and associate ed. Madeleine B. Stern (Athens: University of Georgia Press, 1997); and *The Selected Letters of Louisa May Alcott*, ed. Joel Myerson, Daniel Shealy, and associate ed. Madeleine B. Stern (Athens: University of Georgia Press, 1995). Also of interest is Ednah D. Cheney, *Life, Letters, and Journals* (1889; reprint, New York: Gramercy Books,

1995), although many of the letters and diary entries are excerpted and carefully chosen to project a certain image of Alcott. Important studies of the Alcott family as a group or of individual members include Cynthia H. Barton, *Transcendental Wife: The Life of Abigail May Alcott* (Lanham, MD: University Press of America, 1996); Madelon Bedell, *The Alcotts: Biography of a Family* (New York: Clarkson N. Potter, 1980); Charles Strickland, *Victorian Domesticity: Families in the Life and Art of Louisa May Alcott* (University: University of Alabama Press, 1985); and Caroline Ticknor, *May Alcott: A Memoir* (Boston: Little, Brown, 1928).

Most of the studies that analyze Alcott's writings focus on her children's literature, her sensational stories, and, more recently, her Civil War and antislavery fiction. Of those that examine Alcott's conception of the artist or genius in her fiction, I found the following to be the most significant: Deborah Barker, *Aesthetics and Gender in American Literature: Portraits of the Woman Artist* (Lewisburg, PA: Bucknell University Press, 2000), chapter 4; Christine Doyle, *Louisa May Alcott and Charlotte Brontë: Transatlantic Translations* (Knoxville: University of Tennessee Press, 2000); Elizabeth Lennox Keyser, *Whispers in the Dark: The Fiction of Louisa May Alcott* (Knoxville: University of Tennessee Press, 1993); Natania Rosenfeld, "Artists and Daughters in Louisa May Alcott's *Diana and Persis*," *New England Quarterly* 64 (Mar. 1991): 3–21; and Gustavus Stadler, "Louisa May Alcott's Queer Geniuses," *American Literature* 71 (Dec. 1999): 657–677.

Far fewer studies have been written on Elizabeth Stuart Phelps, and most scholars continue to focus on her protofeminist views and interest in social causes. For biographies, see her autobiography, *Chapters from a Life* (Boston: Houghton, Mifflin, 1895); Mary Angela Bennett, *Elizabeth Stuart Phelps* (Philadelphia: University of Pennsylvania Press, 1939); Lori Duin Kelly, *The Life and Works of Elizabeth Stuart Phelps, Victorian Feminist Writer* (Troy, NY: Whitston, 1983); Carol Farley Kessler, *Elizabeth Stuart Phelps* (Boston: Twayne, 1982); Susan Coultrap-McQuin, *Doing Literary Business: American Women Writers in the Nineteenth Century* (Chapel Hill: University of North Carolina Press, 1990), chap. 7; and Susan Coultrap-McQuin, "Elizabeth Stuart Phelps: The Cultural Context of a Nineteenth-Century Professional Writer," (Ph.D. diss., University of Iowa, 1979). Susan S. Williams, "Writing with an Ethical Purpose: The Case of Elizabeth Stuart Phelps," in *Reciprocal Influences: Literary Production, Distribution, and Consumption in America*, ed. Stephen Fink and Susan S. Williams (Columbus: Ohio State University Press, 1999), 151–172, is an important examination of Phelps's identity as an author. For additional analyses of her artist fiction, see Deborah Barker, *Aesthetics and Gender in American Literature: Portraits of the Woman Artist* (Lewisburg, PA: Bucknell University Press, 2000), chap. 3; Linda Huf, *A Portrait of the Artist as a Young Woman: The Writer as Heroine in American Literature* (New York: Ungar, 1983), chap. 3; Karen Tracey, *Plots and Proposals: American Women's Fiction, 1850–90* (Urbana: University of Illinois Press, 2000), chap. 5; and Jack H. Wilson, "Competing Narratives in Elizabeth Stuart Phelps' *The Story of Avis*," *American Literary Realism, 1870–1910* 26, no. 1 (1993): 60–75.

It seemed as if a renaissance of Elizabeth Stoddard studies was under way with the publication of *The Morgesons and Other Writings, Published and Unpublished*, ed. Lawrence Buell and Sandra Zagarell (Philadelphia: University of Pennsylvania Press, 1984), which includes an authoritative "Biographical and Critical Introduction." However, although some significant essays have appeared, no full-length book has yet been published on Stoddard. The most complete biography continues to be the unpublished dissertation by James Matlack, "The Literary Career of Elizabeth Barstow Stoddard" (Ph.D. diss., Yale University, 1967). Biographical essays include James Matlack, "Hawthorne and Elizabeth Barstow Stoddard," *New England Quarterly* 50 (June 1977): 278–302; and Sandra Zagarell, "Legacy Profile: Elizabeth Drew Barstow Stoddard (1823–1902)," *Legacy* 8, no. 1 (1991): 39–49. Her husband, Richard Stoddard's *Recollections, Personal and Literary* (New York: A. S. Barnes, 1903), contains some useful information. On her husband and his circle, see John Tomsich, *A Genteel Endeavor: American Culture and Politics in the Gilded Age* (Stanford, CA: Stanford University Press, 1971); and Richard Cary, *The Genteel Circle: Bayard Taylor and His New York Friends* (Ithaca, NY: Cornell University Press, 1952). Despite the dearth of book-length and biographical studies on Stoddard, many excellent essays have appeared on her fiction; however, most of them are on her novel, *The Morgesons*. Ann Jerome Croce, "A Woman Outside Her Time: Elizabeth Stoddard (1823–1910) and Nineteenth-Century American Popular Fiction," *Women's Studies* 19 (1991): 357–369, examines her relationship to popular women writers. On her story "Collected by a Valetudinarian," see Lisa Radinovsky, "Negotiating Models of Authorship: Elizabeth Stoddard's Conflicts and Her Story of Complaint," in *Constance Fenimore Woolson's Nineteenth Century: Essays*, ed. Victoria Brehm (Detroit: Wayne State University Press, 2001), 31–49; and Ellen Weinauer, "Alternative Economies: Authorship and Ownership in Elizabeth Stoddard's 'Collected by a Valetudinarian,'" *Studies in American Fiction* 25, no. 2 (1997): 167–182.

The body of scholarship on Constance Fenimore Woolson has been small but steady over the years. Her niece, Clare Benedict, edited an eclectic and fragmentary but nonetheless useful compendium of her private and public writings, *Constance Fenimore Woolson*, vol. 2 of *Five Generations* (London: Ellis, 1932). Studies of Woolson such as John Dwight Kern, *Constance Fenimore Woolson: Literary Pioneer* (Philadelphia: University of Pennsylvania Press, 1934); and Rayburn S. Moore, *Constance Fenimore Woolson* (New York: Twayne, 1963); as well as Leon Edel, *The Life of Henry James*, 5 vols. (Philadelphia: Lippincott, 1953–72), which discusses Woolson's relationship with James, helped pave the way for an outpouring of interest in Woolson by feminist scholars. Sharon L. Dean, *Constance Fenimore Woolson: Homeward Bound* (Knoxville: University of Tennessee Press, 1995); and Cheryl B. Torsney, *Constance Fenimore Woolson: The Grief of Artistry* (Athens: University of Georgia Press, 1989), are the two most comprehensive studies of Woolson's life and works. Joan Myers Weimer, introduction to *Women Artists, Women Exiles: "Miss Grief" and Other Stories* (New Brunswick, NJ: Rutgers University Press, 1988), provides an important overview of her life and her fiction. Cheryl B. Torsney, ed., *Critical Essays on Constance Fenimore Woolson* (New York: G. K. Hall, 1992); and Victoria Brehm, ed., *Constance Fenimore Woolson's Nineteenth Century: Essays* (Detroit: Wayne State University Press, 2001), include many excellent essays on Woolson's works.

Probably the most enduring fascination for scholars has been Woolson's friendship with Henry James. In addition to Edel's biography, see Lynda S. Boren, " 'Dear Constance,' 'Dear Henry': The Woolson/James Affair — Fact, Fiction, or Fine Art?" *Amer-*

ikastudien 27, no. 4 (1982): 457–466; Sharon L. Dean, "Constance Fenimore Woolson and Henry James: The Literary Relationship," *Massachusetts Studies in English* 7, no. 3 (1980), 1–9; Lyndall Gordon, *A Private Life of Henry James: Two Women and His Art* (New York: Norton, 1999); Mary P. Edwards Kitterman, "Henry James and the Artist-Heroine in the Tales of Constance Fenimore Woolson," in *Nineteenth-Century Women Writers of the English-Speaking World*, ed. Rhoda B. Nathan (Westport, CT: Greenwood Press, 1986), 45–59; Cheryl B. Torsney, "The Traditions of Gender: Constance Fenimore Woolson and Henry James," in *Patrons and Protégées: Gender, Friendship, and Writing in Nineteenth-Century America*, ed. Shirley Marchalonis (New Brunswick, NJ: Rutgers University Press, 1994), 161–183; and Joan Myers Weimer, "The 'Admiring Aunt' and the 'Proud Salmon of the Pond': Constance Fenimore Woolson's Struggle with Henry James," in Torsney, *Critical Essays on Constance Fenimore Woolson*, 203–216.

For information on these four authors' female contemporaries, I found the following sources to be the most useful. On Sherwood Bonner, see Hubert H. McAlexander, *The Prodigal Daughter, A Biography of Sherwood Bonner* (Baton Rouge: Louisiana State University Press, 1981; reprint, with a new introduction, Knoxville: University of Tennessee Press, 1999). On Rebecca Harding Davis, see Sharon Harris, *Rebecca Harding Davis and American Realism* (Philadelphia: University of Pennsylvania Press, 1991); Tillie Olsen, "Biographical and Critical Introduction," *Life in the Iron Mills and Other Stories* (New York: Feminist Press, 1985), 69–174; Jean Pfaelzer, *Parlor Radical: Rebecca Harding Davis and the Origins of American Social Realism* (Pittsburgh: University of Pittsburgh Press, 1996); and Jane Atteridge Rose, "The Artist Manqué in the Fiction of Rebecca Harding Davis," in *Writing the Woman Artist: Essays on Poetics, Politics, and Portraiture*, ed. Suzanne W. Jones (Philadelphia: University of Pennsylvania Press, 1991), 155–174. On Emily Dickinson, see Joanne Dobson, *Dickinson and the Strategies of Reticence: The Woman Writer in Nineteenth-Century America* (Bloomington: Indiana University Press, 1989); Alfred Habegger, *My Wars Are Laid Away in Books: The Life of Emily Dickinson* (New York: Random House, 2001); Elizabeth A. Petrino, *Emily Dickinson and Her Contemporaries: Women's Verse in America, 1820–1885* (Hanover, NH: University Press of New England, 1998); and Cheryl Walker, *The Nightingale's Burden: Women Poets and American Culture before 1900* (Bloomington: Indiana University Press, 1982). On Helen Hunt Jackson, see Petrino, *Emily Dickinson and Her Contemporaries*; and Walker, *Nightingale's Burden*. On Emma Lazarus, see Allison Giffen, "Savage Daughters: Emma Lazarus, Ralph Waldo Emerson, and *The Spagnoletto*," *ATQ* 15, no. 2 (2001): 89–107; Dan Vogel, *Emma Lazarus* (Boston: Twayne, 1980); and Bette Roth Young, *Emma Lazarus in Her World: Life and Letters* (Philadelphia: Jewish Publication Society, 1995). On Charlotte Forten Grimké, see Joanne M. Braxton, "Charlotte Forten Grimké and the Search for a Public Voice," in *The Private Self: Theory and Practice of Women's Autobiographical Writings*, ed. Shari Benstock (Chapel Hill: University of North Carolina Press, 1988), 254–271; Geneva Cobb-Moore, "When Meanings Meet: The Journals of Charlotte Forten Grimké," in *Inscribing the Daily: Critical Essays on Women's Diaries*, ed. Suzanne L. Bunkers and Cynthia Anne Huff (Amherst: University of Massachusetts Press, 1996), 139–155; and Carla L. Peterson, "Frances Harper, Charlotte Forten, and African-American Literary Reconstruction," in *Challenging*

Boundaries: Gender and Periodization, ed. Joyce W. Warren and Margaret Dickie (Athens: University of Georgia Press, 2000), 39–61. On Sarah Orne Jewett, see Paula Blanchard, *Sarah Orne Jewett: Her World and Her Work* (Reading, MA: Addison-Wesley, 1994); Richard H. Brodhead, *Cultures of Letters: Scenes of Reading and Writing in Nineteenth-Century America* (Chicago: University of Chicago Press, 1993), chap. 5; Gwen L. Nagel, ed., *Critical Essays on Sarah Orne Jewett* (Boston: G. K. Hall, 1984); and Elizabeth Silverthorne, *Sarah Orne Jewett: A Writer's Life* (Woodstock, NY: Overlook Press, 1993). On Sarah Piatt, see Paula Bennett, introduction to *Palace-Burner: The Selected Poetry of Sarah Piatt* (Urbana: University of Illinois Press, 2001). And on Harriet Prescott Spofford, see Alfred Bendixen, introduction to *"The Amber Gods" and Other Stories* (New Brunswick, NJ: Rutgers University Press, 1989), ix–xxxiv; and Jennifer Putzi, "Harriet Prescott Spofford," *Dictionary of American Literary Biography*, vol. 221, *American Women Prose Writers, 1870–1920*, ed. Sharon M. Harris (Detroit: Gale, 2000), 322–331.

In addition to the above works, I looked to many broader sources to help flesh out my understanding of nineteenth-century American literary cultures. A few of the most influential were Nina Baym, *American Women Writers and the Work of History, 1790–1860* (New Brunswick, NJ: Rutgers University Press, 1995); Nina Baym, "Early Histories of American Literature: A Chapter in the Institution of New England," in *The American Literary History Reader*, ed. Gordon Hutner (New York: Oxford University Press, 1995); Nina Baym, *Novels, Readers, and Reviewers: Responses to Fiction in Antebellum America* (Ithaca, NY: Cornell University Press, 1984); Richard Brodhead, *The School of Hawthorne* (New York: Oxford University Press, 1986); Lawrence Buell, *New England Literary Culture: From Revolution through Renaissance* (Cambridge: Cambridge University Press, 1986); Donna M. Campbell, *Resisting Regionalism: Gender and Naturalism in American Fiction, 1885–1915* (Athens: Ohio University Press, 1997); Mary Kupiec Cayton, *Emerson's Emergence: Self and Society in the Transformation of New England, 1800–1845* (Chapel Hill: University of North Carolina Press, 1989); William Charvat, *The Profession of Authorship in America, 1800–1870*, ed. Matthew Bruccoli (Columbus: Ohio State University Press, 1968); Susan Phinney Conrad, *Perish the Thought: Intellectual Women in Romantic America, 1830–1860* (New York: Oxford University Press, 1976); George Cotkin, *Reluctant Modernism: American Thought and Culture, 1880–1900* (New York: Twayne, 1992); Carol Klimick Cyganowski, *Magazine Editors and Professional Authors in Nineteenth-Century America: The Genteel Tradition and the American Dream* (New York: Garland, 1988); Kenneth Dauber, *The Idea of Authorship in America: Democratic Poetics from Franklin to Melville* (Madison: University of Wisconsin Press, 1990); Joseph J. Ellis, *After the Revolution: Profiles of Early American Culture* (New York: Norton, 1979); Judith Fetterley, introduction to *Provisions: A Reader from Nineteenth-Century American Women* (Bloomington: Indiana University Press, 1985); Michael T. Gilmore, *American Romanticism and the Marketplace* (Chicago: University of Chicago Press, 1985); Nancy Glazener, *Reading for Realism: The History of a U.S. Literary Institution, 1850–1910* (Durham, NC: Duke University Press, 1997); Joan D. Hedrick, *Harriet Beecher Stowe, A Life* (New York: Oxford University Press, 1994); John L. Idol, Jr., and Melinda M. Ponder, eds., *Hawthorne and Women: Engendering and Expanding the Hawthorne Tradition* (Amherst: University of Massachusetts Press, 1999); Carolyn L.

Karcher, "Reconceiving Nineteenth-Century American Literature: The Challenge of Women Writers," *American Literature* 66 (Dec. 1994): 781–793; Paul Lauter, "Race and Gender in the Shaping of the American Literary Canon: A Case Study from the Twenties," in *Canons and Contexts* (New York: Oxford University Press, 1991); Richard S. Lowry, *"Littery Man": Mark Twain and Modern Authorship* (New York: Oxford University Press, 1996); Christopher Newfield, *The Emerson Effect: Individualism and Submission in America* (Chicago: University of Chicago Press, 1996); Patricia Okker, *Our Sister Editors: Sarah J. Hale and the Tradition of Nineteenth-Century American Women Editors* (Athens: University of Georgia Press, 1995); Gilman M. Ostrander, *Republic of Letters: The American Intellectual Community, 1776–1865* (Madison, WI: Madison House, 1999); Kenneth M. Price and Susan Belasco Smith, eds., *Periodical Literature in Nineteenth-Century America* (Charlottesville: University Press of Virginia, 1995); Ellery Sedgwick, *The "Atlantic Monthly," 1857–1909: Yankee Humanism at High Tide and Ebb* (Amherst: University of Massachusetts Press, 1994); G. R. Thompson and Eric Carl Link, *Neutral Ground: New Traditionalism and the American Romance Controversy* (Baton Rouge: Louisiana State University Press, 1999); Jane Tompkins, *Sensational Designs: The Cultural Work of American Fiction, 1790–1860* (New York: Oxford University Press, 1985); Priscilla Wald, *Constituting Americans: Cultural Anxiety and Narrative Form* (Durham, NC: Duke University Press, 1995); and Joyce W. Warren, ed., *The (Other) American Traditions: Nineteenth-Century Women Writers* (New Brunswick, NJ: Rutgers University Press, 1993).

A number of historical works also shaped my understanding of this period, including Barbara Berg, *The Remembered Gate: Origins of American Feminism, The Woman and the City, 1800–1860* (New York: Oxford University Press, 1978); Lee Virginia Chambers-Schiller, *Liberty, A Better Husband: Single Women in America, The Generations of 1780–1840* (New Haven, CT: Yale University Press, 1984); Catherine Clinton and Christine Lunardini, *The Columbia Guide to American Women in the Nineteenth Century* (New York: Columbia University Press, 2000); Wilfred M. McClay, *The Masterless: The Self and Society in Modern America* (Chapel Hill: University of North Carolina Press, 1994); Nancy Cott, *The Grounding of Modern Feminism* (New Haven, CT: Yale University Press, 1987); Philip Cushman, *Constructing the Self, Constructing America: A Cultural History of Psychotherapy* (Reading, MA: Addison-Wesley, 1995); Trisha Franzen, *Spinsters and Lesbians: Independent Womanhood in the United States* (New York: New York University Press, 1996); Nathan O. Hatch, *The Democratization of American Christianity* (New Haven, CT: Yale University Press, 1989); Glenna Matthews, *"Just a Housewife": The Rise and Fall of Domesticity in America* (New York: Oxford University Press, 1987); Stephen Mintz, *A Prison of Expectations: The Family in Victorian Culture* (New York: New York University Press, 1983); Richard Rabinowitz, *The Spiritual Self in Everyday Life: The Transformation of Personal Religious Experience in Nineteenth-Century New England* (Boston: Northeastern University Press, 1989); Carroll Smith-Rosenberg, *Disorderly Conduct: Visions of Gender in Victorian America* (New York: Knopf, 1985); Alice Felt Tyler, *Freedom's Ferment: Phases of American Social History from the Colonial Period to the Outbreak of the Civil War* (Minneapolis: University of Minnesota Press, 1944; reprint, New York: Harper, 1962); and Nancy Woloch, *Women and the American Experience* (New York: Knopf, 1984).

Another significant area of research for me was on the concept of "genius." In addition to many primary sources, I found the following secondary sources particularly helpful: Flavia Alaya, "Victorian Science and the 'Genius' of Woman," *Journal of the History of Ideas* 38 (1977): 261–280; Christine Battersby, *Gender and Genius: Towards a Feminist Aesthetics* (Bloomington: Indiana University Press, 1989); Gene Bell-Villada, *Art for Art's Sake and Literary Life: How Politics and Markets Helped Shape the Ideology and Culture of Aestheticism, 1790–1990* (Lincoln: University of Nebraska Press, 1996); Preben Mortensen, *Art in the Social Order: The Making of the Modern Conception of Art* (Albany: State University of New York Press, 1997); Michael Warner, *The Letters of the Republic: Publication and the Public Sphere in Eighteenth-Century America* (Cambridge: Harvard University Press, 1990); Martha Woodmansee, *The Author, Art and the Market: Rereading the History of Aesthetics* (New York: Columbia University Press, 1994); and Raymond Williams, *Culture and Society, 1780–1950* (New York: Columbia University Press, 1960).

My understanding of women's relation to Transcendentalism was influenced by a variety of sources, most notably Kristin Boudreau, "The Woman's Flesh of Me': Rebecca Harding Davis's Response to Self-Reliance," *ATQ* 6, no. 2 (1992): 132–140; Charles Capper, *Margaret Fuller: An American Romantic Life, the Private Years* (New York: Oxford University Press, 1992); Phyllis Cole, "Pain and Protest in the Emerson Family," in *The Emerson Dilemma: Essays on Emerson and Social Reform*, ed. T. Gregory Garvey (Athens: University of Georgia Press, 2001), 67–92; Lucinda Damon-Bach, "To Be a 'Parlor Soldier': Susan Warner's Answer to Emerson's 'Self-Reliance,' " in *Separate Spheres No More: Gender Convergence in American Literature, 1830–1930*, ed. Monika M. Elbert (Tuscaloosa: University of Alabama Press, 2000), 29–49; Armida Gilbert, " 'Pierced by the Thorns of Reform': Emerson on Womanhood," in Garvey, *Emerson Dilemma*, 93–114; Linda Kerber, "Can a Woman Be an Individual? The Discourse of Self-Reliance," in *Toward an Intellectual History of Women: Essays* (Chapel Hill: University of North Carolina Press, 1997); David Leverenz, *Manhood and the American Renaissance* (Ithaca, NY: Cornell University Press, 1989); Leonard N. Neufeldt, "Thoreau's Enterprise of Self-Culture in a Culture of Enterprise," *American Quarterly* 39 (summer 1987): 231–251; Anne Rose, *Transcendentalism as a Social Movement, 1830–1850* (New Haven, CT: Yale University Press, 1981); Jeffrey Steele, "The Limits of Political Sympathy: Emerson, Margaret Fuller, and Woman's Rights," in Garvey, *Emerson Dilemma*, 115–135; and Christina Zwarg, *Feminist Conversations: Fuller, Emerson, and the Play of Reading* (Ithaca, NY: Cornell University Press, 1995).

My study of the French and British women writers who inspired Alcott, Phelps, Stoddard, and Woolson was most facilitated by primary sources and the following secondary sources: Ellen Moers, *Literary Women* (Garden City, NY: Doubleday, 1976); Avriel H. Goldberger, introduction to *Corinne, or Italy*, by Madame de Staël (New Brunswick, NJ: Rutgers University Press, 1987); Madelyn Gutwirth, *Madame de Staël, Novelist: The Emergence of the Artist as Woman* (Urbana: University of Illinois Press, 1978); Deborah Heller, "Tragedy, Sisterhood, and Revenge in *Corinne*," *Papers on Language and Literature* 26 (spring 1990): 212–232; Maggie Berg, *Jane Eyre: Portrait of a Life* (Boston: Twayne, 1987); Elizabeth Gaskell, *The Life of Charlotte Brontë* (1857; reprint, London: Everyman's Library, 1992); Sandra Donaldson, ed., *Critical Essays on Elizabeth Barrett Browning* (New York:

G. K. Hall, 1999); Holly A. Laird, *"Aurora Leigh:* An Epical *Ars Poetica,"* in *Writing the Woman Artist: Essays on Poetics, Politics, and Portraiture,* ed. Suzanne W. Jones (Philadelphia: University of Pennsylvania Press, 1991), 353–370; Joyce Zonana, "The Embodied Muse: Elizabeth Barrett Browning's *Aurora Leigh* and Feminist Poetics," *Tulsa Studies in Women's Literature* 8, no. 2 (1989): 241–262; George Levine, ed., *The Cambridge Companion to George Eliot* (Cambridge: Cambridge University Press, 2001); and Patricia E. Johnson, "The Gendered Politics of the Gaze: Henry James and George Eliot," *Mosaic* 30, no. 1 (1997): 39–54.

Finally, those interested in studying nineteenth-century American writers' interest in Europe will find the following sources most informative: Van Wyck Brooks, *The Dream of Arcadia: American Writers and Artists in Italy, 1760–1915* (New York: Dutton, 1958); Leonardo Buonomo, *Backward Glances: Exploring Italy, Reinterpreting America (1831–1866)* (Madison, NJ: Fairleigh Dickinson University Press, 1996); James Buzard, "A Continent of Pictures: Reflections on the 'Europe' of Nineteenth-Century Tourists," *PMLA* 108 (Jan. 1993): 30–44; Leo Hamalian, ed., *Ladies on the Loose: Women Travellers of the Eighteenth and Nineteenth Centuries* (New York: Dodd, Mead, 1981); and Mary Suzanne Schriber, *Writing Home: American Women Abroad, 1830–1920* (Charlottesville: University Press of Virginia, 1997).

Index

Douglass, Frederick, 6
Duff, William, 129
Duveneck, Frank, 118

Edel, Leon, 190, 194, 195, 198
editors. *See* Fields, James T.; Howells,
    William D.; Lowell, James
Eggleston, Edward, 29
Elbert, Monika M., 8, 10
Eliot, George (Mary Ann Evans), 10, 25, 26,
    28, 29, 30–32, 34, 79, 101, 104, 112, 128,
    151, 181, 224, 229, 230, 244, 246; *Adam
    Bede*, 75; *Armgart*, 91–93, 96, 98–99, 100,
    104, 113, 128; and genius, 136, 137; *Mid-
    dlemarch*, 75, 156, 159–60; *The Mill on the
    Floss*, 31; Phelps and, 4, 31–32, 74–75,
    228; *Romola*, 75, 119; Woolson and, 4, 25,
    31, 70–71, 150, 153, 181
Emerson, Ralph Waldo, 6, 9, 13, 18–21, 22–
    24, 38, 47, 90, 128, 144, 168, 219, 241,
    243, 244, 245, 246; Bronson Alcott and,
    48, 49, 50; Louisa May Alcott and, 22–23,
    53, 169, 186; "The American Scholar,"
    17, 19; and *Atlantic Monthly*, 202, 210; and
    gaze of artist, 147; and genius, 17, 19, 141,
    148, 149; and individualism, 19–20; influ-
    ence on women writers, 15, 19–21, 22–
    24; Emma Lazarus and, 20, 22, 186, 187;
    Nature, 147; Phelps and, 22, 180, 188;
    "Self-Reliance," 19, 20, 23, 24; Stoddard
    and, 23; Woolson and, 22, 24
Europe: as destination for American writers
    and artists, 105–25; female visual artists
    in, 106–7, 110–11; freedom for American
    women in, 106–7, 109–11, 125; scrutiny
    of American women traveling in, 116–18,
    125
Evans, Augusta Jane: *St. Elmo*, 80–82, 93,
    104, 124
Everett, C. C., 29, 131, 137, 147

Fern, Fanny (Sara Payson Willis Parton), 2,
    14, 32, 34, 248; *Ruth Hall*, 40, 80–82, 93,
    102, 174
Fetterley, Judith, 3
Fields, Annie, 69; Alcott and, 126, 211, 212;
    Boston marriage with Sarah Orne Jewett,

68; and Brontë sisters, 29; as literary host-
    ess, 188, 211; Phelps and, 68, 74, 214–15
Fields, James T., 68, 203; Alcott and, 126,
    210, 211–13; as editor of *Atlantic Monthly*,
    207–8, 210–13, 214–15, 220; as literary
    host, 188, 211; Phelps and, 74, 76, 214–
    15; Stoddard and, 207–8
Foerster, Norman, 242
Foucault, Michel, 154
Freeman, Mary Wilkins, 239, 247
Fuller, Margaret, 24–25, 32, 38, 43, 47, 61,
    75, 80, 141, 149, 245, 249; Alcott and,
    23, 50, 53; authorial identity of, 33; and
    Emerson, 19, 20; and Europe, 106; Phelps
    and, 21–22; *Woman in the Nineteenth Cen-
    tury*, 14, 18, 21–22, 25, 33, 133; and
    women's genius, 21, 24–25, 133, 136; as
    the "Yankee Corinne," 26

Galaxy, 27, 130, 210
Gaskell, Elizabeth: *The Life of Charlotte
    Brontë*, 28
gaze, of artist, 147–49, 155, 156, 157, 162;
    women artists and power of male, 154–55,
    156, 158–60
genius: American, 14, 15–17, 221, 241; as
    androgynous, 133; competing nineteenth-
    century ideas of, 128; democratic concep-
    tions of, 17, 18, 129; as divinely inspired,
    18, 138; elite conceptions of, 17, 129;
    Enlightenment views of gender equality
    and, 35, 133; European women writers
    and, 26–32; feminine, 133–34, 140; his-
    tory of concept, 129; as male, 14, 18, 33–
    34, 129; as masculine, 129, 139, 147; as
    result of hard work vs. inspiration, 140–
    41, 161, 172; romantic, 16, 127–38, 139,
    140, 149, 166, 167, 174, 175, 177, 179,
    183; and sexuality, 129, 130; Victorian
    views of sexual difference and, 35–36, 133;
    women and, 24–25, 33–34, 128–63, 173–
    74, 177, 181–83, 250. *See also* artist
Gilman, Arthur, 205
Glazener, Nancy, 243
Godey's Lady's Book, 62
Greenwood, Grace, 106; *Haps and Mishaps of
    a Tour in Europe*, 106